Lc
AF802816

The United States Discovers Panama

The United States Discovers Panama

The Writings of Soldiers, Scholars, Scientists, and Scoundrels, 1850–1905

EDITED BY MICHAEL LAROSA
AND GERMÁN R. MEJÍA

ROWMAN & LITTLEFIELD PUBLISHERS, INC.
Lanham • Boulder • New York • Toronto • Oxford

ROWMAN & LITTLEFIELD PUBLISHERS, INC.

Published in the United States of America
by Rowman & Littlefield Publishers, Inc.
A wholly owned subsidiary of The Rowman & Littlefield Publishing Group, Inc.
4501 Forbes Boulevard, Suite 200, Lanham, MD 20706
www.rowmanlittlefield.com

P.O. Box 317, Oxford OX2 9RU, UK

Copyright © 2004 by Rowman & Littlefield Publishers, Inc.

All rights reserved. No part of this publication may be reproduced, stored in a retrieval system, or transmitted in any form or by any means, electronic, mechanical, photocopying, recording, or otherwise, without the prior permission of the publisher.

British Library Cataloguing in Publication Information Available

Library of Congress Cataloging-in-Publication Data

The United States discovers Panama : the writings of soldiers, scholars, scientists, and scoundrels, 1850–1905 / edited by Michael LaRosa and Germán R. Mejía.
p. cm.
Includes articles from the Atlantic monthly and Harper's magazine.
Includes bibliographical references and index.
ISBN 0-7425-2721-2 (cloth : alk. paper) — ISBN 0-7425-2722-0 (pbk : alk. paper)
1. Panama Canal (Panama)—History—Sources. 2. Panama—History—Sources. 3. Panama—Relations—United States—Sources. 4. United States—Relations—Panama—Sources. I. LaRosa, Michael (Michael J.). II. Mejía, Germán R. III. Atlantic monthly. IV. Harper's magazine.
F1569.C2U75 2003
386'.44'09034–dc22

2003018046

Printed in the United States of America

The paper used in this publication meets the minimum requirements of American National Standard for Information Sciences—Permanence of Paper for Printed Library Materials, ANSI/NISO Z39.48-1992.

Dedicated to the memory of our mentor and teacher at the University of Miami, Robert M. Levine (1941-2003)

Contents

Acknowledgments

Completion of this book would not have been possible without the help of Nancy Hunt, Elizabeth Porras, and Tim Walsh at Rhodes College, Memphis, Tennessee. Ricardo Pardo of the Pontificia Universidad Javeriana assisted with research in Bogotá. In Miami, the staff of the history department at the University of Miami, and Craig S. Likness, Rochelle T. Pienn and Christine Layton of Archives and Special Collections, Otto G. Richter Library, University of Miami, provided invaluable assistance during the preparation of this manuscript. Lina Del Castillo assisted with indexing in Bogotá.

Michael Conniff graciously allowed us to reproduce the map of Panama which appears in his book, *Panama and the United States: The Forced Alliance.*

Maria Isabel Perdomo, as always, has been a source of inspiration and has supported both of us, not only during the preparation of this manuscript but over the many years of our professional careers.

A Note on Language and Spelling

Throughout the preparation of this manuscript, we have preserved original English usage of spelling, language, and grammar and have only modernized words to facilitate comprehension.

Spanish language words, terms, and proper names have not been changed or modified from the original texts in any way.

Introduction

Michael J. LaRosa and Germán R. Mejía

The separation of Panama and construction of the Panama Canal began, officially, on November 3, 1903 with an uprising in Panama, the declaration of Panamanian independence from Colombia, and immediate recognition of the "new" republic by the Theodore Roosevelt administration of the United States of America. Students, in Latin American and the United States, are taught these basic details of the events of 1903, but the story is far more complex, and reflects the interests, motivations, and specific histories of North America, as well as certain South American and European nations.

Serious interest in developing a transit route across the Isthmus of Panama began as far back as the 1840s and is related, specifically, to two important events of that decade. First, war with Mexico (1846-1848) resulted in the United States expanding its border westward to the Pacific Ocean. The discovery of gold, in 1848, and the promise of quick fortune via relocation west fueled the spirits of adventurers, the landless in the east, and those who envisioned America as a land of endless opportunity. Interestingly, these important historic events coincide with the publication of a new monthly magazine, *Harper's New Monthly Magazine*, which was first published in New York City by Harper and Brothers, Publishers, in 1850. The first volume, June to November 1850, announced that the primary objective of the new magazine was "bringing within the reach of the great mass of the American people, an immense amount of useful and entertaining reading matter." In addition to educating the American people, the editors at *Harper's* hoped "to present . . . every thing of general interest and usefulness which the current literature of the times may contain."[1]

Not surprisingly, an essay in the very first issue of *Harper's New Monthly Magazine* deals with Panama. The article is short, and calls on Americans to cut a canal through Panama. The article cites the German naturalist Alexander von Humboldt's calculations in the early nineteenth century concerning the feasibility of the project (which were far from exact or clear), and suggests that construction of a canal would be relatively easy. Since the people living in Panama are part of an "imperfect civilization," part of the mission of building a canal would involve, of course, the bringing of a more perfect civilization to the tropics.[2]

This first article illustrates many of the themes and issues that would recur in many different publications and settings between 1850 and 1903. North Americans and Europeans would begin, roughly in 1850, to explore the isthmus of Panama, and work to develop some form of transit route across the isthmus. Cornelius Vanderbilt's enterprise in Nicaragua helped move passengers from the cities of the northeast United States to California without having to make the long, dangerous 3,000-mile overland voyage. That route became obsolete, for in 1855 the Panama Railroad opened after five years of difficult work in which thousands died of malaria, yellow fever, and exhaustion from laboring, all day, in the scorching tropics.

This book invites the reader to more fully understand how the tropics, how Central America, and how Panama were, in effect, discovered by North Americans via published articles in *Harper's Monthly Magazine* and *The Atlantic Monthly*. The enterprise of building anything in the tropics was far more complicated and difficult than outlined in the first edition of *Harper's*. We've tried to reproduce the essential debates, during a long period of time (fifty-five years) concerning the canal, and all of the social, political, military, geographic, geological, and technological aspects that would frame the discussions surrounding construction of a canal. The enormous difficulties of building a railroad line through the tropics in the early 1850s gave people pause, and helped promote a wide variety of scientific and military voyages of discovery and inquiry during the second half of the nineteenth century.

The book is organized in five parts and, in each, chapters are arranged in chronological order. The first part deals with the Panama Railroad—two chapters present the completion of the project as a triumph for civilization, while, at the same time, the authors discover the geography, climate, flora, and fauna of the tropics. The next part presents five chapters, organized thematically around the "search" for the ideal route across the isthmus. Scientists, naturalists, military officers, and engineers were sent abroad to describe the isthmus in terms of geology, geography, and climactic conditions. Interestingly, a common theme in all of the chapters is the lack of specific or detailed information on the "people" who inhabited the region; Europeans and North Americans viewed the people of the isthmus as "objects" who would either cooperate with the larger projects being proposed, or they would have to be removed. Thus, the social and political organization, customs, traditions, culture, or language of the peoples of the isthmus is not the focus of a single chapter in this volume. There are, of course, tangential references to the natives, but they are generally discussed and dismissed with a condescending remark or with the racist rhetoric and theories that were very much in vogue in nineteenth-century scientific writing.

Settling the route question, which is the topic of part 3 in this book, was still being debated, in the United States and to a lesser degree in Europe, in the early twentieth century and involved the politics of England, France, Colombia, Nicaragua, the United States—and, after November 1903, the Republic of Panama. The decision had been made, after the Spanish-American War and the birth of an American Empire, that construction of a canal in the isthmus was urgent to connect a two-ocean navy and promote U.S. commerce around the globe. Negotiations with the French gave the United States complete control over the rights to continue the project begun in the 1880s, but treaty terms could not be successfully negotiated with the Colombian government, for reasons explained in chapters that follow.

Part 4 concerns the diplomacy of the isthmian region and contains two chapters from *The Atlantic Monthly* and two from *Harper's*. *The Atlantic Monthly* began publishing in 1870 on topics related to politics and culture and we have included, for the sake of diversity, four chapters from that source. The focus of *The Atlantic Monthly* at this time was more scholarly, perhaps, than *Harper's*, and many of the articles were written by professors of law and diplomacy at prestigious institutions in the United States. The final part of this book deals with the period after separation, or after November 1903, and we have included two chapters that debate the legacy, role, and in fact, future of the Monroe Doctrine (1823) in the events of 1903.

How influential were the articles presented in this book during the period 1850-1905? We believe that the journals, and articles selected in this volume, were of critical importance in shaping public opinion in the nineteenth century on the issue of the isthmus, as they were among the earliest documents that began the process of "educating" a North American public on the strategic importance of the isthmus in terms of both economic expansion and political influence. As such, the articles from *Harper's* constitute critically important primary sources that are virtually unknown among students and specialists of Latin American and U.S. history. Additionally, the articles appear at a time of expanding literacy in the United States. After the 1850s, with the important educational reforms in Massachusetts pioneered by the visionary educator Horace Mann, Americans had access to free public education, and the reading public expanded accordingly. Information and news were spread, in the mid-nineteenth century, via public meetings, churches, gossip, newspapers, and magazines. *Harper's New Monthly Magazine*, appearing in 1850, came to define the territory of monthly news magazines and helped shape a readership in terms of themes presented, style of writing, and political tone. Of course, the magazine appealed to an American elite—a group of Americans who had disposable income to spend on magazines, who had leisure time to read magazines, and who had benefited from some sort of education either at home or school. *Harper's* was not geared to a "mass audience," but persons who were or would become influential in terms of law, diplomacy, and politics in the United States during the second half of the nineteenth century were likely to read the magazine.

This book presents the issue of Panama as complex, and an ongoing academic, legal, and diplomatic debate carried out in the pages of journals, at universities, and in Washington. Opinion varied widely concerning the isthmus and a canal, because the questions involved the very future of the United States and what that nation hoped, or expected, to become in the late nineteenth century and early twentieth. The "debate" over the canal is found, especially, in part 5 of this work, and, interestingly, of the four chapters in the part, three are clearly opposed to the canal, offering diplomatic, cultural, and legal reasons for staying out of isthmian affairs. Two important events, though, would have a critical impact on U.S. consciousness concerning a future canal and American control of that canal. First, the French began, in 1880, digging the canal through Panama; that enterprise ended, about eight years later, in utter failure due to rampant corruption, technical difficulties, and the deaths of about forty thousand workers from yellow fever. The idea, though, of a French company, chartered by the Colombian government to build a canal through the Province of Panama, never received the enthusiastic support of U.S. politicians or diplomats. The question of who would control a French-built canal, through a sovereign Colombia, eluded U.S. policymakers, and, thus, Americans lent little support to this French enterprise and when it failed, by the late 1880s, American policy makers began to believe that there was only one option for an isthmian canal: built by Americans, and completely in American control.

The events of the 1890s—economic depression, the ending of the American frontier (the so-called Turner thesis), and the birth of American imperialism with war in 1898 against Spain and Cuba—ensured that, by the turn of the century, a new canal project would be under way. When the impatient Teddy Roosevelt assumed the presidency of the United States in September 1901, clearing a path to construction of an American canal became a central foreign policy objective. Along the path, of course, lay the ruins of the French enterprise, literally rusting in the Panamanian jungle and the sovereign republic of Colombia.

Colombia, reluctant to negotiate with the United States in 1903, rejected the Hay-Herrán treaty of the same year, which would have allowed for construction and control of a seven-mile strip of land through the Province of Panama, leased for ninety-nine years and occupied by U.S. military forces. Americans considered Hay-Herrán the final piece in a complex diplomatic puzzle, extending back, essentially to the Clayton-Bulwer treaty of 1850, clearing the way for American construction and control of an interoceanic canal through Panama. By 1903, American engineers and scientists believed they possessed the skills and know-how to conquer the complex technical and health problems posed by the Panamanian jungle. Liberal-minded Panamanians saw their economic future tied to the construction of a canal, and the rejection of the treaty by conservative politicians in the capital city symbolized Bogotá's utter lack of interest in the Panamanian's livelihood. The Colombian War of a Thousand Days, which had ground to a halt by 1902, left the country deeply divided and, according to one scholar of the period, "given the fragility of the concept of nation in Colombia, the political structure of the country was in no position to negotiate the most urgent problem of the country's international agenda: the transaction of the rights to excavate and construct—through Colombian territory . . . an inter oceanic canal."[3] The Colombian Senate's rejection of Hay-Herrán provoked an uprising at Panama, and resulted in the birth of a new republic—the Republic of Panama—which was immediately recognized as a sovereign nation by the United States. A new treaty was negotiated with the Panamanians, and work began almost immediately on the canal. Teddy Roosevelt's wish to "make the dirt fly" in Panama came true by 1904, but the political costs of America's heavy-handed tactics, which fell well outside the boundaries of international law and diplomacy, suggested that a new era of aggressive tactics toward Latin America would define U.S. diplomacy in the region—the so-called Big Stick of the Roosevelt era.

The final two chapters in this volume are from 1904 and 1905, and reflect attempts by scholars in the United States to explain, or justify, the actions taken in Panama in 1903. Both pieces allude to the "Monroe Doctrine" of 1823, and John Bassett Moore, a renowned professor of international law and diplomacy at Columbia University, defended Roosevelt's handling of the separation of Panama, writing how the actions of 1903 fell within the best traditions of American diplomacy—that is, supporting peoples in their desire to be free and helping to organize sovereign states. The Colombians, of course, didn't quite see it that way, nor did most Latin American scholars and diplomats. The long, complex path to an American canal, which began in the 1850s with construction of a railway line through Panama, ended in November 1903. A new American imperialism, impatient with the niceties and pace of international negotiation and law, preferred heavy-handed, extralegal measures to achieve its objectives, and U.S. actions in Panama predicted, to a great extent, U.S. policy and attitudes toward Latin America for the remained of the twentieth century.

Notes

1. *Harper's New Monthly Magazine*, vol. 1, June to November 1850, (s/p).
2. "Short Cuts Across the Globe," in *Harper's New Monthly Magazine*, 1:1850, 79-81.
3. Thomas Fischer, "Antes de la separación de Panamá: la Guerra de los Mil Días, el contexto internacional y el Canal," in *Anuario Colombiano de Historia Social y de la Cultura*, 25:1998, 73 (our translation).

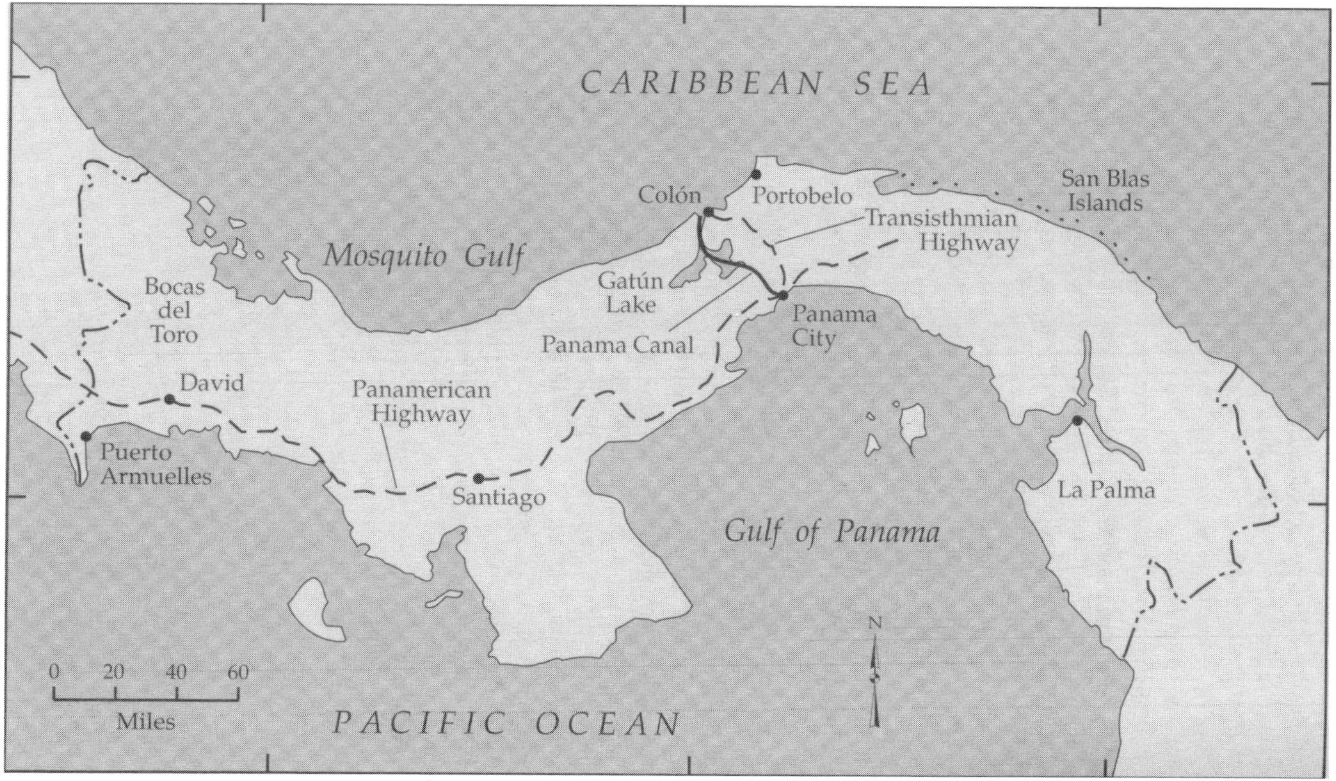

Source: Michael Conniff © University of Georgia Press

PART I

The Panama Railroad

The Panama Railroad was a partial solution to interoceanic communication during the nineteenth century. The fees and risks of losing merchandise grew to be considerable due to the frequent loading and unloading of cargo during a single voyage. However, the problems and costs associated with constructing a canal between the two oceans were much greater. Thus, for a little more than half a century the Panama Railroad was perhaps the best alternative for the entire continent in crossing from one ocean to the other. More than 400,000 persons used the railroad in the first ten years of its operation, and the Railroad Company was one of the most valuable and profitable commodities on Wall Street.

It is interesting to note that the route selected in 1850 for construction of the railroad ended up being, thirty years later, the same route selected by de Lesseps to construct a canal. The French contractor considered it of fundamental importance to acquire the Panama Railroad, regardless of the price he might have to pay. And the price was high: inevitably, the price of shares increased when the digging of the canal, by de Lesseps, began in the 1880s. In this way, the Panama Railroad and canal became part of the same project, and the first became a tool of the second, but, without a doubt, the two ought to be considered part of the same historical reality: they offered the best solution to the problem of interoceanic travel in terms of time and security for passengers and merchandise, and provided earnings for investors.

In this sense, the Panama Railroad project was the first result of a historical necessity turned into state policy and carried out via private capital. The process of territorial expansion of the United States obligated policymakers there to consider, from very early on, viable solutions to the difficult task of connecting the vigorous cities of the east with the "new" but far away west. In effect, many years before the war with Mexico (1846-1848) and the discovery of gold in California in the late 1840s, President Jackson, in 1835, charged a commission with the task of finding, on the continent, the best place to construct an interoceanic railway. Jackson, after concluding that the route through Panama—beginning at the mouth of the Chagres River—was the most adequate, began negotiations with the government of Colombia (at that time, the Republic of New Granada) for the right to construct a railroad through the isthmus. Nothing occurred at this time given that the commissioner of the project, Charles Bridle, died in 1837 before presenting the findings of the U.S. government. However, the seed had been planted.[1]

It took the U.S. government another ten years to begin, once again, the search for an efficient solution to the problem of interoceanic communication. But, now, the urgency was much greater. Not only did the United States possess, after the Treaty of Guadalupe Hidalgo (1848), a Pacific coast with a concurrent migratory movement toward the west, but, also, California—now part of the United States—was the site of the discovery of gold in 1848.

The pressure generated by the growing number of travelers to California was enough to convince North American businesses of the benefits that could be obtained if they participated in the construction of a railroad through the Isthmus of Panama. Of course there were doubts about this route which was perceived as a means to connect the Eastern North American ports with the far-away, and still forming, markets of Asia and Australia, and thus, more of a concern for military men and adventurers than calculating businessmen.

Convinced of the convenience of business, the problems now were of a different nature: they were political and technical. The route was politically complicated by the fact that the entire trajectory crossed through another country, New Granada. Though recognized as an independent and sovereign state by the United States, New Granada was perceived as incapable of guaranteeing neutrality of the use of the railroad and protecting the rights of the investors of the project. However, the Congress of the United States approved, in 1848, a treaty that had been endorsed in December 1846 by the business representative to the New Granadian government, Benjamin Adlen Bidlack; the treaty was approved after equal pressure was applied in Washington by the New Granada government represented by Pedro Alcántara Herrán. Clause 35 of the treaty was the crown jewel for the United States: by that clause, the government of New Granada guaranteed to the United States exclusive rights over all means of existing communication or construction in the isthmus of Panama. In return, the United States guaranteed, positively and efficiently, the complete neutrality of the isthmus and the sovereignty of New Granada with respect to these territories.[2]

Diplomatic initiatives continued, for it was necessary to clearly establish the terms of the arrangement between the investors and the government of New Granada. The contract with the Railroad Company stipulated the exclusive privilege of constructing the rail line and maintaining the monopoly over its use; the company would be given free access to the needed land; the directors of the company would be given 250 acres of land in any part of the isthmus; the initiation and termination ports of the route would be considered "tax-free ports" and the company would have the right to charge freight rates as it saw fit. This contract would be in effect for forty-nine years, allowing the government of New Granada to take possession of the route after twenty years and a payment of five million dollars, or thirty years paying four million, or forty years with a payment of two million. In exchange for all of this, the Railroad Company would pay to the government of New Granada 3 percent of all of its declared earnings. Finally, it was stipulated by contract that the construction of the line would be completed in eight years and that the sum of 120,000 dollars would be deposited as a form of a guarantee: the money would be returned (with interest) to the company if the work were completed within the eight-year limit.[3]

The technical problems were initially related to the selection of the best route and, later, the difficulty inherent in the climate of the Panamanian jungle. The final decision concerning the best route was made after one of the engineers found a section between the mountains, known as "Culebra," in which the maximum elevation was only 286 feet. There was no solution to the problems with the climate and the jungle; since no human being could realistically resist strenuous work in severe jungle conditions, the deaths of workers, from the beginning of the construction of the railroad, began to grow by the hundreds, and eventually by the thousands.

The Railroad Company ended up becoming an excellent business. Of course the company was sold to the French Canal Company in 1881, which proved to be another excellent and profitable deal for the Railroad Company. No one, in the early 1880s, could have predicted the complete failure of the French Canal Company enterprise and, in reality, the Railroad Company was always a North American company—it was registered in New York, its stock was traded on Wall Street, and the grant of the Colombian government remained intact, unaltered, and protected by Clause 35 of the treaty of 1848. Given that the United States remained in the position of guaranteeing the neutrality of the route, its warships maintained a vigilant position at both ends of the railroad line.[4]

Notes

1. Joseph L. Bristow, *Report of Joseph L. Bristow, Special Panama Railroad Commissioner, to the Secretary of War, June 24, 1905*, Washington: Office of Administration Isthmian Canal Affairs, 1905, p. 5.

2. David McCullough, *The Path Between the Seas: The Creation of the Panama Canal, 1870-1914*, New York: Simon and Schuster, 1977, pp. 32-33.

3. Fessenden N. Otis, *Isthmus of Panama: History of the Panama Railroad; and of the Pacific Mail Steamship Company. Together with a Traveler's Guide and Business Man's Hand-Book for the Panama Railroad and the Lines of Steamships Connecting it with Europe, the United States, the North and South Atlantic and Pacific Coasts, China, Australia, and Japan*, New York: Harper & Brothers Publishers, 1867, pp. 17-18.

4. McCullough, pp. 135-136.

1

A Trip on the Panama Railroad*

Robert Tomes

This short article, published in 1855, represents one of the first accounts of travel on the Panama Railroad. After five years of construction, the railroad traversed fifty miles of the isthmus, and ship passengers arriving at the Caribbean city of Aspinwall (now Colon) could arrive at the city of Panama in about four hours. Race, culture, and the insalubrity of the tropics are significant themes of the article. Consider the casualness with which the author reports on the death of laborers who worked on the railroad during a five-year period. The writing presented here is drawn together from a work by Robert Tomes entitled Panama in 1855.

"Would you like to go to Panama?" was the question propounded to one of our esteemed contributors. The track of the Panama Railroad had been completed from ocean to ocean, and the Company that had for five years been so lavishly casting its dollars upon the fever-haunted Isthmus, in the confident hope of finding them again, with increase, after many days, had resolved to give a grand celebration, with wining and dining and speechifying, in honor of the event.

It was January, and the thermometer stood at zero in New York, and mortal man could not be expected to resist the temptation to visit the tropics free of expense. So our friend returned an answer of acceptance to the formal note invit-

* *Panama in 1855: An Account of the Panama Railroad; of the Cities of Panama and Aspinwall; with Sketches of Life and Character on the Isthmus.* By Robert Tomes. Harper and Brothers.

ing him to assist in commemorating the important event, and instituted a search into the receptacles which contained last year's summer wardrobe, in preparation for the trip.

On the 5th of February the good steamer *George Low* left the wharf at New York, bearing, in addition to its usual miscellaneous crowd of Californian emigrants, the company of invited guests, and the United States Minister to Granada. A "Notice" to passengers, conspicuously posted up, intimating that no deadly weapons were to be worn on board, and no fire-arms discharged, and that it was out of order for any person to make his appearance at the dinner-table with his coat off, might have been a little startling to the nerves of a timorous or fastidious person; while the ostentatious display of "life-preservers" hinted at the possibility of drowning too plainly to be altogether agreeable to one who was not insured against that mode of leaving the world, by a premonition that he was reserved for a certain other fashion of exit.

Nobody, however, was shot, stabbed, or drowned, and the brave vessel, passing within sight of the green hills of Cuba and Hayti, and the Blue Mountains of Jamaica, dashed with never-resting wheels among the islands of the Caribbean Sea, and at length, on the eleventh day, lay motionless as a captured whale, at the dock at Aspinwall, the Atlantic terminus of the Panama Railway.

City of Aspinwall

If the map proudly displayed by the enthusiastic draughts-man of the Company is to be accepted as prophetic, Aspinwall is destined to be a wonderful city. Broad avenues—A, B, C, and so on far down the alphabet—are intersected by streets, to designate which whole squadrons of Roman numerals are pressed into service. Magnificent docks give proof that the interests of commerce are to be duly cared for; while the noble Boulevard surrounding the city, as the "ocean stream" girdled the shield of Achilles, and a spacious "Central Park," show that devotion to the "Almighty Dollar," the tutelar genius of America, was not the sole passion in the hearts of the projectors.

It must be confessed that the real Aspinwall hardly corresponds with the ideal existing in the mind of the enthusiastic artist, as our friend the Doctor—for we may as well give him his official title—discovered when he set out on a tour of exploration.

"A hundred or so," he says, "are about the whole number of houses in Aspinwall. Upon the beach at the northern end of the island are few scattered buildings, gay with white paint and green blinds, chiefly occupied by the officials of the Panama Railroad, while to the right of these are the works and depot of the company with machine shops and reservoirs. The shore at the north curves round, leading easterly to an uncleared portion of the island, where a narrow rim of white beach separates the sea from the impenetrable jungle. As we turn westerly and follow the shore, taking the Mess House as the point of departure, we come upon a building of corrugated iron in progress of erection, intended for the residence of the British Consul, if he will ever have the courage to live in what is only a great target for all the artillery of heaven. The lightning during the rainy season keeps it in a continual blaze of illumination, and I mourned, in common with Colonel Totten, whose house is next door, over several prostrate cocoa-nut palms, which had been struck down in consequence of their fatal propinquity to the iron-house. As we proceed we pass three wooden, peaked-roofed cottages, with green blinds and verandas, inhabited by employés of the Company; hurry past some ugly white washed buildings, which the pale-faced sailor and the melancholy convalescent negro, sitting smoking their pipes on the steps, remind us are hospitals, and soon passing by some outlying huts with half naked negresses and pot-bellied children sunning themselves in front, we make our way into the thicker part of the settlement over marshy pools corrupt with decaying matter, black rotten roots of trees, and all kinds of putrefying offal, which resist even the street-cleaning capacities of those famous black scavengers, the turkey-buzzards, which gather in flocks about it. We now get upon the railroad track, which leads us into the main street. A meagre row of houses facing the water, made up of the railroad office, a store or two, some half dozen lodging and drinking establishments, and the 'Lone Star,' bounds the so-called street on one side, and the railroad track, upon its embankment of a few feet above the level of the shore, bounds the other.

"There is another and only one other street, which you reach by crossing a wooden bridge, that a sober man can only safely traverse by dint of deliberate care in the day-time, and a drunken man never, and which stretches over a large sheet of water that ebbs and flows in the very centre of the so-called city. This second street begins at the coral beach at the northern end of the island, and runs southward until it terminates in a swamp. At the two extremities houses bound it on both sides; in the middle there is a narrow pathway over an insecure foot-bridge, with some tumble-down pine buildings on one side only, with their foundations soaking in the swamp, their back windows inhaling the malaria from the manzanilla jungle in the rear, and their front ones opening upon the dirty water, which we have already described, that fills up the central part of the city. The hotels—great, straggling, wooden houses—gape here with their wide open doors, and catch California travelers, who are sent away with a fever as a memento of the place, and shops, groggeries, billiard-rooms, and drinking saloons thrust out their flaring signs to entice the passer-by. All the houses in Aspinwall are wooden, with the exception of the stuccoed Railroad office, the British Consul's precarious corrugated iron dwelling, and a brick building in the course of erection under the slow hands of some Jamaica negro masons. The more pretentious of the wooden buildings were sent out from Maine or Georgia bodily.

"The inhabitants of Aspinwall—some eight hundred in number—are of every variety of race and shade in color. The railroad officials, steamboat agents, foreign consuls, and a score of Yankee traders, hotel-keepers, billiard markers, and bar-tenders, comprise all the whites, who are the exclusive few. The better class of shop-keepers are mulattoes from Jamaica, St. Domingo, and the other West Indian Islands, while the dispensers of cheap grog, and hucksters of fruit and small wares are chiefly negroes. The main body of the population is made up of laborers, grinning coal-black negroes from Jamaica, yellow natives of mixed African and Indian blood, and sad, sedate, turbaned Hindoos, the poor exiled Coolies from the Ganges."

Notwithstanding the profuse hospitality of his hosts, with Champagne cocktails and choice Havanas *ad bibitum*, the Doctor could not find it in his heart to be grieved at the announcement that the grand expedition across the Isthmus was about to be made. In addition to its own habitual fever, Aspinwall was in a fever of excitement in anticipation of the great event. Speeches and counter-speeches were to be delivered, and duly reported for the New York Press. Those who expected to be "most unexpectedly called upon to fill a gap," showed a praiseworthy diligence in preparing the materials, and in rehearsing their speeches to each other, so as to provide against any possibility of failure. The appointed hour at length came and the train left the depot, amidst a general waving of the star-spangled banner from the shipping, and a display of miniature copies of the same from the hotels and drinking saloons; while from the balcony of the Lone Star a single white female waved her white handkerchief in adieu. The negroes were especially delighted. A party of them had taken possession of a rusty old cannon, which they kept firing off with uproarious glee that was soon turned to wailing, when one of them was mortally wounded by a premature discharge. The poor Coolies alone were apparently unmoved amidst the general excitement. They gazed with Eastern apathy upon the scene. What mattered it to them that another link was completed in the chain that binds together the Occident and the Orient?

The Summit, Panama Railroad

"For seven miles the road passes through a deep marsh, in which the engineers, during the original survey, struggled breast-high, day after day, and yet, in spite of such toilsome and perilous labor, fixed their steady eyes straight forward, went on step by step, and accomplished their purpose. These seven miles are firm now as a stone pavement. Piles upon piles have been driven deep down into the spongy soil, and the foundation covered thick with a persistent earth, brought from Monkey Hill, which overhangs the railroad track two miles from Aspinwall.

"On we go, dry shod, over the marsh, through the forest, which shuts out with its great walls of verdure on either side, the hot sun, and darkens the road with a perpetual shade. The luxuriance of the vegetation is beyond the powers of description. Now we pass impenetrable thickets of mangroves, rising out of deep marshes, and sending from each branch down into the earth, and from each root into the air, offshoots which gather together into a matted growth, where the observer seeks in vain to unravel the mysterious involution of trunk, root, branch, and foliage. Now we come upon gigantic *espases* and *coratos*, with girths of thirty feet, and statures of a hundred and thirty feet, out of a single trunk of which, without a plank or a seam, the natives build great vessels of twelve tons burden.

"Again we cross a stream, rippling between hanks of verdant growth, where the graceful bamboo waves over the water its feathery top, and the groves of the vegetable ivory palm, intermingled with the wild fig-tree, spread their shade, and rustling gently in the breeze, whisper a slight murmur of solitude in the ear, and suggest a passing dream of repose."

At Gatun, seven miles from Aspinwall, the first halt was made. We who remained at home read in the papers gorgeous accounts of the triumphal arch flung over the road, and the irrepressible burst of enthusiasm which greeted the passing train. Our author's recollections of the scene hardly come up to the florid description of the enthusiastic reporter. He remembers having seen one white man, two negroes, and a Coolie mounted on the top of a clay hank in front of a ruinous hut, shouting with all their might, and firing a salute from an old blunderbuss.

Passing Bujia Soldado, where stands a picturesque cottage which was formerly the favorite residence of the lamented John L. Stephens, while upon the Isthmus, the train reached Baracoas, where the road crosses the Chagres river by a bridge 600 feet in length. It is built of pine, brought from Georgia. Its massive timbers seemed as though they might endure for ages; but such is the destructive character of the climate that in a twelve month they must be replaced. To the west looms up the Cerro Gigante, the loftiest summit upon the Isthmus, whence Balboa saw at one glance the bright waters of the two oceans. Another short stage brought the train to the spot which had been selected for the site of a monument to Stephens, Aspinwall, and Chauncey, the original projectors of the Panama Road. The train stopped, and two sturdy negroes panted up the gentle acclivity, bearing the corner-stone of the proposed monument, and our Minister to Granada delivered a speech, of which copies were duly forwarded to the papers at home; where we hope it was read with more attention than seems to have been accorded to it by hungry listeners.

Another seven miles brought the train to the summit of the line, 250 feet above the level of the Pacific. Here has been the heaviest work upon the line. A deep cutting, 1300 feet long, and 24 feet deep, has been dug through a soft soil, which every rain washes down upon the road, requiring a numerous force of laborers to keep the track clear. A rapid descent of 70 feet to the mile conquers the descent upon the Pacific side. Then a few miles of level track and the train reaches Panama, stopping on the very verge of the shore of the broad Pacific. The transit from ocean to ocean has occupied just four and a half hours, including the time lost in listening to speeches.

Panama was very quiet just then. The Californians, going and returning, had all left for their several destinations, and the visitors had abundance of leisure to wander about the town and see the few sights, and observe the people. There is the spruce-looking Padre, in long silk surplice, lined with pink satin. A cocked hat, fringed and tasseled, covers his reverend head; and his lower members are encased in silken hose, and polished shoes with golden buckles. His golden-headed cane, the jaunty air with which he puffs his cigar, and the gallantry with which he accosts the females of his flock, show that he is no anchorite. Then came a slouchy negro woman, with long black hair streaming down her back. Her garments are any thing but superfluous, and, in accordance with the custom of the Isthmus, the flounces are at the top, instead of the bottom of the skirt. She carries a child astride upon her hip, which looks as though it was fashioned for that special purpose. She, too, is smoking the perpetual cigar. Next may come a mother and child gayly tricked out in loose calico dresses, of the most flaming colors and startling patterns. Broad-brimmed, bright-ribboned Panama hats cover their heads; and satin slippers are stuck upon the tips of their toes. The child is a perfect facsimile of the mother in all but size. From hat to slipper they are dressed alike. One fancies that he is looking at the mother through a spy-glass reversed. They evidently belong to the upper class, and are fully aware of the magnificence of their appearance, as they pace along in conscious pride through the streets. Another characteristic denizen of Panama presents himself in the person of the water-carrier, mounted on his mule. He is just returning from out-side the walls, where he has filled his kegs from the orange-shaded spring, and is now returning to supply his customers, whose water-jars stand under the balcony, covered with cool moisture. Into the hung-holes he has inserted a tuft of green leaves, by way of cork; so that, at first sight, one might suppose his water-kegs had spontaneously germinated, and were about to grow up, and perhaps produce a crop of diminutive vessels in their own image and likeness. A shackled mule is cropping the grass in the deserted Plaza; a group of naked black children are playing on the church steps; and a file of galley-slaves are marching through the streets. Inside the churches, devotees are prostrate before tawdry images of the saints; and frowzy padres are snuffing the candles and peering into the contribution boxes. To remind you of home you look into a drinking saloon, where the sallow bar-keeper is concocting a sherry-cobbler for a fever-stricken Yankee; a brace of dark-haired natives are making wonderful strokes at the billiard table; and a group of Spaniards and Frenchmen are playing dominoes and sipping absinthe. This appears to be about the sum total of life in Panama.

The rampart speaks of the days when the memory of Morgan was fresh in men's minds. Its solid foundations, laid two centuries ago, still breast the long waves of the Pacific. But the wall is in ruins; the loopholes are rent and jagged; the beautiful guns lie dismounted. A few barefooted mulatto soldiers, clad in loose linen jackets and trowsers, with red woolen caps on their heads, smoke their cigars, and strive to keep up the appearance of a military post. But it is all a sham. The descendants of the Castilian conquerors, here as everywhere else, are a worn-out and effete race. People and town alike have fallen into decay. The government is too feeble to exercise the ordinary duties of police, and has been obliged to give into the hands of foreigners the duty of preserving order on the Isthmus. The right of punishment, even to life and death, without appeal, has been granted to the Railroad Company. What the government is unable to accomplish, is performed by a guard of forty men, headed by Ran Runnels, famed as a Texas Ranger, who have cleared the Isthmus of robbers, and keep the thousands of unruly laborers in awe.

Two centuries ago Panama was the centre of the trade between Europe and Western America. It was a gorgeous city, whose merchants were princes. Their warehouses were filled with gold, silver, spices, and precious stuffs; and their dwellings were adorned with all that wealth could procure. But the discovery of the passage round Cape Horn turned the trade into a new channel. With the decline of the Spanish power the last gleam of prosperity departed; and since the Isthmus has been divided into feeble states, the decay has gone on with accelerated speed. For a short time the California emigration infused a spark of life into the stagnant city. But it was a spasmodic activity. The two thousand foreigners who were there congregated in 1850, have fallen to a few hundreds; and the native population was never fairly aroused from their death-like lethargy. The majority of the natives are a mongrel race, in whose veins White, Indian, and Negro blood is mingled in every conceivable proportion. Yet these are every way superior to the few who boast an unmixed Castilian descent. It is fearfully probable that no race of whites can escape deterioration upon the Isthmus. The indomitable energy, which braves every hardship, and overcomes every visible obstacle, yields to the fatal influence of the climate; and each generation sinks lower than the one that preceded it. Yet the prize of the commerce between the East and the West is too great to be abandoned without a desperate struggle. It is hardly to be thought of that this narrow Isthmus should be suffered to add ten thousand miles to the voyage between New York and San Francisco.

With the commerce between California and the East for a prize, it would at first sight seem to be no extraordinary achievement to construct a railway of less than fifty miles in length, where there were no broad rivers to cross, no rocky ridges to excavate, and no deep valleys to fill up. But the Panama route presented obstacles more formidable than these visible and tangible ones. The materials for the construction and equipment of the road were all to be brought from a distance. Not only were the tools and iron work to be conveyed from the United States and from England, but, although the country abounded in forests, the very wood upon which the rails were to rest, and of which the bridges were to be constructed, was the product of Maine and Georgia, and the food for the laborers must be sought in the markets of the Atlantic cities. The tropical climate, which stimulates the powers of nature, whether of production or destruction, to an activity unknown in temperate regions, wrought in both directions with unresting activity against the enterprise. Thick jungles had to be pierced, which reproduced themselves almost as rapidly as they were cut down. The way once cleared, if left to itself, would be overgrown again in a twelvemonth. The destruction of dead material is as rapid as the growth of the living. A month does the work of a year. The most solid timber, exposed to the action of the climate and the insects, decays in a twelve-mouth. Bridges, stations, tanks, houses must be built of stone or iron to be permanent.

But worse than all these is the pestilential climate, with which no race of men and no strength of constitution can contend; and against which no measure of precaution and no process of acclimation is a safeguard. No man could hope to escape the terrible Panama fever for more than a few weeks, or months at most. If the patient survived the violence of the first attack, the poison remained in the system, and he could hope for no perfect recovery so long as he remained on the Isthmus. And those who had apparently recovered by seeking a more healthy climate, succumbed at once on their return. "I never met," says our author, speaking as a medical man, "with a wholesome-looking person among all those engaged upon the railroad. There was not one whose constitution had not been sapped by disease."

The laborers upon the road were sought from every country, and there was a marked difference in the rapidity with which different races yielded to the miasma. The African resisted it longest; next came the Coolie; then the European races; and last of all the poor China-man, who succumbed at once. A ship-load of eight hundred of these poor Celestials landed at Panama. Of these thirty-two were prostrated almost at the moment of landing; in four or five days eighty more lay by their side; and in as many weeks there was hardly one who was fit for labor. They gave themselves up to despair, and sought for death at once, rather than await its rapid and inevitable approach. Hundreds destroyed themselves. Some persuaded their companions to kill them. Some seated themselves on the beach at low-water, and lighting their pipes, grimly waited for the rising tide to engulf them. Some strangled themselves, in default of a better means, with their own cherished pig-tails. Some impaled themselves upon sharpened stakes or the implements of their labor. In a space of time incredibly short, six hundred of the eight were dead, and the miserable remnant, hardly alive, and wholly unfit for labor, were shipped to Jamaica, where they linger out a life if possible more wretched than that of their countrymen whom a heartless cupidity brought to our own city, and then, failing in its object, abandoned here. Hardly less terrible was the fate of a shipload of Irish laborers, fresh from their green island. So rapidly did they give way to the fearful poison pervading the atmosphere, that not one of them was ever able to perform a full day's labor; and the miserable survivors, shipped to New York, died almost to a man of the fever contracted during their brief stay upon the Isthmus.

Nature seemed determined that the "door of the seas" should not be opened. Yet in spite of the obstacles, which she interposed, and in spite even of the unexpected cost of the work, the enterprise went steadily on, until in five years from the time when ground was first broken, the first locomotive traversed the whole space from ocean to ocean. It is a wonderful triumph of man's indomitable will over the hostile powers of nature, visible and invisible. But the victory has been won at a fearful cost of life and health. Whether—leaving these out of view, and looking at the matter in a merely pecuniary point of view—the enterprise is a success or a failure, is still a question. Wall Street counts up the millions already expended in the construction of the road, and the other millions required to keep it in operation, and seeking a more healthy shaking its head, asks dubiously, "Will it pay?"

We, certainly, most devoutly hope that it may.

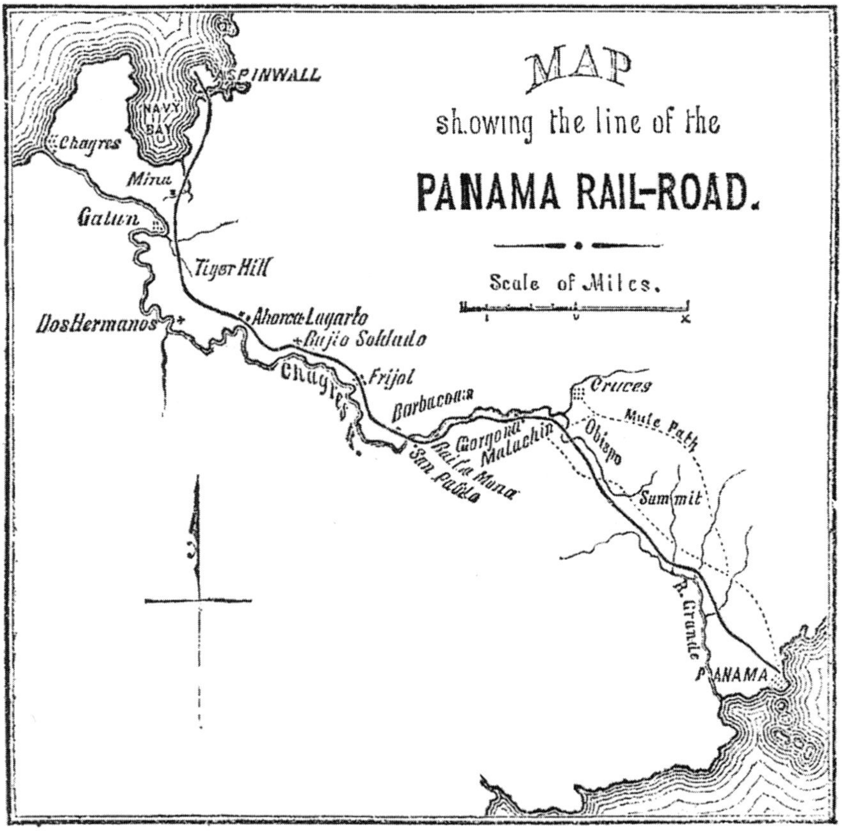

2

Panama Railroad*

Oran

This article reveals the details of the difficulty in building the Panama Railroad. Drawn from conversations with the chief engineer of the project, Colonel Totten, and the general superintendent of the railroad, Mr. Center, and documents supplied by the two men, the author describes the construction as a heroic (American) undertaking. Again, the human toll of the enterprise is described and the author seems much more concerned with the financial rather than the human cost of the project. The author travels the entire length of the railroad by handcar, offering an open-air tour of the railroad route. The article, therefore, provides an excellent description of the flora and fauna of the region.

The return from Portobello to Aspinwall was accomplished with a dash of the pen. We set sail—we arrived. But embodied in that dash were certain incidents which it will be necessary to relate in order to come to the full understanding of certain circumstances which We are to follow. Of first importance was an acquaintance formed with Colonel Totten, the Chief Engineer, and Mr. Center, the General Superintendent, of the Panama Railroad.

Every body ought to know what the Panama Railroad is, and where it is—for *every body* reads the papers. Every body may have had either a neighbor or a

*Entered according to Act of Congress in the year 1858, by Harper and Brothers, in the Clerk's Office of the District Court for the Southern District of New York.

friend, and perhaps dozens of them, who have traveled over that road. Perhaps the reader has been over it himself. He may know that, in the year of our Lord one thousand eight hundred and forty-eight, three bold merchants of the city of New York, after obtaining a contract from the Government of New Granada, memorialized Congress on the subject, and obtained a charter for the protection and prosecution of the work, and that in seven years afterward the road was completed. But *every body* does not know the stupendous and almost desperate character of that undertaking, the means by which it was accomplished, the perils and privations encountered, the labors undergone, the skill, energy, and courage displayed by the pioneers and builders of the Panama Railroad.

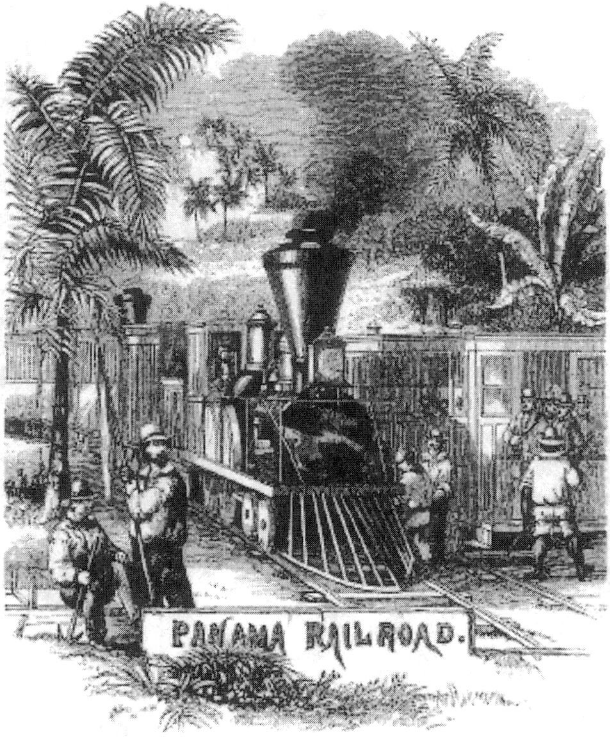

Colonel Totten was one of the pioneers of that work. From its inception to its completion upon him rested the responsibility of its location and construction. He shared the dangers and the sufferings of the builders, and led in the labor and the toil. During the voyage just alluded to I had an opportunity of conversing freely with him upon the subject of this road. I listened with deep interest to its history from the early times to its glorious and successful present. From that and subsequent conversations with him and with Mr. Center—who had been engaged upon the work for several years, first as Vice-President, and more recently as Superintendent—and from documents, letters, books, and sketches, to which I had access through their united kindness, I am enabled to impart the results in the form of a brief history, which, before traveling over the road with the reader, I shall take the liberty of laying before him.

The project of a great interoceanic communication across the Isthmus of Panama had been agitated for centuries, and the whole commercial world was alive to its importance, and coveted its advantages. New Granada, unable herself to attempt so great a work, had freely offered the privilege of so doing to any nation rich and brave enough to undertake it, well knowing the benefits which must accrue to her own citizens thereby. England had looked toward the project with longing eyes, but quailed before the magnitude of the labor. France did more, surveyed and entered into a contract to establish it; but too many millions were found necessary for its completion, and it was lost by default.

Events at last occurred which turned the attention of the American people to this transit, viz., the settlement of the northwestern boundary, by which we came into possession of Oregon, and the war with Mexico, which added California to our possessions. But while the accession of these territories was of the highest importance to us in a national point of view, their distance rendered them almost inaccessible to the class of emigrants who usually settle our new domains, as well as inconvenient to the proper administration of law and government. Still, urged on by that pioneering spirit which seems inherent in the blood of the American, and invited by the prolific soil and genial climate of these distant possessions, and a prospect of a new and enlarged field for commercial pursuits, large numbers of our people migrated thither around Cape Horn. Congress, however, in 1848, in order to render these countries more accessible, authorized contracts to be entered into for the establishment of two mail lines of steamships, the one from New York and New Orleans to Chagres, and the other, to connect with this by the Isthmus of Panama, from Panama to California and Oregon. The inducements to invest in these projects were not sufficient to attract the favorable attention of capitalists, and the contracts were taken by parties without means, who offered them for sale, and for a long time without success.

Men were at last found bold enough to venture upon the enterprise. Mr. William H. Aspinwall secured the line on the Pacific side, and George Law that on the Atlantic. In the Atlantic contract there was comparatively little risk, and a promise of almost immediate remuneration, as it connected with the cities of Savannah and New Orleans, and terminated at the portals of the Pacific Ocean. But the Pacific contract was looked upon by the generality of business men as a certain sequestration of a large amount of property for an indefinite time, with a faint prospect of profit; and the wonder seemed to be that so sound a man as Mr. Aspinwall should have engaged in it. But it soon became evident that he expected no great profit from the steamship line, *per se*; but that, with those enlarged and far-reaching views for which he is so justly noted, this line was only a part of the great plan which he had conceived, the remainder being embraced in the bold design of a railroad across the Isthmus of Panama. And at this time he, with Mr. Henry Chauncey and Mr. John L. Stephens, entered into a contract with the Government of New Granada for the construction of that work. Mr. Chauncey, like Mr. Aspinwall, was a large-minded and public-spirited capitalist, whose integrity and straight-forwardness were undoubted. Mr. Stephens possessed an experience in the country through which the road was to pass, and a knowledge of its geography and its inhabitants, gained by practical study and observation. These three gentlemen were associated together for the prosecution of this great enterprise, and shortly after, Mr. Stephens, accompanied by Mr. J. L. Baldwin, a skillful and experienced engineer, made an exploration of the route, and decided upon its entire feasibility, dissipating the fears entertained by many that no line could be established without such heavy grades as would interfere materially with the paying character of the undertaking, by the discovery of a summit gap no more than three hundred feet above the ocean level.

John L. Stephens William H. Aspinwall Henry Chauncey

A formal contract was then entered into with the government of New Granada, on the most favorable terms, for the exclusive privilege of constructing a railroad across the Isthmus of Panama. Among the most important concessions by the terms of this contract was one guaranteeing that all public lands lying on the line of the road were to be used gratuitously by the Company; also a gift of 250,000 acres of land, to be selected by the grantees from any public lands on the Isthmus. Two ports, one on the Atlantic and the other on the Pacific (which were to be the termini of the road), were to be *free* ports; and the privilege was granted of establishing such tolls as the Company might think proper. The contract was to continue in force for forty-nine years, subject to the right of New Granada to take possession of the road at the expiration of twenty years after its completion, on payment of five millions of dollars; at the expiration of thirty years, on payment of four millions; and at the expiration of forty years, on payment of two millions. Three percent was to be paid to the New Granadian Government upon all dividends declared. The entire work was to be completed within eight years, and a sum of one hundred and twenty thousand dollars was to be deposited at its commencement, as security for the fulfillment of the contract, but to be refunded, with interest, on the completion of the road within the given time.

Up to this period calculations for the ultimate success of the undertaking were based upon the advantages it would afford in shortening, by many thousand miles, not only the route to California and Oregon, but to China, Australia, and the East Indies, and in the development of the rich, but then almost inaccessible, countries bordering the whole Pacific coast. At this time, however (the latter part of 1848), the discovery of gold in California, with its accompanying tide of emigration across the Isthmus of Panama, changed the prospects of this projected road; and, from an enterprise which looked far into the future for its rewards, it became one promising immediate returns from the capital and labor invested, and in which the people, as well as the Government of the United States, must be immediately and deeply interested. A charter was now granted by the Legislature of the State of New York for the formation of a stock company, under which one million dollars of stock was taken—the original grantees having previously transferred their contract into the hands of this Company. A large and experienced party of engineers, under the command of Colonel G. W. Hughes, of the United States Topographical Corps, was sent down, in the early part of 1849, to survey and locate the line of the road. The result of their work not only confirmed the previous reconnaissance in regard to the entire practicability of the railroad, but another summit gap was discovered by Mr. J. L. Baldwin, thirty-seven feet lower than that previously established by him, and a line was run from ocean to ocean not exceeding fifty miles in length. The Pacific terminus of the road was located at the city of Panama, on Panama Bay, and the Atlantic terminus at Navy Bay, on the Atlantic shore.

The character and geographical position of the country through which the line of the road had been carried was such as might well have made the hardiest projectors shrink from attempting its construction. The first thirteen miles, beginning at Navy Bay, was through a deep morass, covered with the densest jungle, reeking with malaria, and abounding with almost every species of wild beasts, noxious reptiles, and venomous insects, known in the tropics. Further on, though some of the land was so fair and beautiful that the natives called it *Paraiso*, the greater part of the line was through a rugged country, along steep hillsides, over wild chasms, spanning turbulent rivers and furious mountain torrents, until the summit ridge was surmounted, when it descended abruptly to the shores of the Pacific Ocean.

Situated between the parallels of 8° and 9° north of the equator, a sultry tropical heat prevailed throughout the year; nearly half of which time the country was deluged with rains that, if they would not seriously damage the works, were certain to impede their progress, and add greatly to the arduous character of the undertaking. The whole Isthmus, though covered with the most luxuriant vegetative growth, possessed little or no timber sufficiently durable to be of use in the construction of a permanent work. The native population, composed of a mongrel race of Spaniards, Indians, and Negroes, were too indolent and unaccustomed to labor to be depended on to any great extent. The resources of the country were entirely inadequate for the support of laborers. Men, materials, and provisions were to be transported thousands of miles. And yet, despite all these obstacles, the dim glimpses of which had, at a previous time, caused European capitalists to shrink back with fear, our bold operators at once, and earnestly, pushed forward this stupendous enterprise.

In the early part of 1849 a contract was entered into with Messrs. George M. Totten and John C. Trautwine for the construction of the road. The services of these gentlemen had been solicited by the Company, not only on account of their previously established reputation as skillful and successful engineers, but from having only a short time before been engaged upon a work of considerable magnitude in a neighboring province—the "Canal del Dique," connecting the Magdalena River with the Caribbean Sea at Carthagena—they had, consequently, a large experience in the character and resources of the country, and the conditions necessary to the success of such a project. The contractors at once proceeded to the Isthmus with a large force, and commenced the final location of the road.

Basing their operations upon the reconnaissance of Colonel Hughes and party, a native town called Gorgona, on the Chagres River, about thirty miles from the Atlantic, was selected as a point for the commencement of the work. This place was chosen on account of the facilities it afforded for communication with the Atlantic by the River Chagres, which was supposed to be navigable to this point for vessels of light draught, by which men, materials, and stores could be transported to a central point on the proposed road; and, on the completion of the Pacific section, traffic between the two oceans could at once be established, while the Atlantic section might be completed at the leisure or convenience of the Company. To this end two steamboats of very light draught were dispatched to Chagres for the navigation of the river. It was soon ascertained, however, that it was impossible to make use of these boats, drawing only from fourteen to eighteen inches of water, and that even the native bongoes and canoes were capable of the service only by great labor and exposure. In addition to this, the rush of California travel, which was then directed through this river as far as Gorgona, had so raised the hire of the native boatmen that the expense of river transportation was enormously increased. It was, therefore, determined to change the point of beginning to the Atlantic terminus of the road.

James L. Baldwin George M. Totten John C. Trautwine

Mr. Trautwine, after a careful survey of the whole line of coast from the mouth of the Chagres to the harbor of Portobello, had located this terminus at the Island of Manzanilla, on the eastern shore of the Bay of Limon, or Navy

Bay, where the city of Aspinwall now stands. It was also found that—instead of a secluded and rarely visited region where laborers and materials such as the country afforded were comparatively inexpensive, as was the case when the contract was framed, and had been time out of mind—it was now swarming with emigrants from all parts of the globe, *en route* for the land of gold. The conditions under which the contract was entered into were changed, the whole *morale* of the country had assumed an entirely different aspect, and it was evidently impossible to continue the work under the arrangement agreed upon. A fair representation of these things being made to the Company by Messrs. Totten and Trautwine, they were released from their obligations as contractors, and retained as engineers, the Company having determined to take charge of the construction themselves.

The plan of commencing at the Atlantic terminus being approved, Colonel Totten left for Carthagena to make arrangements for procuring an increased supply of laborers. Mr. Trautwine, in company with Mr. Baldwin, as chief assistant-engineer, then proceeded to Manzanilla Island with a small party, and commenced clearing in the month of May, 1850. This island, cut off from the main land by a narrow frith, contained an area of a little more than one square mile. It was a virgin swamp, covered with a dense growth of the tortuous, water-loving mangrove, and interlaced with huge vines and thorny shrubs, defying entrance even to the wild beasts common to the country. In the black, slimy mud of its surface alligators and other reptiles abounded, while the air was laden with pestilential vapors, and swarming with sand-flies and mosquitoes. These last proved so annoying to the laborers that, unless their faces were protected by gauze vails, no work could be done, even at mid-day. Residence on the island was impossible. The party had their quarters in an old brig which brought down materials for building, tools, provisions, etc., and was anchored in the bay.

Thus situated, with a mere handful of native assistants—most of the original forty or fifty having previously deserted, on account of the higher wages and easier life promised them by the Transit—Messrs. Trautwine and Baldwin struck the first blow upon this great work. No imposing ceremony inaugurated the "breaking ground." Two American citizens, leaping, axe in hand, from a native canoe upon a wild and desolate island, their retinue consisting of half a dozen Indians, who clear the path with rude knives, strike their glittering axes into the nearest tree; the rapid blows reverberate from shore to shore, and the stately cocoa crashes upon the beach. Thus unostentatiously was announced the commencement of a railway, which, from the interests and difficulties involved, might well be looked upon as one of the grandest and boldest enterprises ever attempted.

Work upon the island was now fairly commenced. A portion was cleared, and a temporary store-house erected from the materials on board the brig. On the 1st of June Colonel Totten arrived from Carthagena with forty natives of that province as laborers for the work. These were descendants of the old Spanish slaves, a peaceable and industrious race, and, from having been employed on the works in Carthagena for several years, proved a valuable accession to their forces. He was accompanied by Mr. John L. Stephens, the President of the Company, who was on his return from Bogota, where he had been to obtain some important revisions in the contract. With their increased corps the clearing progressed rapidly; but the rainy season soon setting in, the discomforts to which they were subjected were very great. The island was still uninhabitable, and the whole party were forced to live on board the brig, which was crowded to its utmost capacity. Here they were by no means exempt from the causes which deterred them from living on shore, for below decks the vessel was alive with mosquitoes and sand-flies, which were a source of such annoyance and suffering that almost all preferred to sleep upon the deck, exposed to the drenching rains, rather than endure their attacks. In addition to this, most of their number were kept nauseated by the ceaseless motion of the vessel. Labor and malarious influences during the day, exposure and unrest at night, soon told upon their health, and, in a short time, more than half the party were attacked with malarious fevers. Having neither a physician nor any comfortable place of rest, their sufferings were severe. At this time the hull of a condemned steamboat—the *Telegraph*—lying at Chagres, was purchased, and sent down as a residence. This proved a vast improvement upon the accommodations afforded by the brig, but still annoyance from the insects was at times almost insupportable.

In the latter part of June Mr. Totten again left for Carthagena to procure more men, and Messrs. Stephens and Trautwine returned to New York to digest further plans of procedure. The work was left in charge of Mr. Baldwin, who continued the clearing with his crippled forces until the latter part of the following month, when Mr. Totten returned with fifty more laborers. Surveys of the island and adjacent country were now pushed vigorously onward. It was in the depth of the rainy season, and the working parties, in addition to being constantly drenched from above, were forced to wade in from two to four feet of mud and water, over the mangrove stumps and tangled vines of the imperfect openings cut by the natives, who, with their *machetas*, preceded them to clear the way. Then at night, saturated and exhausted, they dragged themselves back to their quarters in the *Telegraph*, to toss until morning among the pitiless insects. Numbers were daily taken down with fever; and not withstanding that the whole working party was changed weekly, large accessions were constantly needed to keep up the required force. The works were alternately in charge of Messrs. Totten and Baldwin—one attending to the duty while the other recuperated from his last attack of fever. In the month of July Mr. Trautwine returned with a surgeon—Dr. Totten, a brother of the Colonel—and several assistant-engineers. About fifty Irishmen also arrived soon after from New Orleans.

The line had already been located for two and a half miles, and decided upon for two miles farther. It was so laid out as to strike a range of small hills half a league from the terminus, when it again stretched into the deep morass. The distance now required to be traversed from the work to the terminus was so great, and attended with so much fatigue and loss of time, that it was determined to erect a shanty for Mr. Baldwin and party in the swamp. The lumber for this was dragged on the backs of the men for more than three miles. Here was erected the first dwelling-house, built of rude hoards, high upon the stumps of trees, to raise it above the waters of the swamp; and in the heart of this dank, howling wilderness our hardy pioneers took up their abode.

Large parties of mechanics and laborers were now constantly arriving from Jamaica, Carthagena, and the United States, so that the quarters on board the hulk were no longer adequate to house them. The insects had diminished in numbers as the clearing progressed, and shanties were erected on the high ground before alluded to for the accommodation of the laborers. In August, 1830, the work of construction was commenced at this place. Another station was also established eight miles distant, opposite to the native town of Gatun, on the bank of the Chagres River, which was navigable to this point; and two of the Company's vessels arriving, laden with machinery, building material, and stores, they were debarked here, and the work of piling and grading was carried on from this station toward the terminus. The number of men now employed on both stations was between three and four hundred, among whom were many mechanics. The construction and surveys for a time progressed with vigor, and comfortable dwellings and hospitals were erected; but sickness, caused by exposure to the incessant rains, working waist-deep in the water, and in an atmosphere saturated with malarious poison, soon made such sad inroads among them that, in a few weeks, more than half their number were on the hospital records, and, either frightened by the fevers or seduced by higher wages offered on the California Transit, so many of the remnant deserted that the work came to a pause. Here the bravest might well have faltered, and even turned back from so dark a prospect as was then presented to the leaders of this forlorn hope; but they were men whom personal perils and privations could not daunt, whose energy and determination toil and suffering could not vanquish. Even in this apparent cessation of labor they were not idle; but pushing off into the neighboring islands and provinces, they collected recruits in such numbers that but a few weeks had passed before the work was again forced onward. Colonel Totten now assumed the direction of the work, and Mr. Center, the vice-president of the Company, repaired to the Isthmus to co-operate with him in the rapid advancement of the enterprise, so that by December over a thousand laborers were employed. With the commencement of the dry season the sickliness abated, the hospitals were soon cleared, and by April, 1851, a large portion of the road between the terminus and Gatun was completed. The line had been located to Barbacoas, sixteen miles farther on, while Mr. J. C. Campbell, assistant-engineer, was actively employed in extending the location toward Panama, and work had been commenced at several intervening points.

Docks had been constructed at Navy Bay, and vessels were almost daily arriving from Jamaica and Carthagena with laborers, and from New York with stores, machinery, and materials for the road. On the first day of October, 1851, a train of working cars, drawn by a locomotive, passed over the road as far as Gatun. In the following month two large steamships, the *Georgia* and *Philadelphia*, arrived at the open roadstead of Chagres with greatly passengers from the United States en route for California via the Chagres River transit; but the weather was so tempestuous that, after several lives had been lost in attempting to effect a landing, they were forced to take refuge in the harbor of Navy Bay. It was then proposed that, instead of waiting for fair weather in order to return to Chagres, the passengers should be transported over the railroad to Gatun, from whence they could proceed up the river in bongoes as usual. There was not yet a single passenger car on the road; an accident like the present had never been included in the calculations of the Company. Every objection was, however, soon over-ruled by the anxious emigrants, over one thousand in number, who were then disembarked and safely transported on a train of working cars to the Rio Chagres at Gatun.

At about this time the affairs of the Company in New York looked very dark and unpromising. The first subscription of one million dollars of stock was expended, and the shares had gone down to a low figure. The Directors were obliged to keep the work moving, at an enormous expense, on their own individual credit. Never since the commencement of the undertaking had its supporters been more disheartened; but on the return of the *Georgia* to New York, carrying news that the California passengers had landed at Navy Bay instead of Chagres and had traveled over a portion of the Panama Railway, its friends were inspired with renewed hope, the value of its stock was enhanced, and the steadfast upholders of the work were relieved from the doubts and anxieties that had well-nigh overwhelmed them.

Up to this time the settlement around the terminus at Navy Bay had been without a distinctive name: it was now proposed by Mr. Stephens, the President of the Company, that it should commemorate the services of one of the originators and unswerving friends of the road. On the 2d of February, 1852, it was formally inaugurated as a city and named ASPINWALL. The work during this season progressed with rapidity, for great numbers of laborers were constantly arriving, and the mail-steamers, which now came regularly to Navy Bay, as regularly, on their return, carried away the sick and disabled. By March the road was completed to a station on the Rio Chagres called Bujio Soldado, eight miles beyond Gatun, and passenger trains ran in connection with every steamer; by the 6th of July it was pushed on to Barbacoas, at which point the course of the road was intersected by the Chagres River, making a total distance from the city of Aspinwall of twenty-three miles.

Thus far the work had cost much more than was anticipated; and in the hope of constructing the remainder more economically, it was decided by the Board of Directors to complete the road from Barbacoas to Panama by contract. Accordingly an agreement was entered into with Minor C. Story, as principal, to complete the work. The death of the lamented President of the Company, Mr. John L. Stephens, took place at this time. From the very inception of the original contract he had devoted to the enterprise his active and intelligent mind with a zeal that knew no faltering. Much of his time had been spent amidst the dangers and hardships of the wilderness through which it was projected, and his loss was deeply deplored by the Company. Mr. William C. Young was appointed his successor.

The work under the contract for construction had been commenced by the attempted erection of a bridge across the Chagres River at Barbacoas. The river at this point was about three hundred feet in width, flowing through a deep and rocky channel, and subject to sudden and resistless freshets often rising forty feet in a single night: the bridge was nearly completed when one span was swept away. Work was again commenced upon it, as well as upon several sections of the road between this point and the Pacific terminus. At times there was a force of several hundred men employed; but they were mostly Irish, unable to endure the effects of the climate, and being also badly cared for, their numbers were soon so thinned by sickness and death that the contractor found himself unable to accomplish any part of the contract for the price agreed upon. The work faltered, and at last stopped almost entirely; so that when a year had expired, not only was the bridge still unfinished, but not a tenth part of the work under the contract was completed, and the Company were obliged again to take the enterprise into their own hands and carry it on by the same system pursued before the unfortunate contract was entered into. Mr. Young now resigned the Presidency, and Mr. David Hoadley (the present President) was appointed his successor—a gentleman who deservedly enjoys the respect and confidence not alone of the company which he represents, but also of the entire commercial community.

Valuable time had been lost from the delay occasioned by the non-fulfillment of the late contract. Not disheartened, however, the Company now redoubled their exertions, determined if possible to retrieve the error. Their working force was increased as rapidly as possible, drawing laborers from almost every quarter of the globe. Irishmen were imported from Ireland; Coolies from Hindostan; Chinamen from China. English, French, Germans, and Austrians, amounting in all to more than seven thousand men, were thus gathered in, appropriately as it were, to construct this highway for all nations. It was now anticipated that, with the enormous forces employed, the time required for the completion of the entire work would be in a ratio proportionate to the numerical increase of laborers, all of whom were supposed to be hardy, able bodied men. But it was soon found that many of these people, from their previous habits and modes of life, were little adapted to the work for which they were engaged. The Chinamen—one thousand in number—had been brought to the Isthmus by the Company, and every possible care taken which could conduce to their health and comfort. Their hill-rice, their tea and opium in sufficient quantity to last for several months, had been imported with them—they were carefully housed and attended to—and it was expected that they would prove efficient and valuable men. But they had been engaged upon the work scarcely a month before almost the entire body became affected with a melancholic, suicidal tendency, and scores of them ended their unhappy existence by their own hands. Disease broke out among them, and raged so fiercely that in a few weeks scarcely two hundred remained. The freshly imported Irishmen and Frenchmen also suffered severely, and there was found no other resource but to reship them as soon as possible, and replenish from the neighboring provinces and Jamaica, the natives of which (with the exception of the Northmen of America) were found best able to resist the influences of the climate. Notwithstanding these discouragements, and many others too numerous to be narrated within the compass of this brief sketch, the work continued to advance, so that by January, 1854, the summit-ridge was reached—distant from the Atlantic terminus thirty-seven miles, and eleven miles from the city of Panama.

David Hoadley, President   Alexander J. Center, Vice-President

Simultaneously with the operations toward the Pacific, a large force was established at Panama, under the superintendence of Mr. J. Young, one of the Company's most efficient and energetic officers, and the road was pushed rapidly onward, over the plains of Panama, through the swamps of Corrisal and Correndeu, and up the valley of the Rio Grande, to meet the advancing work from the Atlantic side; and on the 27th day of January, 1855, at mid night, in darkness and rain, the last rail was laid, and on the following day a locomotive passed from ocean to ocean.

During the dry season the early morning of the isthmian climate is indeed delicious. So I thought as I sallied forth for a walk on the one following our arrival from Portobello. Heavy dews had deepened and brightened the rich hues of the landscape, and permeated the air with their grateful coolness; the sun had not yet risen, and the golden colors of the Eastern horizon, where they joined the deep purple of the mountains, appeared like a great conflagration, burning paler and paler as the eye followed it upward, until it faded into the cool blue of the surrounding sky.

My course soon brought me to that part of the island shore where the railway leaves it and crosses over the frith to the swamps of the main. At this point the channel was about two hundred yards in width, broadening rapidly to the eastward into a miniature archipelago, with a dozen little islands lying upon its surface, like emeralds upon a mirror. To the westward it again expanded into a wide placid basin, only separated by a narrow belt of foliage from the waters of the bay. The shores on every hand were skirted with a dense growth of mangrove bushes, which drooped deep into the water; while, looking directly onward through the vista opened by the railway, a tangled forest was seen that seemed interminable.

The track crossed the channel on an artificial isthmus built originally of piles and crib-work, and afterward filled in with stones and earth. At about its middle was a sluice-way several yards in width, through which a connection between the waters of either side was maintained. By the edge of this sluice-way sat a little native boy fishing, who, as I came near, displayed a string of a dozen little fishes. Brilliant with all the colors of a rainbow. In shape and size they resembled the sun-fish of our Northern lakes. Some were bright blue, striped with silver and gold; others crimson barred with blue; some with irregular dark spots upon a silver ground; some entirely green, and others of a delicate orange color. Scarcely two were marked alike; but all were curious and beautiful, and the little fisher, turning them around in the sun cried, "*Flores del mar! dos reales por todas!*" and swashing them down into the water, he again held them out, dripping and glittering, for inspection. *Two rids for the "Flowers of the Sea*!" I gave him a *medio* for the beautiful name, and pushed on toward the main land shore for an exploration among the mangroves; but soon found that, with the most strenuous efforts, only a few steps could be accomplished. Growing like the banyan of India, the branches of the mangrove frequently turn downward, and, interlacing again, take root and form a barrier, requiring the stout hatchet or *machete* to overcome. Many branches of those trees overhanging the water were loaded with a sort of crustaceous deposit, which proved, on examination, to be genuine oysters, varying in size from half a dime to a quarter of a dollar, and as sweet and palatable as "Shrewsburys." Several pounds often hung upon a single bough. Submerged by every tide, they were as fat and jolly as possible, and no doubt if, instead of being suspended, they were put to bed like our Virginian oysters, their increased size would soon leave no fault to be found with them.

It was my purpose to have taken the regular nine o'clock train this morning for Panama; but on visiting the office with that view, I had the fortune to meet there my recent *compagnons de voyage*, Messrs. Totten and Center, who suggested that, while my luggage could go on in the usual way, I might accompany them on a tour of inspection which they intended making over the road in a hand-car immediately after the departure of the train. To this proposal I gladly assented, and at about half past nine a comical little low-boxed car, about six feet square, was rolled up in front of the office. Two brawny natives, stripped to the waist, standing on the after-part, worked a double crank, attached to the axles, by an upright contrivance in the centre. In front was a single seat, just raised enough to permit the pedal extremities of its occupants to swing clear of the track. Mounting upon this, with our faces set toward the Pacific, away we skimmed over the ground at the rate of ten or twelve miles an hour. It would be difficult to conceive a mode of conveyance more exhilarating than a well-manned hand-car. Seated on the front, and out of sight of the propelling power, you seem almost to fly by your own volition; by a word you go swiftly or slowly, and when you add beautiful scenery, pleasant companions, and a perfect day, the enjoyment passes expression.

Away we sped, over the frith and through the swamp, until the tall forest of Mount Hope came into view. This was upon a spur of highland, through which the railway passed by a deep, long cut. On the left, near to its summit, a space of a couple of acres, flecked with small white points, revealed the site of Mount Hope Cemetery. Dense foliage surrounded it on every side, marked by the mourning plumes of the cocoa and the palm. The place was selected for a burial-ground shortly after the commencement of the road, and many victims to the hardships of the work and the climate were borne and buried there by their heavy-hearted comrades. But those days of trial have passed, and the long grass waving over their graves tells of the years since then. A few were recent, and marked by simple stones; among them several of strangers, and two or three of the officers of the U.S. Home Squadron. One at the lower side, under the shade of a lofty palm, was pointed out to me as the grave of the lamented Strain, whose sufferings and heroism, as the leader of the ill-fated "Darien Expedition," are still fresh in the memory of his countrymen. Strange was the providence that returned him almost to the very scene of his terrible experience, to finish his journey of life.

Whirling through the hill, which was cleared at several points and bore marks of recent cultivation, we again stretched away into the marsh, and began to bring into view the wondrous wealth of the isthmian forest. For a space of fifty feet on either side of the solid track embankment the original growth had been swept away, and was replaced by a rich display of aquatic plants, through whose road, shining leaves myriads of callas and long, slim-petaled pond lilies struggled out to fill the air with delicious perfume. The low and recent vegetation along the track was walled in by a primeval growth of a variety and luxuriance that almost defies description. Palm-trees, slender and tall, from under whose crowns hung long scarlet and yellow tassels; palms, low and huge, with trunks scarce lifted above the slimy ooze, sending out graceful pinnate leaves half a dozen yards in length; great cedro and espabe trees, towering up like giants for a hundred feet, then sending out strong arms that almost grasped each other across the clearing, their trunks covered with thick vines and parasites; these, and many other varieties, were so closely set and interwoven together that the eye failed to penetrate into the depths of the forest. The great number and variety of parasitic growths constantly attracted my attention. Almost every tree and shrub supported more or less of these treacherous leeches, in form and size ranging from what appeared a simple tuft of grass to an enormous growth whose branches often exceeded in magnitude the poor victim from which its nourishment was drawn. One specimen had wound itself around what must have been a large and thrifty tree; but unable to support itself under the close embrace and exhausting demands of the parasite, it had decayed and fallen, leaving the well-conditioned leech, though a mere shell, upright, and so like the original tree, that, except for occasional apertures which disclosed the hollowness within, this villainy might at a little distance have escaped detection. Many bore beautiful and fragrant flowers. There was one curious variety, the seeds of which, deposited in the ordure of birds upon the highest trees, sent long fibrous tendrils, without a single twig, down to the earth, where it again took root, growing until it occasionally attained a diameter of five or six inches. Often trees so decayed that otherwise they must have fallen, were, by these supports, retained in position for many years. The smaller ones, combining pliability with great strength, are much used for cordage by the natives. Trailing vines and blossoming creepers were in great profusion and luxuriance, enwrapping the trees, and hanging in variegated festoons from their branches.

As we proceeded, every moment new, and, if possible, richer varieties of vegetation passed in quick review, until I almost lost myself in wonder and admiration. At about three miles from the terminus we cut off a bend in a small, sluggish stream called the Minder River; its waters, almost concealed by the over-hanging verdure, were said to be swarming with alligators. Along its banks the tall and graceful bamboo, that giant of grasses, added a new beauty to the scene. In the immediate vicinity of this stream some of the lands were dry enough to be susceptible of tillage. Two or three native huts were seen on a little clearing near the road, surrounded by patches of plantains, bananas, Indian corn, and sugar-cane; but it was only a moment before we were again scouring through the marsh.

The vegetation was now varied and enriched by a species of the palm, from the fruit of which the palm-oil of commerce is extracted. It differed but little from the tasseled variety, except that it attained a greater size, and instead of the gaudy tassel bore immense clusters of scarlet nuts about as large as a lime. The clusters, shooting out from the trunk of the tree just underneath its foliage, hung by a single stem, and were often two and three feet in length, contrasting vividly with the surrounding verdure. Riding along at our ease upon a firm, well-ballasted track, the gorgeous vegetative display that met our eyes on every side was enjoyable to the last degree; but, underlying it, the slimy pools and yielding ooze upon which, by almost incredible expense and suffering, it had been built, were too often seen not to realize how differently it must have impressed the hardy men who sacrificed health, and even life, in carving through this wild region, and constructing a solid causeway upon its treacherous surface.

At a little after ten o'clock the seventh mile-post was passed, when we emerged from the swamp, and came out upon the eastern bank of the Rio Chagres, which stream is here about fifty yards in width, and making a great curve, opens beautiful vistas through the dense forests, up and down its course. This bank of the river is formed by a ridge of low bills across the foot of which the railway runs. A few yards from the road, on the high ground to the left, were the buildings of the Gatun station; on the opposite shore of the river was the ancient native town of Gatun, composed of forty or fifty huts of cane and palm, situated on the edge of a broad savanna that extended back to a range of hills a mile or two distant. This place is principally worthy of mention as a point where, in the days by-gone, the bongo loads of California travelers used to stop on their way up the river for refreshment; where "eggs were sold four for a dollar, and the ground rent for a hammock was two dollars a night." It was also here that the native inhabitants of the country had their first view of a locomotive engine. On the completion of the road to this place a day was appointed for running an engine over it. The natives on the work having informed their friends far and near of the expected event, an immense concourse of men, women, and children were assembled at the station on tip-toe of curiosity, to see the fabled monster, concerning whom their ideas were by no means definite. The growling of the engine was at last heard in the distance, and in a moment more it came in sight, coughing out volumes of black smoke, and spurting jets of steam from its sides; the excitement was intense, when the engineer suddenly turned on his whistle, and the entire multitude took incontinently to their heels and plunged into the river and the depths of the surrounding forest. In a few moments, however, finding no one killed, they rallied, and from a respectful distance sent forward their native priest to examine and report upon *el animal*. The padre soon returned with an assurance that it was no *animal* but a *machina*, in the interior of which, securely chained, a veritable demon worked the crank by which it was propelled. This solution proved entirely satisfactory, and is said to pass current among many in the interior to this day.

Pursuing our course, which lay along the base of an irregular line of high lands that rise up from the eastern side of the valley of the Rio Chagres, we came in a few moments to the Rio Gatun, a tributary of the Chagres, and crossed it by an iron truss girder bridge of ninety-seven feet span; the dense swamp foliage continued to wall us in, while, rising out of it close on our left, two fine conical peaks, four or five hundred feet in height (called Tiger and Lion hills), attracted the eye by their regularity of outline and the dense and gorgeous character of the forests with which they were covered. We occasionally passed small gangs of natives engaged in clearing away recent growths along the track with their *machetas*. The *macheta* (a sort of hiltless broadsword, from two and a half to three feet in length, and about two and a half inches in width, heavy, straight, and pointed, with a handle of wood or bone) is a universal accompaniment of the native of this country—with it he cuts his path through the tangled forest, builds his hut, clears his little plantation, plants his crops, cultivates and reaps them. It is usually his only weapon of defense or offense; and, from the boy of fifteen to the old and gray-headed man, you seldom find one waking or sleeping without his cherished *macheta.* The rapid growth of vegetation upon the road was said to be a source of no little trouble, as it required clearing along the whole line several times during the year; but it eventually proved beneficial, as stout roots were sent out in every direction, interlacing underneath and around the embankments, adding greatly to their firmness and stability.

At the base of Lion Hill we passed another station with a fine clearing on the high ground behind it. The stations on the road, uniform in size and appearance, are located four miles apart across the whole line, each occupied by a small party of men under a superintendent who has charge of the work and repairs of his particular section.

Leaving Lion Hill the vegetation became less dense and more decidedly aquatic in its character. Large patches of canebrake, liliaceous plants, huge ferns, low palms in great variety, and scrubby mangroves rose out of the dark pools by the roadside until we came to the next station called Ahorca Lagarto, where the land, still low and level, was again covered by a noble forest growth. Just beyond the station we halted beneath the shade of a huge ceiba, known as Stephens's tree. This Titan of the tropics measured not less than five yards in diameter at its base, including the broad plane-shaped roots that extended out on every side like buttresses, and towering up without a branch for nearly a hundred feet, supported a canopy of foliage full fifty yards in diameter. A luxuriant growth of vines decorated the trunk, and, winding out upon its branches, hung down like a thickly woven curtain upon the tree tops below. A little reconnaissance rewarded us with several fine specimens of the *orchidaceae* with which the trunks and branches of many of the trees were studded. Scarlet and purple passion-flowers were occasionally seen, and the delicate sensitive plant, with its feathery pink blossoms, covered the cleared ground like a carpet.

Occasionally, during our journey, we had been regaled with the notes of sweet singing birds, or the harsh screams of the parrot and the toucan; but the sun, being now near the meridian, pouring down his rays in true inter-tropical style, the most profound silence prevailed. With one consent all things animate had sought the deepest shades of the forest. Even the quivering leaves seemed to shrink from the fervent heat; but our stalwart natives, although exposed to its full glare, to which was added severe and continued exercise, were, with their half-hour rest, apparently as fresh as ever.

Again pushing onward, in a few moments I was startled to find ourselves passing through what appeared the overgrown ruins of some ancient city. Walls, watch-towers, tall columns, and Gothic arches were on either hand; and it was really an effort to realize that Nature alone, with a lavish and fantastic hand, had shaped this curious scene out of myriads of *convolvuli*. Whole groves of trees were covered in by them so that they appeared like huge fortifications. Tall stumps of palm, thirty or forty feet in height, were firm columns of verdure, and when they leaned together, as in several instances was the case, great Gothic arches were formed. So dense was this enshrouding web of creepers that not a tree nor a branch could be recognized through it over a space of several acres; and the whole of this wondrous display was decorated with bright blue trumpet-shaped flowers.

Leaving behind us the city of verdure, we brought into view a chain of high, densely-wooded hills on our left, and, winding along its base, passed a new station called Bujio Soldado, opening on our right a fine view of the Rio Chagres; and, about a mile farther on, passing through a fine quarry of freestone, where thirty or forty natives were at work blasting and hewing it for building purposes, we came to a pretty little cottage on the edge of the steep river bank by the road-side, which, from having been a favorite residence of the late J. L. Stephens when on the Isthmus, still bears his name. Here we stopped for a moment. The cottage was a low, wooden building, almost buried in by flowering vines. A stately palm cast its shadow across the little garden, rich in fruits and flowers, with which it was surrounded. From the piazza in the rear beautiful views up and down the river were visible; while, across, the high opposing bank stretched back in a broad plateau, covered with low palm, from among which occasional tall trees shot up, until it met a range of distant hills. It was here that Mr. Stephens, whose fame as a traveler and writer is world-wide, and whose later life was spent in developing this great railway enterprise, loved in his intervals of labor to rest in his hammock and enjoy the luxuriant beauties of the surrounding landscape.

Continuing our course with occasional view of the river, which winds like a great serpent along this tortuous valley, we soon came to the native town of *Bueno Vistita* (Beautiful Little View). This was a collection of thirty or forty rude palm huts skirting the track, and occupied by the families of native laborers on the road. A few native women, bareheaded, in long heavily flounced muslin dresses (off at the shoulder), and a naked "picanniny" astride the hip, formed the principal feature of the population; while the balance seemed made up of pigs, chickens, and children, in a charming state of affiliation. Very few of the aborigines of the country are found on this portion of the Isthmus, the inhabitants being for the most part a mixture of Spaniard and Indian. There are, however, many Africans and half-breeds, descended from the old Spanish slaves of this province, or imported from Carthagena and Jamaica. The former, usually peaceable and industrious, cultivate little patches of land, and occasionally raise a few cattle. But the latter are a restless, turbulent set, requiring a strong hand to keep them in subjection; being, however, hardy and athletic, they have been much employed as laborers on the road.

A couple of miles more of forest, intersected by one or two small tributaries of the Chagres, and we arrived at Frijoli. This station was superintended by a Mr. M'Clellan, famed along the line as a taxidermist and general collector of curios. As we were momentarily expecting to meet the train from Panama, and as lunch-time appealed stoutly to each one of us, it was determined to unship our car from the track and test the hospitality of the superintendent—also, if possible, to explore his collections.

At Work

The Singing Hummer

Here, as well as at most of the stations, was a bright little garden where the roses and rhododendrons, pinks and pansies of our northern clime defied comparison with the orchids, fuschias, and passifloras of the tropics; and there were radishes, lettuces, and cucumbers that had no competitors. The first object that met our eyes on entering the gate was a *small boa constrictor* about ten feet in length, lying directly across the path. After the first shudder, it was gratifying to notice a couple of deep *macheta* cuts through the neck of the beast, and to assure ourselves that life was extinct, though a vicious quivering of the tail secured to the reptile a wide berth. M'Clellan met us at the door with the air of a man laboring under considerable excitement, which was naturally attributed to his encounter with the specimen in the garden. Nothing could have been farther from the fact; he had discovered, only a few yards from his house, a rare variety of the humming-bird in the act of forming its nest. True, the *boa* turned up on his way thither; but a couple of his natives soon dispatched *him*. That was a common affair; but the *hummer* was probably still at his work—if we liked he would show us. Catching his enthusiasm, we followed to a jungle of low palms, where, upon cautiously pushing aside a few branches, he discovered to us a brilliant crested *trochil* spinning swiftly around a bent leaflet of palm in circles of a foot radius, that soon narrowed to the centre, when the bird darted out of sight. Drawing near to examine the result of these novel movements, we found that the ingenious little fellow had weighed down the end of his leaflet with bits of mud until it was sufficiently bent to form a shelter, and secured them by serving it around with threads drawn from the fibrous spatha of the palm. It had already begun to form its tiny nest upon the inner surface. If this was not the result of experience and calculation, how wonderfully like it were the ingenious instincts here displayed! As we retraced our steps toward the station a steam whistle was heard in the distance, and in a moment the expected train swept by, leaving us a comparatively clear track for the rest of our journey.

After a satisfactory lunch we had the pleasure of examining stuffed specimens of several richly-colored varieties of parrots, toucans, orioles, trogans, tangers (blue and scarlet), and hummers. Among the latter was a little dark-brown specimen said to have a beautiful song. A singing humming-bird has not been generally noticed in works upon ornithology; but I was led the more readily to credit its existence from having heard an account from Mr. J. Bell, the celebrated American taxidermist, of a singing hummer which he discovered on the Isthmus of Panama a year or two previous. Its notes were said to be somewhat like those of the wren, and exceedingly sweet and musical. All of Mr. M'Clellan's birds were procured in the immediate vicinity of his station. He had also a live toucan—a dark scarlet-breasted bird about the size of a pigeon, with a heavy serrated bill measuring seven inches in length. Its manner of feeding was very curious. Picking up a bit of banana on the point of its huge beak, by a sudden jerk he would throw it up half a yard, and as it fell catch it, deep in his throat, with perfect certainty. It also made extraordinary motions over the water-dish when attempting to drink. The habits of the toucan in this respect were noticed by the early Spanish American priests, who, averring that this bird in drinking made the sign of a cross over the water, called it "*Dios te de*" (God gives it thee). We also saw several fine skins of the *cougar* (or Isthmus lion, as it is popularly called), of the tiger cat, and tapir; but these animals, though common in the vicinity, were seldom seen near the line of the road.

A curious encounter with a large male cougar was related as having occurred a short time previous—Dr. Gallaer, surgeon-in-chief of the line, while driving over the road in a hand-car one morning, suddenly turned a curve near this place, and discovered a full grown *puma* standing upon the track only a few yards off. The headway of the car was so great that retreat was impossible. Driving on with increased speed, the animal was stricken down and so injured as to be incapable of resistance. On a careful examination the poor creature was found to have been *stone-blind.*

Leaving Frijoli, we passed several fine fields of Indian corn nestled under the hills, and, towering up amidst the overhanging forest trees, whose tops, crowned with scarlet flowers, appeared like great bouquets set into the surrounding verdure. Dense groves of palms, loaded with fruit, and superb displays of convolvuli, were also seen along this section for a couple of miles, when we approached the lofty banks of the Chagres River at Barbacoas, and crossed over it by a huge wrought-iron bridge six hundred and twenty-five feet in length, and eighteen feet in breadth, standing forty feet above the surface of the river.

This bridge—said to be one of the largest and finest iron bridges in the world—was composed of six spans, of over a hundred feet each, built of boiler iron, with a top and bottom chord two feet in breadth and one inch in thickness, and joined together by a web of boiler iron nine feet in height at the centre, and seven feet at the ends. The track was laid on iron floor-girders, three feet apart; and the whole structure was supported by five piers and two abutments of hewn masonry, twenty-six feet wide and eight feet in thickness, increasing in the proportion of an inch to the foot down to their foundations, which were constructed of piles and concrete.

After crossing the Chagres, instead of low grounds and virgin forests, a beautiful stretch of meadow land, bounded by high, precipitous hills, met our view; while the river, broad and swift, curved around like a horse-shoe through its deep channel on the left and behind us, displaying along its banks groups of a gigantic species of the caoutchouc-tree, that broke the outline of dense palm and cocoa groves. The cultivation of the land at this point is said to date back more than a century, and to have been worked originally by the Jesuits.

At about half a mile from the bridge we passed the San Pablo Station, and a little farther on a fine quarry of recent volcanic rock; from thence, through occasional cleared and cultivated land, to the station at Mamer and the native town of Gorgona, noted in the early days of Chagres River travel as a place where the wet and jaded traveler could worry out the night on a raw hide, exposed to the insects and the rain; and in the morning, if he was fortunate, regale himself on jerked beef and plantains.

The road then leaving the course of the river, passed on through deep clay banks and rocky cuts, presenting little novelty beyond the magnitude of the labor expended upon them, until sweeping around a hill the beautiful meadow lands of Matachin were opened to our view. Here, rising in their stateliness, the classic sheaves of the royal palm shed an air of Eastern beauty over the landscape. A native village dotted the foreground. On our left, the waters of the Chagres, broadened at this point by its greatest tributary, the Rio Obispo, was seen through the ceiba groves that skirted its banks; while on our right, and before us, the scene was bounded by a group of conical hills, covered with short grass and studded with palms. The completion of the Panama Railroad in 1855 was here celebrated with great ceremony and rejoicing, and the corner-stone of a monument to its originators and constructors was erected upon the crest of the highest and most beautiful of these hills.

San Pablo Station

The railway has several side branches at Matachin, and is the usual point of meeting for the trains from either terminus. As there is usually a little delay on such occasions, the natives take advantage of it to traffic with the passengers. Almost every hut displayed something for sale. One had a couple of tiger-kittens tied to a stake near the entrance; another, a sloth and a pair of ant-eaters; a third rejoiced in the ownership of a pet crocodile; while monkeys, parrots, and parrakeets, cakes, *dulces*, and a variety of tropical fruits, were exposed for sale on every side. Nor was this all; near the track on our right was a little cottage, containing a Yankefied combination of saloon, variety store, and dwelling, kept by a Frenchman, who was supposed to keep every thing that every body wanted.

From Matachin, passing along the base of "Monument Hill," we entered the narrow valley of the Rio Obispo, and, crossing its waters twice by stout iron bridges within the distance of a mile, passed the Obispo Station, and continued along the course of the Obispo River over a fine rolling and luxuriant woodland, where the delicious wild mango, the zapote, the nispero, and the guava were frequently seen; also occasional native huts, surrounded by cultivated fields.

From the station at Obispo we had been gradually ascending on a grade with a maximum of sixty feet to the mile. Continuing to rise, we passed the Empire Station, and reached the summit, or highest elevation of the railway above the mean level of the two oceans. Here was a little native settlement called Culebra, noted as the terminus of the railroad in 1854. Then, passengers arriving at this place by the cars from the Atlantic shore were compelled to mount upon mules and flounder on through heavy sloughs and rapid streams, along the borders of deep ravines, and over precipitous mountains; exposed to drenching rains in the wet season, and a broiling sun in the dry; not infrequently attacked and plundered by banditti, by which the road was then infested, until, after a whole day's labor and peril, they arrived at Panama, only twelve miles distant.

Monument Hill

Culebra at that time was a thrifty place, boasting of two or three hotels imported ready-made from the United States, into which often more than a thousand men, women, and children were promiscuously stowed for a night. There were also twenty or thirty native huts, about twelve feet square, each of which was considered of ample dimensions to house a dozen way-worn travelers, only too thankful to find a spot of dry ground upon which to spread their blankets. But its glory had departed, and not a vestige of its former prosperity remained except an old sign that some pitying hand had rescued from the ruins, and stuck in the crotch of a neighboring tree. Painted in large, grotesque characters, it ran thus:

"Old Joe" was the enterprising negro owner of the largest hotel in Culebra, And his curious old sign alone remains to mark a spot never to be forgotten by the Isthmus travelers of that time.

From Culebra, pursuing our course through a deep clay cutting, from twenty to forty feet in depth and nearly a third of a mile in length, we entered upon the Pacific slope by a descending grade of sixty feet to the mile. As we advanced the surrounding scenery was bold and picturesque in the highest degree. Lofty conical mountains rose on every side from among the irregular ridges that form the upper boundaries of the valley of the Rio Grande. Our course lay across steep rocky spurs, and deep ravines between them and along their precipitous sides. High embankments and heavy cuttings were frequent. Here, also, the vegetation was profuse and gorgeous. Tall forests covered the whole landscape as far as the eye could reach.

At about a mile from the summit the road plowed along the side of a huge basaltic cliff, whose great crystals (nearly a foot in diameter, and from eight to twelve feet in length), lying at an angle of about forty degrees, with a clear though broken and jagged outline, seemed almost to overhang and threaten the track below. This curious formation can not but strike the beholder with admiring wonder, from the regularity and beauty of its crystallization; and with awe, when he reflects upon the gigantic internal forces that have resulted in its upheaval. It is one of the few known examples in the world where the natural perpendicular which basaltic formations always assume (which is so beautifully seen in the celebrated Fingal's Cave at Staffa) has been so rent and displaced. But this whole region gave evidence that great, and comparatively recent, volcanic forces had been instrumental in its formation. There was no continuity in the mountain ranges. Conical peaks rose up on every side; marine shells and coral were found on their summits; the strata of the rocks they exhibit, exposed by the cuttings of the railroad, were all volcanic. Those great, crystals of basalt—firm and compact but easily dislodged—had been made to form the foundation and ballasting of a large portion of the road along this section.

The Rio Grande, at this place a narrow and noisy torrent, was winding along through the dense forests below us. The caoutchouc-tree, with its tall, gumstained trunk and verdant crown; the caoba and the malvicino trees rose up, like lords of the land, over the endless growths of palm and the innumerable varieties of other tropical woods that interwove below them. After nearly three miles of this, we came to the beautiful undulating valley of *Paraiso* (or Paradise), surrounded by high conical hills, where nature, in wild profusion, seemed to have expended its choicest wealth.

On we went, over ravines, and curving around the base of frequent conical mountains, gradually descending, until low lands and swamps, with their dense growths, were around; and we saw, looming up before us, the high, bald head of Mount Ancon, whose southern foot is washed by the waters of the Pacific Ocean. On our left rose *Cerro de los Buccaneros* (or, the Hill of the Buccaneers), from whose summit the pirate Morgan, on his marauding march across the Isthmus in 1670, had his first view of ancient Panama, and where he encamped on the night previous to his attack and pillage of that renowned city. Crossing by bridges of iron the San Pedro Miguel and Caimitillo, narrow tide-water tributaries of the Rio Grande, we passed the Rio Grande station; and from thence, through alternate swamp and rolling savanna, until the muddy bed of the Rio Cardenas was crossed; where, leaving the Rio Grande to the east-ward, we brought into view a fine stretch of undulating country around the base of Mount Ancon, enlivened by native huts and cultivated fields. A mile beyond us the long metallic roofs of the railroad buildings at the Pacific terminus were seen peeping out from a grove of cocoa-trees; and a little beyond them, and to the right, the cathedral towers, the high tiled roofs, and dilapidated fortifications of the city of Panama; while, through the intervening foliage, occasional glimpses of the "ever-peaceful ocean" assured us that our transit across the Isthmus was nearly accomplished; and in five minutes more we were safely housed in the spacious passenger dépot of the Railroad Company at Panama.

PART II

The Search for a Route

The five chapters in this part cover a twenty-six year period from 1855 to 1881. All of the chapters' articles are focused on exploration of the Central American region, and each offers a unique perspective, and geological site, for possible future construction of a canal. With the Panama Railway opening in 1855, the search began, in earnest, for a broader understanding of the region, in terms of its people, the political organization of the state, geography, and flora and fauna. The interest of the United States in the region took on a compelling, strange turn in the early 1850s, particularly after the war with Mexico which seemed to fulfill the prophecies of those who had spoken, in the 1840s, of an American "manifest destiny" to control the entire North American continent, and maybe even more than that.

The adventures of William Walker are worth mentioning here. A fundamentalist Christian from Tennessee interested in extending slavery a few years before the U.S. Civil War, he arrived in Nicaragua in 1855 and had himself elected president one year later. Walker changed the official language of Nicaragua to English and reinstituted slavery which had been abolished in Nicaragua years earlier. Walker's support came from a group of New Yorkers "who were jealous of Vanderbilt and assisted by Southerners who dreamt of extending the slave states."[1] Cornelius Vanderbilt, it must be remembered, had built a successful and profitable business in Nicaragua by carrying passengers from Greytown on the Caribbean coast by boat up river to the western end of Lake Nicaragua and then forty miles over land (by stagecoach) to the Pacific coast. Vanderbilt's enterprise, of course, collapsed when the faster, more comfortable rail line across Panama opened in 1855, the year Walker appeared on the scene. Walker was captured, eventually, and executed, but the legacy of the "gray-eyed man of destiny" would be felt for many years after his death, especially in Nicaragua where political liberals were discredited for having cooperated with Walker in Nicaragua's ongoing feud between conservatives and liberals.

The Walker affair certainly soured relations between the young Central American republics and the United States. Though Walker was a mercenary, without official sanction from the U.S. government, enough people in the United States supported his antics to cause alarm outside of the country. Walker's tactics and attitudes represented an extreme example of the U.S. presence in the region, yet many citizens of the United States shared Walker's belief that the citizens of Central America were hopelessly backward, lethargic, and in need of the civilizing, energetic spirit of American enterprise and ingenuity. Such an attitude is clearly reflected in the language of some chapters reproduced in this and other parts of the book.

Traveler's accounts, or traveler literature, has become over the past fifteen years or so an important source of information for nineteenth-century Latin American history. Traveler's books were extremely popular in the United States and Europe during the nineteenth century and have been recently "rediscovered" by historians and other social scientists interested in studying perceptions and attitudes of the travelers and comparing their observations with the written (where and when it exists) historical record. John Charles Chasteen has observed, in a noteworthy section on travel accounts in his textbook *Born in Blood and Fire*, how "Latin Americans as a whole did not rate very high in English language travel books."[2] He's right, of course, and what we would clearly consider chauvinistic and unacceptably racist was published and widely distributed in mainstream magazines written by and for the upper-middle and upper classes of America in the nineteenth century.

The first chapter in this part, by J. T. Headley, is from a March 1855 essay and is the first of a two-part series explaining to the reader the mission of Lt. Isaac C. Strain, commander of a mission to cross the isthmus at Darien, the dense jungle region separating what is today Colombia and Panama. The author describes the natives of the regions as "traitorous" and the New Granadians are depicted as pathetic, lazy, and selfish. Interestingly, the author did not make the voyage, so the essay is reconstructed from Strain's official report sent to the U.S. Secretary of the Navy, the diaries of those who made the voyage, and interviews with Strain, as well as conversations with those who survived the expedition. E. G. Squire offers a distinct perspective in his essay "Nicaragua: An Exploration from Ocean to Ocean" published in 1855. Squire provides excellent description of the city of Granada and, in general, of Nicaragua. He concludes, unlike the majority of the authors included in this text, that a canal through Nicaragua is unnecessary—assuming, of course, that one's perspective is British! The author points out that the mileage is about 200 miles greater from London to Canton through a proposed isthmian canal than via the preferred route, around the Cape of Good Hope. Squire states "it is folly to suppose that the enterprise will ever receive the commercial or political support of the powers of Europe."

Another proposal for a canal was presented in *Harper's* in 1861, in an article titled "The New Route through Chiriqui." Here, Thomas Francis Meagher suggests that a route could be competitively constructed at David, about 200 miles north of Panama City on the Pacific. The author, together with other explorers, crossed Panama west to east on foot in six days; he claims that a railroad and/or a canal could be constructed at the site. Unlike other pieces in this book, natives in Meagher's essay are described as noble savages and in language that can be termed picturesque. The next chapter, "The Secret of the Straight," is an excellent, early description of the Colombian cities of Cartagena and Turbo and the Urabá region, as well as the Bay of Darien, which the author claims as the best natural harbor in the world. This chapter, more than others, perfectly combines geography, geology, and politics, and the author calculates that 123 million dollars (U.S.) would be needed to construct a canal through the Darien jungle. Finally, one of the more entertaining chapters in this book was published in 1881 as an essay titled "Tehuantepec and the Eads Ship Railway." The author of this essay suggests that ships could be "dragged" across a narrow strip of land in Mexico powered by parallel railroad lines. This is one of the more innovative ideas designed to move ships from one ocean to the other and suggested, via technical drawings and diagrams, that ships could cross America without having to ever dig a canal. The author estimates that the cost of the project would be about seventy-five million dollars, and would take from four to five years to complete.

The first four chapters in this part, then, fall into the category of traveler's accounts, although Headley never actually "took" the voyage about which he writes with such detail and conviction. Traveler literature, as we can see, often had political ends and the intersection of scientific report, traveler account, political piece, and geographic description is especially evident in the first three chapters of this part. The final chapter is more technical in nature, but it, too, is designed to sell a project to a skeptical and confused society which spent years searching for a route—the best, most efficient (and potentially most profitable) route—for construction of a canal.

Notes

1. Helen Miller Bailey and Abraham P. Nasatir, *Latin America: The Development of Its Civilization*, 2nd ed. Englewood Cliffs, N.J.: Prentice-Hall, Inc., 1968, p. 452.
2. John Charles Chasteen, *Born in Blood and Fire: A Concise History of Latin America*, New York: W.W. Norton, 2001, pp. 114-117.

3

Darien Exploring Expedition, under Command of Lieut. Isaac C. Strain*

J. T. Headley

This essay recounts the Strain Expedition through the Darien jungle, which began in January 1854 at Caledonia Bay on the Caribbean Sea as a search for a route across the isthmus. The author tells the story of the heroic expedition after interviewing Lieut. Strain, reading the official report of the mission submitted to the U.S. secretary of the Navy, and reviewing journals supplied by some of the adventurers. Relying on "trustless" maps and "treacherous" Indians, the Strain Expedition lost its way in the Darien jungle and faced depravation, starvation, and death. Strain and a few of the men lived to tell about the expedition and eventually arrived at the Pacific Coast. This is the first of a two-part story.

[Having from the first become deeply interested in the Darien Exploring Expedition, and afterward doubly so in the fate of Lieutenant STRAIN, I was very anxious to know its history. Subsequent acquaintance with Lieutenant Strain, ripening into a warm friendship, enabled me to gratify this desire. With that grew the wish to make the facts public. At my request, therefore, Lieutenant Strain gave to me his private report to the Secretary of the Navy, whose permission to use it

*Entered according to Act of Congress, in the year 1855, by Harper and Brothers, in the Clerks Office of the District Court for the Southern District of New York.

was cheerfully granted, also the journals kept by both parties, together with the book of sketches made by the draughts-man. Interesting interviews with Lieutenant Maury and civil engineer Mr. Avery, have enabled me to add many details not incorporated either in the report or the journals. For any personal matters relating to Lieutenant Strain I solely am responsible, as well as for any special praise bestowed on him. I know it would be his wish that I should speak of him *personally* as little as possible, but I have thought it best to look only at the truth and interest of the narrative, and make every other thing subservient to these.]

It is not necessary here to speak of the importance to the whole civilized world of a ship canal across the Isthmus of Darien, nor of the different surveys that have been made. The route of the following Expedition, beginning in Caledonia Bay and ending in Darien Harbor, had not been passed over since 1788 and was a *terra incognita.* In 1849, an Irish adventurer published a book, which went through several editions, in which he declared that he had "crossed and re-crossed it several times and by several tracks," and that only "*three or four miles of deep cutting*" would be necessary for a ship canal the entire distance. Aroused by this report—which proved to be a mere fiction—Sir Charles Fox and other heavy English capitalists took up the subject, and sent out Mr. Gisborne, a civil engineer, to survey the route. He pretended to do so, and also published a book mapping down the route, and declaring that it was only "*thirty miles between tidal effects*," and the "*summit level one hundred and fifty feet.*" An English company was immediately formed with a capital of nearly $75,000,000.

Without following the progress of this scheme in England and on the Continent, it is necessary, in this connection, to state only that Mr. Gisborne's favorable report resulted in enlisting England, France, the United States, and New Granada, in exploring together the proposed route for a ship canal across the Isthmus. It will be seen in the succeeding pages that this report was also a fiction; that Mr. Gisborne never crossed the Isthmus at all—never saw across it—never advanced more than a dozen miles inland at the farthest—and, in fact, was afraid to make the attempt, and that, instead of the summit-level being 150 feet, it is at least *one thousand feet.* As an inevitable result, therefore, the various expeditions, relying as they did entirely on this report, with its accompanying maps, would be led into error, and in the end completely baffled. The English one, starting from the Pacific side December 23d, 1853, proceeded up the Savana, and cutting its way more than 26 miles from the place of debarkation on that river, finally became disheartened, and, with the loss of four men slain by the Indians, returned discomfited to the ships. Strain, from the Atlantic side, started nearly a month later. Three days after his departure, another expedition, composed of French and English together, under the guidance of both Dr. Cullen and Mr. Gisborne, set out from the same point, and endeavored to follow in his track. But, notwithstanding they had the men who *said* they had crossed and surveyed the Isthmus—the former having walked it "several times and notched the trees"—they were unable even to get out of Caledonia Valley, and after having penetrated not more than six miles in all returned. Gisborne and Cullen could not follow their own maps, not to mention the notched trees. The Granadian expedition started still later. This was a very large party, under the command of Codazzi, the principal engineer of New Granada. How far it penetrated is not known, but straggling over the space of a mile it was completely broken up, and returned, after having lost several men. It is with feelings of national pride I state that the American expedition, under Strain, alone accomplished the passage, though under an accumulation of suffering rarely recorded in the annals of man.

On the morning of the 17th of January, 1854, the *Cyane*, Captain Hollins, with Lieutenant Strain and his party on board, entered Caledonia Bay, where they were immediately visited by a number of Darien Indians, some of whom spoke broken English and Spanish, which they had acquired in their intercourse with the traders on the coast. They came on board fearlessly, were very intelligent and observant, and, though much below the ordinary stature, were strongly built and athletic.

On the 18th a council was held which lasted about eighteen hours, and finally terminated favorably. For a long time the chiefs resisted Hollins' demand for permission for Strain's party to traverse the Isthmus, and opposed the project of a canal most pertinaciously, insisting that if God had wished one made, he would have given greater facilities (an opinion in which Strain fully coincided before he got across), and that they ought not to be disturbed in the quiet possession of the land which the Almighty had given them. Strain replied that God had created them naked, but they had chosen to clothe themselves, which was as much an infraction of his laws as it possibly could be to construct a canal. To this special pleading they could not reply, and finally, believing that Captain Hollins would send a party through their country with or without their permission, gave their consent, remarking that it appeared to be the will of God that they should cross; and after stipulating only that they should not disturb their women, and respect their property, cemented the treaty by a hearty supper, during which they indulged freely but not immoderately in strong liquors.

Relying on Mr. Gisborne's book, the party took only ten days' provision. Each member of it, with the exception of Mr. Kettlewell, the draughts-man, had either a carbine or a musket, with forty rounds of ball cartridges; while eight of the officers and engineers had, in addition, a five-barreled Colt's revolver, with fifty rounds of ammunition to each pistol. The arms and provisions, in addition to the blankets and minor articles, brought the average weight borne by each individual to about fifty pounds, which was quite as much as they could carry through a pathless wilderness, and in a tropical climate.

The naval officers who were detailed for the expedition were—Passed midshipmen, Charles Latimer and William T. Truxton, and 1st assistant-engineer, J. M. Maury, whom Strain appointed assistant-astronomer and secretary, having obtained sufficient knowledge within the last ten years of his high capacity in each department. Mr. Latimer, however, being taken ill, never started. Mr. Truxton was appointed acting master and executive officer.

Midshipman H. M. Garland, of the *Cyane*, accompanied the party as a volunteer. The assistant-engineers were Messrs. A. T. Boggs, S. H. Kettlewell, J. Sterret Hollins, and George U. Mayo. Dr. J. C. Bird, of Wilmington, Delaware, was the surgeon. In addition to these were three others, volunteers.

Messrs. Castilla and Polanco, commissioners appointed by the New Granadian government, also determined to accompany the party, which numbered, all told, twenty-seven men. Having safely landed his little band, Strain drew them up, read his instructions to them, and then took up the line of march for a small fishing village at the mouth of the Caledonia river, where good water could be obtained.

As the huts were abandoned by the Indians, they took possession of them for the night, and, having stationed four armed men as sentinels, stretched themselves on the floor. But the heavy booming of the surf, as it fell in regular and tremendous shocks at their feet, made it like sleeping amidst the incessant crash of artillery. The billows, as they broke on the beach, swept on through the houses, over the sand spit, and into the river beyond.

On the morning of the 20th, the party was early afoot—and while waiting for some provisions and other articles for which they had sent to the *Cyane*, Strain endeavored to obtain a view of the valley above by opening a path to the summit of a hill on the right bank of the river, near its mouth, and some knowledge of their route by sending a party to cut up the left bank of the river. Here, as he from the top of this hill swept the mountain-range with his glass, the first feeling of doubt and missing arose within him, for in an unbroken chain that range stretched onward till it abutted on the sea, showing nowhere the depression indicated on the maps.

This little band of explorers, as they boldly struck inland and began to traverse the intricate forests of the tropics, presented an interesting spectacle. Officers and men were all dressed alike in blue flannel shirts, with a white star in the collar, blue trowsers and belt. The only distinction between them was, the latter wore blue caps without a front-piece, while the former had Panama hats, and pistols in their belts. These caps were stuffed with tow, which afterward served an admirable purpose in kindling fires. A spy-glass strapped to Strain's shoulders distinguished the leader. The order of march was single-file—the leading men carrying a macheta (cutlass) or ax to clear the way. The others followed, each carrying a blanket, haversack, carbine, cartridge-box, and forty rounds of ammunition. It being necessary that the men should be well armed, not much additional weight could be imposed upon them. Strain, an old wood-man and explorer, thoughtfully put a linen shirt under his woolen one anticipating the want of linen with which to dress wounds. That shirt afterward did good service to his wounded, lacerated men.

The Council

Taking the bed of the Caledonia River—dragging a single canoe after them until the shallowness of the stream compelled them to abandon it—they pushed vigorously up the Pacific slope, and near sunset reached a large island in the river. Following a path, they found deserted huts similar to those they had left at the mouth of the river, and there determined to encamp. The huts had evidently been deserted in haste, for stools, gourds, and cooking utensils, were strewn over the floors. These, as well as the extinguished brands of a recent fire, were all collected together and placed under charge of a sentry. In the morning they were restored as nearly as possible to their original positions, as Strain was determined to give the Indians no pretext for a display of hostility; although he felt sufficiently strong in numbers and preparation to cope with any tribe they would probably meet on the Isthmus. The rancho was surrounded by a plantation of cocoa, which, with the exception of tortoise-shell, is the only exchangeable product of the Darien Indians. A strict watch was kept during the night, there being two seamen and two officers or engineers, armed to the teeth, at all times on guard, while the remainder of the party had their arms beside them and their cartridge-boxes buckled on. These, silent and motionless, kept anxious watch in the midst of those deserted huts, whose very abandonment seemed portentous of evil. At length the wished-for light appeared, when the shrill and protracted boatswain's call, "*hence road*" the cheering strains used to quicken the sailors as they tread round the capstan to heave the anchor to the eat-head-startled every sleeper to his feet. "*Saddle up*," then rang through the encampment; and soon every man had his blanket and haversack swung to their places, and, with carbine in hand, stood ready to march. At half-past six they set out; and now wading in the bed of the river, and again following paths along its banks, through plantations of cocoa, plantains, and Indian corn, they pushed on until they came to a point where a small tributary entered from the southward and westward. Here they had a good view of the Valley of the Caledonia; and Strain, taking advantage of it, carefully examined the range of the Cordillera with an excellent spy-glass, and finding only a semicircular chain, from fifteen hundred to two thousand feet in height, abutting upon the sea-coast ranges to the westward and southwestward, determined to follow the easterly, or principal branch of the river, believing that it offered the stronger probability of a gorge through to the other slope.

Soon after passing the tributary already alluded to, they followed a well-beaten path on the left bank of the river, which soon brought them to an Indian village, containing some forty or fifty houses, grouped among trees and surrounded by large plantations of cocoa and plantains, and a small quantity of sugar-cane.

An occasional glance through the interstices of the bamboo walls at the interior of these houses—which were spacious and well-constructed—showed that, though devoid of inhabitants, much of their personal property still remained. The grunting of pigs and the crowing of cocks left behind by their owners, gave the only evidence of life in this deserted village, except the steady tramp of the heavily armed and overloaded party. These familiar sounds added inconceivably to the desolation of the scene, and impressed deeply the whole band. Strain, with his cocked carbine in his hand, strode on in advance, his eye rapidly, almost fiercely, searching every suspicious-looking spot; while the men, each one with his weapon resting in the hollow of his arm, pressed swiftly after. Not till the last hut was passed did they breathe free again. As they emerged from this village, they found a path which wound down a steep bank to the river, near the opposite bank of which lay a canoe containing women's clothing, abandoned evidently in the haste of their flight. As Strain was about to descend by this path, three Indians suddenly appeared. After an interchange of friendly signs, one of them offered to point out to him, as he supposed, the path leading to the Pacific. He accordingly counter-marched; but, after accompanying his guide a few hundred yards, came to the conclusion that the latter only wished to lead them from the village; for in the direction he took, toward the west and southwest, Strain, as already mentioned, could see no opening whatever in the Cordillera. He accordingly halted the party, and explained to the Indian, as well as possible, that he would proceed no further in that direction, and was determined to follow up the main branch of the river. The latter made no opposition, but shrugged his shoulders; and turning down a ravine to the river, led up its bed until they had passed the village, then courteously took leave. Subsequent events convinced Strain of the good faith of this Indian, who doubtless would have led him into a path across the Cordillera, which he afterward discovered by mere accident. At ten o'clock the order to halt passed down the line; and the party, still suspicious, breakfasted in the bed of the river. A fire was kindled, some coffee and tea made, which, with pieces of pork stuck on sticks and toasted in the fire, made a comfortable meal. The repast being ended, the party started forward, keeping the bed of the stream till mid-day, when Strain ordered a halt, thoroughly convinced from its course—which inclined strongly toward the Atlantic—its rapid fall—which imparted to it almost the characteristics of a mountain torrent—and the aspect of the mountain ranges which crossed his course, towering some two or three thousand feet above the level of the sea, that this route could afford no facilities for a ship canal, and could not be that alluded to by either Mr. Gisborne or Dr. Cullen. While the main body remained halted here, Messrs. Truxton, Holcomb, and Winthrop were sent up the river to reconnoitre, and upon returning reported unanimously that the route in that direction was impracticable. Having received this report, they rapidly retraced their steps, finding, as they had done in the ascent, several canoes containing women's clothing drawn up on the beach. Their owners were invisible, having doubtless hidden themselves in the forest; but the fact of their having fled up this branch of the river to avoid the party, was additional evidence to Strain that he had taken the wrong direction. Marching rapidly past the village, which seemed to be occupied, he followed the smaller branch toward the southward and westward—the India-rubber, cottonwood, and other tropical trees, gracefully festooned with parasitic plants, darkening the way, which was enlivened only by the laugh of the men as their companions, now and then, tumbled over a rock into the water. About sunset they encamped on the right bank of the stream. The officers and men were divided into two messes, each having its separate fire and cook. This second day's tramp had been a hard, exciting one, and the men were glad to halt. After tea, the two groups sat around their respective fires, smoking, telling stories, and singing, till the watch was set. An officer and two sentries formed, this night and for a long time afterward, the regular guard front eight in the evening until daylight. The two fires were kept brightly burning all night, shedding their steady light over

SECTION OF THE ELEVATION OF THE ISTHMUS.

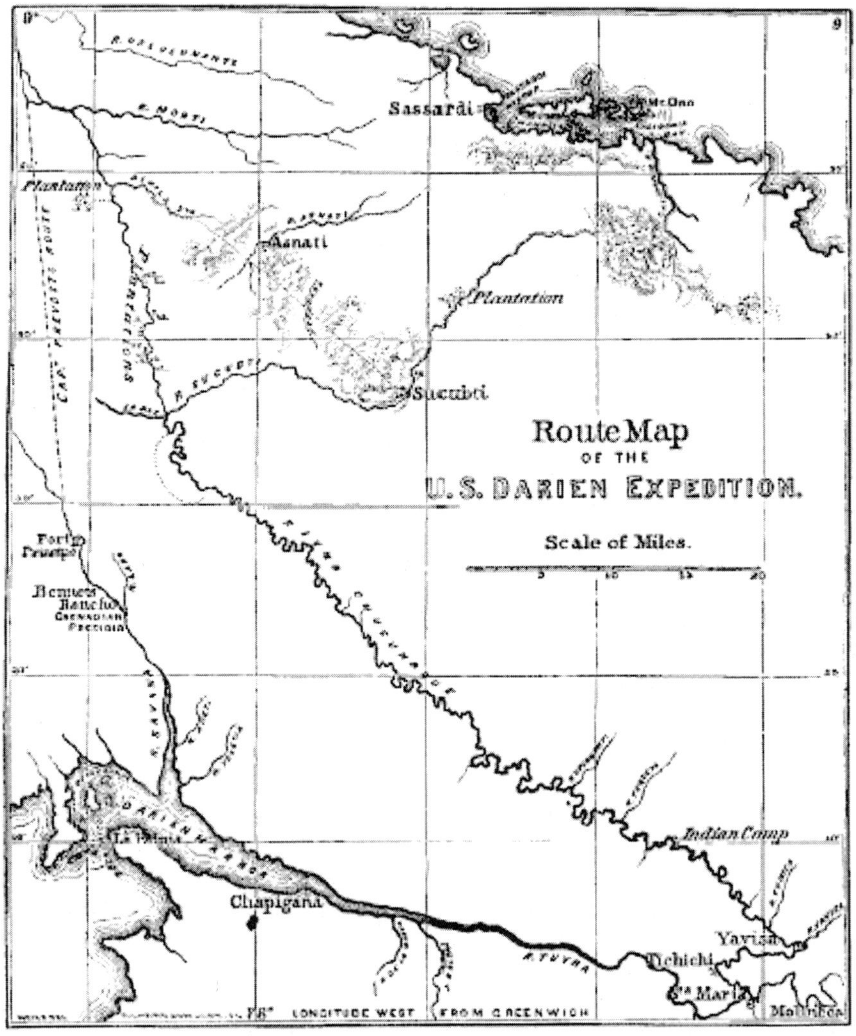

the motionless party as they slept in pairs, with one blanket beneath and the other above them, under the open sky. They were a splendid set of men, and, as they lay there in order of battle, seemed well fitted for the hardships before them.

Roused up by the boatswain's whistle, the party breakfasted, and again set out, wading about a mile up the river, until they arrived at a "caon," in which the water was so deep as to place fording out of the question, while the scarped rocks on either side made the ascent to the bank above very difficult. From the outset as the way became more and more obstructed, Wilson, who had a splendid voice, cheered on the party by making the woods ring with "Jordan is a hard road to travel." While stumbling up the rocky bed of the Caledonia, he had changed his song into "Caledonia is a hard stream to travel," in which there was far more truth than poetry. It was a relief to all, therefore, when Strain ordered a halt, and informed them that it was his intention to leave this river soon, as it was leading toward a very high range of mountains and too far to the southward. Holcomb and Winthrop were for continuing on, and the former having found an accessible point on the bank of the "caon" to ascend, and displaying some impatience to attempt it, and as some of the party appeared anxious to follow, Strain gave permission, but at the same time recommended them to follow him a short distance below, where a more gentle ascent might be found, and one less likely to tire the heavily-laden party. They did so, and soon came to an easy slope, up which they pushed. They had not proceeded far when they unexpectedly stumbled on a well-beaten track leading over the hills to the southward and westward. This was an unlooked-for stroke of good fortune, and Strain was convinced that he had found by accident the traveled Indian route to the Pacific. He now recalled the scattered party—first by shouting, as they were near, then by the boatswain's whistle, and finally by firing his carbine. The stragglers soon closed in, but upon counting the party to see who might be missing, he found that Holcomb, Winthrop, Hollins and Bird, and Roscoe, a seaman of the *Cyane*, were absent. He then fired three carbines in quick succession, the previously established signal to close instantly—the signal also of extreme danger. This signal was answered, but still the missing party did not come up. After waiting some time, several successive shots were fired, when Strain, to his astonishment, heard their carbines far up the river, and apparently near the base of the hill. Unwilling still to believe it to be their wish to separate, he waited some time on the slope of the mountain, firing frequently. But finding that their responses gradually became more and more faint and distant, he determined to proceed, hoping that they were only seeking a lower point in a gorge—which he felt sure existed on his left—to cross over and rejoin him. The path he now followed was clear and well defined, and led by a spur over the Cordillera, or principal chain, which rose in three successive peaks as they advanced. The ascent was very steep, being in many places as much as fifty and sixty degrees, up which the men were frequently compelled to pull themselves by trees. As they were without water, and heavily laden, this proved very fatiguing. Arriving at the summit of the first peak, Strain ordered a halt, hoping that the missing party might come up. In the mean time Edward Lombard, a seaman of the *Cyane*, climbed a tree to reconnoitre the country, but reported nothing but mountains and hills in every direction. Following the Indian trail, at a quarter past one, P.M., the party arrived at a small stream running to the westward. The men, suffering from thirst, stooped down to this, and took long and hearty draughts of water. They then laid aside their arms, blankets, and haversacks, and sat down to wait for the absent-tees, who were expected every moment. The sun at length stooping behind the tropical forest, and no signs of their arrival, Strain ordered a fire to be made, and went into camp. After eating a scanty supper, he seated himself at a point where the Indian trail entered the gorge, and watched long and anxiously for the arrival of the missing men. The shadows of night gathered over him there, yet he still waited until a late hour, when he stretched himself on his blanket in painful suspense as to their whereabouts.

Early in the morning he sent scouts across the mountain, to see if they had not crossed higher up on the Caledonia, and reached the river valley which he was confident must exist on the other side. At half past nine they all returned, unsuccessful, but reported having found a large stream, which they believed united with that on which they then were, which afterward proved to be the fact.

Deeply solicitous as Strain was about the absent men who had been entrusted to his care, and for whom he was in a great measure responsible, he felt the obligation also not to make any delays that should endanger those still under his command nor the success of the expedition, and at ten o'clock gave the welcome order to move forward. Keeping in view this river to its junction with the Sucubti, they followed the latter in its rough and tortuous course, struggling over huge boulders and masses of stones rolled together by the torrent, and which rendered the way almost impassable. Dangerous rapids also intersected their path, skirted by precipitous banks, along and up which, heavily laden, they scrambled with great difficulty, until at last, fatigued and hungry, they encamped at five o'clock at the mouth of a small stream, having made in all not more than eight or nine miles. All day long, whenever they struck a sandy reach, they found fresh Indian tracks always in advance, but as there appeared to be only two men, and they accompanied by a dog, Strain felt no anxiety, as he knew their strategy never admits of a dog on a war-path. On the morning of the 24th, at nine, A.M., they left their bivouac and proceeded down the bed of the river, occasionally pursuing the banks when it was deep or impassable from falls or boulders. The trail of the two Indians and dog was still very distinct, and it was evident that they had slept in the immediate vicinity of the last night's camp. About eleven o'clock, while wading down the bed of the river, a smoke was seen rising through the trees, and immediately the quick order, "*Close up*," passed down the line. Soon after, Strain commanded a halt, and advancing alone, mounted the left bank, and found an Indian hut, apparently just abandoned, and on fire; the roof had already fallen in, while the joists and timbers were slowly burning and crackling in the still air. Two other houses on the opposite bank were also in flames. Strain immediately crossed over, and found that, as in the first, all the stools, pots, and other utensils were left a prey to the flames, but their *arms* and clothing had been taken away. While examining these two houses, Mr. Castilla, the New Granadian commissioner, came up the bank, and seeing a bunch of plantains hanging on a rafter, reached up to take them; but Strain stopped him, declaring that he had promised to respect private property religiously, and was determined to give the Indians no excuse whatever for assailing his party. This destruction of their property looked ominous, and could be construed in no way, except as an evidence of hostility; and Strain now began to anticipate a gathering among them, and an attack at some favorable point in advance. He therefore ordered the men to re-examine their arms carefully, and march in close order. Still leading his little band, he kept on the difficult path, expecting every instant, for hours, a shower of arrows upon his party. He, of course, would be the first victim; and he confessed afterward that he remembered the account given by a comrade in Texas, of the sensation the latter once experienced with two arrows in his body, and the remembrance made him squirm. But compact and silent they kept down the river, generally wading in its bed, and where the water was too deep, selecting the bank which appeared less densely wooded, and always, when practicable, following the trail of the two Indians and their dog. Strain carried twenty or thirty pounds more than any other member of the party; and Castilla, the Granadian commissioner, wishing to relieve him, offered to take the spy-glass, but on being informed that the Indians knew that this was carried by the commander, who would be selected for the first fire, he turned pale, and did not press his offer. Several of the men requested to take part of his load, but he refused, saying, that by carrying more than they, and doing more work, he could better tell how fast to march and when to halt, so as not to overtask them.

At some points the water had attained a great depth, especially where it had caught a rotary motion around some of the smaller boulders, and the traveling not only grew more difficult, but very dangerous. They had lost the Indian trail, and not being able to pass through the forest without the tedious operation of cutting a road with an ax, so thick was the undergrowth, they were forced to climb along the rocky banks of the river, to cross wide clefts in the rocks, and surmount enormous boulders, where a false step or a slip would have led to a broken limb, if not to a broken neck. They made only some ten miles the whole day, and at six in the evening, finding a defensible position, pitched their camp. The men were quite fagged out, and prepared their supper without their usual boisterous merriment. Besides, the consciousness of danger at hand made each one thoughtful. To enliven their spirits they concluded to drink up a bottle of brandy which one in the party carried for medicinal purposes, for the very sensible reason that they feared it would get *broken*. The reason that they feared it would get *broken*. The evening gun of the *Cyane*, rising with a booming sound over the Isthmus, also cheered them, for while that was in hearing, they did not feel themselves so entirely cut off from the outer world.

It was not so pleasant, however, when darkness enshrouded the wilderness; hut the camp fires blazed brightly, and they were all brave hearts. Still many an anxious glance searched the shadowy forest that hemmed them in, and a score of musket-halls or arrows in their midst would hardly have taken them by surprise. Sentries were posted at some distance up and down the bank, to give timely warning. As silence settled on the camp imitations of the cries of wild beasts were heard in the surrounding forest, made evidently by the Indians who were hovering near, in the hope of alarming them. The next morning the boatswain's "*Heave round*" rung far and wide through the solitude, and the tired sleepers arose to another day's toil. On examining the ground near the camp they discovered the tracks of seven men, who had closely reconnoitred them in the night. Strain had already begun to doubt whether he was on a branch of the Savana, owing to the course which the river pursued, but as the number of cascades corresponded exactly with those laid down for that river, he was still partially satisfied, and hoped that the maps might, after all, prove to be tolerably correct.

Leaving camp about half past eight, they followed the river by the bed or banks, just as one or the other furnished best footing. Both were difficult; the former being encumbered with granite boulders, and the water often so deep as to reach nearly to the cartridge-boxes, while the latter was almost closed against them by the denseness of the undergrowth. Their constant companions, the two men and the dog, between whom and them there seemed some strange, mysterious link, still preceded them.

Passing several isolated peaks, some five or six hundred feet in height, they at noon, or in three hours and a half, had made about three miles. At length they came to some plantain fields, while the distant barking of a dog announced the proximity of Indian habitations. A halt was now called, and Strain consulted with his officers upon the best course to pursue. A long straight reach of considerable depth apparently closed the bed of the river against them in front, while on the banks the undergrowth grew so thick that it was impossible to proceed, except by the slow process of cutting a road. At length, however, they discovered a path on the left leading over a steep hill, and which they supposed would intercept the course of the river below. Strain directed Mr. Truxton with a few men to examine it, while he, leaving the main body of the party, many of whom showed symptoms of fatigue, in an open space, where surprise would be almost impossible, continued down the river, to determine whether the reach was passable.

He found it to be, under the circumstances, and considering the evidences of a hostile spirit on the part of the Indians, a dangerous route, as the water was very deep for about a quarter of a mile, the banks on each side perpendicular and about eighteen feet in height; while the ledge at the foot of the right bank, where only they could pursue their way, was not in any part more than two feet wide, and in some places could be passed only with the greatest difficulty, and not without danger of slipping into deep water, where they would sink by the weight of their baggage and accoutrements before assistance could be rendered. An attack in such a place would prove fatal; for the Indians could fire from the bushes while they were on the ledge, where they could neither return the fire nor close with them, nor escape, except by swimming—a resort almost as fatal as to stand and be shot down. At all events, the entire ammunition of the party would be rendered useless. It was a great relief therefore, when Mr. Truxton came down on the opposite bank and pronounced the path practicable, and trending down the valley of the river after crossing the hill on the left. Cheered by the intelligence, the party entered the river, and slowly, and with great difficulty, stemmed the deep and rapid current. Striking the foot of a steep hill on the opposite bank, they clambered up half a mile to the top, where they found a plantain field, in which the path ended. Wholly at a loss what course to take, they retraced their steps to the river, and while rattling down the bill were arrested by the barking of a dog, which was as abruptly smothered, apparently by a muzzle, and by the distant sound of axes struck rapidly upon some hollow substances. These evidences of the vicinity and watchfulness of the Indians made Strain still more unwilling to risk the ledge along the bank of the river; but as there appeared to be no alternative, he gave the reluctant order to advance, he leading the file. They steadily entered the passage, one by one, and crawling cautiously along the precipice, fortunately passed without an attack. With his gallant little band, Strain had felt himself a match for a horde of Indians; but here he was power-less, and a mountain seemed lifted from his heart when he saw the last man through.

At the end of the reach they came upon a house standing a little back from the river, and surrounded by what appeared to be a species of fortification. Not wishing to expose the whole party to the risk of an ambuscade, or to alarm the natives unnecessarily, Strain ordered a halt, and advanced alone to examine it. Like all the other huts they had seen, it had evidently been recently abandoned—the proprietors having left behind much of their furniture, and some provisions scattered upon the floor. Its position was peculiar, and different from any thing they had before seen, having been erected on an artificial mound, scarped and made nearly inaccessible on all sides except through a strong gateway. This mode of construction may have been adopted to guard against inundations; but reference also appeared to have been had to defense against enemies, and the position was certainly one which a few determined men might have held against a large number. Continuing their journey, they soon arrived at a village on the left bank, containing several houses, almost concealed amidst plantain and other fruit trees. They passed this without entering, supposing it to be, like the others, deserted by its inhabitants; the only sign of life being the barking of a dog, which had probably been left when the Indians concealed themselves in the forest. Immediately in front of the village, and on a sloping shingle-beach, they found the remains of seven canoes which had just been destroyed. Their condition satisfactorily explained the sounds of the ax they had heard while in the plantain field on the hill. The destruction of these canoes was complete; for, not satisfied with splitting them up, the Indians had cut them transversely in several places, taking out large chips, rendering it impossible to repair them. This had an ugly look, and was an unmistakable sign of hostile feeling.

The river here was deep and rapid; but Strain leading the way, the whole party crossed in safety, and entered a path which appeared to follow the right bank. Advancing along this, Strain suddenly saw a party of five armed Indians rapidly approaching. Considering all the recent evidences which he had seen of their distrust, not to say hostility, his first impulse was to cock his carbine; but a moment's reflection convinced him it was better not to lose the benefit of their friendship, if it could be obtained, especially as he felt certain that he was not upon the river Savana, as he hoped and at first believed.

He accordingly halted the party, and handing his carbine to one of the men, advanced to meet them, calling out at the same time in Spanish that they were friends. The Indians then came up and shook hands, when he recognized two of their number as having been on board the *Cyane* soon after her arrival in Caledonia Bay. One spoke a little English, and another, who appeared to be the leader, spoke Spanish intelligibly; while the remainder, belonging to the Sucubti tribe, used only their own dialect. The leader informed Strain that he was on the *Chuqunaqua* instead of the *Savana*, but offered to guide him to the latter stream. In answer to a question respecting the distance, he replied that they could reach it in three days. Strain then inquired if he had been sent by the commander of the *Cyane*, or by Robinson, a chief referred to in a letter from Captain Hollins, which reached him during the second day's march. He replied, "Neither;" and did not appear to know who was meant by Robinson—probably not recognizing his English name.

Strain felt that he incurred no little risk in trusting himself to these Indians; but being firmly convinced that they were neither on the Savana nor any of its branches, and knowing that the course which the Indians pointed out would at least bring him nearer to it, he determined to accompany them, believing that he could subsist wherever they could, and that, as a last resort, he could return if they deceived or abandoned him. He was especially induced to this determination by the fact that he had offered this same Indian a large sum of money, when he was on board the *Cyane*, if he would guide him across, and thought it not improbable that he had determined to accept it when once free from the surveillance of his tribe. The order "Forward!" was accordingly given, and they proceeded rapidly, by a well-beaten path, through a cocoa grove and through the forest in a westerly direction. Once in the woods, and finding the path growing less distinct, Strain secretly gave orders to the officers to observe the route carefully, in order that they might return by it, if it was found necessary; and also directed Mr. Truxton, who commanded the rear-guard, to have the trees marked with a macheta as they proceeded.

In silence, and in close order, the little party rapidly followed the Indians, who, leading them over three minor ridges, and one hill nearly six hundred feet high, and through a grove of plantains and of cocoa, arrived a little before dark at a deep and gloomy ravine, through which brawled a rivulet, running apparently in the direction of the river they had left, and as the guide informed them it did.

At this place the Indians left, promising to return in the morning. To this course Strain assented with as good a grace as possible, although very much against his will; for, although he believed them sincere, he felt much more confidence in them while they were within the range of his carbine.

Some of the party asked the Indians to bring some plantains when they returned; which, after consulting with the oldest man among them, the guide promised to do. They then filed away into the woods, and the party pitched their camp. The undergrowth was cleared away, the fires lighted, and the supper of pork and biscuit quickly dispatched. Strain set the watch earlier than usual, as he did not feel perfectly secure in his position, and could not shake off all suspicion of his new friends. He also ordered the fires to be made at some distance from the place which had been selected for sleeping, so as to mislead the Indians if they should attempt to surprise them, and directed the party to lie down in their ranks where the steep bank of the rivulet afforded a certain barrier against an attack in the rear. The two sentries he placed completely in the shade on each wing of the camp, and directed the officers of the guard to keep away from the fire, where the light might guide the aim of any one who should be lurking in the bushes.

Having taken all those precautions which a thorough woodsman alone understands—Strain, keenly alive to the welfare of his party, kept the watch of one of the gentlemen who was somewhat indisposed. After it was over he lay down, but at one o'clock was aroused by a slight noise on the side of the ravine whence he supposed an attack, if any, would be made. Without starting up he turned himself slowly and cautiously over, and saw someone silently climb up the bank close to where he was lying, and look round over the sleeping party. He appeared to be short in stature, as the Indians invariably are on the Isthmus, and by the dim light he could see that his hat closely resembled those which they wear, so, silently drawing his revolver, he thrust it suddenly against his side, saving, in a low tone, "Who's there?" He was answered by Mr. Truxton, just in time to prevent his firing. It was this officer's watch, and having heard a noise in the ravine, he had gone down to investigate it, and was returning by the bank when he thus unexpectedly encountered Strain, and came near losing his life. A moment's delay in answering would have insured his death.

This little circumstance, which was unknown both to the sleepers and sentries, was the only alarm they had during the night. On the morning of January

26th, about half past eight, the guide returned, and announced himself ready to continue the journey. Strain was somewhat surprised to find that, excepting the interpreter and guide, the rest, numbering four, were new Indians.

No plantains were brought as promised; but they continued to give every evidence of friendship, and advised the party to supply themselves with water from the rivulet, as they would have a long and severe march before they reached any more. They therefore filled their bottles and flasks, and, after taking a hearty drink, commenced following a path leading in a westerly direction over a very steep hill about 800 feet in height. Resting but once, and only for a few minutes to recover their breath, they reached the summit, from which could be seen many ranges and peaks, still higher, to the northward, forming apparently a chain of isolated mountains. Hurrying down the opposite slope, which led them at times along the margin of deep valleys with almost perpendicular sides, they reached, about half past ten, another ravine containing water, where they halted to refresh themselves, not having drank since leaving the camp in the morning. In this rapid march Strain had a fair opportunity of testing the comparative endurance of his men and the Indians; and although the latter, being nearly naked, and with no burdens except their arms, took the steep ascents much better than the former, he found his own men fully equal to them, heavily laden as they were, in descending or on level ground.

Having slaked their thirst at this stream, which Strain concluded to be that called the *Asnati* on the old Spanish maps, they pushed on, and soon after, passing another branch of the same stream, and some plantations of plantains and cocoa, commenced ascending another steep hill, still pursuing a course little to the northward of west. Near this point, and in the valley, a village known as *Asnati* is supposed to be situated; but the Indians were always careful to carry them as far as possible from their habitations. The hill which they now ascended was neither so steep or high as the last one, not being more than 450 feet above the level of the valley from which they started. While ascending it, one of the men, Edward Lombard, a seaman of the *Cyane*, and who carried the boatswain's whistle, was stung on the hand by a scorpion, and for some time suffered severely. Truxton had a little brandy left in a flask, and Strain having heard that stimulants were good for poison, told Lombard to drink it. But the latter being a temperance man declined. Strain then ordered him to swallow it, threatening, if he refused, to pour it down his throat. The poor fellow finally swallowed it, and some moistened tobacco being applied to the wound he soon began to rally, and was at length able to proceed slowly, and by night had recovered entirely, and was as active and energetic as before. He said the effects of the sting were like an electric shock, as instantaneous and as paralyzing. While Lombard was suffering and unable to walk, the whole party halted, and Strain asked the Indians if they knew of any remedy for the sting. They replied they did not; but that there were men in their village who could cure it.

Strain, taking Lombard's musket, gave the order "Forward!" and passing the summit of the hill they commenced the descent, when they were suddenly met by some five or six Indians. A halt was made, and a man, who appeared to be a chief approached Strain, and made an elaborate speech, accompanied with all the gesticulation and vehemence of an Indian orator. He concluded by directing the guide to interpret it. During the continuance of this speech, of which Strain could distinguish but one word, "*Chuli*"—No—he carefully watched the countenance of the guide, and thought he could detect an expression of annoyance not unmingled with contempt. The latter would not interpret the speech, though requested to do so both by the orator and Strain. At length, being urgently pressed, he abruptly replied, "*Vamos*"—"Let us go"—and led off. While descending the hill, most of the strange Indians, taking with them some of the party with which they had started in the morning, and replacing them with others, left. From that time the conduct of the Indians changed.

At the foot of the hill they arrived at a ravine leading nearly west, which they followed until sunset, sometimes climbing over boulders, and at others sliding down the face of smooth rocks, where the rivulet formed cascades, and always traveling rapidly and most laboriously. From time to time Strain was obliged to order a halt, to allow those who were most fatigued a little rest. The Indians who had joined that day appeared to enjoy the distress of the men amazingly, and attempted to hurry them on before they were sufficiently rested. Mr. Polanco, one of the New Granada commissioners, laid down, utterly prostrated by fatigue; and Mr. Kettlewell, engineer and draughts-man of the expedition, who was ill the night before, wished the party to leave him to rejoin them afterward at the next camp. Having made only twelve miles, they arrived about sunset at a stream a little smaller than the one they had left two days before, and encamped on an island in front of a plantain grove. The difficulties of the way may be gathered from the fact, that, to make even this short distance, the men were kept all day to the top of their speed and endurance. The whole march was a constant climbing, sliding, floundering over one of the most broken countries imaginable. The ravine which they had traveled was, by common consent, denominated "the Devil's Own." Before the Indians left that evening, the guide, who had appeared some-what depressed since the interview with the strange Indians, informed Strain that, in the morning, he should start on his return to Caledonia Bay; and that he would visit the ship, and tell the Captain how well they had progressed; mean-while, he would leave behind some of his friends, to guide them to the Savana, at which they would arrive in a day and a half.

Strain attempted to dissuade him, offering him any pay he might ask to guide him through; but to no purpose. He then told him that he would send a letter by him to Captain Hollins, which he declined taking, and started with the others, leaving Strain with no very pleasant anticipations for the future, there being seven days' hard march between him and the ship, while it was very doubtful whether he could find the path back; for in many places it was so obscure that the Indians themselves could with difficulty follow it. A fatigued party, who looked back with horror to the last few days' march, and with less than one day's provisions, and very doubtful guides, was not a very pleasant object to contemplate. Believing that there was a large Indian population immediately in the neighbor-hood, Strain ordered an unusually strict watch to be kept. Still he had pitched the camp in so strong a position that he did not believe they would dare to attack him.

The next morning, while preparing breakfast, two strange Indians, with quite a small boy, strolled into camp; and soon after, the old guide, and several others, among whom were the new guides, of forbidding appearance, and who were besides armed with bows and steel-pointed war-arrows—which they never use in hunting—also came in. Some forty more, of different ages and sexes, were seen skulking in a plantain patch on the opposite side of the river, and narrowly watching every movement. Those who were in camp were exceedingly anxious to look into the haversacks of the men and ascertain the amount of provisions they had. These, it is true, were scanty enough, as many of the men had used theirs imprudently, and the New Granadian commissioners, having either consumed or thrown away their rations, had none at any time after crossing the mountains, but lived entirely on those of other members of the party. The officers still having some provisions, which, with greater prudence, they had reserved, Strain directed that they should be divided with the men. All cheerfully consented, with the exception of one, who could not understand why those who had stinted themselves to provide food for the future should now be made to suffer for the reckless improvidence of the others. Strain, who cared little for meat, had eight pounds preserved, all of which he gave up to the men. This left them with nothing on hand but a little bread dust and two or three pounds of coffee. Still, if the Indians fulfilled their promise and took them to the Savana in a day and a half, and they could there obtain boats, they would make a fair journey and escape without great suffering.

Before setting out, Strain took the old guide aside and endeavored to obtain a clew to their intentions and his own prospects. But the frankness and apparent sincerity of his demeanor were gone. He now stated that he would not return to Caledonia Bay until next month, which was only a subterfuge to avoid being pressed to carry a letter. Strain then renewed his offer of large pay, if he would continue to act as guide; and finally asked him his motives in coming thus far. To this he replied, that he had taken an interest in him when they met on board the *Cyane*, and did not wish him to follow the Chuqunaqua, which was a very long route to the Pacific. He still declared that they would reach the Savana in a day and a half and the harbor of Darien in two days and a half; but Strain could not induce him to give the name of the river on the banks of which they then were. He then broached the subject of provisions, and asked him if they could not procure some plantains, offering to pay exorbitantly for them. Being told he could not, he requested that he would ask his friends to give them some, reminding him, at the same time, that in compliance with their promise, they had never taken a single article belonging to the natives. To this he assented, but refused either to give or sell. Strain then told him that if they should become short of provisions, and the Indians would neither sell nor give the fruits which were rotting on the trees, in justice to his own party, he should be obliged to violate his promise and help himself. To this threat the guide made no answer. Finally, Strain offered him money for his past services, which he positively refused to accept; and soon after, as the party was about to set out with their new guides, the former turned to take leave of him, and found he had disappeared. This was a bad omen, as the natives on this Isthmus have a strong taste, whether natural or acquired, for shaking hands when their intentions are friendly.

Setting out under these unpleasant auspices, they followed their guides, who led them rapidly by a trail over a hill and through the forest again, to and down the bed of the river. When about a mile below the camp, Strain was anxious to speak with them, but they would not stop, and were careful to keep some one hundred yards in advance—imagining that at that distance they were out of the reach of their fire-arms. They appeared determined to allow no time for rest, which the lagging of some of the party soon showed the need of; for the climbing over rocks, and floundering through reaches of deep water, at the rapid rate they went, tasked to the utmost the heavily-laden party. At length they struck off from the river, taking a path which led into the wood in a westerly direction. From the moment they left the river nothing more was seen of them. Strain's suspicions were immediately aroused, yet he continued to follow the path for about a mile, when it terminated at a plantation and recently abandoned rancho. Here he halted his men, and waited some time to see if the Indians would return. Finding they did not, he hallooed for them. Receiving no answer, he gave the order to countermarch. Disappointed and baffled, the party slowly and with difficulty succeeded in finding their way back to the bed of the river.

The treachery of the Indians now being evident to the whole party, and hence their whereabouts encompassed with doubt, Strain called the first and last council which he held in the expedition. This was composed of all the officers, the two New Granadian commissioners, and the principal engineers of the party. The maps were brought out and spread before them, and Strain explained to them their position, as he understood it. According to the statement of the first guide, in whom they still had some little confidence, they had left the Chuqunaqua, and were within one and a half day's march of the Savana; and as there was but one river of any importance laid down on the maps, the Iglesias, which entered the Savana near its month, he naturally concluded he was on that river. Besides, this view made the statements of the Indians and the different maps in his possession corroborate each other. On the one drawn by Mr. Gisborne, ranges of hills were put down between the Chuqunaqua and Iglesias, which corresponded to those which they had just traversed. The great object was, if possible, to reach the Savana; but the question arose, whether the risk might not be too great to justify the attempt. The distance was not supposed to be very great, but there was no trail to direct their course, so that they would probably have to cut a path the whole of the way. The journey, therefore, instead of occupying a day and a half might take weeks.

Besides, there was no certainty of finding water on the route, as it was near the end of the dry season, and they would thus perhaps become embarrassed in the wilderness, and perish from hunger and thirst. To effect this seemed to be the object the Indians had in view in leading them away from the river; while, even should they reach the Savana, they would meet no canoes, as the savages who had abandoned them would take care to conceal or destroy them all. The only resource then left would be to make their way for more than forty miles through one of the most impenetrable mangrove swamps in the world, where half a mile would be a hard day's journey. In addition to all this, Strain was also aware that, owing to the slight fall in the bed of the Savana, the tide ascended the whole length of these swamps, so that they might perish for want of fresh water while following its marshy banks. In a mangrove swamp, too, they could not expect to find game, or get it if they did. Neither could they dream of finding timber with which to construct a raft. As if to nail all these arguments for not attempting to reach the Savana, two or three of the men and the junior New Granadian commissioner were already foot-sore and worn out with fatigue, and should they break down entirely, or should any body fall sick, it would be impossible to carry them through the dense forest which they would have to traverse. On the other hand, whether the river they were on was or was not the Iglesias, one fact remained certain, that however tortuous might be its course, it would eventually lead to Darien Harbor, the common receptacle for all the streams in that region. As long as they continued on its banks they could not, at any rate, suffer from thirst, at least until reaching tide-water, which did not run so far inland on any of the Darien rivers as on the sluggish Savana. Until meeting tide-water they would encounter no mangroves to impede their march, and if they should, could return a short distance to the forest growth of timber and construct rafts to convey them through.

On the contrary, if this river, notwithstanding the assertions of the Indians, should prove to be the Chuqunaqua, they would meet with settlements before arriving at the mangrove swamps, which presented the most formidable obstacle to reaching the Pacific shore.

The best chance for game was on the river, where some fish might also be obtained, while there was every reason to believe that, as on the stream they had left, they would find plantains and bananas. These last Strain had already determined no longer to respect, considering that the treachery of the Indians and their refusal either to sell or give had entirely relieved him from his former promise. Finally, by keeping on the river, should any of the party fall ill, they could, as a last resource, always construct a raft for their conveyance, even if they failed in finding canoes farther down, which they hoped to do.

This imposing council was held upon a shingle beach, upon which Strain sat soaking his hard, dry boots in the water while making his final speech. The different members were scattered around, some drinking water and others smoking, listening with the gravity of Indian chiefs to this lucid exposition of these not very flattering prospects. After he had finished, he invited every one to express his opinions freely. Unlike most councils, no one was found in this to suggest objections, and Strain took a vote on the two alternatives, when it was unanimously determined that they should continue down the river on which they then were.

No proposition was made to return to the ship, nor was it hinted at by any one.

To those easily discouraged—if there were any—the obstacles already surmounted must have appeared too formidable for them to wish to grapple with them a second time; while, as far as one could judge, the idea of a return occurred to very few members of the party. If it had been otherwise Strain would have pushed on, for, to quote his own language, he said, "I neither considered it expedient or consistent with our national or personal reputation, that so formidable a party, and one of which so much was expected, should be turned back by trifling obstacles."

Of the seven persons who voted at this council, two perished during the journey, and one afterward, from the effects of starvation and fatigue.

At this point the reader would naturally wish for some clew to unravel the tangled state of things, and know definitely where the party really were, and obtain some explanation of the conduct of the Indians. The river which they had followed for several days after crossing the Cordillera, Strain eventually ascertained to be the Sucubti, a very important stream, utterly ignored in those maps of the moon which Dr. Cullen and Mr. Gisborne—the latter backed by the highest English authority—had published. The Indian guide whom they met on the Sucubti stated that this river was the Chuqunaqua, and that to follow it was a very long route to the Pacific. This, though not literally true, was so in effect, for while it was not the Chuqunaqua, it was a tributary of that river, which certainly did prove to be a most tedious and toilsome route. The river on which they now were was the Chuqunaqua, one of the most tortuous known to geographers—in fact, by looking at the map, one will see that it would be almost impossible to double up a stream so as to get more length in the same space. To all Strain's inquiries respecting the name of this river, he could get no other reply than "Rio Grande" the great river. He therefore remained in utter ignorance respecting it, although, if he gave any credit whatever to the statements of his first Indian guide, that the Sucubti was the Chuqunaqua, he would naturally conclude that they were upon the *next* river to the westward of it, which was laid down by Mr. Gisborne as the Iglesias. On the whole, Mr. Strain was afterward convinced that the Caledonia Indians and their Sucubti friends intended to lead them by the most direct route to the Savana, and that they were prevented from doing so by the Indians of the *Chuqunaqua* or *Chuqunas*, whom they met on their seventh day's march, and who from the first created suspicion. This opinion, which was originally founded upon the conduct of the respective parties, was farther corroborated by the report of a journey made by a Spanish officer in 1788, from the fort of Agla, near Caledonia Bay, to Puerto Principe, on the Savana. He set out under the guidance of the chief of the Sucubti village, who conducted him safely across, cautiously avoiding the Chuquna Indians, who were hostile to the Spaniards. He was prevented from returning, owing to the hostility of this tribe.

It would appear that in 1788, as in 1854, the Chuqunas were on friendly terms with the Indians of the Caledonia and Sucubti valleys, probably on account of their commercial relations but that the latter have not sufficient influence to obtain a passage for a white man through the territory of these intractable savages. To these Indians is attributed the massacre of the four men in the British expedition.

It afterward turned out that when they struck the Chuqunaqua river, they were within five miles of the road cut by this British expedition before it turned back. At first sight, by looking at the map, it may appear a most unfortunate circumstance that this road could not have been struck as they might easily have cut their way to it. Still it is very doubtful if they could have followed the Savana without canoes—owing, as before remarked, to the impenetrable mangrove swamps that stretched so far up with its tides into the interior—and they would have been compelled at last to return to the Chuqunaqua.

It is true that from the termination of Prevost's road to the mouth of the Lara, where the English civil engineers in the service of the Atlantic and Pacific Junction Company had established a station for the purpose of surveying the river, was but six miles; yet, as they were unaware of that circumstance, it could not have influenced their determination. A man with a thousand leagues of wilderness before him may be within one mile of deliverance, yet, with the facts in his possession, to go in that direction would be downright infatuation. The maps on which Strain had implicitly relied proved utterly trustless. The Indians were no better than Gisborne's maps; and thrown wholly upon his own resources, he had, from the meagre facts in his possession, to determine what course to pursue. To have gone in search of a road of whose existence he was ignorant, or to have followed the banks of the Savana toward impassable swamps to find a station he had never heard of would have been the act of a madman. Under the circumstances he took the wisest course beyond a doubt.

After having determined to continue down the river, Strain felt it important to impress on the men the necessity of great frugality in the use of provisions. He endeavored to prove to the sailors and other members of the party, that the idea that men needed such a liberal supply of food was entirely a popular fallacy; and in order to give his views a more practical bearing, declared that a man could live very comfortably three days without food, and *eight* with very little suffering. The men rolled their tobacco quids in their mouths, and tried to *look* their assent to this entirely new doctrine promulgated there on the Isthmus, in the midst of famine, but it was evident Strain could not count much on his converts. The resolution to go on being made, the order to march was given; and now, without a guide, they wound down the crooked banks of the stream.

Soon after leaving the place where the council was held, they passed a river which entered from the eastward, and which corresponded with one put down on Mr. Gisborne's map as an upper branch of the Iglesias.

Subsequent investigations led to the belief that this river was the Asnati (see chart), which Colonel Codazzi in his recent maps has shown to be a branch of the Sucubti, upon information compiled from old Spanish manuscripts, and from conversations held with the Indians. During the afternoon a few plantains were found by the men, and urged upon Strain, who refused, wishing the men to keep them. He and Truxton killed eight birds during the day (though one was an owl and another a woodpecker), which were divided among the party, and none felt the want of the ration, which had given out. This was the first time Strain had fired his carbine at game, and the men, seeing what a dead shot he was, requested him to shoot for the party. While their pieces were echoing through those rarely-trod solitudes, a little incident occurred which caused a thrill of feeling to pass through the band. On looking up they saw a large flock of birds high in the air, and sweeping with great velocity to the west. Down in the forest all was still, but far up heavenward the trade-wind was fiercely blowing, and on the wings of the gale those birds were drifting to the Pacific, now the goal of their own efforts, and the only hope of their salvation. An unknown and toilsome way was before them, while those buoyant forms, borne apparently without effort on, would soon feel the spray of the Pacific. Many an envious glance and envious wish was sent after those birds in their flight. Still the party kept up good spirits, and whiled away the time with jokes and stories. At this camp, and that of the night before, they were first annoyed by sand-flies, and this was the first camp where they met mosquitoes. Fire-flies, too, filled the wood, enlivening the otherwise monotonous gloom. The next morning, January 28th, at half past eight, they continued their journey, and although they had no provisions on hand the party was in fine spirits. The river widened and deepened in parts so much that they were obliged to cut their way across some bends through the undergrowth of the forest. Mr. Truxton shot three birds and caught some fish—among them one cat-fish, six inches long. In the afternoon they had come upon a plantain and banana field, and after eating as many ripe ones as they could obtain, filled their haver-sacks. Finding that Messrs. Castilla and Polanco, the Granadian commissioners, were very much fatigued, they encamped at about half past three, having made only about five miles. In this camp mosquitoes and sand-flies were met in swarms; and for the first time they heard, what is familiar to every woods-man, the falling of forest trees alone, resembling in the distance the reports of guns.

On the morning of the 29th they left camp at nine o'clock, many of the party with legs and hands much swollen from the bites of mosquitoes and sand-flies, and one of the engineers completely speckled with their bites and badly swollen. About two miles from camp they found some dilapidated huts, which had evidently been deserted for a long time, and fields of plantains and bananas. As the Chuquna Indians apparently do not frequent this portion of the country, these plantations probably owe their origin to the Spaniards, who had a garrison in this vicinity about the middle of the last century.

In the afternoon Corporal O'Kelly and Strain together shot a large iguana in the opposite bank of the river, which sunk. Holmes (lands-man) jumped in to bring it ashore, but finding the water deeper than he anticipated, he threw off one of his boots, which sank to the bottom. The recovery of this was of more importance than the iguana, and after feeling around for it in vain, one of the men stripped and dived again and again for it, but unsuccessfully, its dark color rendering it invisible. To this apparently trivial circumstance this poor fellow's death after was partly attributable. This was Sunday. Fatigued with the weight of plantains and bananas, which filled every haversack, and with climbing through gulches and struggling through thickets they went into camp about four o'clock, having accomplished, with hard work, a distance of only seven miles and a half. Opposite to the camp was a plantain field, with its whole vicinity swarming with mosquitoes of such enormous size, that the officers jocosely christened it "*The camp of the mosquitoes elephantes*." This afternoon Strain took off his boots for the first time since starting. It required the efforts of two men to remove them. His feet were very much lacerated, as were also those of the party. The linen shirt which he had put on under his woolen one was now of great service, and Strain tore it up by piecemeal to bind up the wounds, which otherwise would have been dreadfully aggravated.

On the morning of the 30th, after plucking a supply of plantains and bananas from the plantation opposite, they set out on their journey down the river, which now had become so deep that fording was difficult, and they were obliged to hew their way along the banks, and in some cases saved much distance by cutting directly across the bends. About mid-day, being on the left bank, and finding an opportunity to ford, they crossed, as Strain deemed it decidedly best that they should be upon the west side, and between it and the Savana, where, if by accident they should get away from it, they might strike the latter river. During the day a snake about eighteen inches long was killed, which Mr. Castilla said was the coral snake, and very venomous. Strain doubted this, as he had seen such before in Brazil, and found them harmless.

At about three o'clock they encamped on a mud bank, the Granadian commissioners declaring they could go no farther. The day's journey, it is true, had been fatiguing, yet the principal labor, which was cutting the road through the dense undergrowth, was performed by the officers and their men. Mr. Truxton shot a crane just at evening, which was given to the men, some of whom, owing to carelessness and improvidence, were out of provisions. At this camp they thought they discovered tidal influence, and were greatly elated. Camping so early left a long afternoon, and those less fatigued resorted to various amusements to pass the time. One man, named Wilson, had a superb voice, and he made the woods echo with negro songs—"Ole Virginny" and "Jim Crow;" and often during the day his comic songs would bring peals of laughter from the party, and discordant choruses would burst forth on every side. Another had made a fife out of a reed, which he played on with considerable skill, and made the camp merry with its music. The next morning they breakfasted leisurely, and at half past eight commenced again their journey. Having been so successful the day before in cutting off bends by pursuing a fixed compass course through the woods, they set off S.W. by W., and after crossing a bayou with some difficulty, met a deep and turbid river, about seventy feet in width, running from west to east, which they crossed on a large tree. This river was known on the old Spanish maps as *La Paz*, and enters the Chuqunaqua nearly opposite the embouchure of the Sucubti, which was thus passed without being seen. A few hundred yards farther on they again fell in with the Chuqunaqua, which had suddenly become deep, rapid, and much more turbid than where they had left it two miles above. Encouraged by the result of this experiment, they again took a departure from the river, and pursued a S.W. by W. course through a swampy country, where, although it was the height of the dry season, they were obliged to make many *detours* to avoid the standing water and muddy bottom. The country being generally open, they marched rapidly, those behind shouting "Go ahead," as the engineer reported sou'west by west; sou'west. As they tramped along, Strain saw a buzzard sitting on a tree. Turning to Lombard, he asked him if buzzards were good to eat. Lombard being decidedly low in the larder, and withal having a strong appetite for flesh, replied—"Yes, captain, any thing that won't kill will fatten." Strain there upon fired and dropped the buzzard, and advanced to pick him up. But as be drew near, the dreadful effluvia which this bird sends forth made him turn a-side. Lombard approached somewhat closer, but at last was compelled to wheel off also. Each man in his turn, tempted by so fine a bird, pushed for the prize, but each and all gave him a wide berth. In the end they became less fastidious. Avoiding the thick undergrowth instead of cutting through it, and returning to their course when it was passed, they by twelve o'clock had made about four miles and a half. Not meeting the river, the course was changed to S.W., at 3.15 to S.S.W., and from 3.45 to 4.15 to S. by E., when they fell in with a pebbly ravine, containing cool and palatable standing water. As the distance to the river was uncertain, the probability of obtaining water in advance too vague to be risked, and many of the men foot-sore and fatigued, Strain determined to encamp there, although the sun was several hours high. Most of the men had no plantains and bananas, while the officers' messes contained only three or four, so that it now became necessary to examine into the resources which the forest afforded. Some palmetto or cabbage-palm, resembling, but not identical with, that which grows in Florida, was found, and as Strain, on a previous journey into the interior of Brazil, had lived some ten days on a similar vegetable, he had no hesitation in recommending it to the party, and set the example by eating it himself. This is not a fruit, it is simply the soft substance growing upon the top of a tree, and can be cooked like a cabbage. The palmetto of Darien is more bitter and less palatable and nutritious than that of Brazil, but the bitterness was partially removed by frequently changing the water in boiling.

Very little was said in this camp, and there was no mirth or pleasantry; on the contrary, a gloom for the first time seemed to rest on the party. They lay scattered around among the trees, talking in low tones or musing. It was evident they missed the companionship of the river, the only thread that connected them with the Pacific, and the last object at night and the first in the morning on which their eyes rested. Even Strain felt its influence so much, that when the draughtsman, Mr. Kettlewell, came at a late hour of the night to him, stretched on the ground in the smoke from the watch-fire to escape the bites of mosquitoes, and asked what he would have the camp named, he replied the "Noche triste"—the "sad night;" and although many other camps afterward were far sadder than this, and more deserving the title, he nevertheless allowed this name to remain, for it proved the beginning of sorrows. In the morning Strain and Maury took a long walk in the woods to examine them, and held a protracted and serious conversation over their condition and prospects, and discussed the project of making a boat.

Starting about half past eight, they struck off on a southeast course, anxious to reach the river. Hitherto Strain had led the party, every day cutting a path with his cutlass. This was most laborious, and Mr. Truxton now insisted upon taking the macheta, and going ahead in his place. The undergrowth was exceedingly dense, and composed, for the most part, of *pinello*—little pine—a plant resembling that which produces the pine-apple, but with longer leaves, serrated with long spines, which produced most painful wounds, especially as the last few day's march had stripped the trowsers from many of the party. After cutting for some time, he suddenly fell backward, and almost swooned away from the effects of heat, pain, exertion, and fatigue. Strain now saw that he was in danger of overtasking the officers, and detailed two men to cut the path, they being relieved every hour. The rest would sit down till ordered to march. It would take hours to cut a few rods.

This was the severest traveling yet, beating, as Strain declared, the jungles of Brazil and the East Indies, which he once considered without a rival. When they encamped, at half past four, near a ravine containing standing water, they had not advanced more than two miles, or at an average only eighty rods an hour. During the march they fell in with palm-trees, bearing a nut which they found edible, agreeable to the taste, and nutritious, though so hard as to be masticated with difficulty. They cut down two trees, and Strain divided the nuts equally.

Some palmetto was also found, and toward evening Strain was so fortunate as to kill a mountain hen, which was divided between the two officer's messes, as the men had the last bird which was shot. A deer was also started—the first seen—but they could not get a shot at it.

So thick was the undergrowth that it required some time to clear away a place sufficiently large for a camp. Into this crater, as it were, hewn out of the foliage, the tired wanderers, after a frugal supper, lay down, filled with gloomy anticipations, and, strange as it may seem, mourning most of all for the lost river, which had so suddenly changed its direction and gone off no one knew whither.

Edward Lombard, an old seaman and former shipmate of Strain, whose boatswain's whistle had each morning piped the "heave round," and who had shown great energy and activity throughout, now became quite ill and desponding. A little soup, however, and meat of the mountain hen, which Strain gave him from his own mess, appeared to revive him. During his whole life he had been accustomed, on board ship, to a large supply of animal food, and with it he could have endured as much fatigue as any one in the party; but without it, he was perfectly prostrated. Ever afterward, until his death, the state of his health was an indication of the quantity of animal food in camp. There were no songs to-night—the last strain of music dying away in the "*Sorrowful camp*." The distressed commander of this handful of brave men now began to feel the pressure of their fate upon him, and on this night he was kept awake by the groans of those who were suffering from sore feet and boils. But fatigue finally overcame all; and at midnight no one was awake, except the sentries and officer of the guard.

Next morning, February 2d, the party appeared in pretty good condition; and Lombard, after eating a banana which Strain had reserved, and which was the last one remaining in the party, declared himself stronger, and ready to start.

Having thus far failed to reach the river on a southeast course, Strain changed it to east; for he found that the great majority of the men thought only of reaching the river banks. "Oh for the river!" exclaimed one; "it is better than Darien harbor." Fearful lest the supplies of water they had hitherto found so abundant might fail, Strain now directed the few vessels which they had remaining to be filled, and given in charge of the officers, he himself carrying an India-rubber canteen containing about half a gallon, which he served out from time to time to the party. As they groped their way through the wilderness, they came upon trees of enormous size, one of which would have measured forty-five feet in girth.

During the afternoon Strain became somewhat anxious in regard to the supply of water, as many hours had elapsed without meeting with water-holes, and their vessels were empty. He therefore deviated from his course still more to the northward to follow down a slope, and finally meeting a dry ravine, where he thought, as a last resort, he could obtain water by digging, followed it until they met water-holes. Here, although but four o'clock, they encamped, and had quite a feast on the turkeys and small birds, reserving a monkey Strain had shot for breakfast. On this and on all subsequent occasions, all game or fruits obtained was divided equally among the party. Poor Lombard was at last unable to chew tobacco, and brought all he had left—about ten ounces—and gave it to Strain, saying, "Here, captain, take what there is left; I can't chew any more." A little coffee remained, and in order to eke it out as far as possible, the berries, after one steeping, were packed up for a second—then for a third, and, finally, for a fourth, when they were eaten for food.

On the next morning, February 3d, they started about half past eight, the whole party, especially Lombard, much revived by the animal food. Feeling confident that the ravine upon which they were would eventually lead to the river, and also afford a certain supply of water, Strain determined to follow it in what-ever direction it might lead. As they advanced the forest became open, though the vines, swinging from tree to tree and coiled around every bush, made the march slow and difficult. During the day they discovered and tested a new fruit of the palm, an egg-shaped nut covered with an acid pulp. This pulp was tried, and found to be refreshing; while the kernel resembled that of the carosas, which they had already eaten. This nut gradually became the principal article of diet; and they found that even the acid covering would support life, although it utterly destroyed the teeth, and by degrees the digestive power of the stomach. Strain, foreseeing to what desperate straits they might yet be reduced, endeavored to cheer up the men by this new discovery, assuring them that they were very nourishing food. Not to mention the pulp and rind, the oleaginous nature of the nut itself was highly nutritious; in fact, he said, many tribes of men lived almost entirely on oil. Men and officers listened respectfully to his philosophical disquisition; but it was evident, that, as they looked at their attenuated limbs, and felt the gnawing of hunger, it was pursuing knowledge under difficulties. Suddenly, a "turkey, turkey!" shouted one of the men, and, looking up, a fine large bird was seen sitting on a limb, and stretching out his neck in wonder toward the party. Strain asked if any one could shoot better than he; if so, let him fire. All shouted "Shoot, shoot!" He fired, and brought down the turkey. Soon after he shot another, which, with a third killed by Truxton, quite animated the hungry band. At length, at two o'clock, Strain, still in advance, with his cutlass clearing a way for his tired followers, caught, through the dense foliage, the gleam of the water. He immediately passed the word "*river*" back through the line, and "*The river! the river*!" was repeated in still louder accents, till "*The river! the river!*" went up in one glad shout, and then three cheers were called for by the excited men, and "*Hurra! hurra!*" rang and echoed through the forest. The German army, when it caught sight of its beloved river, never shouted The Rhine! the Rhine! with more ecstasy than did this little party over a stream of whose name even, they were wholly ignorant. They found it deep and turbid, sweeping on at a velocity of nearly three miles an hour. Truxton immediately rigged his hook and line, baiting with the intestines of turkey, and commenced fishing, and soon six fine cat-fish were floundering on the bank. Five of these were given to the men, in addition to their share of the wild turkeys, and seemed, after their late privations, a feast, and filled the whole party with high spirits. Besides, they were once more on the river, and as the tropical moon sailed up over the trees, and turned the dark and turbid water into flowing silver, they felt almost on the borders of civilization. From this time on, a marked and striking difference was seen in the power of endurance between the officers and gentlemen of the party and the common seamen (from the Granadian commissioners, of course, nothing was expected); thus proving, what every man has observed who has been in long and trying expeditions, that intellect and culture will overbalance physical strength. The power of a strong will—the effort demanded by the calm voice of reason and the pride of true manhood—take the place of exhausted muscles and sinews, and assert, even under the pangs of famine and the slow sinking of over-tasked nature, the supremacy of mind over matter, of the soul over animal life—no matter how vigorous the latter may otherwise be.

After leaving the ship they all fared alike, and when many of the men were already broken down, physically and morally, the officers and engineers were as active, energetic, and cheerful as at first.

Next morning, at half past seven, they started merrily, down the banks of the river. The woods were, at first, open, and the traveling easy; but after making about a mile, they found their progress impeded by a dense jungle, while the river took another easterly bend, thus leading them entirely off their course. Strain halted the party, and after informing them that it was his conviction they were on the Chuqunaqua, one of the most tortuous rivers in the world in proportion to its length, or upon a branch of it which appeared upon none of the maps, and that their journey might be very much protracted, declared that, in his opinion, they ought to avail themselves of the strong current of the river for assistance, or, at least, to convey the sick and foot-sore of the party. A canoe was, unfortunately, nearly out of the question, as about half the cutting part of the only ax had been accidentally broken off in a hard tree. This would prevent them from felling a tree of sufficient size for a boat; while a raft had thus far been out of the question, as they could find no wood sufficiently buoyant to support more than its own weight. The only resource left them, he said, was to cut down a few moderately-sized trees, split and hew them into planks, and construct a boat which might convey the whole party. "It is true," said he, "we have not a single nail, screw, or any oakum or pitch; but I once constructed a boat on a river in Brazil, secured only by wooden wedges and clamps, and I have little doubt we can do it now within twenty-four hours, if you will join me and work with a will." "Hurra! hurra!" was echoed far and wide; and a "boat! a boat!" repeated with acclamations. The order to encamp and kindle a fire was then given. Truxton, Maury, and Garland, and one man, were sent out to hunt game and obtain food; while the remainder, with every hatchet and cutting instrument they could lay hand on, were soon scattered through the woods, which began to ring with the unwonted sounds of incipient civilization. They vigorously cut down trees for planks, and trimmed up clamps, and wedges for splitting the timber, and by evening they had the clamps all done, and two planks, twenty-four feet long, split out and partially hewn. The hunting party returned before night, bringing only one small monkey, or marmoset, a little palmetto, and some of the acid nuts of the palm. This was a small allowance for twenty-two tired men; and Strain, bearing the cry of hawks near, started off with his carbine, and soon returned with three, which made a meagre addition to the supper. As the men had been hard at work during the day, and were now out of the Indian country, Strain dispensed with the sentries for the night, placing the watch in charge of the officer of the guard; and after this had but one sentry at a time instead of two. The tobacco, their chief comfort, had, at the last camp, given out entirely, and they were driven to all kinds of expedients to supply the deficiency. Some, who were inveterate smokers, gathered decayed dry wood, with which they filled their pipes. The deprivation of tobacco was more severely felt than even that of provisions; and the longings expressed for it greater than for food.

February 5th was Sunday; but, being in no position to make it a day of rest, they were early at work at their boat. In the course of their search after a tree appropriate for planks, they came across some very buoyant wood; and, although it was scarce, Strain immediately determined to build a raft instead of a boat, as the labor was so much less, and so many more men could be employed upon it at the same time. The half-hewn planks were accordingly deserted, and the whole party sent out to seek and cut down these new-found trees. One after another they came dragging them into camp; and, stripping away the bark, peeled off the inner surface for lashings. These strips a part commenced plaiting into ropes, and soon a large quantity of materials was collected on the bank. The officers discovering that animal food went much farther by boiling it into soup, Truxton was selected as cook, to superintend the operations for them, and give to each his portion. Each man carried a cup, and this cup full was the quantity allowed him.

A great misfortune befell them this day, in the loss of their only fish-hook. It was private property, but Strain had appropriated it for the use of the party, and forbidden every one except Mr. Truxton—who was the best fisherman—to use it. He would not even trust himself, so fearful was he of accident. Mr. Castilla had asked for it, and, as he thought that international courtesy would not allow him to refuse, gave it to him. The latter imprudently turned it over to one of the men, who broke it. Had that hook remained to them, no lives need have been lost by starvation, as the river always abounded in fish, their number increasing as they advanced. On such apparently insignificant circumstances do the lives of men depend.

As the man who lost the hook was one of the best in the party, Strain rebuked him only by setting forth what would probably be the consequences both to him and all the party.

By sunset they had collected nearly all the buoyant wood within reach of the camp, and wearied and worn out flung themselves along the bank, and though pierced by thousands of mosquitoes at length fell asleep.

The next morning the boatswain's call from Lombard, "Heave round!" roused all hands at early daylight, and they again went to work upon the raft. By noon it was finished, but upon testing it, they found, alas! that it would support only seven or eight persons. As they had used all the balsa wood there was in the region, nothing more could be done, and so Strain determined to put those who were ill and foot-sore upon it, and proceed by land with the remainder of the party until they could find more timber of the same description.

At a quarter past four the raft, in charge of Mr. Truxton, was headed from the shore, and swung slowly out into the current. On board were the two New Granadian commissioners, Mr. Boggs, Wilson, one of the seamen of the *Cyane*, and the draughts-man, Mr. Kettlewell, whom Strain furnished with a compass, to take the bearings of the river, and thus save them on land this trouble; for, still true to the great purpose of the expedition, Strain, amidst all his sufferings, had carefully worked up the route. The remainder of the party, after seeing the raft fairly moving down stream, turned to depart, but discovered that Lombard, who had already given symptoms of mental aberration, was nowhere to be found. Upon inquiry, Strain ascertained that he had been absent from camp several hours, and had left without permission. Scouts were immediately sent out, but they one after another dropped in, reporting no traces of him. Leaving a note directing him to follow down the bank of the river, Strain ordered the march, intending to re-turn for him as soon as he met the raft. But just as they were moving oft to their great joy Lombard emerged from the wood—having been, as he said, down the river to reconnoitre. The main body then took up the line of march, occasionally exchanging signals with the party on the raft; but at length being forced away from the bank by the undergrowth, they heard nothing more of them, and returned to the river late in the afternoon.

Feeling convinced that they were above, Strain called a halt, and sat down to await their arrival. Very soon the report of a gun above was heard, and then a second. This was the signal to communicate, and Strain set off with two men to ascend the river, leaving the main body to rest upon its banks.

After traveling a mile through the forest they came to a bend in the river, where the raft lay moored, those on it believing that Strain and his party were still above. Undeceiving them in this particular, and directing them to move on he returned; but had scarcely seated himself again when he was startled by another gun, then a second, and a third. This signal was a recall for all parties, and understood to be one also of distress. He immediately took some fresh men, and carrying the ax, hatchet, and macheta, hurried in the direction of the sound.

Forcing his way through the undergrowth and along the bank of the river, he at length came upon Mr. Truxton and the majority of his party seated upon the bank. The latter, as Strain approached, simply made a sign with his thumb over his shoulder, quietly remarking, "There's the raft;" and, true enough, there it lay, jammed against two trees that had fallen across the river from opposite sides, thus forming a complete boom. The bank opposite was high and perpendicular, so that it would be impossible to lift the timbers out and carry them around. Neither could they cut away the huge trees that blocked the stream—it would take, as one of the men said, "a steam snag machine two days to remove it." Strain therefore determined at once to abandon the raft, notwithstanding the labor and time it had cost. Mr. Castilla, the principal New Granadian commissioner, however, still sat on the raft and refused to land, declaring that he was utterly unable to proceed on foot. Strain, knowing better, used every argument to persuade him to come ashore, promising, if necessary, to carry him, but all in vain. At length, becoming provoked at his obstinacy, he told him plainly that he would not, out of mere courtesy to him as a commissioner, sacrifice his own party, and would leave him where he was if he did not come on at once. Seeing that Strain was determined, he crawled ashore, and walked to the place where the main body was halted.

The following extract from the journal of one of the officers vividly portrays the condition of the party: "Proceeded down stream about a quarter of a mile, when finding a place to camp, built a fire and spread our blankets in the mild moonlight. We all feel downhearted to-night, being without any thing to eat, and not having eaten enough each man for the six or eight days to make one good meal; our clothes all in pieces, and nearly all almost shoeless and bootless. Have no idea where we are, nor, of course, when we shall reach the Pacific. The sick almost discouraged, and ready to be left in the woods to take their chances. I would freely give twenty dollars for a pound of meat, but money is of no use here. Thus they lay down, while countless sand-flies and mosquitoes, combined with the pangs of hunger and torture of undressed wounds, made the poor sufferers groan aloud. Their moans were answered only by the screams of the wild cat or cry of the tiger seeking their evening repast of blood. At last fatigue overcame their sufferings, and, save the night sentinel, all at length fell fast asleep. And over them the white moonlight lay, and past them, in quiet beauty, the unconscious river swept onward to the ocean.

Here, on the 7th, Strain again took off his boots, and finding, one of his feet extremely lacerated, put on a moccasin in the place of the boot.

Early in the morning Mr. Castilla asked Strain's permission to return, with Mr. Polanco, his colleague, and one man, in order to attempt the reconstruction of the raft on a small scale, capable of carrying three persons, with which, as it would be more manageable, he expected to reach the Granadian settlements on the river below. This request was acceded to very unwillingly, and only with the condition that no one unless a volunteer should be sent. Finally, Benjamin Harrison, one of the best men, offered to go, and they departed, having first received from Strain good arms in the place of their own, which they had allowed to become unserviceable. The party, which numbered twenty-seven when it left

Caledonia Bay, was now reduced to nineteen on the land, and with this number Strain continued to follow the river. The thickness of the undergrowth soon drove them inland, and they did not reach it again until evening, when it was time to encamp.

The next morning, February 8th, they were about to leave camp 19th, when a shot was heard near by, to which the party answered with a shout. Immediately after the two Granadians and Harrison emerged from the bushes. Their story was soon told: owing to the exertions of Harrison a small raft had been built, but was soon wrecked among the snags and rapids, and a musket, carbine, and hatchet lost. They all seemed delighted to rejoin the main body, especially Mr. Polanco, who threw his arms around Mr. Truxton and Strain, and declared he never would leave them again, saying to the latter as he embraced him, "I know you don't like me, but I like you, and will stay by you." He evidently had gone with Mr. Castilla against his own inclinations. Harrison was utterly worn out, and, moreover, somewhat feverish, but declaring he was able to proceed, the whole set out to follow the river. The Granadians caught this afternoon an iguana, and stealing off into the wood by themselves, built a fire and ate it. The men, who had hitherto generously divided their last morsel with them, on discovering this, became disgusted, and ever after secretly despised them.

During this day's march they found an article of food which afterward became common in the camp, and was called by Mr. Castilla the "monkey pepper pod." It resembled the cocoa-nut (in its exterior) after the husk has been removed. The interior bore some resemblance to the yellow water-melon, though the seeds were not so regularly disposed, nor in the same direction. It grew in clusters like the jack-fruit, or cocoa of tropical climates, and on the most beautiful forest tree of the Isthmus, which sometimes towered to the height of two hundred feet, not a limb or knot breaking the smooth surface of the column-like trunk for a hundred and thirty feet; the fruit, when not quite ripe, as they at first found it, was hard and of a greenish tinge, becoming black by exposure. When ripe it was softer and assumed a yellow color, yielding a most fragrant odor. In either state it had a pungent and peppery taste. In small quantities it was a very agreeable stimulant to them, who had so long been without condiments to their scanty food. They ate it raw, cooked it with soup, made soup of it, which proved very refreshing and stimulating when setting off on the day's journey without any breakfast. For some time previous to using it they had met with it in the forest, but dared not eat it. At length, however, they found one partially devoured by some animal or bird, and concluding that what one stomach was able to digest another could, they used it without fear. This was the more acceptable, as Strain had stopped their allowance of gunpowder which had been used for pepper and salt in seasoning their miserable food; but the Pacific receding like the mirage of the desert, and the ammunition getting scarce, he feared they might need it more in procuring than for seasoning it.

As they had lost their fish-hook, the officers tasked their ingenuity to make others out of the wire in the tin-pots, though without success, owing to their inability to get a barb on them.

The next morning, February 9th, after having been nearly devoured by mosquitoes, the half-starved party set off and being forced away from the river by undergrowth and deep ravines, only reached it again about five P.M. having made an estimated distance of nine miles. The forest during this day's march abounded in swamps and heavy undergrowth, which, combined with Harrison's weakness, rendered their progress painfully slow and laborious. Many very large trees were seen in the woods, which generally abounded in fine timber, though very little of it, except caoutchoue and mahogany, was recognized by the party.

The camp to-night (camp 21) was pitched in an open grove, under a magnificent canopy of an open grove, under a magnificent canopy of trees, and on a bank thirty feet high, from which a long reach of the river could be seen as it swept in a deep strong current on. As the declining sun sent long streams of light through the leafy arcades, and flecked the high bank with shadows, and poured its tropical glories full on the flashing stream, the scene arrested every eye by its picturesque beauty, and with one accord the spot was christened CAMP BEAUTIFUL.

This little band of explorers, as they sat at sunset in their "Camp Beautiful," making soup out of their lean, tough hawks, the dark background of forest casting into still stronger relief their tattered garments and emaciated figures, looked any thing but men on whose fate, for the time being, rested the fate of a ship canal, destined to change the aspect and history of the world.

The next day they continued their march, but were much delayed by Harrison, who, though feverish and unfit to travel, would not permit the party to halt for him, but weak and wretched, kept staggering on. Strain could not see the brave fellow bearing up so nobly, yet painfully, without often stopping to let him rest, and at length at four o'clock encamped on a point abounding in palm-trees, and gave it the name of "Nut Camp." They passed during the day the dry bed of a river of considerable magnitude, coming in on the left side. Its bed and banks were strewn with the trunks of trees, which showed that, though then perfectly dry, it must be a tremendous torrent in the rainy season. Breakfastless and weary the party, now thoroughly crippled with the feeble and sick, renewed in the morning their almost hopeless journey along the banks of the apparently endless river. Harrison was still sick, while the Granadians, as usual, complained much of fatigue, and required great urging to keep up. The Americans, both officers and men, except Harrison, as yet showed no signs of breaking down, although almost all had very sore feet, and their low diet had begun to tell fearfully upon their appearance. Truxton declared he would not wait for the Granadians, who kept constantly crying out "*Halt, halt!*" He finally came forward and told Strain it was of no use marching in this way—they would never get through. The latter had thought so for some time. He, however, halted, and requested an officer to give the Granadians a cat-fish to revive them, which he did. Constantly on the look-out for something on which they might make a supper, he managed during the day to kill six hawks. No order was observed in the march to-day—the line was long and straggling—and, as it crawled slowly and wearily along the winding shore, presented a most piteous spectacle to the commander. Events were drawing to a crisis—each day told fearfully on the party—a few more like the last would compel them to stop, and leave a portion behind to die by slow starvation. Every morning Strain would scrutinize each man anxiously, to ascertain by the increased emaciation how fast they were sinking. At three P.M. they en-camped for the 23d time upon a shelving mud-bank, having made some seven and a half miles by the course of the river. After reaching camp, Strain managed, even with the defective fish-hook, to catch two cat-fish, which were divided among the sick; the hawks being divided equally among the well. When about to start early the next morning, Lombard was suddenly attacked with severe pains, accompanied by dangerous symptoms, which delayed them until nine o'clock. This attack was owing to the diet of palm nuts, which, containing only acid and fibre, the first was absorbed in the stomach, leaving the latter in undigested and matted masses, effectually preventing the action necessary to throw them off. Lombard was the first who suffered severely from this cause, but in the course of the journey no one escaped from the fearful effects of such a diet, which, at the same time that it paralyzed the internal organs, utterly destroyed the enamel of the teeth.

During the day they discovered another species of nuts, the outside covering of which was not unlike the mango fruit. As the tree was large, they did not stop to cut it down, but obtained what they could by shooting into the clusters with their carbines. The complaints of Castilla were constantly heard along the line, while Lombard and Harrison were so ill they could scarcely drag one leg before the other. It was impossible to march, and Strain was obliged to encamp at noon, making only about two miles in all. The serious aspect which affairs were assuming was no longer to be trifled with. There was no concealing the fact that most of the party were failing fast, while the feet of many were sore, and the clothes of all in tatters. Strain had given the last remnant of his trowsers to Ketlewell, and had traveled several days in nothing but his drawers.

Lombard was ill and dispirited, and declared that he would "leave his bones in the woods." The unfortunate Granadians were much alarmed at the protracted journey, but still would make no exertions to advance; on the contrary, they constantly retarded the party by begging Strain to halt at times when his own officers and men could have made three times the distance. Lombard and Harrison were really ill and suffering, yet they still pushed on, and the last early halt was made at the urgent request of Castilla, who, though doubtless fatigued, was in perfect health.

Now nearly certain that they were upon the Chuqunaqua, which, though almost unknown to geographers, was noted for its tortuous course, Strain was aware that marches of two miles a day would never clear them of the forest until all had suffered terribly from starvation or perished from disease, which their diet would certainly engender. He had no direction in which to look for assistance from without. Captain Hollins, as he was well aware, must be already very anxious, but he was utterly powerless to relieve him, as any party which he might have sent would have consumed their provisions before they could reach him, and instead of being serviceable, would only embarrass him the more, by increasing the number to be provided for in the forest.

From below he had no reason to expect any assistance, as he did not suppose any one in that direction was aware of the Expedition, and besides, if they had, he had already had sufficient experience among the New Granadians to feel assured that—their fear of Indians being placed out of the question—their indolence and selfishness would prevent them from making any effort for which they were not well paid beforehand. Having nothing, therefore, to expect from abroad, finding the party daily becoming weaker, he determined at this camp to send forward and have canoes and provisions brought up to meet them.

Soon after encamping, therefore, he called the men together, and explained to them their situation and the necessity for obtaining canoes and provisions. He then told them that he had resolved to build a small raft, capable of transporting three persons, who were to go forward in search of them. Notwithstanding their previous ill-fortune, he believed that, with a small raft, obstacles might be avoided and surmounted which would stop one large enough to transport the whole party. The proposition seemed to meet the views of the whole party, and the poor fellows went to work energetically to fell a tree which he pointed out to them, and which he had himself commenced cutting down; the wood was tested to see if it would float, and the result being satisfactory, they felled it with no little difficulty, cut it into pieces of appropriate length, and peeled it.

At sunset they had, as they supposed, timber enough for the raft, and were about to convey it to the river bank when it was discovered—by throwing a limb into the water—that, though the wood would float, it was just about the specific gravity of water, and would bear no additional weight.

Thus were all their hopes dashed to the ground, and their labor thrown away. They had, however, found some *pussley*, as it was called, which they gathered, but hesitated to eat it; when one of the party said that hogs would eat it in the United States, and if it was good for hogs it was good for men. This was conclusive; and large quantities were boiled, of which they all ate ravenously. Violent vomiting ensued—Strain suffering among the rest. They became so thoroughly disgusted with it, that afterward, though nearly half starved, they could never eat it again.

The camp-fire was kindled, and the dispirited, distressed band flung themselves on the earth around it, and sought that refreshment in sleep which could not be obtained by food. That was a long and gloomy night to Strain. He could not sleep, but lay amidst his suffering men, pondering on their sad condition, and revolving various schemes for their deliverance. He had resolved, if the raft had succeeded, to have sent others forward and remained himself behind. This hope was past; and, turn which way he would, it was clear that the last hope of the party rested on some of the strongest cutting their way through and returning with boats. If they were near the Pacific, so much shorter would be the delay of relief—if far, so much more urgent was it that the attempt to reach it should be made before all were too weak to undertake the journey. The time had come for immediate and energetic action, if they would not all perish there in the forest. He had found by experiment that he could endure more, and on less food, than any other member of the party. Besides, the advance might be more dangerous than the retreat. Before them was all uncertainty. Perils greater even than those they had already encountered, might await those who ventured forward, He therefore felt that it was his duty to go; and, if necessary, sacrifice himself for the rest. Still, to leave his command to a doubtful fate, tried him sorely. They had supreme confidence in him, which they might not transfer to another leader; and should an evil fate befall them, which after events should prove he could have avoided, it would be a blow greater than he could bear. Thus revolving his condition, he out-watched the stars; but when the morning dawned his resolution was taken.

Rousing up the men, he called them together and announced his determination to leave the party, and taking three persons, force his way down the river to the nearest settlement, from whence he would send back canoes and provisions. Not willing to order men on this doubtful undertaking, he packed up his blanket, shouldered his haversack and carbine, and called for volunteers. Several at once stepped forward, out of whom he selected Mr. Avery, originally a volunteer in the Expedition, and Golden and Wilson, two of the crew of the *Cyane*. These men were chosen for no mental qualification, but solely because the state of their physique appeared to promise the greatest endurance of the fatigue which he anticipated.

He then told the men officially that they were placed under the command of Mr. Truxton during his absence; whom he directed to follow under the bank of the river by easy marches—halting whenever it might be necessary—and taking all possible precautions to supply the party with game and other food. In a short conversation with the officers, he expressed his firm conviction that if the nuts, palmettos, and other articles of food which they had met thus far held out, the party might be sustained in camp for six months; but he advised them to change their camp as often as provisions became scarce in the vicinity.

With these parting directions, he, on the 13th of February, took leave of his command, and set out on his journey. As he turned away, he exclaimed "Good-by! good-by!"—"Good-by! God bless you!" came from all, and the forest soon shut him from sight.

This little band of four were well calculated for the terrible trial before them. Strain, the leader, though half naked and a small man, was knit together with iron sinews, and with as brave and resolute a heart as ever beat in a human bosom. Fertile in resources, and with that natural spirit of command which begets confidence and insures obedience, no man could be better fitted for the trying position in which he unexpectedly found himself. Avery was a man of powerful frame, and had already had some experience in tropical travel, having passed some months on the Atrato, and journeyed elsewhere in New Granada. James Golden, seaman, was a young man who had served with Strain in a cruise on the coast of Africa, and had enlisted in the naval service with especial reference to accompanying him in this expedition. Wilson, a lands-man, was also a man of splendid frame, which seemed to have suffered scarcely at all from the privations which he had undergone. Their arms were one Sharps rifle, belonging to Mr. Avery, two carbines, and two Colts pistols. They also took plenty of ammunition. Young Golden, not being so strong as the others, had no arms except a pistol—Mr. Avery, Wilson, and Strain carrying the others. Two machetas and a small pocket-compass, and their blankets and empty haversacks, completed their equipment.

The best compass and the double-barreled fowling-piece were left with the main body, one to direct their course and take the bearings of the river, and the other to provide the party with game.

4

Nicaragua: An Exploration from Ocean to Ocean*

E. G. Squier

The author crosses the isthmus at Nicaragua, which until the completion of the Panama Railway was a popular passenger route. The article provides an excellent description of lake Nicaragua and the city of Granada, as the travelers make their way from the Atlantic city of San Juan de Dios to the Pacific. The piece presents Nicaragua as a "picturesque" paradise, though the author can not help stating that the country and its residents are "uncivilized." The author claims that European capital would be unlikely to finance a canal project through Nicaragua since the voyage from England to Singapore or Calcutta is shorter via the Cape of Good Hope. This is the first of a two-part series.

"El Castillo," or the ruins of the old fort of San Juan, is the first place, in the actual occupation of Nicaragua, which the traveler encounters on the river San Juan. Here, for the first time, he is saluted by the nautical flag of blue white and blue, with a central oval inclosing a triangle and three volcanoes—the latter eminently typical, as H----- suggested, of the political state of the country. Here, too, he will have his gravity put to the test by a squad of hopeless tatterdemal-

*Entered according to Act of Congress, in the year 1855, by Harper and Brothers, in the Clerk's Office of the District Court for the Southern District of New York.

ions, armed with little muskets, who figure in the bulletins of the country as "valientes," and who are supposed to be the garrison of "El Castillo." I say supposed to be, since if they do not occupy the old fort they certainly do occupy a couple of modern shanties on the hill, close beneath its walls. And, moreover, a sentinel paces in front of the gateway of the works, on which there is not a single gnu, and which can be entered only by a rickety bridge of rotten poles laid across the fosse. His responsibility, therefore, is heavy, especially when any one is looking on, at which times his musket is carried with a stiff affectation of the military air quite irresistible. But while the degenerate and amalgamated sons of the Conquistadors excite only mingled pity and contempt, the traveler can not resist a feeling of admiration for those iron adventurers who raised here, in the midst of a vast tropical wilderness, before the Puritans landed at Plymouth, or New York was founded, those massive fortifications which, even in their ruins, seem to bid defiance to the destroyer, Time!

The hill occupied by the fort is steep, and stands in an angle of the river, which, at its feet, is interrupted by difficult rapids. It thus commands the stream, both up and down, for a long distance. The view from its summit is exceedingly fine, taking in miles on miles of emerald forest, relieved by broad, silvery reaches of water. But excepting the small village which the Transit Company has brought into existence at the base of the hill, there is not a sign of civilization—not a single white cottage, not a single green field, but only the silent, interminable wilderness.

We reached the Castillo at night, after a passage of four days from San Juan del Norte, and were received with great cordiality by Mr. Ruggles, the agent of the Transit Company at that point. He gave us beds in his establishment, in which we extended our limbs in happy consciousness that there was "scope and verge enough." H----- nevertheless protested that his experience in bestowing himself on a box three feet by two for the previous four days, had given him an almost irresistible tendency to shut himself up like a clasp-knife. And Captain M-----, not to be behindhand, formally complained of the unsubstantial nature of his pillow, as compared with the pickle-jar and pair of boots which had done service in that capacity on board of our boat.

Rain fell during the night; but, as usual, the morning was clear, and we rose early to aid in tracking our boat past the "Raudal del Castillo." These rapids almost deserve the name of falls, and are only ascended with great difficulty. The steamers of the Transit Company do not attempt to pass them, but land their passengers below, who pass on foot and re-embark in other vessels a few hundred yards higher up. A rude wooden railway is built from the lower to the upper landing, for carrying baggage and freight. A short time previous to our visit, one of the steamers plying above the rapids was carried over the fall, and a considerable number of passengers drowned. The affair was assiduously hushed up, lest its publicity should injure the credit of the route.

At the period of my first visit, a single hut, built on the "plataforma," or ancient water-battery of the fortress, in which were stationed a few soldiers to aid the boatmen in effecting the ascent of the rapids, was the only evidence of human occupation. A year later, when I passed down the river, homeward bound, even that solitary hut had been deserted; its roof had fallen in, it was surrounded by rank weeds, and a lean wolf darted from its open doorway when I approached. Less than three years had elapsed, and now a brisk village of several hundred inhabitants had sprung up at the base of the old fortress; a row of neat cottages, and several large, barn-like structures, facetiously labeled "Hotels," occupied the site of the solitary hut, and lined the previously deserted and desolate shore.

We breakfasted together at the "Crescent Hotel," where we had ham and eggs at California prices, or rather more than twenty times their value and at nine o'clock were again cramped together in our boat, and on our way up the river. About noon we reached the last rapids which are encountered in ascending, called the "Rapidos del Toro." The river here spreads itself out over a broad ledge of rocks, among the detached masses of which the water whirls and eddies in deep, dark pools, rendering navigation both difficult and dangerous. During the dry season, these rapids are impassable for the river steamers, and passengers are obliged to make a third *portage* on foot. We left our men to force the boat up against the strong current, and entered the narrow path which leads through the woods past the rapids. About midway, already surrounded by dank vegetation, we found the ruins of a small thatched hut, and evidences that its former occupant had there undertaken to effect a clearing. A few paces distant from it, two rough crosses, rotting above an oblong hollow in the ground, in which the water of the rains was guttered, green and festering, told too plainly the fate of those who had built it. A few months more, and nothing would remain to attest that they had lived; but perhaps even those lone slumberers have left behind them, on the banks of the bright Hudson or of the turbid Mississippi, hearts that bleed and eyes that weep bitter tears when affection recalls the memory of the loved and lost. Our gay and almost reckless party lifted their hats reverently as they passed in silence the sunken graves in the forest.

Above the "Rapidos del Toro," the river, although still having a strong current, is broad and deep, and almost deserves the name of an estuary of Lake Nicaragua. The banks also begin to subside, and the trunks of fallen trees, still clinging by their roots to the shore, line the edge of the stream. Above them trail long, cable-like *lianes*, or vines, pendant from the loftiest branches of the trees, and often supporting, in their turn, clusters of parasitic plants blushing with gay flowers. As the traveler advances, he observes that the banks become still lower, and that the forest trees, diminishing in size, are interspersed with feathery palms, which gradually usurp the shores with their graceful plumes, to the exclusion of other vegetable forms. They constitute a dense covering to the earth, from which they exclude every ray of the sun, and it lies sodden and lifeless beneath their shade. The streams which wind beneath them are dark and sluggish fit haunts for alligators and unclean monsters such as made horrible the Saurian period, with those huge, misshapen forms which the geologists have pictured to us from casts in rocky strata, within whose stony leaves we can never be too thankful to Heaven that they are securely packed away! The names of these streams correctly indicate the character of the surrounding country. There is the "Rio Palo del Arco," arched with trees, "Poco Sol," Little Sun, and "Rio Mosquito," suggestive of sleepless nights and objurgations bordering on the blasphemous.

The second morning from El Castillo brought us within sight of the drooping flag-staff and thatched huts of Fort San Carlos, which is situated on the left bank of the river, at the point where it debouches from the lake. The old fortress is overgrown with a heavy forest, which entirely conceals it from view. It occupies a commanding position, on a bluff point or headland, that seems to have been planted there to mark the precise spot where the lake terminates and the river begins. Under the crown, it was carefully kept in repair and strongly garrisoned. But its draw-bridge is now broken down, large trees are growing in its ditch, vines clamber over its walls, cluster around dismounted guns, and twine their delicate tendrils through the iron gratings of its deserted cells.

An old friend of mine, Don Patricio Rivas, was "Commandante" at San Carlos, in place of the fat and funny colonel who had done me the honor of parading his scanty garrison in glorification of my previous visit. Don Patricio invited us to the matutinal cup of coffee, and pressed us to remain to breakfast, but we were eager to proceed, and inconsiderately declined. Forgetting my former experiences in the country, I really deluded myself that we might get off in the course of three or four hours, since we had nothing in the world to do but to put up a temporary mast. But no Nicaraguan boat's crew was ever known to get away from San Carlos under a day, for each one has there some coffee-colored inamorata, to whom he invariably brings some article of tribute from the port. We had left the boat with strict injunctions to the men to get it ready for our immediate departure, which they unhesitatingly promised to do. But when we returned, not only had nothing been done to that purpose, but the men themselves were hopelessly scattered throughout the village. We waited for them to return, but in vain, and finally started out, in evil temper, determined to attach their black bodies wherever they were to be found. We succeeded in discovering the *patron* and one of the men, and took them to the boat, whence they soon effected an escape, under the plea of looking up their companions! But hours passed, and the sun grew high and hot; we saw the Commandante's breakfast go smoking and savory from his kitchen to his house, and afterward, with melancholy interest, witnessed time empty plates carried from the house to the kitchen; and yet the obdurate boatmen came not. The sun ascended higher, and the wind, which had blown fairly on our course, died away. It was high noon, and still we waited on the shore. I could endure it no longer, and entered a formal complaint to Don Patricio, who had already retired to his hammock to enjoy his siesta. He shrugged his shoulders, and said it had always been so with the sailors, but nevertheless sent the sergeant of the guard to hunt up the stragglers.

Meantime I had purchased a mast for our boat at ten times its value, and we had fitted it in its place, to obviate any delay which it might otherwise occasion. And then we waited again! Finally, at about three o'clock in the afternoon, after a corrosion of temper which the reader can poorly comprehend, our men were got together. But instead of taking their places, they sat apart, under the shade of a tree, and held a long consultation. The result of their deliberations was, that they had heard the government was enlisting (i.e., impressing) troops in Granada, and that, therefore, they could not possibly go on. It was clear that they imagined we could not proceed without them, and had resorted to this pretense to extract additional pay. They had seen just enough of Americans to comprehend their impatience of delay, and to endeavor to practice upon it in our case. But we were not in a temper to be trifled with, and resolved that, as the wind was fair, we could manage the boat ourselves. So we bundled out a few articles which they possessed, and consigning them with unctuous vehemence to the *Demonio*, as *hombres sin verguenza*, "men without shame," hoisted sail and started, to their great astonishment.

As soon as our boat got out from under the lee of the shore, she caught the strong breeze in her sails, and darted away like a courser on her track. Lieutenant J----- was elected commodore, *nem. con.,* and the other members of the party were assigned such stations as their skill or experience warranted them in accepting. H----- had drawn pictures of many elegant boats, and ships, and steamers, and was able, in most cases, to distinguish the bow from the stern, but his knowledge of navigation was deplorably imperfect. Nevertheless he was installed in the responsible post of watching the stays, or, as he expressed it, "engineering the ropes." The doctor, better versed in nautical affairs, was placed at the halyards; while ponderous Captain M----- was commissioned to "trim ship," by shifting his bulk from one side to the other, as occasion required.

We went off bravely from Fort San Carlos, and fired our guns derisively in the faces of our mutinous crew. Every moment the wind freshened, and our boat seemed to grow buoyant and instinct with life. But our mast was frail, and bent under the strain. By-and-by there was a suspicious crackling, as if it were about to break, followed rapidly by the order, "Let go the halyards!" H----- had already forgotten the difference between stays and halyards, and in his eagerness to "engineer the ropes," made a spasmodic pull at the fastenings, letting down the sail "on the run." In an instant it was blown overboard, causing the boat to broach to with a jerk which tumbled men, oars, and boxes in a heap, and half filled the boat with water. For a little while our condition was perilous, but at the cost of a general wetting, we finally got in our sail. As we were now shut out of sight of the fort by a friendly promontory, we considerately made a reef or two in the canvas, and proceeded on our way with more safety if less speed.

The "Columbus" on the Lake

The afternoon was one of surpassing beauty, and the surrounding scenery harmonized, in all respects, with the skies which bent overhead—here gorgeous with crimson and gold, and there, melting away in delicate pearly hues, just flecked with clouds so downy and light, that they seemed to dissolve in air before the eyes of the gazer. The shores of Italy, and the lakes which are lapped among the snow-crowned Alps, and which gleam at their feet, on the borders of Lombardy, certainly combine almost every element of the grand and beautiful. The azure of their waters cannot be surpassed, and the rugged rocks that frown around them leave little for the imagination to supply in forms of severity and grandeur. But the lakes of Nicaragua super add new and striking features. Here rise lofty volcanoes, the irregular cones emulating the Pyramids in symmetry of out-line. Around their bases cluster dense forests of dark green, as if carved in emerald. Above these, blended with matchless delicacy, is the lighter green of the mountain grasses, while the umber-colored summits, where the arid scoria refuses to nourish life, are plumed with light wreaths of clouds through which the sunlight struggles in a hundred opalescent hues. The islands, too, which gem the waters, are luxuriant with tropical trees. The palm lifts its kingly stem high above the forests, and traces its airy form against the sky, while broad-based plants and vines, in heavy masses, drape over the rocks, or depend from the trees above the water, which darkens, and seems to slumber in their cool shadows. And although there are here no castles perched on high cliffs, or clinging to the faces of precipices, nor yet the white walls of villas nestling on the shore, yet the voyager discerns ocean ward vistas, openings among the trees, terminating with views of huts of picturesque and primitive forms, set round with plantains and papayas, clustering with their golden fruit. Canoes of graceful out-line are drawn up on the shaded shore, and dark figures of men, of a strange and decadent race, watch the stranger with curious interest, as he glides noiselessly by. Such are some of the varied elements of the grand, the beautiful, and the picturesque, which give to the Nicaraguan lakes their indisputable pre-eminence over those allowed by recollections, and immortalized by songs, which claim the homage of Nature's worshipers in the old world.

We sailed gayly past the clustering islets of La Boqueta, and the little village of San Miguelito, situated on the northern shore of the lake. Herds of cattle lingered lazily on the beach in front, and the village girls filled their water-jars under the shadows of the trees, while bright–winged macaws and noisy parrots glanced among the branches, and made the shore vocal with their querulous cries.

It was long after dark when we doubled the high point of black volcanic rocks which shuts in the *playa* of "El Pedernal," and cast anchor for the night under its lee. We had made, in nautical phrase, a splendid run, and had accomplished nearly one-third of the entire distance from the fort to Granada, the city of our destination. We had now passed the region of eternal rain. It was the dry season around the lakes, and the stars shone down with a clear and almost unnatural lustre from a serene and cloudless sky. New constellations wheeled over head, and the Southern Cross jeweled the bosom of the night; while the familiar Polar Star, revolving low in the horizon, was hardly visible above the tree-tops. The tiny waves toyed and tinkled beneath the bow of our boat, while the swell of the open lake heaved with a dull, monotonous sound, against the dark and rugged rocks which protected our little harbor. I lay for hours in a half-slumberous, dreamy state, conscious only of those impressions which go out from Nature herself, and mould and fashion the whole flow of thought in sympathy with her own harmonious beauty. But finally slumber came, quiet and dreamless, and silence reigned supreme until the gray dawn roused the wakeful captain, whose shout of "*Show a leg*!" startled every recumbent form bolt upright, and frightened sleep from every eyelid.

When the sun rose, lighting up the high volcanic peaks of Ometepec and Madeira with its rays, we were in mid-lake, steering boldly for the blue cone of the volcano of Mombacho, which towers over the city of Granada. The sailors on the lake seldom venture across it in their rude *bongos*, but coast along its northern shore, sometimes stretching past the little bays, but oftener conforming to the curves of the land. One reason for this caution is to be found in the turbulence of the lake. Swept by the strong northeast trade-winds, its waves emulate those of the ocean, and roll in majestically on its southern shores. During certain seasons of the year, sudden thunder-gusts, which appear as if by enchantment on the horizon, rush over its surface with impetuous force, often whelming the frail boats which they encounter in their track beneath the seething waters. Fortunately for us the weather was serene and the wind fair, and we sped on our way with exhilarating speed. By noon, the outlines of the high island of Zapatero became clearly defined, and the clusters of islets, called "*Los Corales*," which stud the lake at the base of the volcano of Mombacho, began to rise, like points of emerald, above the waters.

Zapatero, "The Shoemaker," had to me a special interest. Three years before I had spent a week in exploring the ancient ruins which are crumbling beneath its gigantic forests—a week of surpassing interest and excitement; for every hour brought with it some new discovery, and every foot of ground bore some quaint witness of a people that had passed away. I felt half-inclined to turn the course of our boat toward its shores, and to resume the investigations which I had then been obliged to suspend in deference to official duties. Zapatero anciently bore the name of *Chomitl-Tenamilt*; and its distant neighbor, with its two lofty peaks, had the characteristic Mexican designation of *Ometepec*, Two Mountains. With the islands of Solenterami, and the narrow isthmus which intervenes between the lake and the Pacific, they constituted the seat of a people speaking a common language, and having common modes of life and forms of government and religion, with those who dwelt on the plateau of Mexico, and made up the empire of Montezuma. But whether a colony from the latter, or their progenitors, who shall undertake, in the maze of conflicting traditions and the absence of authentic records, to decide?

By the middle of the afternoon we were skirting the fairy-like group of "Los Corales." It comprises, literally, hundreds of islets of volcanic origin, elevated in the form of cones to the height of from twenty to one hundred feet. They are composed of immense rocks of lava, black and blistered by the fire; but their summits are covered with verdure, and long vines hang trailing over their rugged sides to the very edge of the water. Some of them, upon which there is a sufficient accumulation of soil, are crowned with the picturesque thatched huts of Indians, shadowed over by tall palms and surrounded with plantain-trees. But most are left to the dominion of nature, and are the favorite retreats of myriads of parrots and flocks of water-fowl.

Suddenly, doubling the islet of Cuba, the outlier of Los Corales, the *Playa* of Granada, opened before us. There stood the ancient fort as of old, and the beach swarmed, as it had done when I last saw it, with its varied groups of boatmen, *lavadoras*, and loungers. There were the same graceful canoes drawn up on the shore, and the same cumbrous *bongos*, wherein the commerce of Granada had been carried on from the time of the Conquest. But contrasting strangely with all, the only new or novel object in the picture was one of the steamers of the Transit Company, with its plume of escaping steam, and its starry flag streaming in the wind—portentous pioneer in that career of enterprise which must soon give a new life, a new spirit, and a new people to these glorious lands of the sun.

We ran our boat under the lee of the old fort and leaped ashore, having made the voyage from San Carlos—a distance of more than one hundred miles—in the unprecedentedly short space of eighteen hours sailing time. I had hardly landed before I was nearly caught from my feet in the Herculean embrace of Antonio Paladan, my ancient patron, who took this elephantine way of evincing his joy at meeting me again. He had been with me in my visit to Zapatero, and had afterward taken me to San Juan, in his pet bongo "*La Granadina*." Poor Antonio! He was subsequently wantonly assassinated by a brutal captain of one of the Transit steamers, a Portuguese refugee, who only escaped punishment through the interference of an over-zealous American ambassador. I can have no selfish motive in vindicating the memory of the poor *patron*; but it is only a just tribute to humble merit to say, that there never was an honester and truer heart than that which beat beneath the swarthy breast of Antonio Paladan, the murdered and already forgotten patron of Lake Nicaragua.

Granada occupies the site of the aboriginal town of Saltaba or Jaltava. Its position is admirably chosen, on a little bay or *playa* which bends its graceful crescent in the land, so as to afford a comparative shelter from the northeast winds. The beach is broad and sandy, fringed with low but umbrageous trees, beneath which a number of paths and broad cart-roads lead up to the city, completely hidden from view by the intervening verdure. All the water for the use of the town is brought from the lake, and hither the women come trooping, morning and evening, with their red water-jars poised upon their heads, in long and picturesque processions, chattering gayly, and with always an impudent smile and quick repartee for the audacious stranger. Here the *lavadoras*—which is smooth Spanish for our rough English designation *wasker-women*—toil early and late in their indispensable vocation; and here, too, resort the bathers for their daily purification—a process which is conducted in happy disregard of our severer conventionalism. And thus, with the swarthy groups of half-naked boatmen, and the gayly-caparisoned horses which their owners glory in, spurring over the smooth sands when the declining sun throws them in the shadow of the trees, the *playa* of Granada presents a scene of gayety and life which, for its hearty abandon and picturesque effect, can not be surpassed in any part of the world.

Leaving the shore, the traveler ascends a gentle slope, by a series of artificial terraces, to the level of the city. First he encounters straggling huts, some built of canes and covered with thatch, and others plastered with mud, white-washed, and roofed with tiles. A clump of fruit-trees, generally *jocotes*, or wild plums, over-shadows each, and within doors may be seen women spinning cotton with a little foot-wheel, or engaged in grinding corn for *tortillas*. On almost every house are one or two parrots screaming at each other, or at some awkward macaw waddling along the crest of the roof, while all around, pigs, dogs, chickens, and naked children mingle on terms of perfect equality.

Beyond these huts commences the city proper. The buildings are mostly of sun-dried bricks, or adobes, raised on foundations of cut stone, and surmounted by projecting roofs of tiles. The windows are, for the most part, balconied, and protected on the outside by ornamented iron gratings, and on the inside by gayly-colored shutters. They are all low, seldom exceeding one story in height, and built around quadrangular areas, entered by heavy, ornamented *zaguans*, or archways, through which are caught glimpses of orange-trees and beds of flowers with which female taste ornaments the court-yards. The foot-walks are elevated one or two feet above the street, and are barely wide enough to admit one person to pass at a time. The streets toward the centre of the town, or *plaza*, are paved as in our own cities, with this difference, that instead of a convex, they present a concave surface, and form the gutter in the centre of the street.

Granada, like all other Spanish towns, has an appearance of meanness to one accustomed to European architecture. But he soon comes to comprehend the perfect adaptation of the buildings to the conditions of the country, where security from earthquakes and protection from heats and rains are the prime requisites to be consulted in their erection. As the windows are never glazed, and the apartments seldom celled, they are always well ventilated, while the thick adobe walls successfully resist the heating rays of the sun.

Granada was founded by Hernandez de Cordova in 1552, and is, consequently, one of the oldest cities of the continent. The country around it, in the language of the pious Las Casas, "was one of the best peopled in all America," and was rich in agricultural products, among which the *cacao*, or chocolate-nut, had the most value, and soon came to constitute an important article of export. In later times, the facilities which it possessed for communication with both the Atlantic and Pacific made it the centre of a large commerce. It carried on a direct trade with Guatemala, Honduras, and San Salvador, as also with Peru, Panama, Carthagena, and Spain. The old English friar Gage tells us that, at the time of his visit in the year 1665, "there entered the city in a single day not less than eighteen hundred mules from San Salvador and Honduras alone, laden with indigo, cochineal, and hides. And in two days thereafter," he adds, "came in nine hundred more mules, one-third of which were laden with silver, which was the king's tribute."

Filibusters were as abundant in those days as now—less noisy, but more daring; and often, observes the quaint old chronicler, "did make the merchants to tremble and to sweat with a cold sweat." They did not content themselves with cruising around the mouth of "El Desaguadero," or river San Juan, and capturing the vessels which were sent from Granada, but had the audacity, in 1686, to land and capture the city itself That rare old rascal De Lussan, who was of the party, has left us an unctuous account of the adventure, which "upon our side," he says, "cost but four killed and eight wounded, which was, in truth, very cheap!" But the pirates got but little booty; for the inhabitants had embarked their treasures and retired to the islands of the lake, whither the pirates, having no boats, were unable to follow them. So they "set fire to the houses out of mere spite and revenge," and retired. De Lussan describes the town at that time as large and spacious, with "stately churches and houses well built enough, besides several religious establishments both for men and women."

Granada, although its trade has greatly fallen off from the opening of other ports in the various Central American states, has nevertheless continued to be the principal commercial town in Nicaragua. Up to the time of our visit it had suffered far less from violence than its rival Leon, the political capital of the province under the crown, and of the state under the Republic. And while the last-named city had been several times nearly ruined by protracted sieges, during one of which not less than eighteen hundred houses were burned in a single night, Granada had escaped without any serious blow to its prosperity. But in a fatal hour some of its leading citizens became ambitious of political and military power and distinction, and succeeded in placing one of their number, Don Fruto Chamorro, a man of narrow intellect, but great pertinacity of purpose and obstinacy of character, in the chair of Director of the State. The means by which this was effected were somewhat equivocal, and probably would not bear close scrutiny. They occasioned great discontent among the people, which was increased by the reactionary policy of the new Director. One of his first acts was the abrogation of the Constitution of the State and the substitution of another, which conferred little less than dictatorial powers upon the Executive. For opposing this in the constituent Assembly, and upon the pretext that they were conspiring for his overthrow, Chamorro suddenly banished most of the leaders of the Liberal party from the State, and arbitrarily imprisoned the remainder.

These acts precipitated, if indeed they did not bring about, the precise result which they were intended to prevent. In the spring of 1854, a few months after their expulsion, the persecuted Liberals suddenly returned to the State, and were received with enthusiasm by the people, who at once rose in arms against the new Dictator. He was defeated at every point, and finally compelled to shut himself up in Granada, where, supported by the merchants and the sailors of the lake, he maintained a siege from May, 1854, until the month of March of the present year, when the besieging forces retired. But before he could avail himself of his improved position he sickened and died; and although his partisans are still in arms, it is supposed that they cannot long sustain themselves against the undoubted public opinion of the State. Be that as it may, it is certain that the siege has left a great part of Granada in ruins, and inflicted a blow upon its prosperity from which it will be unable to recover for many years.

The population of Granada is estimated at from 12,000 to 15,000 souls, including the suburb and separate municipality of Jalteva. It has seven churches, an hospital, and nominally a university. It had anciently two or three convents, but these were all suppressed at the time of the revolution in 1823, nor has any attempt since been made to revive them. The edifices which they occupied have either fallen into ruins, or been dedicated to other purposes.

Granada de Nicaragua—from the West

I have said that the position of Granada is well chosen. Upon the south, at the distance of a few miles, rises the volcano of Mombacho, with its ragged crater, while on the west, undulating plains and low ridges of land intervene between the town and the Pacific ocean. Toward the north are only broad, alluvial, and densely wooded plains, possessing a soil rich and well adapted to the cultivation of rice, sugar, cotton, and cacao. But from no point of the surrounding country can the traveler obtain a satisfactory view of the city. Its low houses are so overshadowed by the trees which grow in the court-yards, and hem in the city on every side, that little can be seen except long lines of monotonous, red-tiled roofs, and the towers of the churches. The accompanying view, taken from the west, conveys a very good idea of the suburbs, where the houses are straggling and comparatively mean. It has been selected, chiefly for the purpose of showing a deep ravine, which seems to be a chasm rent originally by an earthquake, and subsequently deepened by the action of water. It extends around the city on three sides, and constitutes a natural defense of no insignificant importance. It is from sixty to one hundred feet deep, with absolutely precipitous sides, and can only be passed at two or three points, where lateral inclined planes have been artificially cut from the top to the bottom on one side, and the bottom to the top on the other. This singular feature had probably something to do in determining the site of the ancient Indian town.

The great lake of Nicaragua was called *Cociboeca* by the aborigines. It is undoubtedly the most remarkable natural feature of the country, and, apart from its beauty, has been invested with singular interest from the supposed facilities which it holds out for the opening of a ship-canal between the two great oceans. Modern investigations have dispelled many of the illusions which have existed in reference to that project, and shown that the difficulties in the way of its realization have hitherto been but very imperfectly comprehended. They have shown that the river San Juan can never be made navigable for ships, and that the great difficulty in the way of the proposed work is not, as had been previously supposed, between the lake and the Pacific, but between the Atlantic and the lake—a distance of 128 miles, for 100 miles of which it would be necessary to dig a canal, through a country unhealthy and in the highest degree unfavorable to the prosecution of this work. It has also been found that, while such a canal would greatly facilitate the commerce of the United States, by shortening the passage of ships to the western coasts of America, to the Sandwich Islands, and the East Indies, yet that, so far as Europe is concerned, the aggregate saving over the route by way of Cape Good Hope would be inconsiderable, and in no degree equal in value to the tolls which the canal would require, in order to keep it open and in repair. The voyage from England to Canton would be 200 miles longer by way of the proposed canal than it now is by way of Cape Good Hope; to Calcutta it would be 3900 miles longer, and to Singapore 2300 miles! Under such a state of facts, it is folly to suppose that the enterprise will ever receive the commercial or political support of the powers of Europe, who are already too much embarrassed by American maritime competition, to lend their aid in reversing the favorable physical superiority which they now possess over the United States in the trade with the East.

Lake Nicaragua has a length of not far from one hundred and twenty miles, and is about forty-five or fifty miles in average width. It is deep, except toward its northern shore, where there are extensive shallows, and is supplied by numerous streams, chiefly from the high district of Chontales. An *estero* or estuary, called the "*Estero de Panaloza*," and a small stream, Rio Zipitapa, connect it with the superior lake of Managua. It abounds in fish, and is infested also with a species of sharks, called "*tigrones*" by the natives, from their ferocity. They sometimes attack men with fatal results. There is a kind of ebb and flow in the waters of the lake, which led the early explorers to think that it was an estuary or bay of the sea. The phenomenon, however, is of easy explanation: As I have said, the prevailing wind in Nicaragua is the northeast trade, which here sweeps entirely across the continent. It is strongest at noon and evening, when it drives the waters, piling them up, as it were, on the western shore of the lake; it subsides toward morning, when the equilibrium is restored, and an ebb follows. The regularity with which this wind blows gives a corresponding regularity to the ebb and flow of the lake. Sometimes when it blows continuously, and with greater force than usual, the low lands on the western shores are flooded; but this is of rare occurrence.

Granada, during our brief stay, was in deep excitement. It had been the scene of an occurrence familiar enough at home, but novel and unprecedented here—

viz., a forgery! Subsequently to the opening of the Transit, it had become customary for the merchants to make remittances to their correspondents abroad, in bills drawn by the agents of the Transit Company, thus saving the risk and trouble of remitting coin. Some practiced hand, possibly from New York or San Francisco, a modest gentleman, plainly dressed in black and wearing glasses, one day introduced himself to a leading merchant, and presented a draft for $10,000, which he wished to dispose of for gold and silver. His necessities were urgent, and he was not indisposed to consent to a trifling "shave." The unsophisticated *commerciante*, nothing loath to be looked upon as a banker, and furthermore not indifferent to making "a nice thing," felt flattered, and straightway, from his own means and those of his friends, raised the requisite amount—a strange collection of vagabond silver, Spanish rials, English six-pences, French francs, and Yankee dimes. The paper was duly endorsed over, and the silver given in return. That night a cart was heard to creak its way down to the playa, where its freight was quickly transferred to a "low, dark, and suspicious schooner," which long before daybreak was out of sight of Granada. A few days elapsed before the truth came out. The people could comprehend a robbery or burglary, the forcing of a window or the shooting of a traveler, but this quiet and genteel way of effecting the same object, was a refinement of civilization which dumbfounded all Granada. People looked anxious, and talked in whispers at the corners, and even the eyes of the water carriers grew big with astonishment. Men forgot their prayers, and madly neglected their siestas. The sentinels at the corners of the Plaza forgot to challenge the passer-by, and the officers of the garrison sat on the steps of the cuartel, with their cigars unlighted! They all seemed to be laboring under a vague notion that they had been "done for," or were dreaming, but were not at all clear which.

After a few days the stupor began to lift; some one suggested that the perpetrators should be pursued, whereupon every body said, "Como no?" ("Why not?") and straightway saddled their horses. But then somebody else asked in what direction they should go? Which inquiry put every thing back again, and they unsaddled their horses. But finally, after the "operators" had had ample time to get well off pursuit was really commenced. It resulted in the capture of an English physician resident in the country, who had actually amputated a leg without killing the patient, and who therefore was regarded as too shrewd and sharp to be honest. He was kept in prison for several months, but as no evidence could be procured to convict him, he was finally discharged. And thus ended Granada's first lesson in the art and mystery of modern financiering!

"*Fue cosa muy extraña.*" ("It was a very strange affair.")

"And so it was, amigo; but you should live in New York!"

The volcano of Mombacho, sometimes written in the old maps *Bombacho*, has a broad base and ragged summit. It measures about 4500 feet, or little less than one mile, in vertical height. Very few of the natives have ever ascended it, although nearly every one has some story to tell of the marvelous lake which exists at its summit, and of the wonderful things which the traveler encounters in reaching it. I had great difficulty in persuading an ancient *marinero*, who had gone up, several years before, with the Chevalier Friedrichthal, and spent several days with him at the top, to act as my guide. The face of the volcano toward Granada is inaccessible, and we found it was necessary to go to the Indian town of Diriomo, situated at the southwestern base of the mountain, and take our departure thence.

We accordingly made our arrangements over night, and early on the following morning, while it was yet dark, mounted our mules and started for Diriomo. We passed under the walls of the *Campo Santo*, white and spectral in the uncertain light, and struck at once into a narrow path in the forest. We could barely distinguish the white mule of our guide, who led the way, and had to trust to the sagacity of our animals to follow the road. At intervals the scraping of the drooping branches over the glazed hat of our guide, and his sharp "*Cuidado*!"—("Take care!") warned us to bend to our saddle-bows, to avoid being dragged from our seats. "Stoop and go safe," is a motto of sound application in riding by night through a tropical forest. After an hour or more of this precarious traveling, day began to break, and shortly afterward we emerged from the woods into a comparatively rough and broken country. The slopes of the volcano are cut in deep ravines, which furrow its sides, and radiate from its base. These ravines are filled with trees, bushes, and vines, while the ridges between them are bare, supporting only long coarse grass, now crisp and yellow from the protracted heats. And as we rode on, we were one moment immersed in dark thickets, only to emerge the next on the narrow savannas of the ridges, whence we could catch glimpses of the lake just reflecting the ruddy light which streamed above the hills of Chontales. The morning breeze breathed cool and grateful on our fore heads, and filled our lungs with an exhilarating freshness.

An hour more, and we had reached the base of the high, conical hills of scoria, bare of trees, but covered with grass, which form so striking features in the scenery back of Granada. They are of exceeding regularity of shape, and seem to have been formed of ashes and scoria, ejected from the volcano when in a state of eruption, and carried here by the wind. They are, in fact, the *ash-heaps* of the volcanoes, and as they are found in greater or less numbers near every volcano in the country, they form infallible indications of the direction of the prevailing winds.

Around these cones we found patches of cleared lands, now overgrown with rank weeds, which had been anciently estates of maize and indigo. Beyond these, the road enters a thick forest, and winds over a high ridge of volcanic rocks and lava, which extends off in the direction of the volcano of Masaya. Midway to the summit, sparkling like a diamond beneath the rocks, is a copious spring of cool water, bearing a musical Indian name which I have forgotten, where we stopped to fill our canteens and rest our mules. It is a lovely spot, arched over with trees, which the nourishing waters keep clothed in perennial green. It has been from time immemorial a favorite resort of the Indians, and the rocks around it have been worn smooth by the tread of their myriad feet.

At the summit of the hill we came upon a figure, carved in stone, planted firmly in the ground, by the side of the path. It is of the same character with the idols which I had discovered during my first visit to Nicaragua in the islands of the lake, but is now used—so said our guide—to mark the boundary between the lands of the Indians of Diriomo and Jalteva. Throughout all Central America the traveler encounters piles of stones raised by the sides of the paths, for a similar purpose. With the Indians, as between Laban and Jacob, they certify to the covenant "that I will not pass over this heap to thee, and thou shall not pass over this heap and this pillar unto me, for harm."

After ascending the ridge the ground became undulating, and we came frequently upon patches of plantains, canes, and maize, which looked fresh and luxuriant, as compared with vegetation elsewhere. This is due to the volcano, which intervenes in the direction of the trade-winds, and which intercepts the clouds that they bear on their wings, and precipitates them in showers under its lee. And thus, while the country at large is suffering from drought, this favored spot is cherished by the grateful rain, arid retains its verdure arid its beauty.

It was scarcely nine o'clock when we reached the large but straggling village of Diriomo. But we did not stop there. Turning, abruptly to the left, we rode rapidly through a broad and well-beaten path, to the cacao hacienda of the family of Bermudez. It is a retired and lovely spot, commanding a fine view of the southern declivity of Mombacho. A little lake in the foreground, and clumps of trees, interspersed with patches of dark lava, and occasional fields of reddish scoria, filled up the middle space of a picture of novel and surpassing beauty, in which the volcano rose grandly in the distance.

Leaving the mules in charge of the *mozos* of the hacienda, we lost no time in prosecuting our expedition. Our path for two hours wound through a very broken country. At times we struggled over beds of *crinkling* lava, already hot under the blaze of the sun, and then plunged in thickets of dwarfed trees, to emerge, perhaps, upon an arid slope of cinders and scoria, supporting only the dry spikes of the *maguey* or agave, and clusters of the spiny cactus.

Finally, we began the ascent of the mountain proper. Upon this side the walls of the crater are broken down, exposing a fearfully-rugged orifice, in the form of an inverted cone, walled up with black and forbidding rocks, which seemed to frown angrily upon our approach. The summit now looked twice as high as it had done before, and we strained our eyes in vain to discover the semblance of a path among the jagged masses of lava and volcanic stones piled in wild disorder on every hand. Two of our party, appalled by the difficulties which presented themselves, decided to forgo the pleasure of witnessing a sunrise from the summit, and the prospect of broken necks or shattered limbs in reaching it, for a quiet night in a comfortable hammock at the hacienda. So we drained their canteens for them, under the shadow of a large rock, and separated.

From this point our ascent was simply a fatiguing scramble. Now clinging to rough angular rocks, anon grasping at the roots and branches of gnarled and scraggy trees, or painfully struggling over steep slopes of ashes and volcanic and, which yielded beneath the feet, we toiled slowly up the mountain, the summit of which seemed to lift itself higher and higher in the air, while the clouds rushed past it with dizzy velocity. The sun, too, shone down upon the arid declivities with fervent heat, and the radiations from the blistered rocks fairly seared our eyes and blinded our sight. At the end of two hours we had gone up so far as scarcely to be able to distinguish our friends below us, and yet, as we gazed up-ward, it was impossible to discover that we had made any perceptible progress in our ascent.

Still we kept on, and on, tearing our hands and bruising our limbs, in our eagerness to reach the summit before the setting of the sun. At three o'clock we were brought to a stand-still by the sudden fainting of Señor Z-----, a young gentleman of Granada, who had volunteered to accompany us. Fortunately I saw him stagger, and was able to catch him in my arms before he had lost all consciousness. A moment later he would have fallen among the rocks, and inevitably have been killed. He soon recovered from the attack, and, after resting a while, attempted to proceed. But his efforts were feeble, and another recurrence of faintness, and indications of a suffusion of the brain, rendering it evident that he could neither go on nor return that afternoon. There was but one alternative left, and that was to encamp where we were for the night. But he would not listen to the proposition, and insisted on being left with the guide until our return. So we led him to a cleft in the rocks, where he was sheltered from the sun, and, supplying him with water and food, bade him farewell, and continued our ascent.

The lead, now that we had lost our guide, devolved upon me. It was a position of some responsibility, for the mountain was here rent in numerous deep rifts or chasms, some of which were hundreds of feet deep, and it was difficult to select a course which should avoid them, and yet conduct us toward the top of the mountain. Besides, we had now reached the region of clouds, which often obscured the summit, and enveloped us in their dark and damp, but refreshing folds. While they were passing we could not move, for a single incautious step might now be fatal.

I had directed my course toward a high angular peak, which, to us, seemed to be the highest part of the mountain. But when, after prodigious toil, we had attained it, I found that it was only one of the broken lips of the crater, and that the true bulk of the mountain lay far to the left, separated from the point on which we stood by a deep cleft, which could only be passed by descending the rocks again for the distance of nearly a thousand feet. This was a severe disappointment in some respects, yet we felt glad that we were not obliged to pass the night there. Before retracing our steps, I crawled cautiously to the very edge of the rock. It overhung the ancient crater, which yawned like a hell beneath. I recoiled with a shudder; but not until I had observed, at the very bottom of the rocky gulf, a little lake of water, which gleamed brightly in its rough setting.

After regaining the body of the volcano, we came upon a comparatively smooth slope, supporting a few bushes and a little hardy grove; and, just before sunset, after passing several small craters or ancient vents, succeeded in attaining the summit of the mountain.

I had abstained from looking around me while ascending, anxious to witness the glorious prospect, which, I knew, must open upon my vision there, in all of its vastness and beauty. Worn, weary, bruised and bleeding, yet that one sublime view compensated for all! Language can faintly picture it. The great Pacific, all golden under the setting sun, spread away boundlessly in the west; and Lake Nicaragua, its glowing waters studded with islands, lay motionless at our feet. Beyond it rose the umber-tinted hills of Chontales, and still beyond these, rank on rank, the high, blue ranges of the silver-veined Cordilleras of Honduras! I turned to the southward, and there, piercing the clear air with their lofty cones, towered the graceful peaks of Ometepec and Madeira. And yet beyond these, rose the volcano of Orosi, with its dark banner of smoke trailing away, league on league, along the horizon, and tracing an ebon belt across the gigantic bulk of cloud-crowned Cartago, proudly dominating over both great oceans! To the northward the view was equally varied and extensive. There, cradled among hills of eternal green, spread out the large and beautiful Lake of Managua. At its further extremity loomed the high volcano of Momotombo, watching, like some gigantic warder, over the slumbering waters. And more distant still, terminating the dim perspective, were the receding peaks which bristle around the plain of Leon. And, apparently at our feet, although ten miles distant from the base of the mountain, stood the broad, low volcano of Masaya, in the midst of a wide expanse of lava fields, which, rugged and black, strongly contrasted with the adjacent forests and cultivated grounds. The white churches of Granada and of the surrounding villages appeared like points of silver in the slant rays of the sun. Rarely, indeed, has the eye of mortal looked upon a fairer scene!

But as we gazed with unwearying delight the sun declined, and broad purple shadows crept over lake and plain, while every peak and mountain shone with increased brightness, like fairy islands in some enchanted sea. Soon the shadows began to invade their slopes, mounting higher and higher, and wrapping them, one by one, in their cool embrace. At last, only the topmost crests of Ometepec and Madeira were left, and around them the sun's rays dallied, as lover dwells upon the lips of his mistress, in fond and lingering adieus.

The glow and the glory passed; and the stately night in her glittering robe came on, in calm and majestic beauty. And then, face to face with the stars, we wrapped our blankets around us, and lay down upon the bare earth. The silence was profound, and almost painful, and deepened rather than disturbed by the subdued and distant, but distinct pulsations of the great Pacific. Suddenly we heard the bells of Granada chiming the passing hour. The sound was almost startling from its apparent nearness, yet softened and harmonized in the rarified atmosphere, so as to resemble the swelling notes of the Aeolian harp when struck by a sudden breeze.

The early part of the night was deliciously cool, but toward morning we were all awakened by a cold mist, which settled upon the top of the mountain, covering the rocks with big drops of moisture, and which was not dispelled until long after the sun had risen above the horizon.* We thus lost the principal object of our visit, but consoled ourselves with the reflection that our imaginations could picture nothing more glorious than the sunset of the preceding evening, It was past ten o'clock before we were able to extend our vision beyond the little circle within which we stood, or advance toward the eastern declivity of the mountain, where an abrupt depression, and the cries of birds, seemed to indicate that we should find the lake of which we had heard so much. We were not disappointed, for we came suddenly upon the edge of one of the subordinate ancient craters, or lava rents of the volcano. It was not so deep as the others we had seen, and its gently converging sides were covered evenly with grass. It was, to borrow a homely comparison, a beautiful saucer-shaped depression, something more than a quarter of a mile broad, and about two hundred feet deep. At the bottom slumbered a small lake, fringed round with trees and bushes, loaded with vines, which drooped over the water in luxuriant masses. Among the trees were a few *coyol* palms, dwarfed, but otherwise flourishing. But most remarkable of all, growing between some loose rocks, and partly shadowed over by other trees, were several tree-ferns—the first we had seen in Nicaragua. I never met with them elsewhere in Central America, except in the great *barranca* of Guaramal in San Salvador. Their tender leaves seemed translucent in the rays of the sun, and as ethereal and delicate as the tracery of the frost on our Northern window-panes. Among the trees, and occasionally glancing out and in, were hundreds of noisy paraquets. As we advanced, a troop of Indian conies, a species of hare common to the tropics, suddenly lifted themselves on their hind legs above the grass, looked at us in evident amazement for an instant, and thou scampered off for the covert. I fired at them fruitlessly with my revolver. The effect of the discharge was marvelous. A cloud of paraquets rose above the trees, and darted in wild confusion around the ancient crater. A couple of ravens, which we had not seen before, also rose and circled over the pool, uttering their harsh, discordant croaks, and a number of toucans fluttered heavily from one tree top to another. In fact, all that there was of life in that secluded spot seemed to have been frightened into wild activity. We were ourselves a little startled by the sudden rustle of wings.

---

*At dawn the thermometer marked 65° Fahrenheit, while at Granada, at the same hour, it stood at 79°, a difference of 14°.

But soon the tumult subsided, and the frightened birds again entered their leafy coverts, whence they watched us in silence. We endeavored to penetrate the thicket around the little lake, but it was so matted together with vines, and the soil withal was so marshy, that we gave up the attempt, and contented ourselves with making a cup of grateful coffee beneath the shadow of an overhanging tree. By barometrical measurement I found this mountain lake to be 4420 feet above the level of the sea.

About noon, after taking a final survey from the summit of Mombacho, we commenced our descent. This was more rapid and less fatiguing than our ascent, but more dangerous. We were far more alarmed in getting down some of the rocky and almost perpendicular declivities than we had been in surmounting them. Once or twice, indeed, we could scarcely persuade ourselves that we were re-turning by the same path we had ascended. Nevertheless, without any greater mishap than the usual one attendant on such adventures, of breaking our barometer, at two o'clock we reached the place where we had left our exhausted companion. To our surprise and momentary alarm he was gone. But after a little search we found a scrap of paper beneath a little pile of stones, informing us that his night's rest had restored him, and that he had availed himself of the freshness of the morning to return. Thankful that we were not to be embarrassed by a sick man, we continued our descent, and at sunset were seated to a cup of fragrant chocolate beneath the hospitable corridor of Bermudez.

We passed the evening in recounting the wonders of the mountain to a bevy of attentive Señoritas, who opened wide their big lustrous eyes, and ejaculated *mira*! at every pause in the narrative. All but the dreamy Dolores, who fabricated *cigaritos* with her tapered fingers, and spoke not at all, except through glances, so earnest, that the speaker faltered in his recital, and forgot his story when they met his gaze! As thou valuest thy peace of mind, oh, stranger! Beware of the dreamy Dolores!

5

The New Route through Chiriqui

Thomas Francis Meagher

The author takes a journey to the city of David, about 200 miles north of Panama City and finds there an unspoiled town with excellent resources, numerous French citizens, and few Americans. The author and a small party cross the isthmus in six days; Indians, unlike in other places, are described as "faithful," noble, and heroic. Essentially, the author is calling for further exploration and exploitation of this land and states, with certainty, that a new, competing railroad line could easily be built across the isthmus, connecting the Chiriqui Lagoon on the Atlantic side with the Gulf of Dulce on the Pacific.

There were jagged rocks, up through the slippery grooves of which, worn by itself, the sea went splashing. Thousands of brown gulls and thousands of pelicans, surfeited and drowsy, clung to them—now and then opening an eye or flapping a wing—otherwise showing little or no concern for the balls which our rifles dropped about them. There were clusters of islands—islands with steep white cliffs and thickset lofty trees, and here and there a cane-built hut, palm-branches fanning it and burnished children frolicking in front of it—and there were lonesome sandy nooks, high up into which deserted canoes were drawn, and over the beach of which the volumed surf rolled calmly in, leaving sheets of thin silvery froth to mark its inroads, as it receded to roll in again. At times from some little bay—the smooth rocks walling one side of which were richly tufted with glossy shrubs, the leaves of which were green and gold and crimson, while those, opposite them, were broken into arches and seemed a pile of feudal ruins—a rough-hewn *bungo*, laden deep with pearl-shells, sail set and coppered faces gleaming from the gunwale, would slip out, and all a-beam slide by us.

Then, as the calm sea darkened—and as the trees and cliffs, the loftiest and most striking of them, softened into one great shadow, and the scene, so tranquil in its beauteousness and grandeur all day long, seemed to settle down still more and grow entranced—high in the dim heavens, with its cloven ridge touching the few pale stars there, and these trembling as the black crest touched them, the volcano of Chiriqui loomed up. Far off, but all the gloomier and all the grander for the distance from us at which it towered, that vast mountain—where, according to Indian tales, the angry spirits and demons of a lost race dwell—seemed, every instant we gazed at it, to grow vaster still. Of all the great mountains bounding the wide plains of Chiriqui, that alone was visible. Every soaring rival seemed to have shrunk away before it.

Still rippling through those quiet waters—still slipping past those palm-crowned islands—still giving the booming breakers a wide berth and rounding many a scowling point—still, with the faintest breath whispering against our torn and discolored sails—with more or less to thwart or puzzle us, making our way through a glowing, and then a clouded labyrinth of lakes and woods, over beds of pearl and past reefs of coral, in the midst of a hundred mingled perfumes—still, from sunrise to sundown at the work, sluggishly nearing that huge volcano, and, if it be not harsh to tell the truth just here, despite of all the sweetness and richness of the picture, growing wearied and verging on vexation—the schooner we were in dropped anchor in the Boca Chica, one of the mouths of the river Pedrigal, our destination being the city of David, two hundred miles and more to the North of Panama.

It was an aged schooner that brought us there—built in Newburyport for the rice and rosin trade—having long kept up a thriving connection between Boston and the Carolinas—having sprung an irreparable leak, been sold, and then miraculously brought round the Horn—she was twenty-eight years old. In the days of her youth she was known as the *Sibyl.* Under her new masters, in the ebb of her industrious life, she was known as the *Fruta Dorada*—a name which seemed to indicate that her Spanish-American owners valued her decayed timbers as though they were as precious as the auriferous trees of the Hesperides. The sails had been so frequently patched, very little of the original canvas remained. She was porous all over. The sailors pumped her every three hours, and then never thought of pumping her dry within three or four feet. The rigging in every direction was constantly snapping. Blocks and ring-bolts, cleets, thimbles, main-topsail sheets, bob-stays and shank-painter, all were woefully out of repair. Rust and worms had fed on them luxuriously for months. A twelve-penny nail, driven into the mizenmast, six feet from the deck, kept the bell for a while in suspense. The bit of spun-yarn, however, which kept it up there, breaking one day, the bell, striking all hours, came with a crash to the deck. It was never replaced. From that out a wooden clapper was used. Cockroaches, spiders, ants, three or five scorpions at least—all of a first-class description, and, with the exception of the latter, all utterly fearless and incessantly busy—had the principal cabin to themselves. No one could sleep there—no one could sit there. The plagues held undisputed possession. Besides, it was a musty little cavern, and one might have died of suffocation in it, if he had not been crawled or stung to death. It answered the purposes of a store-room, or steward's pantry, well enough, but that's all it was good for. The sugar, the rice, the mustard, the coffee, the vinegar and onions, the claret, the knives and forks, the pliant spoons, the tumblers, the red cabbage, the cork-screw, the lemon-squeezer, the ladle of a lost soup-tureen—all the appliances of our breakfast and dinner table were stowed away there, underneath or along the bunks, and both sides of the ladder which descended into it from the quarter-deck. It was furnished, moreover, with a looking-glass the size of the Ace of Clubs, peering into which a gentleman had the average of seeing more faces than one, and of ascertaining many of the mutations which the human countenance, without incurring any torture or permanent mischief, is enabled to undergo. To stand up to this glass, correct the slightest irregularity or effect the slightest improvement of feature, was a triumph which all the ingenuity and nerve the *Fruta Dorada* could boast of, this trip at all events, completely failed to achieve.

It was in this infirm schooner we had come from Punta Arenas, in the Gulf of Nicoya. For nine wearisome, blistering, deadening days, were we imprisoned in her. A slack breeze, a seething sun—at times a fierce shower which left the deck and rigging steaming for an hour after it had ceased—these were the consolations of that captivity. Reconciling us all the more to it, there were the grand mountains of Costa Rica ever within sight—oftentimes within pistol-shot—glittering in their dark-green and purple glory, from the rising to the setting of each sun, and at night deepening with their majestic forms the darkness of the sky. Pictures of shadowy deep ravines—great leafy branches overarching them, their walls trickling with moisture, and a full stream, cold and bright, bounding over rocks, plunging into green transparent basins which the sunshine veined with gold, and then with a smooth swiftness widening off between two strips of sand and pebbles—the fragrance of flowers and the notes of birds, the most beautiful and wonderful on earth, pervading all—such were the appeasing pictures which those mountains ceaselessly suggested. Dwelling on them—filling them up with bright-eyed friends and all the accessories of an Arcadian feast—it is not difficult to conceive the rapt pleasure with which our detention on board the *Fruta Dorada* filled us.

Steaming past with an accelerated speed, it seemed to us, as if in derision of our slow and awkward pace—for we were dawdling about and wabbling up and down in the most ignoble style imaginable, as the heartless Levite, scorning our distress, swept by—the Panama Railroad Company's steamer, the *Guatemala*, which we had left in Punta Arenas the night before, furnished us with an additional reason for congratulating ourselves on the age and comfort of our craft. Lest we might omit to do so with all the heartiness and zeal to which the *Fruta Dorada* was entitled, the gay Captain of the *Guatemala* called out to us to know what we had for dinner, while the solid Doctor put other interrogatories of an equally friendly, soothing, and exhilarating nature. In half an hour there was a small black cloud ahead, and that was all that remained to us of the *Guatemala*. The next night she was in the Bay of Panama, and we had not made a knot from the point at which she passed us.

The dullness of our sailing, however, was in great measure compensated by the variety of character which the company on board presented. The Captain was a Frenchman, a native of Marseilles. Frolicsome, good-natured, active, profuse with his claret and absinthe, running over with song and anecdote, voluble on all subjects, festive at all hours, and a finished comedian—he was the brightest star of the luminous group on board the *Fruta Dorada*. In this group was included the owner of the schooner.

A Panamanian by birth, he was studded with pimples, had very feeble pink eyes, and in every feature revealed an exuberant condition of scrofulous taint. Solemn to the gravest excess, he spoke little, smiled none, drank deeply, and profoundly slept. He slept all night. Were it not that he had to open his eyes in the sunlight, now and then, to imbibe and eat a little, he would have slept all day. He slept in the principal cabin—in the midst of the cockroaches, the spiders, the ants and scorpions—an astounding fact, demonstrative of his imperviosity to intense heat and venom. Solemn as he was, however, on more than one occasion he proved himself amiable, and of his honesty in matters of business, the Captain told us, there was the brightest of evidence. His father and mother are old residents of David. Foremost of the wealthiest people there, they own and inhabit a two-storied house, pushing a prosperous custom with English calicoes and cottons, French wines, and Dr. Barth's electric oil.

Besides the Captain, there was another Frenchman on board. Escaping from Paris, early in 1852, the Vigilance Committee of Louis Napoleon being keen on his track, he waved his *adieu* to France from the breakwater of Ostend, crossed over to the land of Alfred and Shakespeare, and thence steamed to Jamaica. Dissatisfied with the liberty vouchsafed to that opulent island—eager for new worlds to conquer—the proscribed Republican made for the Boca del Toro, crossed the Cordilleras, and, finally, dropped down into David, where, in course of time, he married into a family having fifty head of cattle. Mottled and slim as she is, he adores his wife as the perfection of beauty. She, in return, adores her husband as the superlative of all that is graceful, chivalrous, and most fascinating. It is a charming delusion. They, also, have a two-storied house, and, no doubt, as sparkling testimonies of their superior respectability, have broken glass chandeliers swaying from the naked beams of their somewhat vacant and airy parlors. The adored husband is engaged in the pearl-trade—makes frequent trips up and down the coast in search of the lustrous shell—and, with great gentleness and suavity of manner, combines a strong love for commercial speculation with the neatest dexterity in clenching a bargain.

The most remarkable of the group—though the accomplished gentleman may have been somewhat less brilliant, perhaps, than the Captain of the *Fruta Dorada*—was a retired Colonel of the Indiana militia. A tall, thin, rigid gentleman, with a frosty bald head and a tight red skin drawn over his face, he stood straight and high and stiff as a flag-staff, whenever the superiority of his favorite profession was questioned. A lawyer of five-and-twenty years standing, in constant requisition and flaming repute in all cases of divorce, afflicted with a raging ardor for political distinction, and ever ready to spread himself with eagle's wings and talons upon every question of the day, nevertheless he preferred the Camp to the Court-House, and a campaign garnished with bullets to one the issue of which was quietly lodged in the Ballot-Box. His fingers were surprisingly slender and long, and, whether he described a charming scene or denounced an enemy, he seemed to claw the air with more or less eagerness for a feast of blood. Fluent as a tropical stream in the month of October, he never ceased speaking of the time when he commanded the Catawba Grenadiers of Terre Haute—the time when he was elected Major of Brigade and had a shaving-box and pair of spurs presented him by the Common Council of Fort Wayne—the day when in his shirt-sleeves and worsted slippers, at the head of the New Albany Fusileers, he tore his way through miles of *cacti* to the bastions of Chapultepec—the evening when specially invited by the President of Peru to a grand ball and supper, in recognition of his eminent rank and exploits, he had to apologize for not bringing his Colonel's uniform along with him, informing his Excellency that he made it a point to travel as Sir Charles Napier advised the officers of the East India army to do—that is, with a towel only, a tooth-brush, a bit of soap, and an old pair of boots.

These references of his to the salient points of his splendid military career—recurring every half hour or so—became somewhat irksome to us the second or third day out. But, then, he was so genial, so accomplished, so vivacious and fresh—spoke with so gallant a temerity the strangest of tongues, under the impression it was the purest of Spanish—bowed so dutifully whenever the faintest compliment was paid him—displayed his long fingers with such flexible significance in his controversies and polite conversations—altogether bore himself with such assiduous magnificence and nicety on the smallest occasion, that, in a resigned though tortured audience, he secured a privilege, which, had he been less accomplished and splendid, would have been briskly denied him. Judged by his own representations, he was one of the most distinguished men of the United States. The annals and newspapers of his native State, however, are wholly uncommunicative concerning him. So, too, are the several histories of the Mexican war. Nevertheless we have no disposition to question his celebrity, but, admitting it fully, must be permitted to express our regret, that such men do so much without their leaving the smallest record, or the world knowing the least about them.

An apothecary from Leon, in Nicaragua, was the least celestial star of the group. Squint-eyed, knocker-kneed, with a broad baggy face the color of treacle, two teeth alone visible in the front of his head, and these set together in the upper gum, long and sharp as a rabbit's—he was the damaged picture of a fallen star. Bound for the *Huaccas* of Chiriqui, he wore a very short coarse trowsers of Guatemalian manufacture, a pair of untanned shoes with murderous soles, and a frowzy red silk sash about his loins—his luggage consisting of a soiled pocket-hand-kerchief stuffed with sausages, hard-boiled eggs, cheese and garlic, and a brass-hooped box of patent medicines. Morose, dogged, beetle-browed, he opened his lips to no one the nine dreary days we were on that trip, but, the live-long day, sat upon a water-cask, musing and frowning to himself, beating one untanned shoe against the other, at times cleaning a lancet or a forceps, greedily swallowing a morsel out of the provisional handkerchief; or at full length, with his shaggy head upon a scroll of ox-hide, fried himself in the forecastle, and took to the basest snoring.

The morning after the *Fruta Dorada* had dropped anchor in the Boca Chica, just at sunrise, the passengers, with the exception of the apothecary from Leon, left the schooner and proceeded up the river to the village of Boca Chica. The Captain of the schooner, with two of his men, one of them a lively round-limbed Chilian, accompanied them.

A calm, soft, clear morning—the dew dropping in large diamonds from the trees which overhung the river—the pale sky reddening as the sun came up from behind the Cordilleras—white birds on the wing, darting from the water into the dense rich foliage on the banks as we swept toward them, the swift powerful stream eddying and gurgling among roots and rocks, or bearing mercilessly seaward some noble tree which it had plucked down miles above—most of the beauteousness of the previous evening was here revived. True it is, we missed the islands, the sparkling beaches, the shady nooks, the pearl-laden *bongos*, the steep cliffs worn into feudal ruins, the dusky crowds of gulls and pelicans clinging to the slippery rocks, up the wave-worn grooves of which the sea went splashing. But the birds in those vine-laced trees, darkly bending overhead, were brighter far than poor gull or pelican could be, and the forest, to the right and left of the hurrying river, showed us aisles and arches, porticoes and columns, statelier and richer far than any ever wrought from stone. And there—in the midst of oranges and *mangos*, the fragrance of which was borne upon the fresh bright waters of the Pedrigal far out to sea—was a swarm of huts, with the shy Naiads of the river gliding in and out of them in their white *chamisettes*, and a pack of hungry hounds yelping and frothing on the bank, as though some bronzed Diana had been surprised, and the Colonel from Indiana had been the rash Actaeon. Besides all which, there was the Volcano of Chiriqui towering sternly and darkly in the sweet light of the morning—the peaks, into which its huge crest is broken, looking blacker than they did at twilight—the unknown forest, with which it is matted from base to summit, looking as though it were a wilderness of purple heather—and the gorges and abysses into which its enormous slopes are rent, and down through which the steadiest looks with an aching eye, closing up in the hazy distance, giving one at the Boca Chica a vague idea, if any, of its terrors and sublimities.

Beyond the volcano, round and tapering as the spire of a great cathedral, and loftier by thousands of feet than that of St. Gudule and Strasbourg, the peak of the Boquete, nineteen leagues to the northeast, shone like a pile of bronze. So, too, did the peaks overlooking the old Provincial road to the Atlantic, and the summits of the San Juan Mountains. Nearer to us were the lesser mountains which intercept the road to Panama—mountains fashioned into striking and wondrous shapes—into churches, roofs of houses, hulls of ships, keel uppermost—and the largest of which is overrun with the fieriest and deadliest vipers—reptiles which do not wait to be attacked or injured accidentally but glide forth and strike fiercely the instant a strange foot approaches. Between us and the mountains were the plains of Chiriqui—immense pasturages over which thousands of cattle rove, and the healthfulness and fertility of which are owing to the abundant waters that break the soil.

Having breakfasted at the village of Boca Chica, we started further up the Pedrigal, on our way to David, parting in the friendliest manner with Phillipe Jean Molyneaux, the Captain of the *Fruta Dorada*, to which frail craft, notwithstanding her multiplied infirmities and age, we drank in bowls of the tartest claret many a golden cruise!

It was at the house of a Spaniard, a citizen of the United States, we breakfasted. From the same gentleman we hired a *bungo* for the river-trip to David.

Five-and-twenty feet in length, two feet deep and three feet broad, painted black and white, furnished with a light canvas awning at the stern—under which awning a bullock's hide, the hairy side uppermost, was stretched for carpeting—four lithe, mirthful, musical young fellows swept this *bungo* up, at the rate of four miles an hour, against the stream. The oars they used were long tough poles—eighteen feet in length and from two to three inches thick—to which a blade, something like a shingle, but broader a good deal at the lower end than at the upper, was nailed. As they rose from the thwarts and gave the stroke, a strange, wild, mournful but ringing *whoop* broke from them; and thus rising to the stroke, bringing their bending oars with a long strong sweep through the swift current, that peculiar cry of theirs, at measured intervals, echoed far and wide beyond the river, from noon to close on sundown.

The same trees, the same birds, the same rich verdure and gorgeousness of foliage we had seen at the Boca Chica in the morning, were visible all day long. The same great mountains we had gazed upon at dawn, were ever present in the wide sunny scene. The same swift powerful river, to which we had descended from the schooner, bore us onward to the city. For seven glaring hours there was no change, unless, indeed, the setting of a leg-of-mutton sail, whenever we came to where the river widened and the breeze from the sea had play, may be set down as something new.

At last, about half past six in the afternoon, we reached our destination. This was an umbrageous tree of prodigious girth, the limbs of which were laden with *epiphytes* and the gaudiest macaws, and up the bare roots of which we had to climb from the *bungo*, to reach the top of the bank, five feet above. David lay four miles off. We had to tramp to it across a plain crowded with cattle. There were neither mules, nor carts, nor *cargueros* to be had for hire. So the young Frenchman led the way, carrying a bundle, an umbrella, and a broad flat pasteboard box containing a white muslin frock, embellished with pink satin bows, for his little boy—the heir-presumptive to the fractured chandeliers and a moiety of the fifty head of cattle. The Colonel from Indiana brought up the rear, painfully dragging his legs and a ragged old carpet-bag after him—one of his war-boots, owing to the state of his corns, being slung over his shoulder, while an enameled slipper, shabbily cracked, flapped on the sole of his most sensitive foot.

As the evening darkened, his tall spare figure, flickering in the star-light half a mile behind, reminded us of the forlorn schoolmaster of Sleepy Hollow. The dramatic effect of the apparition was powerfully heightened by all the mules, colts, and staid gray asses of the plain herding toward it, following it inquisitively, whisking their tails and pricking their ears in its wake, and, finally, when their curiosity appeared to have been satisfied, flinging up their hoofs with a simultaneous snort, and vanishing in a whirlwind of derision from it.

A few yards from the tree at which we disembarked, we came to the hacienda of Don Jose Obaldia, recently the Governor of the State of Panama. All the cattle within sight were his. The wealthiest man in the State, he is at the same time one of the most urbane, liberal, and enlightened. Half-way across the plain we were overtaken by his *mandador* or steward, mounted on a sprightly little horse. For the consideration of one dollar, this good Samaritan undertook to relieve us of our carpet-bags, fire-arms, the Colonel's *impedimenta*, including the discarded war-hoot, and convey them to David for us. Thus relieved, an hour's trudging and stumbling brought us to the outskirts of the city, and, ten minutes more, we were in the *Hotel Francesca*, cooling ourselves with copious draughts of Benicarlo and lemonade. Twenty minutes after that again, we were seated at an excellent supper, and, in due time, the neatest and whitest beds received our wearied frames. It was late next morning when we left them. The sun was showering down a blinding light on David as we went forth to view the city.

Planted in a corner of the great plain of Chiriqui—having wide though rugged streets, well-built houses for the most part, several of them two stories high, and these furnished with balconies and piazzas, the faces of the houses being variously colored—having tall cocoa-nut trees, here and there, with a graceful languor swaying above the plantain—thatched or red-tiled roofs, and that vast volcano ever overlooking it—the city of David, in spite of all the blistering and warping it has got from its exposed position, is an attractive picture. It is at first sight at all events. And on Sundays, when the Senoritas flash upon the scene in all the effulgence of crisped and snowy muslin, beaming jewelry and flowery sunshades, and the snug French Consul displays the *tri-color* over his bright green balcony in the principal thoroughfare of the city, and all the young *caballeros* in glossy suits saunter or dash about—some on foot and others in silver-bowed and embroidered saddles—the picture is quite brilliant. Not until one has been a week or two condemned to loiter through its broiling streets—for the city is exposed to the fiercest sun on every side—not until one has found that his aching feet can stand no longer the ruts, the stones, the broken tiles and other snares with which those streets abound, and finds, moreover, that among the inhabitants of the place, buzzards and corpulent negroes and strolling pigs preponderate—not until then does one begin to criticize, in a doubtful spirit, the hues and outlines of the first impression.

The Plaza is an ample square, tufted with burned grass, having on one side the *Hotel Francesca*, a blank *adobe* wall, and the *Botica Francesca*, where a filibuster of French birth—a spry young gentleman who sports a white *burnouse* and a profound mustache—dispenses calomel and Brandreth's pills. On another side there are four or five two-storied houses, one of which is in a slimy state of disintegration, and has two naked children perpetually oozing in and out of the doorway. A German butcher owns another; Mr. Haws, of Panama, the clean and freshly painted one at the farthest end. But, at present, this handsome house is in a state of deep repose, the doors being padlocked and the windows shuttered. The Parochial Church stands in the middle of the Plaza. Built of *adobe*—and the dusky bricks never having had a spattering of whitewash, while the worm-eaten beams, supporting the roof project like wooden legs a foot and a half beyond the eaves—the uncouth structure has none of those architectural incentives to piety which men of austere creeds are sometimes moved to rebuke. The chamber in which the Provincial Legislature of Chiriqui used to sit, previous to the recent subdivision of New Granada into States and the absorption of the Provinces, must have been just as poor as the Church.

The French flag has been mentioned. France is the only foreign Power that has a representative in this remote Department of New Granada. Many Germans have settled here, but the French exceed them. They constitute the most influential portion of the foreign population of David, confining themselves, however, to the little city, while the Germans disperse themselves over the neighborhood, bridge the rivers, climb the mountains, penetrate and hew down the forest, advance and plant their new homes in the regions of the palm and cedar, proving themselves better emigrants, more adventurous and aspiring, than their brethren of Burgundy and Champagne. As for the United States, they are completely in the background here. Texas, I believe, has sent one of her citizens, and New Hampshire another, and Connecticut a third—but at this point, for the present, the contributive enterprise of our great Republic to Chiriqui ceases.

Nevertheless there is much to tempt it here. From the shores of the Pacific, to the slopes of the Cordilleras, the soil is fertile to excess. While it affords pasturage for countless herds, it yields all the inter-tropical grains, fruits, vegetables and esculent roots, in marvelous abundance. The sugar is the best on the coast. It has a finer grain than the sugar of Louisiana. The tobacco is superior to that of San Salvador. Cotton might be cultivated to any extent. Rice is produced in astonishing quantities, and this, not on lands artificially inundated as in Bengal and South Carolina, but on a surface simply irrigated by rains, two and three crops being had in the year. Perfectly free from swamps and stagnant waters, the land from the sea to the mountains, a distance of five-and-thirty miles at the narrowest interval, is sound and wholesome. The sun is powerful, indeed, and there are few trees on those vast plains to shelter one, but no rank matter exists for it to work upon. The climate, therefore, is pure and healthful—so healthful, that at Dolega, about thirteen miles from David, and situated very nearly in the centre of the plains, people are said to die of sheer old age, and of that alone. Mr. Power, the genial and accomplished editor of the *Panama Star and Herald*, eloquently enumerates these and other characteristics of Chiriqui, in a memorable article which appeared in that paper, the 9th of July, 1853. In this article, having stated that the few foreigners, who had visited that part of the coast during the two previous years, had taken so much pains to develop the advantageous position and internal wealth of the country, that it was already attracting too much attention to be neglected in the future, Mr. Power gives it as his conviction, that "had the same knowledge, relative to the Province, been acquired four years before, Chiriqui would this day have been the leading route between the two oceans, instead of Panama."

At present, however, notwithstanding the extraordinary facilities it presents for immigration and interoceanic transit—the Atlantic and Pacific ports, terminating the route, being pronounced by Mr. Power, who is a practiced engineer as well as a clear and conscientious writer, to be superior in safety and convenience to any on the coast—Chiriqui is little known to the commercial world. Half a dozen schooners—every one of them just as crippled and precarious as the *Fruta Dorada*—more than suffice for its trade along the coast. They bring a few casks of rum—and excellent rum it is, that, especially manufactured by Messrs. Wagner and Campbell—to Panama, Bonaventura, and one or two Peruvian ports. They bring pearl-shells hither and thither—sometimes to Panama—sometimes to Punta Arenas—and once or twice a year they take a cargo of hides down to the first-named place. Pigs and horned cattle, too, are exported in small quantities. The latter, however, are driven in considerable numbers, in the months of March and April, overland to Panama.

With these exceptions, Chiriqui may be said to have no foreign trade whatever. The Panama Railroad Company, when they first started them, made the Boca Chica a port of call for their Central American steamers. But after two or three trips the experiment was pronounced a failure, and now the handsome

Guatemala passes up the coast in all the pride of a fortunate career, leaving the boundless pasturages, the sugar fields, the palm-groves, the great forests of oak and sandal-wood, and teak and caoutchouc, and all the luscious and all the solid wealth of Chiriqui, idly sleeping in the azure or golden mist ten leagues away. The discovery of those strange relics in the old Indian graves, in the month of August, 1859, gave the country for a short time a vivifying impulse. Hundreds of foreigners poured in. The merchants of David quadrupled their purchases. Monsieur Quelquejeu, of the *Hotel Francesca*, enlarged his establishment—built a row of neat and commodious sleeping-rooms—laid in a prodigal supply of wines and all sorts of liquors, making every arrangement which an agreeable and enterprising host could devise for the accommodation of his expected guests, and they were counted with a military arithmetic nothing short of a battalion. The Guatemala herself, punctual and inflexible as she is, was unable to resist the impulse, and in she went with a score of plunderers for the graves. But the *huaccas* soon gave out. Gold-hunting among the ancient dead of Chiriqui, in a month or so, was declared to be a lottery in which there were ninety-nine blanks to every prize, and to secure that one prize much labor and suffering had to be endured. One by one the foreigners drew off. The natives only, it seemed, could stand the work.

And so the precious soil, sown with golden bats and alligators, with golden birds and scorpions, with golden obscenities and gods, was abandoned to the children of the soil. They are reaping the fitful harvest still. To their patient toil, scantily clothed and nourished as they are, but enduring and persistent, and proof against the rains and heats, those undeciphered graves are to this day yielding up their treasure. The *Guatemala* made but one trip to aid the spoliation. A second would have been worse than profitless. As he surveys his vacant rooms and undiminished stock of cobwebbed bottles, Monsieur Quelquejeu wrings his hands, and with the wildest maledictions averts his eyes from those costly evidences of his infatuation. Pick-axes, India-rubber leggings, red flannel shirts, frying-pans, tin dishes, hatchets and revolvers, all the accessories of a California mining-camp are to be found in the principal stores of David, and would be sold by auction, at any moment, were two solvent purchasers within hail.

Had the *huaccas* been more prolific, Chiriqui, in half a year, would have become one of the busiest and wealthiest countries within the tropics. As it is, the gates of the Cordilleras have to be driven in, the country has to be thrown wide open to the world, the noble harbors, between which it lies, have to be united by an iron pathway, before it can hope to receive a useful and powerful accession to its population, and grow glad in the full exposition of the riches with which it has been so sumptuously blessed.

Ten days after his arrival in David, the writer of this narrative set out for the Boca del Toro. For a week he had been busy procuring information, guides, mules, and provisions. The trip between the oceans being seldom made—four or five times a year at most—it is necessary to make inquiries as to the state of the rivers, etc., and, moreover, it takes some time to secure the services of competent guides. Neither are mules so easy to be had in Chiriqui. Horses abound—quick, hardy, showy little fellows—but their more demure kindred are scarce, and for hire or sale command a high figure. Two hundred dollars is an average price for a serviceable mule.

The expedition, at last, set out. Three Indian guides led the way on foot, costumed in blue and white cotton shirts, with white cotton handkerchiefs bandaging their heads, and large *javas*—wicker-work baskets—slung upon their backs. In these they carried the provisions, the cooking utensils, the blankets, and every thing else that was considered essential for the road. Each had a load of seventy-five or eighty pounds. There was Jose, a boy of splendid shape, immense strength, and mysterious silence. There was Camillo, a noisy scapegrace, sinewy and gigantic, good-natured, officious, reckless, jovial, enraptured with song and absorbed in liquor. There was Eduardo, a quiet, gentle, patient, indefatigable fellow, the most civilized and refined of the three.

Jose, however, was the surest guide. His memory and keen instinct never failed him. On more than one occasion, when the track was lost under the fallen leaves or a fresh growth of prickly shrubs and Indian plantain, or when the marks of the *machetta* on the blazed trees were difficult to be made out, this powerful creature—whose limbs one would fancy were the texture as they were the color of cast iron—used to unsling his *java*, and gliding into the depths of the forest, disappear, perhaps, for an hour. His appearance as he returned to us—his step, his attitude, his look—would make a glorious painting. With the right hand up-lifted, the forefinger pointing to the sky, his naked feet gliding through the florid dense foliage over roots and stones, as though they were shadows only, his dark brown features flashing with happiness and triumph—at such times he looked like some young conqueror bearing tidings of freedom to a race in chains!

Besides the Indian guides, there was Don Carlos Wagner, a most hospitable and hearty German gentleman, who had in the friendliest manner offered to accompany the writer as far as the Boquete. Don Carlos has been nine years a resident of Chiriqui—lives, two miles outside David, on a fine farm, to which he has given the name of Buena Vista—and by precept and example has done much to excite an intelligent industry throughout the country. He is, of course, particularly interested in the success of his countrymen who have made it their home, and is ever ready to encourage and befriend them. They, in return, look up to him with confidence and very grateful feelings, regarding him as their oracle and leader in the Battle of Life they have crossed the seas and continents to fight, and upon which, not forty centuries, but all the cycles of creation, from the summit of the volcano of Chiriqui, look down.

The brave old Indiana Colonel, too, was in the cavalcade, wearing a blood-red shirt and a green bough in his hat, which, being of straw and having seen a world of service, was chipped and tarnished. And so was the Captain of the *Fruta Doroda*—not chipped and tarnished, indeed, but in the best condition and cricket-like spirits—astride of a pony, four hands high, and draped in a Peruvian *poncho* colored like the rainbow. Mr. William Campbell, the brother-in-law of Don Carlos Wagner, undertook not only to accompany the gentleman from Costa Rica as far as the Boquete, but made up his mind, with all the chivalry of a Highland Scots-man, to be his escort to the shores of the Atlantic. For such a journey—through mountains so wild and lonesome, in such appalling rains as fall there, over rivers such as thunder through those solitudes, in the midst of the dismaying perplexities to which such dark tracts of forest oftentimes give rise—day after day advancing through the undisturbed domain of the wild beast and reptile, between dawn and sundown ascending and descending thousands of feet with torn hands and swollen ankles, lying down for the night under a roof of woven palm-branches, with Indian followers snoring and steaming to the right and left of you, and a pile of green logs crackling and sputtering, and sluggishly rolling up a smothering cloud of smoke, through which the bat and fire-fly never cease to flit—for such a journey, than William Campbell, of *Gualaca*, no cheerier nor brighter escort could be had.

The first thirteen miles of the journey were easy work. No road, indeed, could possibly be easier. From David to Dolega it is a perfectly level plain, broken only by the rivers bearing the same names. In the rainy season these rivers are dangerous to ford, but in the dry season, though their beds are full of deep pools and heaped with boulders, they are passed on horse-back without the slightest difficulty. Thousands of cattle clouded the plain, and, here and there, shaded by noble *mangos*, orange-trees, the sweet lemon and, *maranone*, were farm-houses shaped like old hay-ricks, and looking just as bleached and wilted. Here and there, too, was a *trapiche*, creaking and groaning as the ponderous oxen walked their slow rounds, and the crushed sugar-cane spirted into the basin of cemented clay underneath the cylinders. At these mills and farm-houses there were curious groups—groups with beaming faces and airy garments—eyeing us wonderingly as we saluted them and rode on. Two or three times we were offered fruit, *agua dulce*, small plates of honey, and brimful cups of a stronger distillation. But the sun was too fiery for such draughts, and we still rode on, cooling our parched lips with a slice of pineapple only, or a howl of the *agua dulce*.

A mile outside Dolega the party stopped at the house of Don Roberto Sees, the discoverer of the golden relics in the Indian graves of Chinqui. All the way from David we had ridden through thousands of these disemboweled and ransacked graves, and in every direction, for leagues and leagues, from Terraba and Boruca to Santiago de Veragua, we might have seen tens of thousands more.

A calm, noiseless, smiling little gentleman is Don Roberto. Bending his wiry frame and stroking his scant gray beard—his small white teeth shining through his opened lips and his small black eyes bubbling with light and pleasure—in bare feet, and with head uncovered, he invited us to dismount. In acknowledgement of so much graciousness we complied. But rich as he is—Don Roberto has taken $20,000 from the graves, and can lay his hand any day, they say, on $20,000 more—his house suggests the idea of mendicancy and misery rather than that of good luck and comfort. In a dark corner of it, stretched upon an ox-hide, his eldest son was lying wretchedly sick with fever. The Colonel—professing a knowledge of pharmacy, as well as of law, theology and arms—undertook at once to prescribe for him. He would have bled him profusely on the spot had not the rest of the party protested.

Seven miles further on, we stopped to dine at the house of a lemon-colored gentleman who had congestion of the liver, and who, stripped to the waist, was plucking a fowl as we rode up. His wife—a pretty, sprightly, olive-complexioned girl, with two pearl-headed and brass-rimmed combs in her luxuriant black hair—was seated upon a block of *guapinol* at the door, busy on a shirt for her nude lord, at the same eventful moment. But as we dismounted, and the guides, having unslung their *javas*, led off the horses to the *potrero*, she laid aside her work, welcomed us to the house, offered us *guavas* and bananas right away, and then, finding we had stopped for dinner, set about putting the kitchen, that is the whole house, in order. In repulsive contrast, her husband kept his seat and held his tongue, still continuing to pluck the grizzly fowl between his knees, never lifting his head, even once, to welcome us. In the same dogged mood he remained all evening, taking to a red clay pipe when he had stripped the fowl and stowed away the feathers in a bag. He was jealous of that guileless hospitable young wife—so Jose told us—and wanted no strangers near the place. Never was there a liver so green with bile.

It was, however, a glorious feast we had that evening. While Isabellita tended the fire, put the water on, sliced the plantains, and warmed into a more sparkling prettiness every second that she tripped about the fire-place, Captain Molyneaux prepared the meats, superintended the cooking, tried his hand at a tasteful dish or two of vegetables, mixed the mustard and achieved a sauce—leaving the Colonel, in his blood-red shirt, to open the tins of salmon and green peas, and at his leisure compound the punch. Mr. Campbell looked after the horses, saw them watered, plentifully supplied with chopped sugar-cane, and safely padlocked for the night.

Five or six minutes' walk from the house, a beautiful little stream trickled through a deep, dark-some, rugged bed. Great shadowy oaks overarched it, and burly rocks, belted with the tenderest green moss, formed basins underneath them, from which the most delicious water, fresh as the dews of a northern climate, gently overflowed. In one of these basins Don Curbs Wagner, having charge of the wine-department, sunk two bottles of pale sherry, and then stretching himself upon a sandy couch close by, with a heavy *meerschaum* between his lips, kept watch over the cooling vintage until dinner was announced. In this duty he was ably assisted by the gentleman who records these facts.

A long slow ride over an immense *savanna* thickly strewn with calcined rocks and other evidences of volcanic action—with a biting wind beating us breathless in the face as it swept down from the volcano—the guides breasting it manfully under their burdens—Captain Phillipe Jean Molyneaux, his distempered straw-hat tied close down about his ears with a flagrant yellow and scarlet handkerchief, complaining dismally of *catarro*—Don Carlos Wagner deploring the absence of his great-coat and hoots, the beaming Teuton having come along in the lightest plaid summer trim and pumps—the Colonel, reduced to a mere skeleton; freezing in the saddle, his eyes and teeth in hysterics—the roar of unseen waters heard at times above the wind—cloud after cloud with torn edges flying across the face of the mountains—a comfortless, wild, raw, disordered morning—it was to all this gall and wormwood we awoke, at four o'clock A.M., six hours after that dinner had been disposed of.

Nearing the volcano—the mighty peaks which form its jagged crest, and the black ravines into which its forest-burdened slopes are rent, growing more and more distinct, and the tumult of rushing waters deepening in the troubled air—we came to a broad stone wall, very nearly six feet high. It was the boundary wall of the great cattle-range of Don Lorenzo Gallegos, the polite and well-informed Prefect of David, and next to Obaldia, the late Governor of the State, the wealthiest gentleman in Chiriqui. Passing it, we found ourselves at the brink of a ravine, a quarter of a mile in breadth, and fully 800 feet in depth. This was to the right of the gateway through which we passed. The side of the ravine next us was precipitous and bare. The side opposite was densely wooded. Between them, in the bewildering depth below, the River Caldera raved and foamed, sweeping furiously through the chasm, as though, whirled away in an agony of vengeance, it were bent upon some terrible work of devastation. To the left, also, was another ravine, broad and deep, four or five hundred yards apart from that through which the Caldera tore its way, and in the abyss of which the Cocheo hoarsely thundered, as the whitened flood broke against enormous rocks and flashed in sheeted froth across them, volumes of glistening mist rising midway between the billows and the green ledge on which we stood. Niagara, with all the power and terrorism of its exhaustless waters, fails to impress one more thrillingly than those fierce rivers do in the inviolable depths of their ravines. Motionless, silent, breathless almost, standing by our patient horses, we looked down with strained and aching eyes, until the rivers seemed to grow more riotous and convulsed, the black depths to deepen, the glistening foam and mist to rise to our very feet, and the ground, on which we stood, to tremble and give way.

At noon, having ridden against that biting wind for eight long hours, most of the time over the same immense *savanna*, but, for the rest, through broken ground and varied scenes—now close to the great volcano, and then down-hill through little groves and shrubberies where the air was chill, the trees were so thickly interwoven, and such faint sunshine stole through them, and, last of all, along the base of the majestic cliffs that on one side, for two leagues fully, overlook the valley, at the head of which, commanding it to the furthest point, the peak of the Boquete stands as a watch-tower for the eagle, and as a pillar of light to those who pass that way from sea to sea—at noon we reached the Culebra, and having spurred through its dangerous current, which is impassable in the rainy season and when a Northern blows, reached, at last, the *ranch* of Santa Maria, at the foot of the Cordilleras.

It was on a round high hill covered with long, wiry, whitish grass, the earth being thrown up here and there, and all about, wherever the *huaccas* had been broken into, while, far and wide, the noble herds of Lorenzo Gallegos were to be seen—above, below, close to us, and leagues away—the only living figures visible in the scene. The *ranch* itself was a doleful wreck, looking, for all the world, as though it were the roof of a hut which had plopped through the side-walls and settled permanently on the floor. Decayed and loose, it must have been a winterish homestead for the raw-boned Indian who owned it, and who, dressed in a velveteen waistcoat and shirt, the latter all smeared and frayed, complacently awaited our approach, being seated on what, the brevity of his garments considered, must have been to him an extremely cold stone.

Here, after a hearty breakfast and a round of enthusiastic toasts, the Captain of the *Fruta Dorada*, Don Carlos Wagner, and our heroic old friend, the Colonel, took leave of the party bound for the Atlantic.

It was an affecting separation. The historian of the party clasped the Colonel's hand, and shook it till it burned. The Colonel, in return, threw his head over the shoulder of the historian, and when he withdrew it, his eyes looked waterish and inflamed. Don Carlos, the big hospitable soul, to smother his melancholy, had recourse to the hamper which Eduardo carried, and there dried up. Phillipe Jean Molyneaux declared that his sun had set, hinted at suicide, vowed he should never forgive himself for not making arrangements to accompany the party the whole way across, beat his breast with a *mea maxima culpa*, was seized with a violent coughing, and, having got through with that, nearly gasped his last in a state of collapse.

In half an hour, these three sad gentlemen might have been seen slowly riding, homeward to Dolega, along the base of the lofty cliffs on the opposite side of the valley of the Boquete, the Culebra swooping and roaring between them and the friends, who, from the top of the hill on which the *ranch* of Santa Maria stood, waved their hats to the solitary horsemen, and discharged their guns in a mournful farewell. In less than an hour, Don Francisco and his friend, Campbell, of Gualaca, were in the heart of the forest on the slope of the Cordilleras, the guides, in single file, speeding along in their bare feet and legs, Jose taking the lead, Eduardo following him in silence, while the exuberant Camillo danced under his load, whistled and sang, uttered mock lamentations over the mules and horses we had left at the *ranch*—for we had to foot it the rest of the way—and, in a word, abandoned himself, at the very outset itself; to a full swing of native good-humor and wit.

The first four hours, the path was exceedingly easy to travel. The trees were well marked. The ascents were gradual. The descents were neither steep nor slippery. One large tree alone lay across the track. There were neither protruding roots, nor trailing vines, nor any thing of the *cacti* growth to trip, strangle, or impale us. A walk through a richly-timbered avenue in some old-country *demesne* could not have been more pleasant. The day was dry though clouded, and even this latter circumstance was most propitious, since it enabled us, with little or no fatigue, to break ourselves in for rougher work. An hour before sundown we crossed a beautiful stream—a sparkling succession of fretful little cascades it was, the lower branches of the trees which darkened them, dipping into the waters by fits and starts, chafing them, then rebounding, and then striking them again before they had time to smooth themselves and look bright—and here, coming to a halt, we determined to build our *ranch* and locate for the night.

The *ranch* is quickly built. Jose and Eduardo unsling their heavy baskets. Setting them against two brawny trees, they leave them covered with the ox-hide they lashed over them when starting. Camillo does the same, disencumbering himself with a fiendish yawn, and, an instant after, airs his limbs in a frantic horn-pipe. The two former, *machetta* in hand, disappear for a little. The latter clears a plot of ground, sixteen feet by twelve, felling half a dozen young trees, kicking three or four sharp good-sized stones into the stream, bundling off all the dead leaves and rubbish, and, finally, running a narrow water-course, with an outlet to the stream, two inches deep all round the clearing. This done, with two or three pieces of charcoal he has brought along in his *pannier*, he lays the foundation for a fire; and having procured a supply of the driest dead wood at hand, arranges it outside the charcoal, filling up the intervals with splinters of fresh resinous wood. In ten minutes the fire is smoking. In twenty it is crackling. In thirty it is ablaze. In less than sixty there is an iron pot warming itself right over the red embers, and in this pot four pounds or more of jerked beef lie buried in three times as many pounds of rice.

In the mean while, Jose and Eduardo have been cutting uprights and rafters for the *ranch*, and peeling off narrow strips of bark to lash them together with. Down they come, at last, from the forest above the stream, dragging great sheaves of palm-branches after them. With these the *ranch* is thatched half a foot thick at least. Six forked uprights, the prongs uppermost to receive the cross-ties, are driven home six inches deep into the earth—two of those uprights, a foot and a half longer than the other four, planted midway at the gable-ends between the corner ones, give the roof a good drainage slant—the frame-work of the roof is laden with palm-branches, these being so arranged as to dove-tail into and lap securely over one another—and in half an hour the ranch stands complete. An India-rubber blanket is spread upon the floor within. Other and warmer blankets are thrown over this again. Logs of wood, saddle-bags stuffed with socks and flannel drawers, all such things serve as pillows. Fowling-pieces, hunting knives, powder flasks and rifles swing from the rafters. Wet shoes and clothing are thrown off, and, when the cooking is all over, are tied to a cross-stick, three feet above the fire, to dry. The iron pot is emptied, the last pipe is smoked, the travelers stretch themselves in their blankets for the night, the faithful Indians fall asleep with their feet to the replenished fire, the forest grows quieter and quieter in the gathering darkness, and the first day of the strangers, in those solitary mountains, is at an end.

The next morning, an hour after daybreak, ascending through a cold, wet, dark and tangled path, the trees for the most part being indistinctly marked, they came upon a deserted ranch, entering which they found half a sack of flour, a tin case of lard, a brass bedchamber candle-stick, and an old boot containing two flasks of powder. A pair of linen drawers, smudged and torn, dangled from the roof. Camillo thought it a pity to leave so valuable an addition to a gentleman's wardrobe mouldering there, and so with an unruffled conscience walked off with them. Then our work began in earnest. The spur of the Cordilleras, on which we were, abruptly rose against us.

Looking up, it seemed a stupendous wall, horizontally pierced with trees, ten thousand feet in height. The sight of it, towering gloomily up there as far as the eye could reach, and then no summit visible, was enough to dismay the boldest heart. The thought struck us, it would take hours and hours, days, perhaps, to climb it. At nine o'clock we were masters of it.

Looking down through the drizzly clouds, and for miles over the sloping forest, we beheld the valley out of which we had come, and the vast plain we had traversed from David to the foot of the Boquete. Beyond that again—separated darkly from it by what appeared to be a narrow belt of palm, but in reality by an unmeasured tract of that glorious tree—the golden Pacific seemed to pulsate in the sun. Nearer to us by ten leagues—jutting right overhead, indeed, so close did they appear—were the cloven heights of the volcano, ever the great central figure of the scene, reared in steep black masses against the cloudless sky. Turning toward the north—on the extreme verge of a whole world of mountains, all buried in what seemed to be an impenetrable forest, and barely discernible through the hazy atmosphere—the waters of the Atlantic, hushed within the islands of the Chiriqui Lagoon, glimmered in the twilight of the horizon. But the cold up there was piercing—we were on the highest ridge of the great dividing range and the dense mist, in a few minutes, had drenched us thoroughly. So, taking a last look at that transcendent scene, turning from the Atlantic to the Pacific, and from the Pacific to the Atlantic waves once more, we rapidly descended.

Yet hardly had we reached the foot of that commanding height, when another, as abruptly as the former, rose against us, and for two hours more we had to climb, and sweat, and ache, clinging to roots and branches, burrowing our knees in the fresh earth, and, all-fours most of the time, tearing our hands and ears with thorns, had to wriggle our way under fallen trees, stride over them if that were easier, but in either event, from first to last, strain ourselves to an apoplectic pitch.

It is an exquisite relief to draw off from all this burning and breathless work beside such a glorious wild river as the Robalo or the Balsa, and with cataracts, white and soft as masses of falling snow, leaping from one black edge to another through gorges a thousand feet in depth—with deep green pools glowing with golden ripples at your feet—with the overhanging foliage, silvered with the spray of splashing waters, breaking the light which would otherwise be deadening—with the torrent, quieted in that sweet cold shade, looking as though it had run its desperate race and was at rest forever, but, for all that, stealing away until it nears some smoking gulf into which it leaps, and then, frenzied and free once more, thunders away through the wildest solitudes and horrors to the sea—in the midst of all this changeful grandeur, it is a luxury, indeed, to take breath, ease the strained limbs, give way to memories and dreams of scenes dearer to the heart, and thus, by the gentlest enchantment tranquilized, renew the strength that has been exhausted. It is more than a relief, it is a rapturous pleasure after a fevered night—in the darkest hour of which a black skeleton, with a tuft of grizzly-gray beard upon the chin, encircled with a pale yellowish light, stood over you, and a long thin finger-bone was uplifted, and quivered as though it gave a stern warning—and after a merciless wet morning, during which you had again to make your way up and down many a rough spur and chasm, the loosened earth and slippery rocks throwing you back every now and then, the rain and wind beating the branches against you, and the lightning causing you to start and reel every twenty paces for two remorseless hours and more—after such a night and morning, it is a rapturous pleasure to find yourself in the midst of a scene like that which the Tres Brasos—uniting in a channel deeply worn in an enormous slab of granite—vitalize and pervade. Down they hasten, those three beautiful young rivers, in a succession of gentle rapids, from three densely-wooded gorges, and as they joyously mingle, they form a broad swift river, borne upon which one can pass from this point, the greater part of the year, in a *bungo* to the Lagoon. Both sides of it there are smooth pebbly beaches, and over these the most luxuriant trees in the whole forest seem to have woven the darkest canopy, for scarce a ray of light penetrates the rustling web, and it is chill and cloister-like beneath it.

A lovelier picture it would be hard to find within those mountains. The wildness and terrorism of nature here subside. No longer haughty, stern, and defiant—no longer throwing up high walls and monstrous fortresses to resist invasion, and, with the torrent, hurling down huge stones and trees to smite and overwhelm the intruder—she surrenders to him, and soft and murmuring as a bride, beautiful as Ruth among the reapers, invites him to repose. For days and weeks we could have gratefully rested there, soothed by the subdued chorus of those confluent waters, and, from the resemblance the picture bore to one made famous in the songs of Thomas Moore, have been lulled into a loving though mournful remembrance of an island, the great hope of which can not perish while the mingled waters of Avoca repeat the name of the minstrel to whom they owe their fame.

One night more in the Cordilleras—the sixth and last on foot—one more supper on pheasant and wild turkey, for the forest of the Cordilleras is alive with game—one sleep more in a palm-thatched *ranch*, Camillo mirthful and boisterous as ever, Jose fresh as though he had come one day's journey only, and Eduardo obliging and gentle as he was the hour we started—one night more, and there were the wide peaceful waters of the Chiriqui Lagoon throbbing at our feet in the auspicious light of the Easter morn!

Of these calm and glorious waters—shut in from the Atlantic by a rampart of large and luxuriant islands, upon which a Spanish scholar, writing from Costa Rica to Madrid, two hundred years ago, declared that another Venice, richer and nobler than that of the Adriatic, might be planted, the region was so bounteous, and the sea so safe, tranquil, and commodious—of those calm and glorious waters, which, according to the English naval report of 1839, every where afford secure anchorage, multiplying harbors within harbors that admit of ships of the heaviest burden, it is unnecessary here to speak. The Commission, authorized by Congress at the close of the last session, have returned, and their report is before the public. The party, charged with the partial survey of the route between the oceans, appear to have had an easier trip across the mountains than has been here described, and, what is infinitely better still and worthier of happier congratulations, have ascertained, beyond all doubt, the practicability of a railroad connecting the Chiriqui Lagoon, on the Atlantic side, with the Golfito, within the Gulf of Dulce, on the Pacific. The energy, quick intelligence, nerve and enterprise of Mr. Ambrose Thompson, Jun.—a young and successful representative of that spirit of practical and enlightened adventure which so strongly marks the American character and is destined to achieve for the American people so vast a measure of prosperity and national power—these have principally led to this result, Mr. Thompson having, in the month of February last, discovered a canon, or chain of narrow valleys, which avoids the spurs and precipices, and most of the difficulties which this narrative in a familiar and convivial way sets forth.

The discovery of this canon overcomes the only difficulty which was at any time supposed to render the project of such a road impracticable. Every thing else was obviously in its favor. Two-thirds of the way across the land is almost as level as a macadamized road could be. Were the rivers bridged—and there are but four between David and the Boquete—a spring-wagon might be driven at full speed from the Pacific to the slope of the Cordilleras, without a stone or any other impediment having to be removed. Perfectly free from swamps—the writer having crossed on foot from sea to sea without once wetting the sole of his shoe, except, indeed, when he had to ford the rivers—not a dollar would have to be sunk, at any point, in the construction of an artificial foundation. The work being upon solid dry soil all through, the sacrifice of human life, which the Isthmus of Panama entailed, would find no counterpart under the pure sky of Chiriqui, and this of itself would save thousands and thousands of dollars in the construction of the road. The eloquent and philosophic Member of Congress, who, beaming forth from one of the Arcadian Districts of New York, spoke in the last session so alarmingly of the embarrassments and horrors of the route, alluding in freezing terms to the snakes and tigers with which, he understood, that region was infested, may be inclined to regard it with a less frenzied and a friendlier eye, when he reads this narrative and learns that the travelers, of whom it speaks, saw but three snakes the entire of the trip—one, it is true, of the Boa species, being fifteen feet in length, while the longest of the other two was not as many inches, though both were poisonous, the smallest one especially—and that, as for the tigers, their howlings were heard on one occasion only, the last night of the trip, when the party were slipping along at midnight in their *bungo*, from the Frenchman's Creek, where they had debouched from the mountains, to the little village of Boca del Toro, on Columbus Island, a distance of forty miles.

For the support of the men employed in the construction of the road, the country furnishes any quantity of food, and that of the best description. Beef, sugar, rice, coffee, potatoes, corn, venison—every thing is to be had in the greatest abundance. Not a tree has to be felled along the proposed route, nor within half a league of it, where the forest most closely approaches it. Nevertheless, an inexhaustible supply of fuel can be easily obtained, and, for building purposes, the forest on the slopes of the Volcano, and all through the Cordilleras, is stocked with the soundest material, such as Spanish olive and mahogany, *guyaca*, cedar, caoba and live oak.

Last of all, there are the unrivaled harbors themselves. Perfectly easy of access at all hours and in every season—deep and ample enough to shelter the navies of France and England, as Admiral Pelion and Captain Barnett long since reported them to be—the islands of the Lagoon teeming with the most serviceable description of coal a steamship can use—fresh water pouring into them in every direction from the impending mountains—magnificently fitted for all the requirements and the highest ambition of commerce, nowhere between the Poles can the New World match those harbors. The railroad once built, ships of the largest size can lie broad-side on to the wharves, and transfer their freight and passengers right off. Neither tug, nor lighter, nor breakwater will be required; nor will it be necessary for cars or ships to wait three minutes, much less three hours, for the tide to suit.

All this being said, nothing more remains, perhaps, satisfactorily to close the narrative, but the expression of an ardent wish, that, before another winter comes, some one, inspired or trained to use a brighter and bolder pen than that which has left its feeble traces on these leaves, shall enter the Boca del Toro, the last great gate-way of America that flew open to challenge of Columbus, and, circled by companions not less genial or amusing than the Captain of the *Fruta Dorada* or the old warrior from Indiana, who has disappeared forever, shall, with a grandeur worthy of it, describe the scene, of which the Cordilleras, the forest, the islands, the cloudy domes of Blanco and Robalo, and, above all, the steeps of the volcano of Chiriqui are the transcendent features, and which, from a deep sense of its sublimity, is here left not unfinished only, but untouched.

6

The Secret of the Strait*

G. A. Maack

This article describes, in great detail, the feasibility and advantages of constructing a ship canal through the Darien jungle, or the area that today constitutes the border between Panama and Colombia. The geographic descriptions of the region are detailed and informative, not surprising since a Dr. Maack, geologist and botanist, accompanied the expedition. The plan, to build a canal through Darien, was estimated to cost 123 million dollars: one of the unique features of this project was the cutting of a five-mile "ship tunnel" (measuring 120 feet in height and 75 feet in width) through solid rock. The engineering obstacles of this tunnel led, eventually, to abandonment of the Darien project.

The Isthmus of Darien, a land of tropical richness and beauty, where the precious woods of southern climates flourish in abundance and where flowers bloom and fruits ripen the whole year round, is placed by nature as a natural barrier between two great oceans. Narrow, and interspersed with many rivers, it would seemingly be an obstacle easy to overcome; but through its whole length stretches a mountain chain, a massive backbone, as it were, defying the science and mechanical skill of the world.

Ever since 1513, when Vasco Nuñez de Balboa stood alone on the summit of the lofty Sierras, and looked out over the vast expanse of the "Great South Sea,"

*Entered according to Act of Congress, in the year 1873, by Harper and Brothers, in the Office of the Librarian of Congress, at Washington.

a water connection between the Gulf of Mexico and the Pacific has been desired by the commercial interest of the world. It is needless to dwell upon the advantages to be gained by something which has been demanded and sought after for more than three centuries. Numerous explorers have searched in vain for what in earlier times was supposed to exist, and it remained for the advanced and enlightened spirit of the nineteenth century to set about the work with a determination leading directly to practical results.

Entrance to Cartagena—Picturesque Gateway

When Cortez was exploring the coast of Mexico and Nicaragua, the Emperor Charles V bade him search diligently for the "secret of the strait," believing that this secret once unraveled, he should become lord of the world, and hold all the balms and spices of the Indies in his hands. Cortez's search was unavailing. After coasting along the sunny shores for months, and ascending the Atrato River for some distance, on whose waters shall perhaps before many years float the commerce of nations, he gave up in despair, and pronouncing the "secret of the strait" unfathomable, devoted his energies to exploits of a less peaceful character.

In later times many expeditions were sent out from different countries to search if possibly some way might be devised to pass by water directly from the Gulf of Mexico to the Pacific. Commercial calculations were made regarding the time and money to be gained by a water connection between the great commercial centres of the world and the rich Pacific coast of South America and

Mexico, which should avoid the long and stormy passage through the Straits of Magellan.

The Panama Railroad was built; but although this served for the passage of travelers across the isthmus, it was found to be insufficient to accommodate the immense quantity of freight which would naturally pass over that road; and the great expense of handling at each end of the route caused merchants, as a rule, to choose the longer but cheaper way of transportation round Cape Horn.

Meanwhile it was determined that the isthmus should receive thorough examination by competent parties, to ascertain if it was possible to break through the barrier between ocean and ocean, and construct a ship-canal which would admit the passage of vessels of all descriptions. Many different routes have been proposed, and shared, in their turn, public interest and confidence. Tehuantepec, Honduras, Nicaragua, Panama, and various routes leading westward from the Atrato River, have all been taken into consideration. It would seem from a study of the map that the Nicaragua route was the most likely to be successful, as so large a portion of the whole course would lie through the lake bearing that name, and the canal leaving the gulf at Greytown and following the line of the river San Juan would find a channel partially prepared by nature. Practical surveys of this route, however, have discovered many obstacles: the summit level is so great that between thirty and forty locks would be required; and although by running in a northerly direction the western side might be reached without the difficult task of tunneling the Sierras, the great outlay necessary on account of the immense length of canal, and the total absence of a good harbor on the Pacific side, have caused this route to be abandoned as impracticable.

The exploring party under command of Lieutenant Strain, which left the United States in 1854 to survey the route from Caledonia Bay to the Gulf of San Miguel, met with adventures of a most discouraging character. They lost their way in the dense forests, and after living for many days on roots, and a few loathsome birds of carrion which they shot in the woods, they succeeded in reaching the Pacific coast, having left many of their number dead in the wilderness. The scientific and practical results from an expedition which terminated so sadly could scarcely be of importance.

The explorations made in the same year by Mr. Kelly's expedition were of a more successful character. Commencing at the mouth of the Atrato, a river already prepared by nature for the passage of vessels of the largest class, Mr. Kelly proposed to follow its channel as far as the mouth of the Truando River, a distance of about sixty-three miles from the Atlantic. The Truando was here taken as a line for the proposed channel, and followed for thirty-six miles. From here to the Pacific would lie the most difficult portion of the route. Mr. Kelly claimed that by this line a practicable route could be secured without the use of locks, and with engineering expedients of less magnitude than many which have been successful in Europe. The plan, however, was pronounced against by good authorities, and has never been brought to any practical application.

In 1781 a survey was made by Colonel Andres de Ariza, and nearly one hundred years later, in 1867, a Mr. De Gogorza, after studying carefully the old Spanish maps of the isthmus, passed over the same ground as the Spanish governor had done before, surveying carefully the rivers Tuyra and Cacarica and the mouth of the Atrato. The general results of his survey may be summed up as follows: 1. Excellent ports on both termini—that of Candelaria or the Gulf of Uraba, on the Atlantic, and the inner and outer bays of San Carlos (San Miguel), on the Pacific, whose entry remains free at all times. 2. A stretch of about fifty-two miles of artificial canal through alluvial soil, without obstacle of intervening mountains, from the deep waters of the Atrato to those of the Tuyra. 3. An extreme elevation of 186 feet above tide-water, and composed of slate and sandstone. 4. A superabundance of water even above the extremist elevation. 5. All this not in a pass or a depression of the chain of mountains, but in a spot of complete separation between the Cordilleras in the north and the Andes in the south. 6. The best and friendliest intercourse with the Indians, wrongly called savages. The route of a ship-canal built along this line would run as follows: Leaving the Atrato at about 7°52′ north latitude, through or near the mouth of the Cacarica, and following a west-northwesterly direction to the highest point, at a distance of about twelve miles; continuing in a straight line, west 20° north, to the nearest navigable point of the Tuyra below the Isleta, at a distance of about forty miles, of which, sixteen are below tide-water; total length of the canal, fifty-two miles.

For many years careful explorations have been made across the isthmus from the mouth of the Atrato River to various points on the Pacific coast, in the hope of settling upon the most feasible plan for the union of the two oceans. At different times Trautwine, Colonel Michler, Kamish, and other skillful engineers have surveyed from the Atrato to the Pacific at different points, and the result of their explorations has been given to the public in a form which has added much to the geographical and scientific knowledge of the isthmus.

The expedition under Commander Selfridge has given the fullest and most complete report of the character and resources of the isthmus, and the most practical calculations regarding the expense of a canal through to the Pacific coast.

The United States store-ship *Guard* sailed from New York on the 4th of December, 1870, and after an uneventful passage of two weeks, arrived one bright afternoon at the port of Cartagena de Las Indias. Cartagena, like most other Spanish-American towns, presents an appearance of former strength and glory, now fast decaying and crumbling to ruins. The massive walls of the city are over-grown with long hanging grasses, and the picturesque finger of time is visible every where. The houses inside the walls are built mostly of boulders of coral reefs, which are found all along the shore. The general character of the place is lazy and indolent, like all other tropical cities. There appears to be little of interest in this old town, and beyond the cathedral and a few half-ruined convents, there is scarcely any thing to attract the eye. Even the cathedral possesses but little exterior beauty. The locality appears to have been interesting only to the geologist of the expedition, Dr. Maack, who found there abundance of fossil corals, especially of the genus *Meandrina*, and also a well-developed tertiary formation in the hills about the city.

After spending a short time only in Cartagena, where the open-handed hospitality of the inhabitants more than atoned for the dreariness of the town itself the expedition sailed for the mouth of the Atrato, and on December 29 dropped anchor in the Gulf of Darien del Norte, or Uraba, where active operations were to begin. In Cartagena Commander Selfridge had engaged a number of *macheteros*, men who were to cut passages through the dense forest of the isthmus with the machete, a kind of broad sabre.

Before proceeding to work, Commander Lull and some other gentlemen connected with the expedition proceeded to make friends with the people of Turbo, a small village lying on the shore near the anchorage ground. The government of New Granada had given the commander an official letter to the alcalde. This chief received his visitors very kindly, and made them as comfortable as possible in his little hut. The inhabitants of the town were at first very suspicious of the strangers, following them in a crowd, many being armed with sticks and stones, ready to give fight at the least provocation. After the friendly reception by their municipal chief, however, their suspicion changed to eager curiosity; and when told that the strangers had come with the intention of remaining for some time in their swampy, feverish country, their astonishment was intense.

Most of the huts of Turbo are raised upon poles a few feet above the ground. This is done on account of the heavy falls of water during the rainy season. In the night all the dogs, pigs, and poultry of the village gather under the shelter of the huts, and amuse themselves with making darkness hideous with their howls and cries.

The principal occupation of the people of Turbo is the collection of India rubber, a work which can only be carried on during the spring months, when the country is dry and least exposed to overflows. The India rubber is sold to merchants at Cartagena, and forms almost the sole support of this indolent people, whose necessities are limited to very small supplies of groceries, and articles of clothing so slight as to be scarcely worthy of mention. Plantain and cocoa-nut grow without cultivation, and the sea yields an abundance of flue fish; so it is not surprising that this rude, uncultivated people prefer lying all day in their hammocks and smoking to laboring for things which to them possess no value—money and luxurious living. It is hard to imagine a place so isolated that its inhabitants have no ambition beyond basking in the sun all day; but the people of Turbo have no desires to gratify except hunger, and nature has placed food in their hands with almost no labor.

It is not surprising, then, that the appearance of a band of working-men excited much astonishment and curiosity among the natives. All the while that preparations for permanent head-quarters in the Gulf of Darien were going on the expedition was subjected to constant watchfulness. As it was probable that for some time this locality would serve as a fountain-head for supplies and other necessities of the exploring parties, various stations were established upon the small islands scattered about the gulf near the mouth of the Atrato. Mr. Blake, the astronomer of the expedition, erected an observatory, and commenced taking observations. There were shops built for the carpenter and the blacksmith; a kitchen-garden was planted, and a stout hen-coop prepared which should protect the poultry from the attacks of alligators. Tide-gauges were erected; the draughts-men and the photographer made every thing ready in their special departments, and careful soundings were taken of the Gulf of Darien and of the mouth of the Atrato.

Meanwhile Dr. Maack, geologist and botanist of the expedition, made his head-quarters in the village of Turbo. He secured a very good hut for his special residence, and it was an object of great wonderment to the natives, ignorant, of course, as to his purpose, that a man should leave his hammock to swing empty all day, and spend his time collecting stones and dried flowers and grasses, preparing skeletons, and embalming all kinds of animals.

One fact ascertained by Dr. Maack may be of importance, should the work of building the canal be prosecuted from this point. He discovered the existence of coal near several rivers. This coal, according to a chemical analysis made by Professor Barker, of New Haven, would be of small service for steamers, but would doubtless prove useful as fuel for numerous purposes in the construction of a canal. It consists of 40.49 fixed carbon, 48.74 water and volatile matter, and 10.77 ash.

"These coal layers," says Dr. Maack, "being covered by a flue green-colored clay, belong evidently to the tertiary formation, which extends not only along the eastern side of the Gulf of Uraba, but upward to Cartagena. These tertiary beds on the Atlantic side of the isthmus are probably of the same geological age as those which extend along the whole Brazilian coast downward to Rio Grande do Sul, and farther south, upward the river Parana and thence downward the coast of Buenos Ayres and Patagonia. It seems that layers of more or less compact tertiary coal beds extend through the whole of Central America. It is a question of geological interest, in what relation these coal deposits stand to those of the Mississippi Valley, and to those of Concepcion, Sota, at the mouth of the river Saraquita, near Senbu, southward of Arauco, in Chili, and at the Straits of Magellan. These latter coal beds were believed to be of tertiary age; but according to Professor Agassiz, who has recently visited the coal mines at Sota and found 'baculites,' a characteristic cretaceous cephalopod, in a sandstone over-lying those beds, they belong to the cretaceous period."

On the 2d of January, 1871, the steam-launch of the expedition, together with several flat-boats, was in readiness for the departure of the first exploring party, consisting of Commander Selfridge, Messrs. Barnes and Beach, civil engineers, several other gentle men, and a sufficient number of workingmen. They proposed to follow the Atrato to the Cacarica River, from which point they would endeavor to reach Paya, an Indian village lying near the Paya River on the Pacific slope. The party took with them provisions for a twelve days' journey in the interior. That time passed and still the party did not return. As no provisions were to be obtained in the country, Commander Lull began to feel much anxiety, remembering the sad fate of the expedition under Lieutenant Strain, and in company with one of the surgeons of the ship started for the Cacarica River to look for the missing companions. He returned after a few days spent in fruitless search.

Every one on board the ship was nearly worn out with anxiety and watching, when one evening, nearly three weeks after the departure of the party, the distant puffing of the steam-launch was heard, and soon the missing boats came in sight. The wildest excitement reigned on board at the return of the first exploring party from the unknown world of the isthmus, and news was eagerly awaited; but this time there was nothing pleasant to be learned. Commander Selfridge came very slowly up the steps to the deck, and greeted his companions with the simple words, "I feel very sick." The other members of the little company were in the same prostrate condition, and for some weeks the ship Guard was transformed into a hospital, where hope and despondency struggled hand to hand. The difficulties in the way of thorough exploration of the swampy and feverish isthmus became more and more apparent; but after rest and careful nursing the health of Commander Selfridge became restored, the United States man-of-war *Nipsic* arrived, bringing mails, fresh supplies, and more men, and the prospects of the expedition were again brightened.

As soon as Commander Selfridge had gained strength the work was immediately resumed. The chief engineer, Mr. Barnes, was sent out with a guide to make a reconnaissance in a southward direction from the Cacarica River toward the tributary Peranchita, that from the result of his excursion final arrangements might be made for a thorough exploration of that region, as Commander Selfridge was determined not to leave any point uninvestigated which had reference to the grand question of an interoceanic ship-canal.

After an absence of six days Mr. Barnes returned with favorable reports. Immediately a new expedition, provided with the proper number of men, boats, provisions, and other necessities, was fitted out for making an exact survey across the isthmus toward the Gulf of San Miguel on the Pacific side.

When all was in readiness an event occurred which delayed the departure for several days. The guide, Remejio Pita, an old native of that country, and well acquainted with its rivers and backwoods, died after a short illness. He had returned from the last excursion sick of fever, and as he had indulged too freely in the native alcoholic drink at various Indian villages along the route, there was no hope for him. This old fellow was a true sample of the isthmus population, and possessed a very high reputation among the natives. He had been an India rubber collector, and in roaming about the woods had acquired a thorough knowledge of the country. When shown all the various scientific instruments and other conveniences of the party, he shook his head knowingly, and exclaimed that his memory, his eyes, and his shoulders were all the helps he needed to take him through the woods.

The death of this man was a great loss, but fortunately Commander Selfridge had heard of another valuable guide, a native of the village of Sucio, on the Atrato River. Lieutenant-Commander Schulz departed immediately on the steam-launch for that place, and was fortunate enough to engage the services of this man, and also to secure a *champa*, the light canoe of the natives of the Atlantic side.

After every thing had been arranged, Commander Selfridge, accompanied by a corps of officers, sailed for Aspinwall in the *Nipsic*, with the intention of crossing the isthmus by railroad, and proceeding down the Pacific coast to the Gulf of San Miguel, from which point he intended to push the exploration of the Tuyra River Valley.

The division for the exploration of the Atrato, under command of Master Couden, were to survey the valleys of the Atrato and Peranchita, intersecting, if possible, with Commander Selfridge somewhere in the valley of the Tuyra.

The famous Atrato River, or Rio Grande de San Juan, pours its waters into the Gulf of Darien through thirteen large mouths. It rises two hundred miles southward in the swampy plains of New Granada, and during the rainy season, when the inundations take place, often mingles its head waters with those of the San Juan do Sul, which empties into the Pacific a few miles north of the bay of Buenaventura. In 1788 a canal was dug between the head waters of the two rivers, which was practicable for the passage of small boats between the two oceans.

The Atrato Valley is a large alluvial plain, with an average width of sixty to seventy miles, resembling very much that of the Lower Mississippi. From the east and the west, tributaries, both large and small, mingle their waters with this great artery of the isthmus, which rushes northward with such impetuosity that its banks for sixty miles above the mouth are too low and swampy to be suitable for human habitation. Sucio, the first village on the Atrato, lies about sixty-one miles above the *Boca Coquito*. Its levees have a height of five or six feet above low-water mark. This region is submerged during nine months of the year, and deep and wide-spread *cienagas*, or lagoons, have been formed on either side. The river-banks, the result of the constant decomposition of the mountains, are abrupt, and the river affords plenty of water for the largest ships. At present, however, a few small *bungoes*, engaged in the India rubber and ivory-nut trade, are the only objects which break the solitude of this grand and beautiful stream.

Below the most recent deposits, which consist of muddy swamps, layers of firm clay and vegetable mould are found. These overlie, varying in thickness from a few inches to several feet, the gold-bearing clay and gravel, which are washed by the natives at various places along the river. This gold is derived from veins of the Cordillera of Antioquia, which is rich in mines of gold and platinum.

No rocks of any kind exist either in the river or the valley, and the vegetation is every where luxuriant and gorgeous. The different banks of the river present opposing botanical characteristics. The convex sides of the bank, being flat and marshy, are covered with various kinds of rank grasses and cane-like plants, while on the concave bank many varieties of trees grow in great abundance.

A tall water-grass, called by the natives "gramalotte," together with another water-plant called "tabaquills," covers a large area of the lowland along the Atrato and its tributaries, sometimes growing so abundantly as to give the impression of solid meadow land. The lowlands can be traversed, however, in a champa without much difficulty; even in the dry season, when the grass becomes a little stiff, the natives push the rude canoe through the swamp with long forked poles.

As soon as the soil gains a little more consistency other species of plants begin to appear, and great varieties of palms rear their stately heads above tile lower growths. Among these is one species with a curiously curved trunk, whose *spatha*, a large leaf in the shape of a bag, is used by the natives as a covering for the head. Other palms furnish the native population with substitutes for bread and yeast, sugar, wine, oil, vinegar, milk, wax, resin, fruit, various medicines, and material for weapons, cordage, and household furniture. What wonder that this simple people regard the palm with almost superstitious reverence, when it satisfies so many of their necessities!

The animal life is according to the rich vegetation, abundant and varying. Many varieties of water-birds, herons, snipes, sandpipers, kingfishers, and others peculiar to that region, make their home among the long reedy grasses; alligators bask in the sun upon the slime and clay of the river-bank; and the rich tropical forests seem alive with monkeys, ant-eaters, wild turkeys, toucans, parrots, woodpeckers, and many other varieties of birds with brilliant plumage.

The month of the Atrato proper is at present very difficult to enter, even for canoes and bungoes, on account of the many sand-bars which are formed there by the opposing action of the river current and that of other streams which flow into the gulf from the eastern side. But there are thirteen other mouths or *caños*, which have acquired a very considerable width, and are deep enough to admit large vessels. The Gulf of Darien, or Uraba, is a large and magnificent harbor, where great numbers of ships could ride safely at anchor. The Isla de los Muertos protects it from the violent north winds which prevail all through these latitudes in the winter season; it is entirely free from reefs, so frequent in nearly all Southern American harbors, and possesses a depth of anchorage sufficient at all times for the largest vessels. Open beaches do not exist along the borders of this gulf, as is the case in many other bays on the Atlantic coast. This is the result of the tidal movement. The equatorial current of the ocean flows through nearly the whole length of the gulf, and is forced backward by all the large and small streams which flow into the gulf from all sides. Mangroves, palms, and various other species of a delta vegetation grow directly at the water's edge, and help, in many respects, the formation of the sand-bars. At the eastern side of the gulf is a small hay, protected by a point of land called "Sandy Point." This little quiet bit of water serves as a harbor for all the boats engaged in the caoutchouc trade, which ply between Cartagena and Turbo.

Some days after the departure of the exploring party under command of Master Couden, Dr. Maack, accompanied by Chief Engineer Barnes, set out for a short trip to the interior. They left the ships boat at the mouth of the Cacarica River, and embarked in a canoe with two native oars-men, to explore the wonderful mysteries of a tropical wilderness. After paddling across the Cacarica Lake, whose waters abound in fishes, and where the huge manatus makes its home, they entered a great swamp where the canoe seemed to have no path among the thickly matted water-plants and grasses. The natives, however, found their way easily by means of long forked poles, and after traversing this watery wilderness for two hours the canoe entered a broad river called by the natives "Raya." After half an hour's clear sailing, among scenery of the most gorgeous richness, the gramalotte swamp began anew. The rest of the day was hard fighting. The gramalotte, or swamp-grass, was thickly matted together, and the burning sunbeams serving to aggravate the combined attacks of flies and mosquitoes, made the passage extremely difficult, and sweltering in the heat of a tropical afternoon, the party began to realize some of the trials of isthmus exploration. Just before sunset another clear stream was reached, which was bordered on both sides with high timber. Although the trees stood in the water, it was still a sign that the laud was rising, showing above the dead level. Before long patches of muddy soil appeared here and there, and the river-banks rose above the water, which in some places was so shallow that all hands were obliged to go overboard and drag the canoe across the flats.

Early in the evening the party reached the camping ground of Master Couden, where all were already under the mosquito-bars, it being almost impossible for any human being to exist at night in this wilderness with out protection against the attacks of that persistent little insect. Vampire bats, too, are very numerous, and often inflict severe bites upon the unwary and unprotected sleeper. In this tropical region, where the productive power of organic life is developed to the highest degree, the nights appear given over to rampage and rioting. The many species of frogs crowd the air with the noise of their singular concerts. Crying monkeys and all kinds of night-birds scream and hoot, and at times, when for a few moments stillness reigns, suddenly a troop of peccaries, scratching their way through the underbrush, awaken all other animals in their path, and a grand chorus of screams and yells arouses the distracted sleeper.

But during the day all is quiet, and the silence is unbroken, save when some decayed monarch of the forest, crashing down from its immense height, fills the air with the news of its dire and utter desolation. Lofty trees, of many precious woods, twine their branches together, forming grand avenues of Gothic architecture, whose pillars and arches are beautified with most delicate and fantastic tracery of creeping vine and graceful fern.

On the return of the exploring party the dry season had already lowered the depth of the Peranchita River, and in passing through the swamps it was almost impossible to drag the canoes.

Dr. Maack spent several days at the hills near the mouth of the Cacarica River, in order to make a geological examination of the surrounding country. These *Lomas del Cacarica*, as they are called, form the lowest range of the Western Cordilleras, which strike in several parallel ranges, like a terrace, now higher, now lower, from the east to the west. They are about one hundred feet in height, and from the summit one may have a magnificent view of the whole Atrato Valley, and obtain a clear idea of its geological development. The large numbers of rivers and streams which pour down from the Eastern and Western Cordilleras into that great artery, the Atrato, bring down a large quantity of fine decomposed material mixed with their waters, which sinks gradually to the river-bottom. When the opposing ocean current meets the powerful outflow of the river the accumulation takes place rapidly. This has been the case in times past, and the same causes are at work today forming the sand-bars at the mouth of the Atrato. The whole Atrato Valley, geologically considered, is nothing more than a great estuary, which was once in the sole possession of the Atlantic Ocean, whose waves at that time washed the very base of the Cordilleras. The slow upheaval of the former ocean bottom has during the progress of ages removed the sea more and more from the mountain ranges. But even now during the prevalence of the powerful north winds the sea seeks to regain its former mastery, and at times floods the Atrato for twenty miles up the valley.

The rock of the *Lomas del Cacarica* is different in its structure from that found between Aspinwall and Panama, or farther south about Cupica Bay and the Napipi River. The geological character of the Cordilleras has undergone in this particular latitude a change in its height as well as in its whole orographical structure. This mountainous system forms several parallel ranges of considerable elevation and extent, and sends out from the main range transverse ridges, which enclose deep valleys. The rock is almost everywhere in a state of disintegration, which renders it very difficult for the geologist to determine its true petrographical nature. It has at some places a soft, sandy texture; at others the slate-like structure prevails; while in some localities it shows through the whole mass so many different colors, the result of its decomposition, that it has lost entirely its stony character. Dr. Maack made a short excursion through the forest in company with two *caoutcheros*, or India rubber gatherers, where he found some large boulders whose internal structure had suffered very little from the disintegrating process. The texture was crystalline, and the mineralogical constituents were mixed very intimately. The boulders split unevenly; the surface had a rough appearance, and was of a dark, blackish color resembling *melaphyre*; but as the upheaval of these mountain chains occurred, according to paleontological facts preserved in the sedimentary strata, during the tertiary period, this rock can not be *melaphyre*, the ejection of which took place in a far remoter time. Different varieties of quartz, such as horn-stone, jasper, chalcedon, and agate, are frequently found along the river-course, often composing the sides of ravines. All these geological developments, differing in their character from those of the ranges farther to the north or south, place the Cordilleras of the province of Darien as a connection between the two, on account of its transitional petrographical character.

While sojourning in the wilderness the exploring party enjoyed many hearty dinners of manatus, or sea-cow. This huge, clumsy creature lives among the swamps of the Atrato, and its meat is considered a great delicacy by the natives. The cormorant, too, is much sought after for food. It is a bird about the size of a wild turkey, and falls a very easy prey to the native hunters. Its loud, harsh cry may be heard all along the shores of the river and through the swampy portions of the country.

While various parties from the *Guard* were pushing the exploration of the valley of the Atrato and its western tributaries with great vigor, Commander Selfridge had crossed the isthmus, and proceeded southward from Panama to the Gulf of San Miguel.

A landing was made at Chipigana, a small village on the shore of Darien Harbor. This village contains about four hundred inhabitants, of mixed descent, who are engaged principally in the caoutchouc and ivory-nut trade. It lies in a semi-circular basin, enclosed by hills, from whose summit a magnificent view may be had of the broad, winding valley of the Tuyra River. Chipigana presents a very curious picture, with its steep thatched roofs crowded together with little attention to convenient arrangement; and the utter lack of clean water, and the oppressive sultry atmosphere, render it a forlorn place of residence. During the day there is no breeze stirring, and the heat becomes so intense that swinging in the hammock is the only occupation possible for white men. In the evening a fresh breeze springs up from the Pacific, and a little relief is had from the suffocating air of the afternoon.

Commercial and industrial enterprise and progress have done little for this benighted region, and the whole country has remained almost unchanged since the time when the Spaniards held possession of it. Only small schooners come up with the high tide from Panama, bringing clothing, provisions, and other necessities, which they exchange for caoutchouc. During the spring tides these trading schooners sometimes proceed up the Tuyra River as far as Santa Maria del Real, an old Spanish settlement, but are prevented from ascending as high as Pinogana on account of numerous sand-bars. The caoutchouc is brought down from Pinogana in the native canoes, called on the Pacific side of the isthmus piragua.

At Chipigana, and for some distance up the Tuyra Valley, rocky masses, covered with a green-colored clay, dip gradually toward the river, having mostly a slate-like structure, and being in a state of great disintegration. Various quartz breccias may be found, as well as single specimens of flint, born-stone, and jasper, which increase in quantity, and fill the river-bottom more and more higher up the Tuyra Valley, spreading out into stony beaches above the village of Pinogana.

The rocks of the hills surrounding Chipigana vary much in their color, from dark blackish to reddish-brown, according to the more or less advanced stage of disintegration. Nearly all of them have a micro-crystalline texture, and are often vesicular, containing various small crystals of feldspar, of hornblende, or minute grains of titanic iron—being similar in character to the rocks of the Cacarica region, and possessing the same lithological character as hornblende-andesite.

For several miles beyond Chipigana the country has a low, swampy appearance, and mangroves and plants of that nature grow to the water's edge, while the distant mountain ranges form a sharply outlined background. The Tuyra flows through this region in long reaches, and has for many miles a considerable depth and breadth. Overlooking one of these reaches the picture presented is like that of a lake.

Passing up the Tuyra River, a few miles below Santa Maria is a small island where hundreds of alligators make their home. It is known by the natives as Alligator Island. Dozens of these hideous reptiles may be seen there, stretched quietly upon the sand, enjoying the hot noonday sun. When disturbed by a passing boat they open their broad jaws and crawl slowly into the water.

At this point the Cordilleras rise majestic and grand in the background, and the curved course of these mountain ranges from east to west may be distinctly traced.

The river-banks here are of red clay, and still very low, but at Santa Maria they rise from ten to fifteen feet, and form a level land upon which the old Spanish village is built. Between Santa Maria and Pinogana the country is of an undulating character, and covered with red clay. No rocks are to be found in this locality, except a few scattered varies of the common quartz.

Pinogana is the last village on the Tuyra River. It has about the same number of inhabitants as Chipigana, but its situation is far pleasanter and healthier. The houses are scattered on a comparatively large plain, the river water is drinkable and well suited for bathing, and a refreshing breeze gives an invigorating quality to the air.

The first reach of the Tuyra above Pinogana is long and but slightly curved. Near the town small banana and cane plantations are seen along the bank, but soon all signs of culture cease, and the explorer finds himself alone with the wildest nature. The whole character of the country changes. Hills begin to show themselves on all sides, and the river diminishes perceptibly. Huge trunks of fallen trees lie scattered in all directions over its bed, sometimes rendering the passage among these natural barricades very difficult, even for a small canoe managed by the skillful arms of a native boatman. Rocky masses begin to appear near the river-bank, and stony beaches are formed. On one of these beaches Dr. Maack landed to examine some water-worn boulders of a darkish green color.

They were very difficult to split with the hammer, but when once broken disclosed the fact that the whole mass was thoroughly filled with small marine shells. Many other boulders afterward examined revealed the fact that the rocks in this locality were all of *pliocene*, or younger tertiary formation. Still higher up the river, where several hills approach the bank, this formation shows an extensive development, and is rich in shells, which, unfortunately, break very easily in the sandy clayish strata. Some well-preserved fossils, however, may be found, which prove by their marine character that this whole region was submerged by the Pacific before the upheaval of the tertiary beds. Shellfish of the same character as these fossils may be found living in both oceans at the present time. A stratum of grayish-green sandy clay and another of yellow sandy clay are clearly distinguished, the latter holding the upper position. Both are covered in some places by an alluvial layer of small pebbles, varying in thickness from one to four feet, and made into a solid mass by a ferruginous sand. These two strata are not always found lying together, and are often very much displaced from their horizontal position, the layers being broken up, and stratified masses filled with shells turned over in different directions, a good illustration of which occurs near the mouth of the tributary stream Paca. This dislocation gives an idea of the powerful force by which this region has been upheaved and made to form a natural barrier between the two oceans.

The bottom of the Tuyra River is, in the upper portion, literally sown with pebbles of various sizes, the result of the destruction of the breccias by the erosive action of the air and water on the crests of the mountain ranges, where they form walls along the slopes. At many places these pebbles have accumulated in such quantities as to form extensive beds, which produce more or less effective changes in the river's course. Of not less importance in this respect are the many islands which are met with throughout the upper section of the Tuyra. Their basement consists of pebbles imbedded in a ferruginous sand, which is covered by a thin humus layer, in which many varieties of rank tropical plants fasten their roots, and make the island beautiful with always green foliage.

The tertiary formation has a vast extent in the Tuyra region, and spreads over the dividing ridges, where fossil shells are found at the height of 763 feet.

These facts lead to the positive conclusion that the Atlantic and Pacific oceans mingled their waters during the early tertiary period, and that their separation is the result partly of an eruption of crystalline rock, such as trachyte, andesite, and propylite, partly by the decomposition of these rocks, under the united action of air and water. Facts leading to the conclusion that an open sea existed until the pliocene period are also found farther north, between Panama and Aspinwall, and south throughout the regions of the Truando and Napipi rivers.

This conclusion once established upon the proper paleontological facts is of the greatest importance to the naturalist, as it gives a key to the right understanding of the geo graphical distribution of the plants and animals in that latitude.

Another fact observed in the region of the isthmus is that the river system on the Pacific slope is far superior to that of the Atlantic slope. In South and North America the contrary is the fact, as the rivers flowing into the Atlantic are of considerable breadth and depth, and of much commercial importance, while those which empty into the Pacific are small streams in comparison. The explanation of this fact lies in the orographical structure of the isthmus. While in South America the main chain of the Cordilleras runs near the western coast, near the Gulf of San Miguel a sudden change takes place, and the bulk of the mountain range is turned away from the Pacific and transferred to, the Atlantic side, where in several places it approaches boldly and abruptly to the sea, the country to the westward running into low bills and broad savannas.

Between the Gulf of San Blas and the mouth of the Chepo River lies the narrowest portion of the isthmus. On this account this locality has been looked upon by the whole geographical and commercial world as the proper point for a connection between the two oceans. But all the expenses and hardships attending various explorations of this particular point have been in vain; for, as if it would form an offset to the weakness of the narrow strip of land, the Cordilleras tower here to a height of several thousand feet, reaching its highest isthmus elevation, and rendering all connection between the two oceans at this point impossible.

After making a thorough geographical and geological survey of the Tuyra River Valley, Commander Selfridge and his company left the Gulf of San Miguel in the United States man-of-war *Resaca* for Cupica Bay, where Master Collins, assisted by Ensign Paine, had already commenced the survey of the famous Napipi route. At Turbo Commander Selfridge had conversed with two natives who had crossed over this route, passing from Cupica Bay through the Napipi and Atrato valleys to Uraba; and in ancient times the line was well known to the Spaniards, who had carefully concealed their knowledge of it, fearing that access to the west coast of America might lead to a discovery of the renowned mining localities on the Caña River, from which Spain derived more revenue in a single year than was exported from all other American mines. These celebrated gold mines are now destroyed, and no trace can be found of their whereabouts. Although they lie in that region of the isthmus where the mountains consist principally of *andesite*, still it is very probable that the ore was worked in quartziferous propylite, which always holds a position at the bottom of volcanic rocks, and is overlaid by *andesite* and *trachyte*.

After passing out by Punta Garachine, the southern promontory of the Gulf of San Miguel, the low swampy land ceases, and the coast presents a hold and mountainous appearance. No beaches exist, and Puerto Piñas is the only harbor where a vessel may seek shelter. The main range of the Cordilleras appears to form a very complicated centre, from which lower ranges spread out in fan-like lines northward and southward. This makes it clear that one mountain range approaches the Pacific behind Punta Ardita, while the other, taking a direct north-easterly course, forms the western boundary of the Atrato Valley, and approaches the Atlantic Ocean north of the Gulf of Darien.

At Humboldt Bay flat beaches come in sight, but Punta Marzo, at the southern end of the bay, is bold and rocky, and the surf beats upon it with such violence as to render it dangerous and difficult to land. The elevation of the mountain ranges lessens, and the country has a broken, hilly appearance.

At Cupica Bay, the external portion of Limon Bay, there is a fine sandy beach, deepening very gradually from the shore outward, which extends in a semi-circular line along the base of the mountains. The waves of the Pacific Ocean break on the beach in long continuous lines of surf dashing up here and there in clouds of spray where a detached rock stands out into the water. The rise and fall of the tide in Cupica Bay is about sixteen feet. The smooth sandy beach is crowded by the hermit-crab, which carries a commodious shell on its back, into which its head and claws can be drawn at pleasure.

Coming from the Atlantic coast, where reef-building corals inhabit the waters of the gulf, and build their reefs in all the bays along the shore, the explorer is surprised to find no traces of this minute insect life on the Pacific coast. The question arises regarding the cause of this phenomenon, which is especially puzzling when we consider the former existence of a channel between the two oceans. It is a well-established fact that all the prominent genera of reef-forming corals are abundantly represented in the central and western Pacific within 15° to 18° of the equator, where the temperature of the surface is never below 74° F. during any season of the year. A cold and strong oceanic current takes its course in a westerly direction all along the South American coast, and consequently forms an obstacle against the distribution of mid-ocean corals toward the coast of the isthmus. Fossil corals of the same species as those of the Atlantic coast have been found in Obispo Valley, on the line of the Panama Railroad, proving the inward extent of the Atlantic Ocean in former times. One more fact may be stated in connection with these corals, which is that even during the tertiary period the Pacific coast was disturbed by volcanic activity long after the eastern shores of the isthmus were tranquil, and the Gulf of San Blas and Caledonia Bay afforded quiet places for the development of reef coral when no such thing would have been possible in the bays of the western side.

It becomes evident from all these facts that reef-building corals did not exist on both sides of the isthmus even at the period when the waters of both oceans were mingled.

Generally speaking, animal life is more developed on the Atlantic side of the isthmus. The forests of the Atlantic slope are full of different kinds of monkeys, and the loud cry of the howling monkey, called by the natives *mono colorado*, is heard every where. But many varieties make their home on both coasts, and the zoology may as a whole be considered of the same character. The reptile life is everywhere well developed. Alligators, lizards, iguanas, turtles, and snakes are all largely represented. There are several varieties of poisonous snakes whose bite proves fatal in a very short time, but as these snakes hunt their food mostly at night, they are rarely encountered. Spiders are represented by many genera and species. Crabs, mollusks, and radiates occur in great abundance in both oceans.

The scenery around Cupica Bay is wild and magnificent. Large boulders of every size and shape lie scattered in wild confusion, all thickly crusted with shells and sea animals. The waves, dashing through ages, have undermined the rocky wall in many places, forming caves and fantastic grottoes, where the sea foams and boils as if eager to carry its work of destruction still further. In the background rise the mountains, covered to their very summits with luxuriant tropical vegetation, and afar off may be seen the great falls of the Limon River plunging over a precipice 250 feet high, and pouring down an immense body of fine pure water to mix with the ocean at Limon Bay.

Examining the mineralogical composition of the rock, it appears that the prevailing colors vary from dark green or greenish-brown to yellowish-red, and that the outside of the rock is generally in a state of decomposition, rendering it very easy to split with a hammer. On examination with a magnifying-glass the internal structure of this rock appears of a fine crystalline character, with mineralogical constituents probably of hornblende and oligoclase feldspar. All these rocks, where the mineralogical constituents are so finely mixed as to be scarcely discovered without a chemical analysis, have been generalized by the Swedish name of "trap." This name, however, is very indefinite and of small service to the geologist. More scientific distinctions are necessary, since the so-called trap rocks belong not only to different geological ages, but possess many different qualities and various mineralogical constituents.

These green-colored rocks of Cupica Bay belong to the tertiary period. The mountains in this locality consist principally of what has been called "propylite," a rock in which the petrographical properties of diorite are united with those of andesite and oligoclase trachyte. The color and structure of this rock vary very largely, but it is nevertheless possible after an examination of several specimens to recognize some general characteristics which are common to all. The darkish green color, caused by very minute particles of hornblende, which are intimately blended with other materials, is the prevailing one. Little pores filled with minute crystals are found sometimes in the crystalline variety, and also thin veins of quartz. One variety may be distinguished in which hornblende and feldspar form crystals of nearly the same size in a dark green or gray matrix; another in which hornblende alone forms crystals, while the feldspar is mixed up with the matrix; a third in which the reverse is the case; and a fourth in which the rock is so homogeneous that no crystals of any kind can be recognized without the assistance of a magnifying-glass.

The effect of air upon this rock is different according to its structure. Fine granulated masses resist the disintegrating influence much longer than those which have a slate or porphyritic structure. The result of this disintegration is a red-yellow clay, which contains a large quantity of oxidized iron. On account of its porphyritic structure, which is sometimes very perfect, this rock has been called porphyry.

The mountains of Cupica Bay, striking in a northeasterly direction, rise almost abruptly from the shore. The mountainous system here has a different geological character from that of the Tuyra and Cacarica regions. The crystalline rocks along the Pacific side of the isthmus are, as before stated, of tertiary formation, but the mountains about Cupica Bay being of "propylite" rock, represent the oldest group, as the andesite of the Tuyra region came to the surface at a later period, and the trachytic and basaltic rocks about Panama represent the last volcanic ejection of the tertiary age. The San Blas Cordillera of the Atlantic coast belongs to a still older geological period, having evidently at one time been an independent island. It is composed of plutonic rocks, such as granite, syenite, diorite, and metamorphic slates. This is another proof that the Atlantic slope had been already upheaved and was in a state of tranquillity when the waters of the Pacific Ocean still covered the whole area which forms the present Pacific slope.

An old Indian trail crosses the crests of the Cupica Bay mountain ridge, leading over the divide at an altitude of 612 feet. After a walk of about an hour the path descends to the Limon River, the bottom of which is filled with pebbles and boulders of every size and shape. All these water-worn rocks have a dark green color, and are very smooth and shiny. They are very hard, and it is almost impossible to split them with a common hammer. The structure is a fine crystalline one, and it appears as if the river water running over them continually acted as a protection against the disintegrating influence of the humid air, as those rocks which crop out from the river-banks are much decomposed, and split far easier. The decomposition has advanced so rapidly that a reddish-yellow clay, as an alluvial product in various stages of induration, covers nearly the whole surface of the country. This yellow clay becomes very slippery during the rainy season, rendering it difficult to walk over the steep mountain passes.

In a few localities are deposits of a grayish-blue clay, underlying the yellow layer, which dates from the younger tertiary formation. This blue clay is used by the natives for making pipes and pottery.

The Indian trail ascends again at the Limon River, and the gorgeous vegetation grows more dense with every step forward, shutting out both air and light from the forest, where profound silence reigns supreme. Even from the summit of the divide, 612 feet high, it is impossible to survey the surrounding country on account of the mat of foliage which shuts in the explorer on every aide. This is a great obstacle in the way of a thorough knowledge of the orographical character of the isthmus. What lies hidden in those deep valleys and ravines? And who shall venture to predict the advantages to be gained should the enterprising commercial spirit of the age open this hitherto unknown region, and lay bare its riches for the benefit of the world?

It is well known that in those countries where "propylite" has been found—in Hungary, Mexico, Bolivia, and other countries rich silver-bearing veins are always connected with it. It seems natural to suppose that the lands situated on Cupica Bay and the Napipi River, as they possess the same geological character, should also be rich in gold and silver. In 1865 gold was discovered on the southern boundary of the province of Cauca, in the Cordillera of Barbacoas, and in 1866 not less than $485,000 was brought to Panama.

Great Falls, Limon River

After passing an elevated plateau 560 feet high, the Indian trail leads down-ward to the river Napipi, whose bed, like that of the Limon River, is filled with pebbles and boulders of various sizes. The trail crosses and re-crosses the river many times, and again leads upon table-land, interspersed with low hills. The vegetation here is very luxuriant, and ferns and palms of every description crowd the thicket, or, rising above it, wave their long leaves in the clear upper air.

This table-land is about three miles long, and is very healthy, being well suited for human settlements. The trail traverses this plateau, and strikes hills about eighty feet high. Following the path, the *Rancho Grande*, or *Embarcadero*, is reached soon after. It lies about 250 feet above ocean level, and is about halfway between the divide and the Atrato. The natives have built a comparatively large hut at this point, which serves as a stopping-place during their travels through this portion of the country. The hut was occupied by a few Indians, who showed themselves very friendly, and immediately offered all the hospitality in their power to the exploring party.

At this place the Napipi becomes navigable for canoes, although still farther below are several rapids of no inconsiderable size. For about thirteen miles from the dividing ridge the country is broken and mountainous in its character, but assumes a flat appearance where the Doguado River flows into the Napipi—a point lying twenty-five miles inland from the Pacific Ocean.

Beds of clay and gravel form the river bank, but gradually the levees become lower and lower, and the gravelly shores give way to long stretches of soft mud, in which are imbedded logs and all kinds of river stuff, like the shores of the Atrato. This lower portion of the river is subjected to violent freshets.

The Napipi flows in a very crooked course of 68 miles through an area measuring but a little more than 27 miles in a straight line, emptying into the Atrato in latitude 6°35′ north, 150 miles from the Gulf of Darien. It is about 100 feet wide at its mouth. The height of the Atrato above mean tide is 41 feet at this point, while its levees have a height of about twelve feet.

The survey of the Napipi Valley by Master Collins and Ensign Paine shows that the divide of the Napipi line has an altitude of 612 feet at a point lying very near the Pacific coast. After passing the Limon River the land forms an elevated plateau, with a rise of about twenty feet, and a total height of 560 feet. The country here assumes the general character of table-land, interspersed with low hills, until a range 400 feet high is encountered, through which the river has cut its way, bounding along a rocky gorge.

The hilly country ends at *Rancho Grande*, and after passing the Doguado no more tributaries of any size are met with, and the river-bottom becomes level and pebbly, and the rapids less frequent.

The survey also shows that the Napipi is an extremely crooked stream, following a serpentine course of sixty-eight miles, while the distance in a straight line from its source to the mouth is less than thirty. Its general width is 120 feet, and the current at the end of the dry season about one and a half miles per hour, giving a volume of flow of 510,300 cubic feet per hour. During the rainy season its banks are overflowed from two to four feet. The Atrato at the mouth of the Napipi is 1500 feet broad and thirty feet deep. Careful experiments at the mouth of the Atrato for three months show that the evaporation amounts daily to one-fifth of an inch. This small quantity is explained by the extreme humidity of the atmosphere.

Commander Lull surveyed the Atrato as far up as the mouth of the Bojaya River, and found its depth to be not less than twenty-eight feet, while in the bends it reached the depth of sixty feet.

The Gulf of Darien may be called one of the finest harbors in the world for the safe anchorage of vessels, and Limon Harbor, an indentation of Cupica Bay, which would form the Pacific terminus of the proposed Napipi ship-canal, possesses no less important qualities for the convenience of shipping. At a distance of 1,000 yards from the shore there is fine anchorage in ten fathoms of water. The bay is spacious, and open only to the southwest wind, which at that latitude rarely blows strong enough to become dangerous, as may be seen from the facts that luxuriant vegetation grows in some places to the very edge of the water, and that the natives have built their frail huts all along the beach. There are no swamps in this locality, no mosquitoes, no dangerous reefs, and the Indians are all peaceful and friendly. The dry season continues longer than at the Atlantic side, which renders the atmosphere invigorating and healthful. There is fine pure water both for drinking and bathing. The salutary effect of this climate was visible at once upon all the members of the exploring party, and although they were subjected to much exposure, no cases of sickness occurred during the survey of this locality.

The fact that this section of country is of the oldest tertiary volcanic rock is of great importance in the construction of a ship-canal for which security and permanency of the level are one of the chief things to be demanded; and while active volcanic forces are still at work along the western coast of South America, and in Central America as well, this particular locality has remained quiet and undisturbed for ages.

The surroundings of Limon Harbor offer healthy and delightful situations for residences, where people employed on the work of the canal could live without suffering any of those inconveniences which are the usual accompaniments of humid and tropical climates. As all the heaviest and most expensive portion of the work lies within five miles of the Pacific coast, this would be an important Item toward the success of the enterprise. The sixteen feet rise and fall of the tide in Cupica Bay would admit the construction of a large dry-dock without too great expense. This is a very important fact, as the lack of dry-docks along the Pacific coast is felt more and more as the commercial interest there increases.

Here the question arises, is a tunnel of five miles in length, 120 feet in height, and seventy feet in width, practicable or not for an interoceanic ship-canal? Judging from the lithological character of the rock, an excavation through the dividing ridge could be executed without encountering any serious obstacles. It is impossible, however, to make a certain statement whether the tunneled rock would sustain itself, or if supporting arches would be necessary.

Mr. J. B. Francis, of Lowell, one of the first hydraulic engineers of America, says of the Napipi tunnel: "As a simple question of engineering it seems to be perfectly practicable. The completion of the Mont Cenis Tunnel and the rapid progress at the Hoosac are highly encouraging, and if climatic difficulty can be overcome, it becomes simply a question of time and money."

Mr. Walter Shanley, the present contractor and engineer of the Hoosac Tunnel, writes: "The section shown me presents a much less impracticable route than from all I had learned of those previously explored I imagined could be obtained. A tunnel of the dimensions contemplated is *not all tunnel*, in the tunneler's sense of the term; that is to say, the work would not all have to be done by the expensive process incident to boring. First drive a tunnel, properly such, say ten or fifteen feet high on the top, and all the rest could and should be treated as an open cut, and as such need not cost more per cubic yard than a cubic yard of similar rock on other parts of the work."

Commander Selfridge, in his report to the Secretary of the Navy, says: "The dimensions for the proposed canal by this route are a depth of twenty-six feet, and a width at bottom, in earth, of ninety feet, in rock of 100 feet, or a general surface width of 120 feet; the sides sloping, in earth, two horizontal to one perpendicular; in rock, one horizontal to four perpendicular.

"Locks 436 feet long and sixty feet wide, with a lift of ten feet each, are used to reach the summit level of 130 feet above the sea. The Atrato River at the mouth of the canal being forty feet, there are required nine locks on the Atlantic side and thirteen on the Pacific. While locks are not a necessity to this route, a moderate number interfere but little with the transit of the canal, and reduce vastly the amount of cost and excavation. Whole length of canal from Atrato to Pacific, 31.2 miles. The canal is filled at the summit level by the Napipi River, distant but a few hundred yards. Ten lockages a day would represent about what would be required, supposing a yearly transit of 3,000,000 tons. At this rate the quantity of water required daily would be

	(in cubic feet)
Ten lockages per day	2,592,000
Leakage per day, 2,500 feet per minute	3,600,000
Evaporation per day	288,000
Waste, filtration	100,000
Total	6,580,000
Daily volume of Napipi, low stage	12,241,200
(difference)	5,661,200

"This amount could be doubled by a feeder, three miles long, from the Boja-ya River, and the leakage could be pumped back into the locks, if necessary. The canal excavation being mostly in rock, there will be only a small amount of waste and filtration; besides, there will be, in consequence, but little expenditure for masonry."

In estimating the expense of the canal, the ground has been divided into four divisions: Division One extends from the Atrato River to Lock No. 9, a distance of twenty and a half miles; Division Two, from Lock No. 9 to east face of tunnel, a distance of five and four-fifths miles. The last half of this division is among the hills, and the cutting is through solid rock, which would greatly increase the expense. The amount of cutting at this point might be lessened by following up the valley of the Guinea River, but as yet no survey has been made to ascertain the practicability of this plan. Division Three is the tunnel, 9,010 yards in length. Estimating the cost of excavation at $5.35 per cubic yard, the whole expense of the tunnel might be reckoned at $39,719,684.

"In the execution of this tunnel," says Commander Selfridge, "shafts should be sunk at every mile, giving sight faces to work upon, expediting the work by allowing the employment of more labor and increased opportunity for removing the rock. On account of the lowness of the hills through which the tunnel passes, the total length of this series of shafts would not exceed 1,100 feet, which is not greater than the depth of the central shaft at Hoosac Tunnel.

"The western end being but about 4,000 feet from the sea, there are great facilities for the rapid removal of the *débris*, which would be dumped into the ocean, forming a breakwater.

"Division Four would be from the end of the tunnel to the sea, a distance of 3,250 feet. This division lies in the valley of the Limon River, which reduces very much the amount of excavation. It includes the system of thirteen locks by which the descent is made."

Commander Selfridge has made a careful estimate of expenses, which is of interest even to the general reader. He considered that the canal proper could be constructed at a cost of $95,555,494. The improvements of the Atrato River are estimated at $500,000. These, together with the expenses of the various departments, light-house, and pier at Cupica Bay, and a large margin for contingencies, form a sum total of $123,200,617.

The survey of the Napipi having proved so successful, it was thought advisable to gain a more thorough knowledge of the country in the vicinity. Commander Selfridge expressed his conviction that further survey would develop opportunities for shortening the route and decreasing the expense. Accordingly in the later part of 1872 he was placed in command of a new surveying expedition, which sailed from Panama in the United States sloop *Tuscarora* on the 23d of January, 1873. After a pleasant sail of twenty-two hours the ship arrived at Cupica Bay. Commander Selfridge has made his base of operations for this year's survey at a point called Chiri-Chiri, located some fifteen miles south of Limon Bay. His present plan is to survey the valley of the Bojaya River, if possibly it may develop better advantages, or lead in some way to increase those gained by the survey of last year.

7

Tehuantepec and the Eads Ship Railway

John A. Dillon

The article describes a scheme, developed by the American engineer James Buchanan Eads, whereby railroad cars carry ships across the Isthmus of Tehuantepec, Mexico. Stating that engineers in England and the United States viewed the project as "scientifically sound," the article, with diagrams, makes the case that the project should be developed. Ships would pass from one port to the other (143 miles) in less than twelve hours. A "liberal" concession was granted by Mexico to Eads—more clear evidence of the Porfirio Díaz government's overzealousness in its desire to please foreign interests. The project was estimated to cost 75 million dollars, and would be complete in four or five years.

The latest railroad maps of Mexico could hardly fail to excite the fears of Mexican patriotism if our neighbor republic had any fear of that Yankee invasion which is now going on. From the northern frontier no less than four lines of invasion, more or less advanced, pierce the interior. The Mexican Central company has its main or international line extending down from El Paso, while its interoceanic branches meet the Gulf at Tampico, and the Pacific at San Blas; the Palmer and Sullivan narrow gauge, or the Mexican National, invades the country from Laredo on the frontier, and Manzanillo on the sea. The omnipresent Jay Gould is said to own a third concession, from the frontier to the capital. Eagle Pass, on the Rio Grande, is the starting point of an American road to Topolorampo, on the Gulf of California. South of the city of Mexico the Grant concession occupies the territory from sea to sea, and guards the western coast from Anton Lizardo across to Acapulco, and thence to the southern limit of the republic.

Instead of dreading this invasion, however, the Mexicans welcome it as the harbinger of the new age of gold which is to succeed their brazen age of pronunciamento and of civil war, and they have given the full measure of their enthusiastic approval to the daring scheme of the American engineer James Buchanan Eads, who proposes to make Mexico the highway of the worlds east and west ocean commerce by taking up the ships, crews, cargoes, and all, and carrying them on railroad cars across the Isthmus of Tehuantepec. Of the many American projects in Mexico, none is so popular as this one, which appeals alike to their imagination, their pride, their patriotism, and their incidental desire of prosperity.

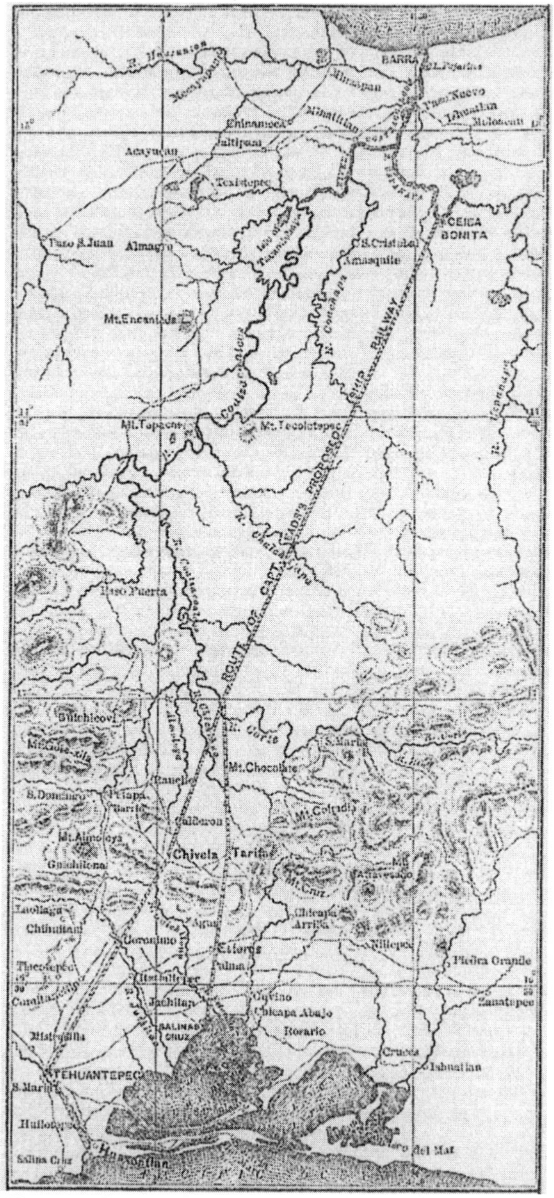

The suggestion of a ship railroad dates back from the adventurous epoch and from the busy brain of Cortez. The "wild surmise" which held Balboa "silent upon a peak in Darien" very soon gave way to a depressing conviction that there was an obstacle in the way of Columbus's idea of reaching the East by way of the West, and Cortez was not content with merely conquering Mexico as long as anything remained beyond. He made a personal exploration of the Coatzacoalcos, the river of the isthmus, with a view of establishing a portage across the short path to the South Sea, for the rich commerce of Zipangu and far Cathay. Spain thought well of the project, and after three hundred years of thinking, issued a decree in 1814 authorizing the attempt. But the revolution had already started, and prevented all further proceedings until 18-12, when the republic granted a concession to Don Jose de Garay to build a railroad there. The Garay concession lapsed, although the government of the United States was prepared to pay fifteen millions of dollars for a right of way across the isthmus, and authorized the commissioners of the boundary treaty to offer that sum to Mexico. This too fell through; but after the gold discoveries of California our government kept its eye on the isthmus, and has since made two surveys for the purpose of deter-mining the practicability of a canal. These surveys were made by General Bar-nard in 1851, and by Commodore Shufeldt in 1870; but it looks as if the isthmus was waiting for the ship railroad, for in the interval three successive concessions were made to Mexicans, and one to an American company, yet the Panama Canal, twelve hundred miles further away from us, was begun before the Mexican government turned a willing ear to the idea of Eads.

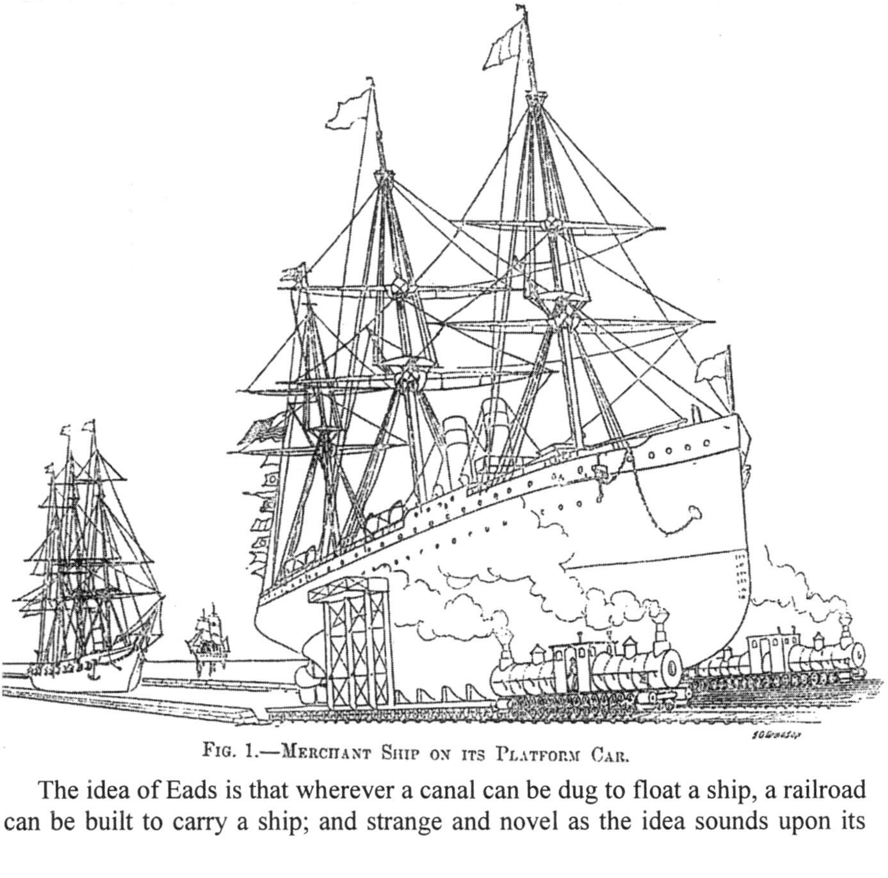

FIG. 1.—MERCHANT SHIP ON ITS PLATFORM CAR.

The idea of Eads is that wherever a canal can be dug to float a ship, a railroad can be built to carry a ship; and strange and novel as the idea sounds upon its first mention, the most sober-minded and competent engineers of this country and of England declare that it is scientifically sound and quite practicable. The illustrations which we give explain themselves so easily that they hardly need detailed elucidation. Fig. 1 represents the ship on its platform car, or cradle, or dry-dock, or whatever one chooses to call it, resting on even keel and bilge blocks, and braced as if it had gone on the ways for repairs. The car is designed to move on twelve rails spaced the standard width, and its wheels are placed as near together as their diameter will allow, or three feet from axle to axle. The tractile power is furnished by four locomotives, each with fivefold the capacity of an ordinary freight locomotive. The non-scientific mind begins to ask at once, How can the ship get there, how is she secured from bending or twisting strains while there, and how does the railroad meet the demands of the pressure on its road-bed, and of the grades and curves involved in a hundred miles of mountain location?

The ship gets on the railway very much as it gets on any other ways. The railway begins thirty feet below the surface of the harbor, in a land-locked basin, as shown in Fig. 2 in elevation, and Fig. 3 in plane. A slope of one in a hundred brings the railway down to thirty feet in depth at a distance of three thousand feet from the land terminus. The cradle is run down this incline to the depth at which the ship's keel rests on its bearing; the vessel is secured to the cradle and braced, and stationary engines at the land end of the basin draw it to its level on *terra firma*.

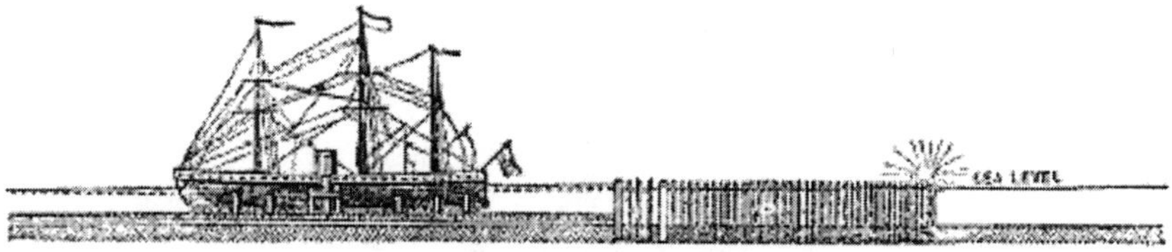

FIG. 2.—LAND LOCKED BASIN—ELEVATION.

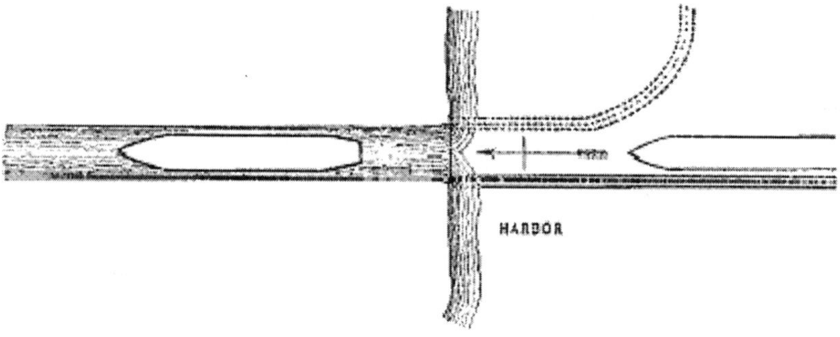

FIG. 3.—LAND-LOCKED BASIN—PLANE.

The sectional view in Fig. 4 and the enlarged section of Fig. 5 show the way in which it is designed to support the weight and to brace the ship. The car is made of cross girders of plate iron, with each wheel bearing on an independent axle, and with its separate set of springs. A car three hundred feet in length, such as would carry a ship of four thousand tons, would have one hundred wheels on each rail, or twelve hundred wheels under each car. This would give a pressure of five tons on each wheel, which is not as great as is borne by the road-bed of an ordinary railroad. Any one who has traveled at the rate of forty miles an hour on the two rails of such a road as the Hudson River road, where the motion is hardly felt, will have no difficulty in believing that a vessel securely braced can be moved on an elastic cushion of twelve hundred springs, distributed across twelve rails, without any disturbance or strain, as long as the road is straight and level. In the ship railway, curves are out of the question, and a change of direction is made by a turning-table. The surveys of the road have shown that a maximum grade of fifty feet in the mile is easily obtainable. Mr. Fuertes, who is now the dean of the engineering department of Cornell College, and who assisted in Shufeldt's survey of the isthmus in 1870, is authority for the statement that the maximum grades need not exceed twenty-five to thirty-five feet in a mile. A cradle three hundred feet long would be exposed to a maximum flexure of six inches in its centre in passing directly from a level to such a grade.

Fig. 4.

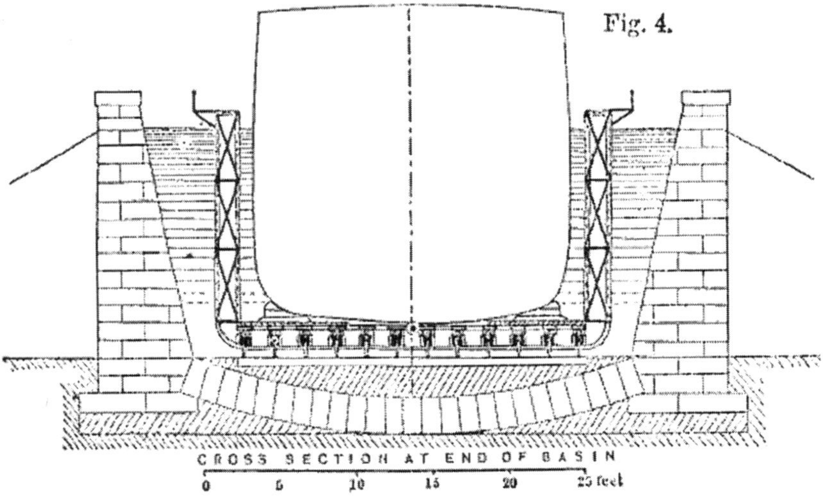

There is a popular delusion that a ship, which represents the highest perfection of human skill in the harmonious adjustment of its proportions, is so delicate that it would give way if any part were left unsupported. Few people are aware that Lloyds' Rules, which are the basis of ocean insurance, require a sea-going vessel to be so strong that it would sustain no injury if supported on a single bearing across its centre, or if suspended between two supports at its ends. A ship that cannot stand this without injury is not fit to go to sea, yet there is no room on the ship railway for any such strain as this.

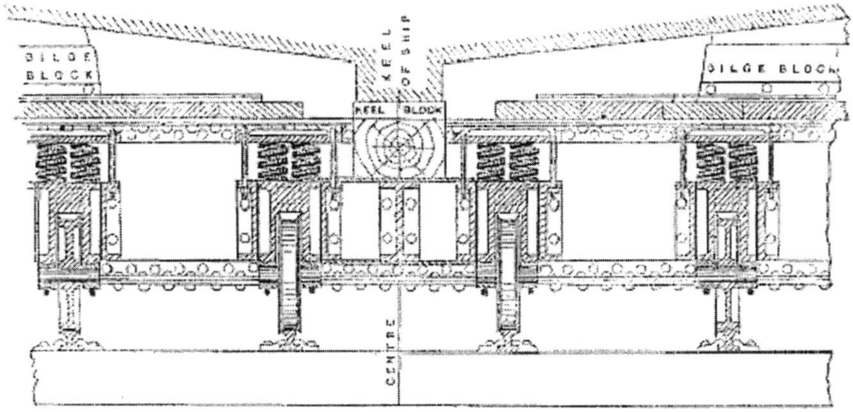

Scale 1 inch to the foot

The easiest way to dispose of these questions is to bear in mind that they are purely technical questions of mechanics, to be decided by the opinion of experts. Captain Eads has demonstrated by his success with the bridge at St. Louis that his opinion as to the possibilities of engineering construction, especially in resisting strains, is very valuable, and he has on his side the support of such men as E. I. Reed, for many years the chief constructor of the British navy, and who holds the first rank in all the world as an expert in naval construction; of Edwal D. Hartt and H. L. Fernald, the experienced naval constructors of the United States navy; and of such military and civil engineers as Barnard, and Gillmore, and Shufeldt, Beauregard, Flad, and others. This should be sufficient to relieve all non-scientific minds of apprehensions which are not shared in by any impartial scientific opinion.

The value of a new idea may generally be gauged by the host of objections which are made against it, and it would be too long to catalogue the unnumbered difficulties which non-professional critics have raised. While, on the one hand, the loaded ship is supposed to have so tremendous a weight as to crush in the road-bed, we are told that it is so light that it can not stand the exposure of its surface to the wind. Ship captains have declared that the seams would dry and crack and open under exposure to the hot sun; to which the projector answers that he will transfer every ship from harbor to harbor within twelve hours, and if the ship's seams can not stand that exposure, it is a sign that they need calking and tarring, for which the passage will furnish an opportunity. In fact, the conservative old salts look upon the audacious attempt to lift their craft out of the water and haul it across dry land very much as the old Shiver-my-timbers and Benbows of sailing three-deckers looked upon the introduction of steam and of Monitors. But science has no sentiment, especially when pressed into the service of trade, and the testimony of science is to the effect that, spite of old salts and salt-water sentiments, ships will yet sail on dry land across the isthmuses of Tehuantepec and of Corinth, across Florida, and over the Landes of Southern France, between Biscay and the Mediterranean.

The Tehuantepec project is already well advanced, and under circumstances that promise speedy success. The concession which the Mexican government gave to our fellow-countryman is the most liberal that any government ever granted to a private individual. It exempts his company from taxes and duties of all kinds, gives him right of way and full control of tolls and regulations. As one of the few opponents of the bill in the Mexican Congress put it, the grant made Eads sovereign of the isthmus in place of Mexico, which had abdicated. Its importance to us consists in the fact that the charter permits the company to discriminate in favor of the commerce of any nation which aids in building the work. If this provision is made use of, it may open to us a way of building up that ocean commerce of which we mourn the loss.

Our country, which possesses the largest coast-line and the finest harbors in the world, and which, in its lusty and adventurous youth, ranked second only to the mother country in the strength of its merchant marine and navy, has fallen so far to the rear that it hardly carries one twenty-fifth part of its own foreign commerce. We have lost our vessels, our seamanship, our prestige, our naval strength, and those substantial profits which flow from ocean transportation and from the industries connected with it. The most liberal of all people toward foreigners in all other respects, we have sunk to the level of the old Spanish exclusiveness in Mexico with regard to our coastwise trade, and we do not allow an Italian, or a Norwegian, or an Englishman, to trade along our coast, well knowing that if we allowed them to compete with us, we would be driven out of the competition. The problem of remedying this disgrace and restoring our commerce to its natural position is one which statesmanship and self-interest have both failed to solve. If the building of the Tehuantepec ship railway should open the way to a solution of it, it would be worth more to us than the fifteen millions we offered thirty years ago for the mere right of way. This is the consideration which leads the projectors of the enterprise to count on the aid of this nation. If the world's commerce can be carried across the isthmus more cheaply than around Cape Horn, it will go there; if it can be carried more cheaply in American bottoms than in English bottoms, it will go in American bottoms; and it is a question in which American capitalists and American citizens all have an interest, namely, to discover whether a rebate of thirty-five or fifty per cent on transit dues would enable us to compete with England—our chief competitor—while at the same time permitting the company to make enough money to earn interest on its cost. This is the question which was before Congress last winter, and which will be submitted to its wisdom again next winter.

The Isthmus of Tehuantepec becomes, in the light of its possibilities, one of the points of interest on the map. At its narrowest part it is 143 miles wide, from the bar of Coatzacoalcos on the north to the chain of natural harbors at the south end. The Coatzacoalcos River is a broad and deep stream, with twenty-five feet of water from the mouth to the town of Minatitlan—a sleepy, ragged, and tumble-down settlement thirty miles up. This is a port of some importance for the trade in mahogany and other precious woods. The whole Atlantic side of the isthmus is a low, marshy, unhealthy forest for fifty or sixty miles back from the coast. Below Minatitlan the tributary stream of the Uspanapa comes in from the south, and carries the deep channel twenty miles further inland to a bend where a conspicuous cottonwood-tree has given the name of "Ceiba Bonita" to the point where the work of the ship railway will begin. Here the land is so marshy that a canal of ten miles in length will probably need to be dredged out to the beginning of track-laying. The railway itself will run through a country of exuberant fertility, of beautiful scenery, and of healthful climate. The mountains present no especial obstacle, for at three different points the Sierra Madre lowers itself to an elevation of only 650 feet, as if bending to the yoke of commerce. These are the passes of Chivela, Tarifa, and Masagua, through one of which the road will run; and thence southward there is a choice of routes either to Salina Cruz, on a large lagoon, or by the town of Tehuantepec to the harbor of Ventosa, on the sea.

A corps of engineers, under the direction of Mr. J. J. Williams, and Captain Flores of the engineer corps of the Mexican army, are now on the isthmus completing the surveys on which the course of the road and the estimates of its cost were based. The choice of a best location for the road is a matter of more than usual importance, as Captain Eads estimates that his railway will cost half a million dollars a mile; the estimate for the total cost of the road, including equipment and harbor work, is placed at seventy-five millions; the period needed for its completion is not to exceed four or five years.

After leaving the fevers of the marshland the chief obstacle is the tropic luxuriance of vegetation, which here grows so rankly as to obstruct all passage. The first step in running a surveyor's line is to send forward a Corp of *macheteros* or choppers, who with their heavy *machetes* cut a *picadura*, or passage, in the direction indicated; a gang of four men will cut a *picadura* four feet wide through three-quarters of a mile of forest in a day. A farm abandoned for a year shows no sign of cultivation through the thicket that springs up, and in two years the very farm-house itself disappears. It is a land of tropic storms, of six months of rain and six months of dry weather; its inhabitants are a few half-civilized tribes of Indians; its woods abound in every species of game; its soil has a capacity for every tropical cultivation. On the Pacific coast there is a wholly different climate, haciendas and villages diversify a landscape which opens out upon glorious views of the far-off Pacific, and peace and primitive prosperity mark it as a fit habitation for man. When the dream of Cortez is realized, and the portage is made, not for such light craft as he built on the lake of Tezcoco, but for the monster ships which now interchange the grain of California and the silks and teas of Cathay and Zipangu with the productions of civilized Europe, two statues should crown the summit of the pass—one of the great conquistadors of the sixteenth century, and one of the modern American citizens whose genius has shown itself not less daring in the paths of peace.

PART III

Choosing the Route

The collapse of the De Lesseps enterprise in the late 1880s clearly demonstrated to policymakers, engineers, entrepreneurs, and business people the extreme complexity of the Central American canal project. Ferdinand de Lesseps, who had designed and built the Suez Canal project in the 1870s, founded the Universal Inter-Oceanic Canal Company of Panama after obtaining a concession from the government at Bogotá. That company went bankrupt in 1889 due to poor administration, yellow fever that killed about 40,000 workers, and massive fraud, graft, and corruption. Part of the problem, of course, was technological in that de Lesseps and others used the same assumptions that had guided their construction of the Suez Canal to work at Panama; but the mountainous, swampy Panama jungle was far more of a challenge than the sandy, flat desert of Egypt. Approximately 40 percent of the canal had been dug by 1889,[1] leaving investors and policymakers, in the United States and Europe, wondering about the future of the canal project.

A series of critical historical circumstances, all occurring in the 1890s, helped the United States move on the canal question. Much had been learned from the French fiasco and the great economic depression of 1893, together with Captain Mahan's forceful writing on the need for a two-ocean navy. In addition, the "acquisition" of Puerto Rico, Guam, the city and Harbor of Manila in the Philippines, and Cuba after America's 1898 war with Spain, Cuba, and the Philippines represented a rapid, unequivocal march toward Empire.[2] All of these factors strengthened the hand of those who wanted to see a canal built, financed, and controlled by the United States. One of those people was Theodore Roosevelt, who assumed the presidency of the United States in September 1901 after an anarchist assassinated President McKinley.

Roosevelt, who had been secretary of the navy and vice president, played a pivotal role in the Cuba campaign and moved quickly to ensure construction of a canal. The first step was to abrogate the inconvenient Clayton-Bulwer Treaty of 1850 and that was accomplished via signing of the Hay-Pauncefote Treaty with England, allowing the United States to construct and fortify, on its own, the canal. The next step was to secure, from the French, the concession and machinery that they had left behind in Panama. With the help of Philippe Buneau-Varilla, agent of the bankrupt French Canal Company and a man who stood to make a hefty profit from the sale of the French concession, the French sold everything to the United States for 40 million dollars.

Choosing the route for the canal was facilitated, of course, by the work carried out by the French in the 1880s and new discoveries concerning yellow fever and malaria. American medical doctors in Cuba, building on the work of the Cuban Carlos Finlay, discovered treatments for both diseases and worked energetically to protect humans from the mosquito. Still, thousands died of exhaustion, heat stroke, malaria, and yellow fever during the early days of the "second" phase of constructing a canal through Panama, the American phase, which lasted from 1904 to 1914.

The five chapters in this part of the book deal with the specific problem associated with constructing the canal from the perspective of the United States. They span a fifty-two-year period, and, taken together, present an ongoing dialogue of interest, intrigue, and advances in terms of U.S. thought on the question of the canal. The first chapter, "Short Cuts across the Globe" from 1850, is an early call for the United States to built a canal through Panama. The author describes Panama as an "imperfect civilization" and states that the canal would bring to the world "concord, prosperity and peace." The author claims that constructing a canal would be "easy" and cites the German naturalist Alexander von Humboldt whose own observations on the canal question, made early in the nineteenth century, were far from conclusive.

The final four chapters cover a four-year period, from 1898 to 1902—the critical period in terms of changing political circumstances in the United States and abroad and a renewed, energetic interest in constructing an interoceanic canal. The Honorable David Turpie debates the problems associated with financing a canal in his 1898 article, "Projects for an Isthmian Canal." He focuses on the many "schemes" that had been advanced as legitimate projects; the author clearly insists on the need of a canal, under American control, and favors the route through Nicaragua. He concludes, though, that the question of financing and constructing any canal in Central America needs to be thoroughly and carefully studied. The technical problems and history of the canal are discussed, in great detail, in Col. William Ludlow's essay from 1898 titled "The Trans-Isthmian Canal Problem." The essay is a thorough overview of the many ideas, proposals, and projects advanced in the past with a clear focus on the difficulty inherent in committing to such a massive project. The chapter should be compared to the first chapter in this part to help the reader appreciate the distance traveled, in terms of technical knowledge and the understanding gained by failed attempts, over a forty-eight-year period.

Henry L. Abbot provides an excellent, clear summary by way of comparison of the Panama and Nicaragua routes. It should be remembered that in December 1900—when this essay was published—the Nicaragua route was very much "on the table" and serious discussion still focused on the benefits of a Nicaragua route. Panama was viewed as tremendously complicated due to political considerations (how should we negotiate with Colombia?), the density and complexity of the Panama jungle, and the proven failure of the French to overcome the daunting power of nature. The chapter titled "The Tropical Renaissance" focuses, briefly, on how humankind had overcome tropical diseases via scientific discovery, control of certain species of mosquito, drainage of swamps, and taking care to eliminate stagnant water. The tropics had, in effect, been conquered and people should not be afraid to venture there. The author states, "with healthier existence made possible in substantially all parts of the tropics, the development of an advanced civilization there should be as practicable as it has been in many northern localities." Civilization could be brought to the tropics, and, though the essay in question does not deal directly with the Panama Canal, the implications were clear: science has conquered the diseases of the tropics, and now a higher form of civilization could be brought to the tropics and could, perhaps, even flourish there.

Choosing a route for construction of the interoceanic canal was in no way a simple matter. The process of "choosing" involved political, military, scientific, geographic, and geological questions, and it would take decades to sort through all of the data, scientific reports, reports of travelers, and political considerations. Theodore Roosevelt's unexpected rise to the presidency in 1901 proved to be a decisive factor in the construction of the canal, but a long, complex history of interest, travel, and debate on where and how to construct such a canal preceded Roosevelt by decades. A complex, international web of information and intrigue led, finally, in 1903 to construction of a canal by the United States, financed by the United States, and controlled by the United States. U.S. domination of the Canal Zone would last from November 1903 through December 31, 1999, which is when the zone was officially turned over to the government of Panama.

Notes

1. See Helen Miller Bailey and Abraham P. Nasatir, *Latin America: The Development of Its Civilization*, 2nd ed. Englewood Cliffs, N.J.: Prentice-Hall, Inc. 1968, pp. 675-677.
2. See Charles Sellers and Henry May, *A Synopsis of American History*, 2nd ed., Chicago: Rand McNally & Company, 1969, pp. 272-280.

8

Short Cuts across the Globe*

This early call for construction of a canal makes the work seem almost simple and straightforward. Why, posits the article, have we not constructed a canal of twenty-eight miles which would prevent a journey of eight thousand miles around the Cape Horn in order to move from one U.S. coast to the other? Two factors, of course, help explain this sudden emphasis on the need for a canal: the conclusion of the Mexican-American war in 1848 which added west coast ports to the U.S. nation, and the discovery of gold in California in 1849. The author suggests Nicaragua as another potential site for construction of a canal, and points to the growing commercial benefits of a canal, as well as the resultant "concord, prosperity and peace" offered by "closer communion" with distant neighbors.

To a person who wishes to sail for California an inspection of the map of the world reveals a provoking peculiarity. The Atlantic Ocean—the highway of the globe—being separated from the Pacific by the great western continent, it is impossible to sail to the opposite coasts without going thousands of miles out of his way; for he must double Cape Horn. Yet a closer inspection of the map will discover that but for one little barrier of land, which is in size but as a grain of sand to the bed of an ocean, the passage would be direct. Were it not for that small neck of land, the Isthmus of Panama (which narrows in one place to twenty-eight miles) he might save a voyage of from six to eight thousand miles, and pass at once into the Pacific Ocean. Again, if his desires tend toward the

*From *Household Words*.

East, he perceives that but for the Isthmus of Suez, he would not be obliged to double the Cape of Good Hope. The eastern difficulty has been partially obviated by the overland route opened up by the ill-rewarded Waghorn. The western barrier has yet to be broken through.

Now that we can shake hands with Brother Jonathan in twelve days by means of weekly steamers; travel from one end of Great Britain to another, or from the Hudson to the Ohio, as fast as the wind, and make our words dance to distant friends upon the magic tight wire a great deal faster—now that the European and Columbian Saxon is spreading his children more or less over all the known habitable world: it seems extraordinary that the simple expedient of opening a twenty-eight mile passage between the Pacific and Atlantic Oceans, to save a dangerous voyage of some eight thousand miles, has not been already achieved. In this age of enterprise that so simple a remedy for so great an evil should not have been applied appears astonishing. Nay, we ought to feel some shame when we reflect that evidences in the neighborhood of both isthmuses exist of such junction having existed, in what we are pleased to designate "barbarous" ages.

Does nature present insurmountable engineering difficulties to the Panama scheme? By no means: for after the Croton aqueduct, our own railway tunneling, and the Britannia tubular bridge, engineering difficulties have become obsolete. Are the levels of the Pacific and the Gulf of Mexico, which should be joined, so different, that if one were admitted the fall would inundate the surrounding country? Not at all. Hear Humboldt on these points.

Forty years ago he declared it to be his firm opinion that "the Isthmus of Panama is suited to the formation of an oceanic canal—one with fewer sluices than the Caledonian Canal—capable of affording an unimpeded passage, at all seasons of the year, to vessels of that class which sail between New York and Liverpool, and between Chili and California." In the recent edition of his "Views of Nature," he "sees no reason to alter the views he has always entertained on this subject." Engineers, both British and American, have confirmed this opinion by actual survey. As, then, combination of British skill, capital, and energy, with that of the most "go-ahead" people upon earth, have been dormant, whence the secret of the delay? The answer at once allays astonishment: Till the present time, the speculation would not have "paid."

Large works of this nature, while they create an inconceivable development of commerce, must have a certain amount of a trading population to begin upon. A gold-beater can cover the effigy of a man on horseback with a sovereign; but he must have the sovereign first. It was not merely because the full power of the iron rail to facilitate the transition of heavy burdens had not been estimated, and because no Stephenson had constructed a Rocket engine, that a railway with steam locomotives was not made from London to Liverpool before 1836. Until the intermediate traffic between these termini had swelled to a sufficient amount in quantity and value to bear reimbursement for establishing such a mode of conveyance, its execution would have been impossible, even though men had known how to set about it.

What has been the condition of the countries under consideration? In 1839, the entire population of the tropical American isthmus, in the states of Central America and New Grenada did not exceed three millions. The number of the inhabitants of pure European descent did not exceed one hundred thousand. It was only among this inconsiderable fraction that any thing like wealth, intelligence, and enterprise, akin to that of Europe, was to be found; the rest were poor and ignorant aboriginals and mixed races, in a state of scarcely semi-civilization. Through out this thinly-peopled and poverty-stricken region, there was neither law nor government. In Stephens's Central America, may be found an amusing account of a hunt after a government, by a luckless American diplomatist, who had been sent to seek for one in Central America. A night wanderer running through bog and brake after a will-o-the-wisp, could not have encountered more perils, or in search of a more impalpable phantom. In short, there was nobody to trade with. To the south of the isthmus, along the Pacific coast of America, there was only one station to which merchants could resort with any fair prospect of gain—Valparaiso. Except Chili, all the Pacific states of South America were retrograding from a very imperfect civilization, under a succession of petty and aimless revolutions. To the north of the isthmus matters were little, if any thing better. Mexico had gone backward from the time of its revolution; and, at the best, its commerce in the Pacific had been confined to a yearly ship between Acapulco and the Philippines. Throughout California and Oregon, with the exception of a few European and half-breed members, there were none but savage aboriginal tribes. The Russian settlements in the far north had nothing but a paltry trade in furs with Kamschatka, that barely defrayed its own expenses. Neither was there any encouragement to make a short cut to the innumerable islands of the Pacific. The whole of Polynesia lay outside of the pale of civilization. In Tahiti, the Sandwich group, and the northern peninsula of New Zealand, missionaries had barely sowed the first seeds of morals and enlightenment. The limited commerce of China and the Eastern Archipelago was engrossed by Europe, and took the route of the Cape of Good Hope, with the exception of a few annual vessels that traded from the sea-board states of the North American Union to Valparaiso and Canton. The wool of New South Wales was but coming into notice, and found its way to England alone round the Cape of Good Hope. An American fleet of whalers scoured the Pacific, and adventurers of the same nation carried on a desultory and inconsiderable traffic in hides with California, in tortoise-shell and mother of pearl with the Polynesian Islands.

What, then, would have been the use of cutting a canal, through which there would not have passed five ships in a twelve mouth? But twenty years have worked a wondrous revolution in the state and prospects of these regions.

The traffic of Chili has received a large development, and the stability of its institutions has been fairly tried. The resources of Costa Rica, the population of which is mainly of European race, is steadily advancing. American citizens have founded a state in Oregon. The Sandwich Islands have become for all practical purposes an American colony. The trade with China—to which the proposed canal would open a convenient avenue by a western instead of the present eastern route—is no longer restricted to the Canton river, but is open to all nations as far north as the Yang-tse-Kiang. The navigation of the Amur has been opened to the Russians by a treaty, and cannot long remain closed against the English and American settlers between Mexico and the Russian settlements in America. Tahiti has become a kind of commercial emporium. The English settlements in Australia and New Zealand have opened a direct trade with the Indian Archipelago and China. The permanent settlements of intelligent and enterprising Anglo-Americans and English in Polynesia, and on the eastern and western shores of the Pacific, have proved so many *depots* for the adventurous traders with its innumerable islands, and for the spermaceti whalers. Then the last, but greatest addition of all, is California: a name in the world of commerce and enterprise to conjure with. There gold is to be had for fetching. Gold, the main-spring of commercial activity, the reward of toil—for which men are ready to risk life, to endure every sort of privation; sometimes, alas! to sacrifice every virtue; one most especially, and that is patience. They will away with her now.

Till the discovery of the new gold country how contentedly they dawdled round Cape Horn creeping down one coast, and up another: but now such delay is not to be thought of. Already, indeed, Panama has become the seat of a great, increasing, and perennial transit trade. This cannot fail to augment the settled population of the region, its wealth and intelligence. Upon these facts we rest the conviction that the time has arrived for realizing the project of a ship canal there or in the near neighborhood.

That a ship canal, and not a railway, is what is first wanted (for very soon there will be both), must be obvious to all acquainted with the practical details of commerce. The delay and expense to which merchants are subjected, when obliged to "break bulk" repeatedly between the port whence they sail and that of their destination, is extreme. The waste and spoiling of goods, the cost of the operation, are also heavy drawbacks, and to these they are subject by the stormy passage round Cape Horn.

Two points present themselves offering great facilities for the execution of a ship canal. The one is in the immediate vicinity of Panama, where the many imperfect observations which have hitherto been made, are yet sufficient to leave no doubt that, as the distance is comparatively short, the summit levels are inconsiderable, and the supply of water ample. The other is some distance to the northward. The isthmus is there broader, but is in part occupied by the large and deep fresh-water lakes of Nicaragua and Managua. The lake of Nicaragua communicates with the Atlantic by a copious river, which may either be rendered navigable, or be made the source of supply for a side canal. The space between the two lakes is of inconsiderable extent, and presents no great engineering difficulties. The elevation of the lake of Managua above the Pacific is inconsiderable; there is no hill range between it and the gulf of Canchagua; and Captain Sir Edward Belcher carried his surveying ship *Sulphur* sixty miles up the Estero Real, which rises near the lake, and falls into the gulf. The line of the Panama canal presents, as Humboldt remarks, facilities equal to those of the line of the Caledonian canal. The Nicaragua line is not more difficult than that of the canal of Languedoc, a work executed between 1660 and 1682, at a time when the commerce to be expedited by it did not exceed—it is equaled—that which will find its way across the Isthmus; when great part of the maritime country was as thinly inhabited by as poor a population as the Isthmus now is; and when the last subsiding storms of civil war, and the dragonnades of Louis XI, unsettled men's minds, and made person and property insecure.

The cosmopolitan effects of such an undertaking, if prosecuted to a successful close, it is impossible even approximately to estimate. The acceleration it will communicate to the already rapid progress of civilization in the Pacific is obvious. And no less obvious are the beneficial effects it will have upon the mutual relations of civilized states, seeing that the recognition of the independence and neutrality in times of general war of the canal and the region through which it passes, is indispensable to its establishment.

We have dwelt principally on the commercial, the economical considerations of the enterprise, for they are what must render it possible. But the friends of Christian missions, and the advocates of universal peace among nations, have yet a deeper interest in it. In the words used by Prince Albert at the dinner at the Mansion House respecting the forthcoming great exhibition of arts and industry, "Nobody who has paid any attention to the particular features of our present era, will doubt for a moment that we are living at a period of most wonderful transition, which tends rapidly to accomplish that great end—to which, indeed, all history points—the realization of the unity of mankind. Not a unity which breaks down the limits and levels the peculiar characteristics of the different nations of the earth, but rather a unity the result and product of those very national varieties and antagonistic qualities. The distances which separated the different nations and parts of the globe are gradually vanishing before the achievements of modern invention, and we can traverse them with incredible speed; the languages of all nations are known, and their acquirements placed within the reach of every body; thought is communicated with the rapidity, and even by the power of lightning."

Every short cut across the globe brings man in closer communion with his distant brotherhood, and results in concord, prosperity, and peace.

9

Projects for an Isthmian Canal

David Turpie

This article deals with the financing and planning for a Nicaragua canal. The author challenges the reports and figures of a "Maritime Canal Company," calling the company's desire to secure concessions to construct a canal little more than a "scheme." The author notes the importance of constructing an interoceanic canal, but states that it should be commissioned only after thoughtful deliberation with funds being furnished exclusively by the U.S. government. With complete U.S. government financing, the world would be given "an American canal under American control."

All the commercial countries of the civilized world have for more than a century heartily favored the construction of a navigable waterway across the Central American isthmus. There is not a member of any government or legislative assembly in Christendom who has ever entertained or declared any sort of opposition or hostility to that enterprise. The execution of such a design has been the desire of all nations, often attempted, anxiously waited for, baffled only by the extreme difficulty of its accomplishment.

Various routes have been at different times suggested and explored for a ship-canal across the isthmus, but the two most prominent thus far in the history of the undertaking are those by the way of Lake Nicaragua and Panama. A canal by the way of Lake Nicaragua has always been favored by the government of the United States, for the reason that it would be nearer to our great coast-lines on the Atlantic and Pacific, and also that as compared with different routes it seems to be quite as practicable, and perhaps even attended with somewhat less difficulty than any other.

There is nothing new in the project of the Nicaragua canal, in the concessions made to promoters by the two governments through whose territory it runs, in the interest taken therein by the people of the United States, or in the chief problem to be solved in its construction. Indeed the project is a very old one. Before the existence of the present republics of Central America, and while the country traversed by the route was yet under the dominion of the Spanish crown, this canal route had attracted marked attention, had become the subject of careful survey and reconnaissance with a view to its cost and feasibility. In 1781 an exploration and survey of this route was made by Manuel Galisteo, under the authority of the Spanish government. This was followed by an order and decree of the Spanish Cortes for the construction of the canal, but the enterprise was subsequently abandoned. After this successive concessions were made to Danes, Englishmen, Frenchmen, and others, followed by surveys and examinations of the route made with more or less precision and expenditure; but no further action was taken by the parties interested. As early as 1826 Governor DeWitt Clinton, of New York, so justly celebrated for his achievements in the building of canals, caused a full survey of this same route to be made for himself and his associates, but upon the report being filed, no further action was taken. In 1851-52 a survey and estimate of the cost of a canal by the Nicaragua route was made by Colonel O. W. Childs, of Philadelphia, for Cornelius Vanderbilt, of New York, and his associates. This survey was made at great expense of time and money, and is conceded to have fully conformed to every requirement of engineering science. The persons interested therein, Vanderbilt and his associates, were at that time largely engaged in isthmian transportation and commerce. They were men of abundant wealth and resources. When the report and estimate were submitted, no further steps were taken in the enterprise.

General Grant, when President of the United States, gravely impressed with the importance of this proposed work, and always very favorable to the Nicaragua route, recommended to Congress the appointment of a commission to make an inspection and examination of the same. This commission was duly selected, performed the duty assigned to it, and made its report, together with an estimate of the cost of the construction. This estimate, provisional in its character, placed the necessary expenditure for the building and completion of such canal by the Nicaragua route at $140,000,000. After this report, which was made November 18, 1874, nothing further was done by President Grant or by Congress in the premises.

This brief account of failed and suspended projects for the construction of the canal by the Nicaragua route very fully discloses the reasons for the extreme care and caution which have been since used by Congress and the government of the United States in dealing with this subject.

The chief problem, the main design, of all these surveys and explorations has been one and the same. It is that of making much the longest part of the voyage through the navigable portion of Lake Nicaragua and the San Juan River, and then to use and control the waters of the lake and the adjacent streams so that they may be safely and permanently navigated as a canal for the remaining distance westward to the Pacific and eastward to the Atlantic, thus connecting the two oceans.

The whole length of the proposed line of transit, from Greytown on the Atlantic to Brito, the Pacific terminal, is 169½ miles. Of this distance 133 miles is made by the use of the lake and of a part of the San Juan River. The canal is to be made by excavation, 14½ miles on the Atlantic side, and about 12 miles on the Pacific side, so that the canal proper is only of the length of about 26½ miles.

The inquiry may be made, as the San Juan River is to be used in part for canal navigation on this route, why may it not be used for the whole distance from Lake Nicaragua to the Atlantic? The answer is that the San Juan River runs through a region of country where the average rainfall is 275 inches annually, sometimes as much as 300 inches. The consequence is that this stream with its tributaries, swollen by enormous tropical rains during the wet season, becomes, as it approaches the ocean, uncontrollable. The San Juan River, after leaving the high-lands around the lake, sometimes chooses one course and sometimes another in its flow to the sea, frequently leaves its banks and submerges the whole tract of land lying between the foothills and ocean with its flooded waters. No engineer has ever advised the prolongation of the line of a ship-canal by this river to the sea. The forces of nature have here placed in the way obstacles so irresistible that no amount of skill, of labor, or of expenditure has been deemed adequate to their removal.

The Suez Canal is about 100 miles in length, and cost one million dollars per mile for its construction. The Corinth Canal is 4 miles in length, and cost completed, with its approaches, one million per mile. The proposed Nicaragua canal will cost per mile with its terminals and approaches, certainly not less and probably more than the sum named. The canals of Suez and Corinth are real maritime canals, built without locks, upon the sea-level. The one, that of Corinth, is situated in the temperate zone, where the rainfall is 37 or 40 inches per annum. The other, that of Suez, is located in a region without rain. Neither of these is threatened in its course by streams liable to sudden and perilous floods, so common in the tropical region of Central America. These two great works afford no real parallel to the Nicaragua project, either as to cost or feasibility. The one work parallel to this undertaking is very near, very like it, both in place and circumstance; it is that of the Panama canal across the Isthmus of Darien. This canal has been in process of construction now for many years. The route is about 46 miles long. Two hundred and forty millions of dollars have been thus far expended in the enterprise without success, and hitherto without any return. A large force is yet at work upon the Panama canal, and since the De Lesseps failure the new organization is hopefully and energetically engaged in its prosecution. We do not know what may be the result. No friend of mankind can wish that it should fail. The whole world would rejoice at its completion; yet such success would furnish, so far as mere pecuniary profits are concerned, a strong competing rival to the Nicaragua route for the tolls and tonnage of maritime commerce.

It is proper to say that the Panama Canal Company has always been, and yet is, a private corporation. It is not a government work, and no congress or parliament has ever appropriated a dollar or pledged the public credit in any way in aid of the enterprise.

The most recent attempt to exploit the project of a canal by the Nicaragua route has been made by a corporation styled the Maritime Canal Company of Nicaragua. It began, as others before it had begun, by obtaining concessions from the two Central American republics which own the territory passed through by the line of the projected canal, Costa Rica and Nicaragua. These concessions bear date April 12, 1887. They allowed ten years for the building of the canal, and the Nicaragua concession expired, by its own terms, on the 12th day of April, 1897.*

The company, in accordance with the provisions of the concession, for the purpose of raising funds for the prosecution of its work, advertised proposals for subscriptions to its capital stock in London, Paris, and New York, inviting the people of all nations to participate.

No subscriptions followed. The initial strength and credit of the undertaking upon which large expectations had been founded produced no fruits. The very great, almost insurmountable natural obstacles to the success of the work were as well known at that time as they are today. The project as a financial investment had been blacklisted upon every exchange and market of both Europe and America for fifty years before. Capitalists had no confidence in the company, or in its plan of execution. The movement for stock subscriptions was a total failure. The company was left without money or credit, just as it had been in the beginning.

There had been incorporated and organized about the same time in the State of Colorado what is known as the Nicaragua Canal Construction Company, composed, as stated in the Senate debate upon the subject, "of substantially the same *personnel* as the principal company." This secondary company, a sort of tender to its chief, acting under large promises and imposing prospects of making lucrative profits out of the construction of the work, and out of the contracts and subcontracts incident thereto, sold or disposed of some of its stocks or bonds, and in various ways raised some moneys for its use. This Construction Company bought and removed to Greytown, the place of its operations, quanti-

---

*The full text of these concessions may be found in Report 1142, 2d Session, 52d Congress, pages 110 and 134.

ties of machinery and materials, built a wooden dock or sea-wall on the site of the proposed harbor at Greytown, and in 1891 had excavated about one mile of the canal, extending from the outer line of the proposed harbor towards the foothills in the direction of Lake Nicaragua. Having done this much, the Nicaragua Canal Construction Company went into the hands of a receiver. Its tangible property at Greytown was sold there under legal process, its paper assets were sold at marshal's sale in the city of New York, and its condition is that of utter bankruptcy and insolvency; but it is yet in existence, awaiting its share of an anticipated Congressional subsidy. After this failure of the Canal Construction Company the work on the canal ceased; it has never been resumed. The last work was done in 1891.

The Maritime Canal Company of Nicaragua transferred its attention to another field of operation. Like Governor Clinton, Vanderbilt, and its other predecessors, it abandoned the work on its canal scheme; but, unlike them, it came to Congress for an appropriation, first of seventy millions, then of one hundred millions, to be expended by it in the enterprise.

The Maritime Canal Company of Nicaragua had been incorporated by an act of Congress on the 28th day of February, 1889. One of the provisions of its charter is as follows:

> Provided, however, That nothing in this act contained shall be so construed as to commit the United States to any pecuniary liability whatever for or on account of said company; nor shall the United States be held in any wise liable or responsible in any form or by any implication for any debt or liability in any form which said company may incur, nor be held as guaranteeing any engagement or contract of said company, or as having assumed, by virtue of this act, any responsibility for the acts or proceedings of said company in any foreign country, or contracts or engagements entered into in the United States.

This corporation had publicly proclaimed that it wanted and needed neither public credit nor money from the government; that it had abundant funds and resources to make the work an assured success; that all it wished was a charter from Congress; but, in direct violation of this provision in its own charter, it now approached Congress for immediate pecuniary aid. Under these strange circumstances it became the duty of Congress to make a somewhat careful examination of the claims of the company, of its concession, of the practicability and probable cost of the work upon the line adopted by it. The company had submitted and published its report, containing in detail the profile of its scheme arranged in separate divisions, with the estimated cost of each. In an analysis of this report, during a prolonged debate thereon in the Senate of the United States, it was disclosed that many of the items of the work plainly required by the terms of the company's concession, such as the harbor and light-house at San Carlos, the eastern lake terminal of the canal, the harbor and light-house at Lajas, the western lake terminal of the canal—works of main importance to the safety of canal navigation—had been wholly omitted in the company's estimate. Others of equal importance had been undervalued as to their cost; and as to other items, like that of the Tipitapa canal, connecting Lake Managua with Lake Nicaragua, a waterway required to be built by the terms of the concession within three years of the date of the same, and which should have been completed in that time, no survey or examination had been made, and the estimate of its cost was wholly conjectural.

What added largely to the distrust and suspicion of the company's plan and estimate was the fact that the same had been submitted to a committee of skilled experts in civil engineering for examination and approval. This committee met in New York city, and after careful inspection of the maps and profiles of the line adopted by the company, of the specimens of the rock, earth, and other materials furnished by such borings as the company had made on the route of its survey, filed a written report,* making very large and material increases in the estimated cost of the work. This committee placed the total cost of the company's scheme at eighty-seven millions of dollars, being an excess of twenty-two millions over the company's estimate. And as to the practicability of the company's line of construction, the committee closes its written report, of date May 9, 1889, with language of such guarded significance as to fall somewhat short of approval. The summary of their opinion is in these words:

> In conclusion we think it proper to express our opinion that the exploration and studies of the region have been sufficient to warrant the conclusion that unless hindered by obstacles or sinister influences, such as would, if permitted to weigh, for-bid the success of all ventures, this enterprise is full of promise.

This commendation had in it such felicitous ambiguity of expression as to give pause to any hasty consideration of the company's project. Congress adhered to its former action, and did not grant any subsidy to the company. In deference, however, to the character of the enterprise, and to the interests of our sister Central American republics, a law was passed appropriating a sum of money and authorizing the appointment of a commission of three engineers—one from the army, one from the navy, and one from civil life—to make an inspection of the line and route of the proposed Nicaragua canal as laid out by the company, and especially to make a detailed estimate of the cost of execution. This commission went personally to the site and line of the canal route. They made a skilful and careful examination of the line, a particular calculation by itemized sections of the cost of completion, returned home, finished their report, and filed it on the 7th day of February, 1896.

---

*See Report No. 331, 2d Session, 53d Congress, page 147.

This report by the government board of engineers, compared with the report of the engineers of the company, became the subject of quite animated discussion and of special notice in the Senate in the winter of 1897, a bill being then pending, the third of its kind, to subsidize the Maritime Canal Company to the amount of one hundred millions of dollars. All were surprised by the very great differences appearing between the estimates of the cost of construction by the government board and those made by the engineers of the company. A few of these will be noted with their comparisons.*

The estimate of the government board for the construction and completion of the harbor at Greytown, the entrance of the proposed canal on the Atlantic side, is $4,480,000. The estimate of the Maritime Canal Company's engineers for the same work is $2,151,000. The estimate of the government board of engineers for building and completing the harbor at Brito, the Pacific terminal of the canal, is $4,398,000. The estimate of the company for this work is $1,920,000. The estimate of the government board for the section of the work called the Nicaragua Division, which relates to the extension of the canal from the shore line of the two lake terminals at San Carlos and Lajas to the deep-water line, is $3,907,000. The company's estimate for the same work is $1,969,000. The same discrepancy appears in the two estimates for the Ochoa Dam. This is a dam to be built across the San Juan River at the place where the canal leaves the channel of that stream and passes, by a series of locks of the largest lift and dimensions, from the summit level of the lake and river to the level of the sea on the Atlantic side. This dam is the key to the whole eastern division of the canal. On its permanence, stability, and preservation the safety of the locks and of the line of navigation depends. The estimate of the government board for the Ochoa Dam is $4,000,000; that of the company is $977,000—less than one million.

The La Flor Dam is a structure upon the line of the proposed canal, located in the western division, between the lake and the Pacific, and, like the Ochoa Dam in the eastern, is the key to the western division. It is, in the plan of the company, an embankment 70 feet high and 1,800 feet long, intended to enclose the waters of the streams adjacent in an immense basin, or reservoir, for use in canal navigation, to be let down by a series of locks to the sea-level of the Pacific Ocean at Brito.

The estimate of the company for the La Flor Dam is $1,306,670. The government board decline to make any estimate for this work; they say it is wholly impracticable; they select and recommend another route for this part of the line, one which they say is quite safe, practicable, and capable of execution, and submit their estimate of its cost in their report.

---

*The report of the government engineers is found in H.R. Doc. 279, 1st Session, 54th Congress.

One of the main parts of the canal route is known as the San Juan River Division. It covers a distance of about 69 miles, in which the channel of the San Juan River is to be used as a part of the canal. The San Juan River runs from Lake Nicaragua to the Caribbean Sea. It is a stream at its average stage in the dry season of the width of 800 feet, with an average channel depth of 10 feet. Between the place where it leaves the lake and the Ochoa Dam there are four principal rapids, with rock bottoms, and the cost was to be estimated of removing these obstructions, and making such excavation in the channel that it might have the proper depth of water for the intended ship-canal. Every part of this channel was easily accessible, susceptible of measurement by line and level, and the nature of the rock and other obstructions was subject to precise and scientific examination. The depth of the water was easily ascertainable, and the cost of re-moving the obstructions and deepening the channel was not a problem of difficult solution.

The estimate of the company for the expense of completion of this division is $1,975,000. The estimate of the government board is $14,866,000, a difference of more than $12,000,000. The estimate of the government board was made by engineers of approved skill, experience, and integrity, men wholly disinterested as to the scheme of the Maritime Canal Company, impartial in their judgment and calculations.

It is fair to assume that some mistakes, miscalculations, or underestimates of such an extensive design may have been made by the engineers of the company, but that these mistakes should have been so constant, so successive, and so large in amount seems to be more than can be charged to mere inadvertence. Such errors tax even credulity beyond endurance. The conclusion, upon a comparison of the two estimates, is almost irresistibly forced upon the reader that the Canal Company either intended to suppress the real cost of its undertaking, or that it took no great pains to ascertain and determine it.

That the estimates and calculations of the company are founded upon a very great reduction or suppression of the real expenditure of money needed for the construction of its work is plain. The explanation of its action in this regard is not so apparent. To summarize this state of affairs, the total estimate of the Canal Company for the construction and completion of the canal is $66,466,880. The estimate of the government board of engineers is $133,472,893, twice that of the company, and within $7,000,000 of the former estimate made by the commission appointed by President Grant in 1874.

These large discrepancies in the calculated expense of the proposed work put Congress upon its guard. Both Houses adjourned without any action upon the subsidy bill, and thus the paramount design of the company, which had been to obtain a large amount of cash or credit from the government of the United States, was again frustrated.

The bills introduced granting a loan of credit or subvention by the government of the United States to the Maritime Canal Company of Nicaragua did, it is true, provide for a mortgage and statutory lien, for a sinking-fund to be created from the net earnings of the canal when completed, to repay the loan to our government, or save it harmless from its guarantee of the company's bonds; but these same expressions, mortgage, statutory lien, net earnings, and sinking-fund had all been used before in the act granting subsidies to the Pacific Railway Company, and the memories of that transaction were so recent and unsavory that members of Congress were very loath to repeat an experiment so costly and unprofitable. To add $100,000,000 to the national debt to be expended in a foreign country upon a line of work wherein the company had itself made a total default appeared to be an investment even more doubtful and hazardous than that of the Pacific Railway bonds.

During the last days of the session of Congress in 1897, while the subsidy measure of the Maritime Canal Company was under consideration, a communication was received from the Secretary of State upon the subject, which instantly attracted great attention. This was a letter of protest from the Hon. J. D. Rodriguez, minister of the Greater Republic of Central America, to the government of the United States, of date January 22, 1897.*

The Greater Republic, recently formed by a joint convention between several of the Central American republics, now includes Nicaragua as one of its states. The Nicaragua canal route lies mainly within the territorial limits of Nicaragua. The letter of Minister Rodriguez is written in behalf of the rights and interests of Nicaragua, as set forth in the concession granted by it to the company. He charges that the provisions of the pending subsidy bill are at variance with the stipulations of the contract of April 12, 1887, between Nicaragua and the company, from which contract (the concession) the company derives its existence, and which is the basis of its enterprise. He cites the 8th article of the concession as providing "that the contract shall in no case be transferable to any foreign government, or foreign public power," and the 53d article, providing "that any contravention of this stipulation shall entail a forfeiture of the concession." He states that the subsidy bill effects a transfer of the concession to the United States, and that the inevitable result is the forfeiture of the concession. He shows that the 47th article of the concession, providing that the canal shall be located by the engineers of the company, two of whom shall be appointed by the government of Nicaragua, is violated by the provision of the bill "that the route of the canal shall be determined by engineers to be appointed by the President of the United States," and that an infraction of this provision is made, in article 53 of the concession, a cause of forfeiture of the contract. He states that under article 14 of the concession the company contracted to build, at its own expense, within the term of three years, reckoned from the time of the commencement of the work on the interoceanic canal, a navigable canal between Lake Managua and the navigable part of the Tipitapa River, that this time had expired long be-

*See Doc. 78, 2d Session, 54th Congress.

fore, but the company, notwithstanding the most earnest solicitation, had made no pretence of meeting that obligation, or of adjusting the damages which it ought to pay in order to be discharged therefrom.

Minister Rodriguez in this communication shows other violations of the concession by the company in very material parts of the same. He concludes with a practical suggestion of the greatest importance. He affirms that it is evident that the company is unable to raise the money to fulfil its contract unless the United States shall furnish it, and proposes that the two governments, relying upon the favorable disposition of the United States, shall come to a direct understanding upon the subject of the construction of the canal on the basis of a former treaty made between them, and endeavor to reach an arrangement with the Maritime Canal Company, so that it may renounce a concession whose conditions it is unable to fulfil.

Now this is precisely the course heretofore suggested by those who have been adverse to the subsidy scheme. There is surely no valid reason why, if our government is to furnish the funds for the construction of the canal, it should not also directly control and administer the same, in conjunction with the Central American governments interested, under a treaty with them concluded for that purpose.

There is certainly no reason why the government of the United States, in relation to the building, completion, and future operation of this great canal, should treat with a private corporation whose only claim to consideration rests in the total discredit and disaster which have accompanied its attempt in the execution of the work.

And it is to be especially noted that although the government of Nicaragua publicly charges the Maritime Canal Company with violations of the concession, and with inexcusable breaches of contract, yet neither of the Central American republics has made any opposition to the enterprise itself, or to the construction of the canal by our government.

A condition quite fortunate is thus shown, because it is not possible that any power could build or operate this ship-canal in the country of an unfriendly population. This work is not like that of Suez or Corinth. Those are canals built by excavation on the sea-level, as before stated. To destroy them would require the slow process of the excavation of another channel to drain away their waters, or the filling up of the present one in use; but the Nicaragua canal, with its double system of dams and locks, would be peculiarly sensitive and liable to injury, by either public or private enemies, as there are many places along the line at which an hour's work with the pick and shovel, to say nothing of the use of explosives, would let the water rapidly escape, and so wreck the whole system.

The commission appointed by President Cleveland, whose report has been before cited, expressly stated that the existing data are inadequate as a basis for estimating the cost of many of the structures along the line of the proposed ship-canal. They recommended an additional appropriation, and that eighteen months time, covering at least two dry seasons, be given for obtaining the necessary data for the formulation of a final estimate.

Congress, in accordance with this recommendation, on the 4th day of June, 1897, authorized the appointment of a commission of engineers to make another survey and estimate of the cost of construction, and to further examine as to the proper route, and as to the feasibility of the Nicaragua canal.*

This commission has since been appointed by President McKinley, and is now engaged in the performance of its duty. Our government is awaiting its report.

Three things are necessary to the consummation of this enterprise: First, funds to be furnished by the government of the United States. Second, the perfect amity and friendly co-operation of Nicaragua and Costa Rica in the work. Third, a reasonable assurance of its feasibility, and of the amount of money needed to construct and complete it.

The three republics could under such auspices thus give to the world an American canal under American control. It is a grave misconception, a disparagement of the dignity and grandeur of such a design, to suppose that its success is in any way dependent upon or necessarily related to the scheme of the Maritime Canal Company.

There may be many and potent reasons for the building of the Nicaragua ship-canal aside from those that would regard it only in the light of a commercial investment. In the voyage from New York to San Francisco it would save the long passage round Cape Horn. The Strait of Magellan would be removed thousands of miles toward the north; the two Americas would be united by closer commercial relations than ever before; but none of these considerations should induce our government, hastily or incautiously, to engage in a work of such magnitude. Vast national enterprises of this character are best preceded by the most careful preparation, by a thorough knowledge of the hindrances and impediments in the way of their achievement, and by an estimate as accurate as can be made, of the amount of expenditure necessary to their execution.

---

*See Act of June 4, 1897, page 55.

10

The Trans-Isthmian Canal Problem

William Ludlow

In 1898, the United States still believed that a canal through Nicaragua would be the best alternative over the Panama route. The financial embezzlement, the difficult tropical climate, and the enormous technical problems that resulted in the collapse of the canal company directed by Ferdinand de Lesseps provided more strength to those who argued for the Nicaragua route. This article is a detailed examination of the two options, and provides important information concerning all of the routes and the diverse projects proposed, from the sixteenth century, concerning the construction of an interoceanic canal through Central America.

Chimeras are long-lived, and their pursuit will continue to be a fruitful source of discovery while man has ideals and the will to realize them. The dream of a direct westward passage for ships from Europe to Asia led Columbus, four centuries ago, to the shores of a new continent, and the problem still engages the interest and attention of the world.

The Spaniards and Portuguese swarmed in the wake of the pioneer, and the isthmian coasts were industriously swept until, in 1536, the Gulf had been explored from Darien to Florida and the Pacific to the Gulf of California, and it became evident that nature had omitted to furnish a waterway. The question then resolved itself into finding a practicable site for a ship-canal. By 1551 enough was known to indicate three possible localities, viz., Tehuantepec, Nicaragua, and Panama; and the construction of a canal at Panama was formally authorized. But the Spanish power had begun to falter, and its waning energies were narrowed to guarding what it had and stifling new discoveries that rival powers might seize. Explorations were forbidden under penalty of death; and a long lethargy ensued.

The next adventurers were the buccaneers, mainly English, who fed on the Spanish traders in the seventeenth century, and conceived the idea of expediting their gains by direct attack upon the Spanish settlements where the booty was stored awaiting shipment. The Indians, hating their oppressors, piloted the Free-Bands to the Spanish quarters by routes known alone to them, and much valuable incidental information was thus gained.

The Spaniards were finally expelled after three centuries of barbarous misrule, having stamped an enduring distrust of strangers in the hearts of the natives, whose hostility has continued to be a serious obstacle to the exploration of the Isthmus.

With the present century a new era began in connection with the so-called republics formed in 1820-23 upon the debris of the Spanish rule.

In 1803 Humboldt had studied personally the physics of Central America, and retained until the end of his life an enthusiastic interest in the question of ship-transit. It was his belief, based on erroneous information, that the lowest depression would be found near the junction with South America, but his numerous letters and publications stimulated explorers and promoters to renewed struggles.

The alternatives at this time were to find a pass of such moderate elevation as could be overcome by hydraulic engineering, or boldly to tunnel through the Cordillera where the conditions should seem least unfavorable. Reconnaissances were multiplied, schemes industriously advertised, concessions from local governments secured, and thereon stock companies formed for the exploiting of the several routes advocated by their promoters.

But a singular fatality seemed to attend all these projects, each proving a phantasm when probed, while large sums of money were expended and numerous lives wasted in the repeated endeavor to confirm or correct the conflicting and fallacious statements. Too many of these schemes were based on misinformation, and no serious endeavor was made to secure authentic data.

The Isthmus was practically a wilderness, and its exploration invested with extraordinary difficulties. The tepid, saturated, and malarial atmosphere, the extensive swamps, the dense tropic jungles, the immense expanse of forest, the steepness and complexity of the hill ranges, the excessive downpour of rain, the frequency and violence of floods, the venom of serpents and insects, and the opposition of the natives, made investigation both arduous and perilous, and elaborate and costly preparation necessary for the attainment of reliable results. Most of the examinations were quite superficial, and even the more important little more than fairly good reconnaissances.

The newly constituted republics lent encouragement to these numerous schemes, and granted concessions with a free hand, finding therein a valuable source of revenue, which the prevalence of internal disorder rendered scanty and precarious through the regular channels.

In 1838 Salamon of Paris organized the Franco-Granadian Company, having procured a concession to build an open sea-level canal in the vicinity of Panama, substantially on the lines of De Lesseps's subsequent attempt. This scheme had for its basis the statement that a summit-level had been found only twelve meters above sea. Salamon's representations were so serious, and at the same time so difficult of acceptance, as an English engineer, Lloyd, had levelled across in 1827, that the French government, in 1843, sent an engineer, Garella, to investigate. The error in this case seems to have been the not unusual one of a displacement of the decimal point, as the least altitude of the divide was proved by Garella to be 120 meters instead of 12. His survey was the first endeavor to get authentic information for a canal project, and has constituted the basis of subsequent Panama schemes. Like others who preceded and followed him, he could not refrain from making elaborate plans and estimates for a combination lock canal and ship tunnel through the divide, although his surveys were mainly transit and level work, and did not include borings for geologic data, gaugings for volume of streams, floods and rainfall, and other necessary particulars.

In 1850 a Dr. Cullen of Dublin, a Fellow of the Royal Geographic Society, declared that he had crossed on foot several times between Caledonia Bay and the Gulf of San Miguel, and that the divide did not exceed 150 feet above sea.

This was a very taking project, as the two bays were regarded as favorable terminals, and Cullen's statement having been corroborated by the report and map of an English engineer, sent out from London to examine the route, an association was formed, containing important European names, with a capital of $75,000,000. This bubble had an extraordinary vitality, and was not fully pricked even after Lieutenant Strain, of the United States Navy, had wrecked his volunteer party and nearly lost his own life in 1854 in demonstrating that at no point of the divide could there be a less elevation than 1,000 feet. The association thereupon dissolved; but Cullen still had his concession, and later revived his project, which did not receive its quietus until the United States naval expedition in 1870 confirmed Strain's observation, and dissipated all idea of a waterway except by tunnel.

In matters of this nature there is no excuse for misinformation or guess-work. Explorations and preliminary surveys are, of course, indispensable, but for serious engineering projects competent engineers must be employed, and the field parties fully equipped to cover the entire range of conditions touching the work geologic, hydraulic, meteorological, and climatic as well as matters affecting the supply and renewal of labor and materials, work-shops, hospitals, transportation, landing and storage facilities, and other adjuncts of construction and maintenance—all of which must be known before the proposed engineering constructions can be properly conceived and specified, and the estimates of cost be even an approximation to the amounts required to execute them. In the case of the

Isthmus it happens that the natural conditions are exceptionally unfavorable, and, in the absence of similar work conducted elsewhere under like circumstances, data for comparison are lacking, and a corresponding uncertainty as to methods and cost is involved, even assuming the most mature investigation by capable and disinterested experts.

The entire region is volcanic; and has been subjected to tremendous convulsions—eruptive, seismic, and cataclysmal. Evidences of subterranean activity still exist, but over a century has elapsed since the last great outburst occurred, and there is reason to believe that the destructive forces of this nature, other than an occasional earthquake of no excessive severity, need not cause serious apprehension for the safety of engineering works.

The geology is in general chaotic, consisting largely of volcanic and igneous products and their derivatives, with variations due to submergence and glacial action. The result is that the materials to be encountered in excavation are of various degrees of solidification and resistance to pressure and moisture, ranging from solid to friable, with immense deposits of clay, and all so diversified and incoherent as to be full of surprises. The precise conditions at any given locality must therefore be ascertained.

The climate, of course, is tropical, which means, in this case, not an excessive temperature at any time, but a uniformly high one at all times, the thermometric range, for example, in the lower altitudes being from 70° to 90° Fahrenheit, and averaging day and night throughout the year between 73° and 86°. Near sea-level, therefore, it is perpetual summer; from 2,000 to 6,000 feet elevation, perpetual spring; above that, a moderate coolness; and at 10,000 feet or over there may be frost and a sprinkle of snow, which, however, does not lie. These conditions favor a wide range of natural products, which exist in great variety.

The rainfall follows the sun in its annual oscillations, north and south, causing two seasons, wet and dry, the latter being comparative only, and with marked local differences. The prevalent trade-winds, from east-northeast, are laden with moisture from the heated Caribbean, and deposit the greater part of it on the Atlantic slope. The precipitation is persistently and phenomenally heavy, varying, for example, from 10 or 12 feet in a year at Colon to 20 or 25 feet at Greytown, and diminishing to a third, more or less, of these amounts at Panama and Brito, the respective Pacific termini of the Panama and Nicaragua canal routes. Local rainfalls of a foot in a day, and three inches in a single hour, have been noted.

The Isthmian climate therefore presents a combination of atmospheric saturation with continuing high temperature that is as favorable to an immense and incessant activity of growth and decay in the vegetable kingdom as it is discouraging to human exertion. Prolonged labor, mental or physical, becomes exhausting, and the effective output is greatly reduced in comparison with what is common in cooler, drier, and more variable climates.

Minor organisms and bacteria swarm in the warm, moist atmosphere and soil, and fevers are common, varying from mild, yielding to treatment, to pernicious and swiftly fatal. Temperance in food and drink is essential.

These are all considerations that enter directly into questions of construction and cost, and must be taken into account in designing work, arranging for its execution, and computing the cost, on penalty of inviting disaster.

Needless to say that the United States evinced a continuing and lively interest in all the canal projects, and took means to keep informed as to the progress of the matter through diplomatic channels or special agencies. Investigations were ordered and valuable reports made from time to time. The gold discoveries in California in 1849 aroused a greater urgency for Isthmian transit, resulting in the procuring by Vanderbilt of a ship-canal concession from Nicaragua, the establishment of a steamboat route *via* the San Juan River and Lake Nicaragua, and thence by wagon to the Pacific, and the making of a survey and project for a canal over the same route by Colonel Childs in 1852.

The American concession for the Panama Railroad was also obtained, and the road built between 1850 and 1855. This was the first important construction on the Isthmus, and furnished clear indications of the contingencies involved in isthmian undertakings. Although carefully studied and intelligently conducted, with no specially difficult engineering features the work cost per mile four times the average cost in the United States, and the working force was recruited and maintained with great difficulty, by reason of the heavy mortality. The natives are neither apt nor willing for such work, and unacclimated Chinese and West Indian negroes had to be imported.

But this same period was one of activity in projecting and surveying the numerous Pacific railroad routes in the United States, and, the civil war intervening, public attention was diverted from canal projects until 1870, when an extended series of observations by United States naval expeditions was authorized, with the object of examining all the Isthmian routes that offered any probability of advantage, and eliminating the persistent uncertainties and discrepancies that characterized them all. These expeditions, while not equipped for making complete engineering projects, accomplished valuable results by covering nearly the entire field, demonstrating the impracticability of most of the schemes, and narrowing the consideration of the subject to the two or three that possessed any verity or merit.

The half-dozen routes in Darien were shown to be invested with grave difficulties; for example, the most favorable, viz., the Atrato-Napipi, involving 140 miles of river, 30 miles of canal, and a ship-tunnel through the Cordillera 3½ miles long. The Caledonian-San Miguel route, heretofore referred to, was hopeless; there was no supply of water for the summit-level, and a ship-tunnel would need to be 10 or 12 miles long. The route from San Blas Bay to Panama Bay, which had been investigated, at his own expense, by Mr. Kelly of New York, and advocated by him, was the shortest of all, 30 miles, and seemed to be the only possibility for a sea-level passage through the Isthmus, but the ship-tunnel would be 7 or 8 miles in length. It must be admitted that so long as a waterway open to the sky could be reasonably projected, the ship-tunnel project would not be likely to find favor with either mariners or investors, particularly in a region of known volcanic history and formidable possibilities.

At Tehuantepec the canal would be 144 miles long, with an elevation of 680 feet to overcome, and much doubt as to the possibility of supplying the summit-level.

There remained the rival projects of Panama and Nicaragua, both of which have had their earnest and persistent advocates. The United States naval expeditions examined these also, and the commission appointed by President Grant to sum up all the evidence that could be gathered on the subject reported in 1876 that, on the whole, the Nicaragua route presented the most advantageous features, both as to practicability and cost, taking occasion to indicate, however, that the estimates prepared in connection with the several projects were not based upon sufficiently definite and, accurate information to be reliable in such formidable work in such novel conditions.

The Panama project has claimed serious attention from the outset. With the exception of San Blas, it is the shortest; with the exception of Nicaragua, its summit-elevation is the least; and the natural harbors at each end are capacious, and can be made to accommodate the heaviest class of vessels.

By the construction of the Panama Railroad it gained the additional important advantages of rail transportation throughout its length, and of established lines of communication with foreign centres by sea from both ends.

The principal drawbacks are the heavy rainfall 10 to 12 feet at Colon—the heavy floods of the Chagres and the necessity of controlling them, and the evil repute of the vicinity for unhealthfulness. To these another formidable obstacle is added in the treacherous nature of the materials through which the cut has to be made, but this was not known until the excavations were actually begun in 1884.

The most moderate estimates that could be made of the cost of the work discouraged undertaking it, until the brilliant success of the Suez Canal, under De Lesseps, concentrated French interest on the project, and stimulated the expectation of a still more important conquest and even greater pecuniary rewards.

A concession was procured in 1877 for a French association by Lieutenant N. B. Wyse, of the French navy, and surveys were made covering four or five months of field-work, during which none of the several lines examined for comparison was actually carried through from sea to sea. On this slight basis, supplementing the prior examinations by Garella and others, elaborate plans and estimates were prepared, the principal one being for a tide-level canal from Colon to Panama *via* the valleys of the Chagres and Rio Grande. This project involved a ship-tunnel nearly five miles long, and was estimated at $95,000,000.

In 1879 an international conference was held at Paris, to which were submitted for consideration the Nicaragua, Panama, San Blas, and Atrato-Napipi

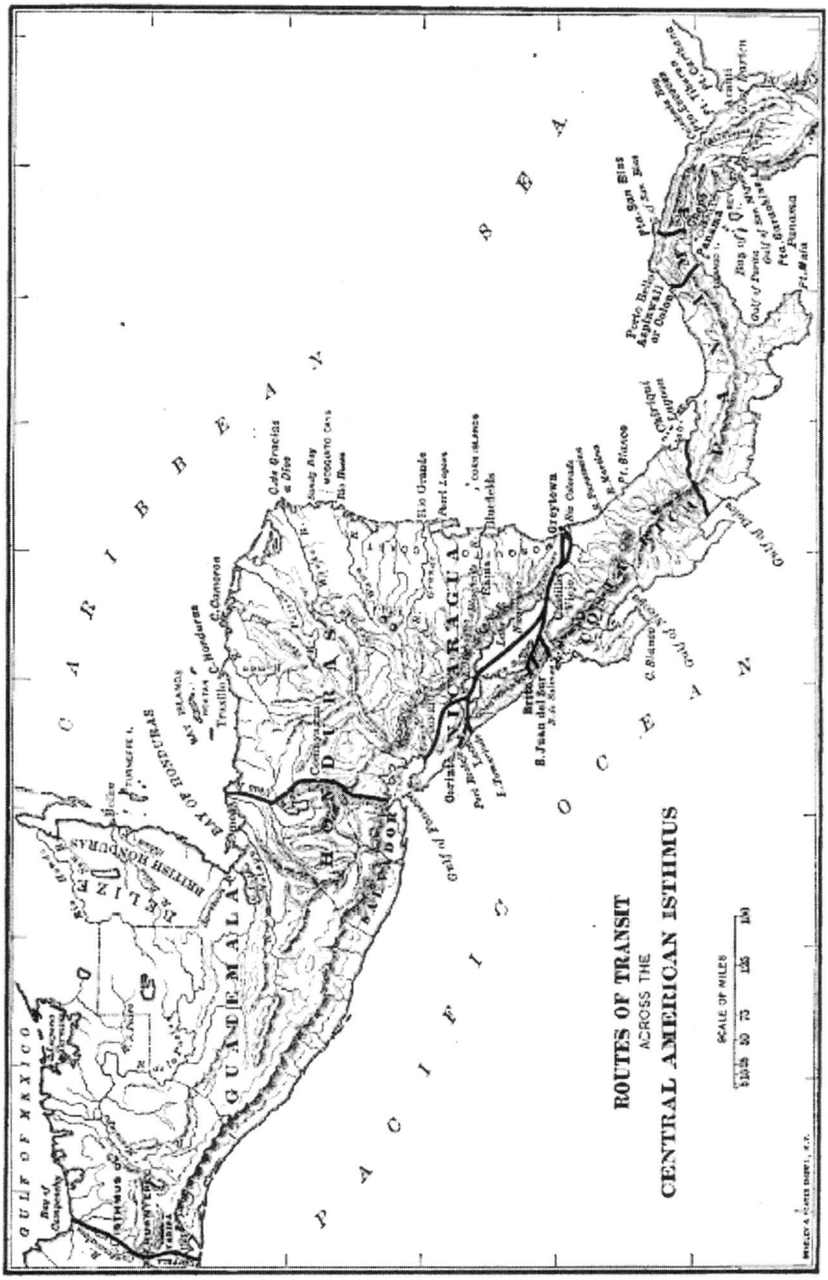

schemes. The project advanced by the Panama concessionaires was triumphantly adopted, after De Lesseps had secured the abolition of the tunnel and the substitution of an open cut throughout at the sea-level, by the declaration that nothing else would meet the requirements of commerce. The cost of the project as thus augmented, and including harbor improvements and 10 per cent for contingencies, was estimated in detail at $170,000,000, or, adding expenses of financing and other incidentals, an aggregate of $210,000,000.

The United States Commission, in 1876, in view of the meagre engineering data available and the uncertainties attending hydraulic constructions on so large a scale, adopted 100 per cent as the amount to be added to the detailed estimates to cover contingencies, and, in the light of subsequent events, it is shown that the French promoters would have been wise to adopt a similar course, and wiser still to have made a thorough research and study of their problem before inviting subscriptions and beginning work.

It is needless to follow in detail the history of this gigantic enterprise, that, at the time of its collapse in 1888, after five years of active prosecution, had absorbed a total expenditure of $300,000,000, with the work less than one-third done, the worst of it yet to do, and none of the serious problems, such as the control of the Chagres and the practicability of making the deep cut, even approximately solved.

The Isthmus was an orgy of reckless expenditure, and the millions poured in from Europe disappeared as if by magic, until at last the stream ran dry, and wholesale ruin ensued.

The *coup de grace* was delivered by the Culebra Mountain, through which the huge cut, ultimately intended to be 330 feet in depth, was in progress. The heterogeneous mass, whose unstable and treacherous constitution had not been investigated before attacking it, included clays of various kinds, some of them extremely plastic, and when the excavation had reached a comparatively early stage the south slope slipped gently forward and paralyzed the undertaking by a silent demonstration of its futility.

The fundamental error made by De Lesseps and his associates was in basing the Panama plans and estimates upon the most favorable results obtained in the Suez constructions, without making adequate or any allowance for the radically different conditions. Suez was merely 100 miles of level digging through sand, in a region where the rainfall is but an inch or two in a year, the climate comparatively cool and healthful, a large supply of native labor, and the mechanical resources of Europe at no great distance; but, notwithstanding these advantages, the work, planned on an estimate of $40,000,000, cost $110,000,000, on a reduced cross-section, before it was opened.

The physical conditions on the Isthmus are the precise reverse of those in Egypt, and the cost of every item of work was enormously greater. A material increase was inevitable, even with the most careful and economic management. The scarcity and diminished effectiveness of labor, losses from disease and sickness, the interference and burden of the heavy rainfall, would at least have doubled cost, and to these drawbacks were added political disturbances and local acts of violence, with a home administration of unparalleled extravagance.

The old company left behind it assets that have been reasonably computed as amounting to $60,000,000 or $70,000,000, including the ownership of the Panama Railroad, and estimating the actual value of the work done and the immense plant collected—much of it in readiness to use.

With this as a basis, and with a working capital of $12,000,000 or $15,000,000 restitution-money recovered from bankers, contractors, and others who had unlawfully obtained possession of it, a new company, with a total change of *personnel* and methods, has been for three years pursuing an extended system of engineering research into the particulars affecting construction and cost-boring, gauging, levelling, experimenting, and computing—with the purpose of effecting a thorough study, and making final plans and estimates, before again submitting the project to public consideration. At the same time a considerable amount of actual work has been done, as set forth in the annual printed reports, and a force of between 3,000 and 4,000 men been kept at work, mainly at the Culebra Pass, but with preparations for extending the work to other points. During 1897 a million and a quarter cubic yards of material were excavated, making a total for three years of over two and a half millions, and deepening the cut some 60 feet. At Panama a channel 26 or 28 feet deep has been dredged from the off-shore anchorage, 3 miles distant, to La Boca, the canal terminus; a basin, wharves, and store-houses have been constructed, and the railroad extended to the same terminal, to enable ships to discharge and take freight directly from the cars.

The canal design has been quite changed, and two projects are now under investigation. One involves a dam on the upper Chagres to store the floods, with a conduit of 10 miles thence to the summit-level of the canal, which is maintained by a dam at Bohio in the lower Chagres, about 15 miles from Colon, converting the middle Chagres into a large lake, the ascent to be made by five locks on each side, of 29½ feet each, making the summit-level about 147 feet above sea. A modification of this reduces the summit-level by a deeper cut through Culebra and uses four locks, and substitutes for the dam in the upper Chagres and the supply conduit, a dam at Gamboa, in the immediate vicinity of the canal.

The second project would still further reduce the summit-level to about 100 feet elevation, with a corresponding increase in the depth of excavation through the divide, and use three locks of 33 feet lift. If the investigations in progress show this to be practicable, a single great dam at Bohio would convert the middle Chagres into a lake of such capacity as to take care of the floods without assistance.

Pending the completion of the studies in the field, an engineering commission has been formed, to whom the finished plans and estimates are to be submitted for consideration and report; and if this commission, which, it may be stated, includes a distinguished American engineer, General Abbot, of the United States army, shall confirm the results of the latest examinations, and find the proposed constructions practicable and adequate, and the estimates sufficient, the project is to be made public, and endeavor made to secure the financial aid to carry the enterprise to a conclusion. The reports state that this is to be done during the present year.

The Nicaragua project is one that has long commanded the interest of the United States, and held the first place in the consideration of our people as free from the financial and other complications of the Panama route, presenting features of much advantage for construction and maintenance, and having the stamp of a specially American enterprise, the execution of which, it is generally thought, will effect valuable commercial and national results.

The physics of the route are unique. Near the northern borders of Nicaragua the Cordillera separates into two branches, one closely following the Pacific coast line, the other diverging towards the Caribbean, both with diminished elevations, and enclosing between them the broad valley occupied by Lake Nicaragua and the smaller Lake Managua, the former covering some 2,700 square miles, and the latter 500 or 600. The water-shed of the two includes about 12,000 square miles, the surplus drainage of which escapes from the southeast corner of the larger lake, forming a noble river, the San Juan, which has a course of 120 miles, with an average fall of about 10 inches to the mile, and discharges into the Caribbean through an extensive delta. During the rainy season the river has a powerful flow, and is navigable for light-draught steamers, but in the dry seasons it is obstructed by sand bars in the lower reaches, by several rapids of considerable extent, and by shallow channels in the upper reaches. There are several affluents, of which the chief is the San Carlos, draining the lofty ranges of Costa Rica to the southward, and joining the San Juan about 65 miles below the lake.

The surface elevation of the lake above the sea varies with the seasons with an indicated maximum range of 12 or 14 feet, and an average low stage of about 102 feet above mean sea-level. Its western shore is only 12 miles from the Pacific, and the height of the intervening divide, 154 feet above sea, is the lowest that has been discovered on the Isthmus. The region between the lake and the Pacific has been thoroughly surveyed, and there are no serious obstacles of any kind to the construction of a canal from the lake to Brito, which would complete the water-way between the two oceans, with a total length of 170 or 180 miles. The natural advantages of this route *via* the river and lake are conspicuous, and have claimed attention from the beginning. The main disadvantage is the absence of terminal harbors. Greytown, the Caribbean outlet, was formerly a fine harbor, with 30 feet depth of entrance and anchorage; but the advance of the delta, and the drift of the waves and littoral currents, have enveloped the entrance with a sand bar, and converted the harbor into a shallow lagoon, with not more than 4 or 5 feet of water on the bar.

At the Pacific end the conditions are also difficult; the natural harbors in that vicinity, owing to formidable intervening elevations, are not accessible from the lake by canal, which must therefore have its terminus at Brito, a mere indentation in the coast-line, with deep water a short distance seaward. At both ends, therefore, adequate harbors must be created; in the one case by massive breakwaters constructed in the open Pacific of such materials and dimensions as shall withstand the ocean surges, and in the other carved out of the delta by extensive dredging, and protected by piers of such extent as to prevent choking by sand-drift.

Another formidable difficulty is the rainfall, which at Greytown exceeds that known elsewhere on the Western Continent. Observations for the three years 1890, 1891, and 1892 gave a minimum of 214 inches, an average of 267, and a maximum of 297—nearly 25 feet of water. On the Pacific side these amounts for the years 1880 to 1894 are reduced to a minimum of 32 inches, mean 65, and maximum 105. In fact, the conditions on the western side of the lake are in several respects far more favorable than on the eastern. The climate is drier, the country more level and open, communication much easier, and the population is mainly grouped there. The soil is of volcanic origin, and wonderfully fertile, with a wide range of natural food products. On the Atlantic side the country is practically a wilderness of steep clay hills and swamps, densely forested, and drenched with moisture, through which the river is in effect the only thoroughfare.

All the projects made have accepted the river and lake as the essential feature, and in 1826 De Witt Clinton secured a concession for a project, economically estimated at $5,000,000, intended for vessels of 400 or 500 tons only. In 1831 a Dutch charter was procured, to which the King of Holland was the principal subscriber. In 1847 Louis Napoleon interested himself in furthering a project to cost $20,000,000, following a route through both lakes, and thence to the harbor of Realejo on the Pacific farther north. In 1849 and 1850 a charter was obtained by Commodore Vanderbilt for a ship-canal, and in 1852 he opened a transit, *en route* to California, by boat up the river to the lake, with transfers at the rapids, and thence by wagon to the little harbor of San Juan del Sur, southeast from Brito, and at the same time procured the first authentic survey and actual location for a canal route by employing Colonel O. W. Childs, an American canal and railroad engineer of distinction, to make them. Childs's work and reports are still the most reliable sources of information, and constitute the basis for all later investigations.

The proposed navigation of that day was restricted to 17 feet depth, and Childs's plans, which were carefully worked out from actual data, held the lake-level at 108 feet above tide, by dams in the San Juan and Rio Grande rivers—the latter discharging into the Pacific at Brito—making a summit-level 103½ miles long, locking down to the Pacific on the west side, and canalizing the San Juan by additional dams on the east side. At a point 90 miles from the lake the river was abandoned, and a canal went through the delta to Greytown; in all, there were to be 14 locks on each side. The estimated cost of his project was $31,500,000, the unit prices being double those for similar work in the State of New York.

In 1873 the United States naval expedition under Commander Lull re-examined the Childs route for a canal of 26 feet depth, substantially on the same lines; and in 1890 the Maritime Canal Company, which had acquired a concession from Nicaragua, and secured a charter from the United States Congress, made public the particulars of its project, invited subscriptions, and began work on the formation of a harbor at Greytown. Operations continued until 1893, when they were terminated by lack of funds, and Congress was appealed to make the enterprise a national one, and to carry it to completion by a guarantee of bonds and loan of public credit. When work was suspended the actual constructions that had been effected by the company were 12 miles of railroad through the swamp to the foot-hills, a thousand feet of jetty, three-quarters of a mile of canal, and considerable dredging in the harbor—all at the eastern end. In addition, there had been erected at Greytown several buildings, including hospital, storehouse, barracks, and offices, a workshop, etc.; and a portion of the line, in both the eastern and Pacific divisions, had been partially cleared of timber.

After discussion, Congress, in the act of March 2, 1895, authorized the appointment of a commission of three engineers for the purpose of reporting on the feasibility, permanence, and cost of completion of the company's project as detailed in the final report by the chief engineer in 1890; and in November, 1895, having spent two months in field-work on the Isthmus, and three in examining all the engineering data in the possession of the company, the commission submitted its report, which was published as Document No. 279, H. R., 54th Congress, 1st session.

The commission believed a ship-canal project entirely feasible, but found it necessary to withhold approval of several features of the company's plans, and in particular deemed it prudent to double the estimates of cost, viz., from $67,000,000 to $133,500,000, as representing the minimum sum that could safely be charged to the construction, administration, and contingent account—this estimate not including some possibly large sums as damages for submerged lands, and the like, for the computation of which no data were at hand, and for other charges incidental to the maintenance of the concession.

The company's project, based partly on the surveys in 1852 and 1873 by Childs and Lull, supplemented by additional surveys made under its own direction at intervals between 1887 and 1893, embodied constructions of a formidable and unprecedented character, the execution and maintenance of which, if deemed practicable, would involve heavy expenditures and be invested with serious hazards. The lake was to be raised to 110 feet elevation, and the summit-level extended in both directions with a length of 155 or 160 miles, the total distance from Greytown to Brito being about 175 miles. To effect this, two immense dams were projected, one across the San Juan River at Ochoa, 70 miles below the lake, and the other at La Flor, less than 4 miles from the Pacific, where the valley of the Rio Grande was contracted between hills.

The La Flor dam would convert the upper Rio Grande Valley into a basin 4½ miles long, to be connected with the Pacific by 3 locks and a short canal, and with the lake by 9½ miles of canal excavated through the low range of hills which constitute the west divide, with a maximum depth of cutting of 75 feet.

The dam was designed with a length of 2,000 feet, and would have to sustain a head of water of 90 feet. The company proposed to build it of loose rock backed with clay, and later changed this to a concrete core, with stone and earth embankments on both sides; but as borings on the site showed that no solid foundation existed, it would be prudent to abandon the dam-and-basin scheme, and have recourse to a low-level canal, which would involve no difficulties in construction.

The Ochoa dam was to raise the San Juan River to the summit-level, and thereby effect a canalization of the entire distance of 70 miles to the lake, saving a large amount of excavation in the river-bed for the ship-channel, designed at 28 feet depth. The dam would be 1,900 feet long, and have to sustain a head of 60 feet. It had to be built in the bed of the stream, and subject to the action of the floods. The company proposed to build it of loose stone, backed with smaller materials and clay, with the expectation that it would be tight enough to maintain the head of water, and at the same time endure the passage over its crest of such floods as the river might discharge. As the bed of the river is sand to an unknown depth, and there were indications that the floods—which had never been measured—might reach as much as 150,000 cubic feet per second, it is doubtful if these expectations could be realized, as a structure for such purposes is without precedent or comparison.

Assuming the maintenance of the summit-level as proposed, the canal was to leave the river at the dam and direct itself for Greytown, 30 miles distant.

The summit-level was to be carried 12 miles through the San Francisco basins, an intricate region of clay hills and mud bottoms, by means of an extensive series of 67 clay dams, some of great magnitude, one of them 1¼ miles long, with a height of 100 feet above its foundations. It is not easy to see how, under the tremendous rainfall prevalent in their vicinity, these huge masses of clay are to be either constructed or maintained. Passing the embankments, the canal winds through the east divide—a rock and clay mass over 3 miles across, with a maximum cut of 324 feet, in materials shown by the few borings made to be of all degrees of hardness, from trap to volcanic ash, in which the side slopes are designed as five vertical on one horizontal. Thence the canal descends the valley of the Deseado, with 3 locks separated by short canals and basins, and reaches tide-level 9½ miles from Greytown.

It is evident that with constructions so novel and formidable, and conditions so difficult, the utmost care must be given to the procuring and study of all obtainable facts, including complete hydraulic and geologic data, variations of lake and river levels, velocity and volume of streams, quantity of rainfall at different points, violence and frequency of floods, and all the other detailed and particular information the engineer requires for the completion of his project, the preparation of his plans and estimates, and the drafting of his specifications. In the case of Nicaragua, as of all the other isthmian projects, the information of this nature is still scanty and incomplete, and the materials composing the bed of the San Juan River for the 30 miles over which large under-water excavations were necessary have not been investigated at all. The project as formulated by the company is manifestly in its preparatory stage only.

The fact is that the possibilities affecting the final location between the San Juan River and the sea have been but superficially examined. The sandy bottom, marshy banks, and turbulent volume of the river through the low-lying delta furnish serious obstacles to the creation of a deep channel following its main course down the Colorado. On the other hand, the company's ambitions high-level project as above indicated presents equally obvious difficulties and special dangers. But it has not been shown that we are in fact restricted to these alternatives, and it is quite possible that a conservative middle course would be at once safer and less costly. For example, at Machuca Falls, 18 miles above Ochoa, a rocky reef crosses the river valley, and the construction of a high dam with locks would be quite practicable. A low dam and lock at Ochoa, and another at a site farther down, would carry the navigation to a point whence it could proceed at the low level direct to Greytown, substantially as projected by Childs. For the solution of these and other similar problems, a thorough investigation and accurate data for comparison are needed before the question of final location can be settled.

In accordance with the recommendation made by the commission of 1895, Congress, in the act of June 4, 1897, has provided for a second commission to finish the investigation and make final plans and estimates.

This commission is now in the field fully equipped for its work, and there is reason to believe that within a year or two it will be possible to decide how the Nicaragua canal should be built and what it will cost, and which of the two great rival projects, Panama or Nicaragua, will be the first to get itself completed, and constitute the most notable achievement in the annals of engineering.

11

The Best Isthmian Canal

Henry L. Abbot

The author of this article presents the precise technical reasons for which the Panama route was considered the best canal route and completely ignores the Nicaraguan alternative. The author notes, in support of his claim, the existence of excellent natural ports at both extremes of the projected canal and a relatively short land distance between the two points. Also, given the natural characteristics of the Chagres River, less digging would be involved in the Panama project, and Panamanian geography, in this article, is described as relatively earthquake free. Finally, the author gives important consideration to the fact that the canal in Panama would pass entirely through one country, which would facilitate diplomatic matters.

While the importance of connecting the seaports of our Atlantic and Pacific coasts by a short water route has been long appreciated in a general way, it needed the exciting incident of the passage of the Oregon around Cape Horn to develop a strong popular sentiment on the subject. The demand would naturally have been limited to the best possible ship canal, leaving the question of route to be determined in the usual technical manner; but, unfortunately, remembrance of the disastrous failure of the old Panama Canal Company ten years ago, and total ignorance of the work accomplished by the new company, were widespread through the country, and it was currently believed that that route had been proved to be impracticable, and that Nicaragua afforded the only possible solution of the problem. Having personally traversed both routes, and given over three years to a professional study of the details of one of them, I may be pardoned for believing that these circumstances have placed us on the verge of a very serious mistake in this important matter.

The question is now narrowed down to selecting the better of two possible routes—that by Panama and that by Nicaragua. Their respective merits have received technical discussion, and the following natural advantages possessed by Panama over Nicaragua will hardly be disputed by persons conversant with the subject. (1) Good natural harbors, familiar for many years to navigators, opposed to artificial harbors, one of which at least will demand constant outlay for maintenance. (2) A land route less than a quarter as long; a summit level to be surmounted of only about half the height, involving only half the number of locks. (3) Curvatures more gentle than on any existing or projected ship canal, contrasted with curves too abrupt for rapid passage. (4) Far less danger from earthquakes than exists in Nicaragua; no troublesome winds or river currents to be encountered; much less rainfall where heavy excavation is demanded. (5) And finally, location in a single country where every interest will favor the canal, and thus render its protection against malicious injuries far easier than in Nicaragua, where for many miles the route lies close to the border of two states which are often hostile, and are always jealous of each other.

There are besides economic considerations, such as very considerable progress in actual construction—about two fifths of the canal bed is actually excavated; important facilities for completion, including a parallel railroad, numerous quarters for laborers, many locomotives, dirt cars, dredges, excavators, and other tools on hand. At Panama there is a fortunate absence of the troublesome engineering problems which beset the way in Nicaragua, such as the maintenance of the level of the lake, a vast inland sea, within the narrow limits of six feet—and this notwithstanding natural fluctuations about double that amount, due to phenomenal evaporation and very heavy rainfalls. This regulation of level is absolutely necessary, on the one hand to avoid drowning valuable private property on the border of the lake, and on the other to maintain the depth needful to navigation over the rocky bed of the San Juan River, which constitutes an important part of the route for shipping. Another great difficulty is to prepare appropriate foundations for the dam at Boca San Carlos, at about one hundred feet below mean water level—and this in a great river a third of a mile wide, that cannot be temporarily diverted during the progress of the work. Last, but not least, there is the advantage of vastly less cost for operation and maintenance when completed. As to all these matters there is absolutely no contention possible between the two routes. It appears, judging from recent discussions, that the advocates of the Nicaragua route appreciate these facts, and now put forth only two claims that come fairly within the province of an engineer. These are: (1) that the distance between our Atlantic and Pacific seaports is considerably less, and hence that the time of transit must be materially less, by the Nicaragua than by the Panama route; and (2) that the trade winds on the Pacific are more serviceable to sailing ships, and will favor their passage by Nicaragua more than by Panama. These claims will now be considered.

The latter may be conceded, but is entitled to little weight. Very few sailing ships pass through any existing canal. That class of vessel is not suited to navigate contracted channels, and greater or less facilities for approach would not be likely to exert a controlling influence between two routes, one of which is short, and the other long and difficult. The relative cost of towage would have to be considered, and would probably decide the choice. As to the actual facilities for approach, Admiral Walker covered the ground in his testimony before the Senate Committee on Interoceanic Canals, on May 11, 1900. He said: "Between Colon and Greytown, for sailing ships, there is not very much difference as to winds; but between Panama and Brito the advantages for a sailing ship would be decidedly with Brito;" adding, "The shipping in these days is going to steam, so that the question of wind is of very much less importance than it was fifty years ago." It would appear that the least of the Panama advantages enumerated above should outbalance this questionable one on the side of Nicaragua.

The other claim, that there would be an important gain in time for our coastwise steamers by the Nicaragua route, is worthy of careful investigation. The first element to consider is the actual relative distance. The following figures have been stated on the authority of Commander Todd, of the Hydrographic Bureau of the Navy Department, the unit being the statute mile: New York to Colon, 2,281 miles; New York to Greytown, 2,372 miles; New Orleans to Colon, 1,589 miles; New Orleans to Greytown, 1,448 miles; San Francisco to Panama, 3,777 miles; San Francisco to Brito, 3,109 miles; New York to Honolulu via Panama Canal (47 miles), 7,699 miles; New York to Honolulu via Nicaragua Canal (190 miles), 7,438 miles.

From these data it appears that the gain to a steamer in a voyage from New York to San Francisco via Nicaragua would be 434 miles; from New Orleans to San Francisco, 666 miles; and from New York to Honolulu, 261 miles. Assuming an average sea speed of 10 knots (11.5 statute miles), these gains in time will be 37.7 hours, 57.9 hours, and 22.7 hours respectively. It remains to inquire how much of this seeming advantage will be offset by longer delays in traversing a canal via Nicaragua than one via Panama. Such delays result from lockages, and from difficulties in maintaining full speed arising from curvature, strong winds, and local currents, if such exist on the route.

The delays to be caused by lockages in the two canals raise the question of the total height to be overcome. For the Nicaragua route, nature has fixed this at the level of the lake, about 107 feet. For Panama, it is a matter of choice, to be determined within the limits of economical excavation by the parties in interest, but it will always be less than 107 feet—a fact of much more importance than the original heights of the divide, so often quoted. The new Panama Canal Company, contrary to what has been repeatedly asserted, has adopted a *single definite project*, but one carefully adjusted to permit a decision as to the height of the ultimate summit level to be deferred until progress in the construction shall make known which of two heights is preferable. These two heights are 102 feet and 61 feet, the latter to attain 67 feet in great floods of the Chagres, which occur only at long intervals. The higher level has been adopted provisionally, to guard against interest costs resulting from any delay in completing the cut at the Culebra; but if the United States government adopts the route, the lower level will doubtless be given the preference, and it will therefore be assumed in the following comparison:

Delays from lockages result from two causes: (1) loss of time consumed in actually raising and lowering the ship, and (2) loss of time in the needful preparations for so doing. The former admits of exact estimate, based on experiments at our great lock Poe at Sault Ste. Marie, and confirmed by experience there and on the Manchester Ship Canal. The limit of speed in raising and lowering which is found to be safe is two and a half feet per minute. This calls for 86 minutes for overcoming the ascents and descents on the Nicaragua route, and 49 minutes for those via Panama. The delays in the needful preparations depend on the number and adjustment of the locks. Careful observation of the passage of great ships through the Manchester Ship Canal has furnished the following figures, including the slackening of speed in approaching the lock, delays in entering and making fast, time spent in maneuvering the gates, delays in unlashing and leaving the lock, and time lost in regaining full speed. For each passage of a single lock these delays aggregate 21 minutes; and for two locks in flights, 30 minutes. On the Panama route there will be five locks, four of them disposed in flights of two. On the Nicaragua route the Walker Commission propose ten single locks. These data give the following as the total loss of time in lockages in traversing the two canals: via Nicaragua, 8 hours and 26 minutes; via Panama, 3 hours and 32 minutes: gain for Panama, 4 hours and 54 minutes.

The speed which can be maintained in traversing the water way will be governed by the dimension of cross section, the curvature at changes of direction, the force and direction of the prevailing winds, and the currents when any are to be encountered. Experience on existing ship canals has also shown that a limit is imperative to protect the banks from erosion. This limit is generally fixed at 6 knots (6.7 miles) per hour. Another important element in determining the practical rate of transit is the length of the levels between the locks; for if short a high speed cannot be attained in traversing them. The routes will now be compared as to these elements.

In the matter of dimensions of cross section both conform to modern requirements; in all other respects Panama possesses great advantages.

For facility in navigation an absolutely straight canal would, of course, be the ideal one; but such perfection is hardly to be attained in practice. The canal which most closely approximates to it, or, in other words, which has its route determined by curvatures of the longer radii, has obvious advantages in respect to ease and safety of operation.

On the Panama route the minimum radius of curvature is 1,900 meters, and only one per cent of the entire distance between oceans approaches this limit (2,078 yards). The ruling radii are 3,000 or 2,500 meters (3,281 or 2,734 yards), and 42 per cent of the route lies between these limits; 57 per cent follows straight lines. For Nicaragua, the report of the Walker Commission is not very definite as to this important element. It gives (page 16) 1,000 yards as the minimum curvature in the canal proper, but does not specify what it is in the 57 miles of the crooked San Juan River; where Lull's survey, adopting the five cutoffs planned by him, indicates for the deep water channel six curves with radii between 233 yards and 1,500 yards; fifteen curves, between 500 and 833 yards; and twenty-one curves, between 833 yards and 1,170 yards. Many of these curves have hills abutting on one side or both. The total change of direction in the entire distance amounts to 4,607°, or about 13 complete circles. This matter of curvature is of immense practical importance. The Suez Company has been compelled, since the canal was opened to traffic, to increase its radius from a minimum of 700 meters to a minimum of 1,800 meters (736 yards to 1,968 yards).

In conducting a ship through a canal or narrow river, where currents are to be overcome, or where strong winds are to be encountered, either blowing across the route or acting from the rear to force her from her course in passing curves, the difficulties and risks of navigation are vastly increased. In this respect there is absolutely no difficulty on the Panama route. In Nicaragua ships must navigate for 57 miles the crooked San Juan River, which must carry the greater part of the lake drainage, and which traverses a gorge that Admiral Walker states is swept by strong trade winds during the greater part of the year.

As to length between locks on the Panama route, there is only one level (1.3 miles) less than 15 miles in length. On the *project* of the Walker Commission the following lengths appear: 3.5 miles, 4.6 miles, 0.8 of a mile, 0.9 of a mile, 1.9 miles, and 2.4 miles.

In view of these facts, it would appear reasonable to accord an average speed of transit to the Panama route equal to that authorized by existing canal regulations (6.7 miles per hour), especially as for some miles in Lake Bohio it can be largely exceeded. The Nicaragua route is manifestly subject to unusual difficulties. On the Suez Canal, in 1898, the average rate of speed was only 5.5 miles per hour, and this with curves of nearly double the radius of those projected for Nicaragua, and with no winds or currents to cause delays. It would seem a very liberal estimate to accord an average speed of 5 miles per hour, allowing full sea speed (11.5 miles) in the 58 miles of deep lake.

Adopting these figures, we find for the relative times of transit by the two canals the following figures:

	Hours	Min.
By Panama, 46 miles at 6.7 miles per hour	6	52
Loss in lockages	3	32
Add 20% for contingencies	2	5
Time of transit	12	39

	Hours	Min.
By Nicaragua, 132 miles at 5 miles per hour	26	24
58 miles at 11.5 miles per hour	5	3
Loss in lockages	8	26
Add 20% for contingencies	7	58
Time of transit	47	51

These figures, allowing full speed by night, show that a steamer crossing the Isthmus from ocean to ocean will require 35 hours more time if going by way of Nicaragua than if going by way of Panama. This practically offsets the seeming advantage of Nicaragua, given above, due to shorter ocean routes. In other words, a steamer leaving New York via Panama is really 12 hours nearer Honolulu, and less than three hours further from San Francisco, than if she went by way of Nicaragua. Even as between New Orleans and San Francisco the advantage of 666 miles in favor of Nicaragua counts for only 23 hours in time. Such gains are unworthy of serious consideration in voyages of this length; but even they are overstated. Further allowance must be made for increased probabilities of detention, arising from inferior harbors, and from having to traverse a land route four times as long, and a much longer part of it by night (as must be done if the transits are to be made in 48 hours and 13 hours respectively). No attempt will be made to assign a numerical value to this additional loss of time, which may vary between wide limits in different transits of the Isthmus; but evidently the loss via Nicaragua will be very important, and it much more than covers the insignificant gains indicated by the above figures. As a matter of fact, the advantage as to time lies decidedly on the side of Panama.

In fine, this claim of gain of time by Nicaragua must be relegated to the class of visionary arguments so often advanced to offset the solid merits of the Panama route. It is certain that if we are to have the best possible canal to connect our coasts, one not liable at any time to be superseded by a rival with which it could not compete, it must cross the continental divide at Panama. Nature has so decreed, and it is idle to contest the decision.

12

The Tropical Renaissance

Sylvester Baxter

This article is an example of how the public began to learn of what was already known in narrow scientific circles at the beginning of the twentieth century, namely that medical doctors could control malaria and yellow fever. The endemic presence of these diseases in Panama was one of the central arguments that favored the Nicaraguan canal route as the most appropriate: Not only had tens of thousands of workers died in the so-called French canal zone (Panama) as a consequence of the above mentioned diseases but, additionally, hundreds of North American soldiers died from the tropical diseases in military camps set up by the United States in Cuba. But, as indicated by the author, there was no reason to think that the diseases would continue to be a problem given that scientists had connected carriage of the sickness to the mosquito and incubation to stagnant waters. Science, developed by white western civilization, had once again conquered nature, which meant that "civilization" could now return triumphantly to the place of origin of malaria and yellow fever: the tropics.

Modern civilization, long barred from the tropics, has lately turned thither with determined purpose, and in strange coincidence science cast down the mightiest barrier in the way. There was the primitive home of man, but the white race, man's standard-bearer, domiciled in rigorous latitudes, has been deemed incapable of flourishing in the lands where it was cradled.

But now the world has just learned that climate in itself has little or naught to do with the chiefest ills of tropical existence. With the knowledge that malaria is solely caused by a certain species of mosquito, and that yellow fever likewise has its source in another species, climate is seen to be blameless. So soon has it become possible to deal unerringly with those two diseases, their source definitely located, that already certain localities, historic and hopeless plague-spots, have been quickly and permanently rid of their curses. The drainage of marshes and swamps, and the covering of stagnant waters with petroleum. Prevent the breading of mosquitoes; screening keeps them from houses; and even travelers and explorers can guard themselves in the wilderness under due precautions. Besides, there are the successful inoculative measures of Professor Kosh against malaria, and of Doctors Sanarelli and Bellanzagui against yellow fever. Altogether the dangers from the terrible diseases now appear to have been reduced to a minimum.

What will be the outcome? Must not the old theory that climatic conditions are adverse to the white race in the tropics be radically revised? In fact, civilization in the higher latitudes is comparatively of yesterday. Only a few centuries have passed since the rude barbarians of the North came under the influence of the southerly branches of the white race. On the other hand stand the ancient civilizations of Egypt, the Semitic races there and in Arabia, the Aryans in India, both white races commingling in the mild Mediterranean lands. At the most, the influences of wintry climates upon civilization appear to have been but subsidiary. Some of its highest developments have been seen in lands of gentle climates—centres for the intensest human energies, both physical and intellectual.

The most productive parts of the world should belong to the most capable among men—those best fitted to put the land to the best use. The parable of the ten talents applies here. If the peoples in possession are slothful, incapable, and socially inefficient, only a fraction of the soil's wonderful potentialities will be developed. But the full fruitage will be needed in the world, and eventually the tenure must pass to them that can do the work. This does not imply the extermination or the expulsion of existing populations. But the guiding powers, the directive authority, must rest with the superior race.

Climate has undoubtedly done much to modify and differentiate civilization. Wintry climates have probably had their chief influences by inducing more intense physical activities. Not only have men had to do a deal of "thrashing around" to get warm, but they have had to thrash around after the means to keep warm. Hence the need of increased earning capacity with the need of more clothing, fuel, and shelter; hence a great diversification of wants, a multiplicity in manufactures, an extension of mercantile activities, a branching out of commerce; hence a competition for new markets, an invasion of lands where climate makes no need for most of these things, and where many of them may be positively detrimental.

Commercial activity is fundamentally a beneficent force. But with the exploitation of mankind regarding selfish profit solely as its motive it develops vicious tendencies. And precisely for this end are artificial wants stimulated among primitive peoples: cravings for intoxicants and narcotics are fostered, together with demands for unnecessary raiment. Physical and moral uncleanness, disease, and increased mortality have been chief results. On the whole, however, the proportion of benefits conferred by civilization appears to be greatly in excess of evils induced. The loss of primitive simplicity is a price paid for parting with much that is bad. A truer civilization may eventually return to a higher simplicity.

In the high latitudes the dormant tendency of all nature in winter extends even to man, who then inclines to hibernation. More sleep is needed then. In the tropics the blood circulates quicker, and in various ways a greater vital energy is indicated there. In tropical dietaries the fuel foods predominate—the carbohydrates: rice, oil, sugar, and sweets in general, though modified by cooling fruits.

Visitors in the tropics are disposed to regard the lack of hustle and bustle as indicating a defect in popular character. But why should there be hustle and bustle? In Northern lands is not the stress to support physical existence so great as to preclude, on the part of the many, due attention to life's loftier aspects? In tropical lands, however, together with the milder temperate-zone regions, nature favors a more genial civilization: less pressure upon life, social benefits more accessible and more widely diffused. This is peculiarly a comfort-commanding age, and it has seen an extraordinary democratization of luxury, in countless things that lend pleasure, worth, and graciousness to life. Under the simple and slightly varying conditions of tropical climates, and with the resources of modern science at command, it is comparatively easy to secure comfort. The element of pure air immensely favors life there. In the higher latitudes the great majority passes the most of the time in air more or less foul. A most potent cause of many diseases is the noisome atmosphere of our shut-in winter life.

The climate aspects of tropical regions cannot be classed under one caption any more than many of those of the so-called temperate zone. There are enormous differences between the steaming atmosphere of the Brazilian lowlands, of the Isthmus of Panama, or of the Malay Peninsula, and the oven-like dryness of Sahara and Arabia, or the delightful equability of the islands of Polynesia; just as between New England, the Mississippi Valley at Memphis, the Canadian north, the south of England, or the Russian steppes. But with healthful existence made possible in substantially all parts of the tropics, the development of an advanced civilization there should be as practicable as it has been in many Northern localities where thermometers record terrific fluctuations in temperature. But the ideal regions for agreeable habitation are the tropical uplands, which, of all parts of the world, seem best adapted for high civilizations. The climates are the most genuinely temperate on earth. From day to day and from season to season the weather changes just enough for a gentle variety, with transitions seldom violent and never extreme. Mexico, Central America, a large part of the Andean region, portions of Brazil, much of central Africa, exhibit these conditions. Civilized or partially civilized peoples occupy some of these countries. But their vast natural resources, yet but slightly utilized, offer immense possibilities for great and enlightened populations.

Perhaps ages will pass before the tropical civilization differentiates itself from the cultures of today, free from hampering precedents and entangling conventions. But humanity grows plastic with enlightenment; race tends to adapt itself to environment; and so we may look for the flowering of a tropical renaissance.

Our race has reached no loftier levels in intellectual and spirit than were obtained in India and Greece under tropic suns and in soft Mediterranean air. May not the zone where man was created some day become the theatre of his highest life—the same simplicity of the Greeks underlying a culture savored by the essence of the best that modern science and art can give, leading to heights yet unimagined?

PART IV

Diplomacy and Strategy of the Isthmian Region

The four chapters in this part range from 1889 to 1897; there are two articles from *Harper's* and two from *The Atlantic Monthly*. The events that transpired during the nine years covered by these essays are of critical importance in shaping the debate that emerged over the canal question. Three major events would occur during the time period under study here, one military, another academic, and a third economic.

In 1890 Captain Alfred T. Mahan published his seminal work *The Influence of Sea Power on History* whereby he explained that every great, powerful, and influential empire in the history of the world had become great via dependence on naval force. Mahan's objectives were clear: if the United States ever hoped to become an influential world power, it would have to build up its naval forces, acquire bases in other regions of the world, and move forward with a plan to construct an interoceanic canal to connect an Atlantic and Pacific fleet. Mahan's views were popular during the 1890s, and he published widely in magazines and journals, including an essay in 1897 "The Strategic Features of the Gulf of Mexico and the Caribbean Sea" in *Harper's Monthly Magazine*. Mahan, in the piece included in this section, argued that Cuba was central to the security and commerce of the United States due to its unique location. Is it, then, mere coincidence that the United States would, one year later, intervene in Cuba in the name of expelling the Spaniards and fostering Cuban independence (under U.S. tutelage, known formally as the Platt Amendment), Mahan was considered the primary expert on naval history and naval matters, and his compelling prose was widely influential in decision-making circles in Washington and elsewhere.

The historian Frederick Jackson Turner, in 1893, announced the end of the "frontier" in American history. This announcement came in the form of a scholarly paper read at the American Historical Association meeting. Jackson's claim, that the frontier had closed, lent itself to an obvious question: where would Americans turn, in the future, to acquire land, trade goods, and exploit resources? The answer and solution to the nagging historical problem posed by Turner could be found in overseas markets. Though Turner never explicitly stated that the United States should concentrate on developing foreign markets and trade routes, the implications of his scholarly paper were clear: if the United States wanted to continue to grow, and avoid social and economic tensions at home, markets outside of the continuous borders of the United States would have to be aggressively sought and maintained.

The year 1893, interestingly enough, represented one of the most severe economic downturns in the history of the United States, up to that point and up until now. The crisis lasted through 1895, and economists pointed not to a flawed system but to an industrial structure that had overproduced during the 1880s and early 1890s. Economists saw a relatively simple solution to the over saturation of the American economy: exports to foreign countries and peoples. Mahan, Turner, and the economic crisis of the early 1890s all pointed to a need for increased trade, better trade routes, more sophisticated marketing techniques abroad, and greater reliance on naval power and sea-routes for shipping goods. An interoceanic canal, then, became the focus of attention of not just U.S. military personnel and politicians, but of business people, shippers, and merchants, and even academicians in the United States.

Two chapters, both articles published in 1889 in *The Atlantic Monthly*, are presented in this part. The two authors are for the most part critical of U.S. policy objectives and actions in the Caribbean region. Stuart F. Weld writes critically of the United States' history and attempts to dominate and militarize an inter- oceanic canal, and shows how the United States had manipulated international law and international treaties all in an attempt at control of the Caribbean. The piece is important for it shows part of the academic and internal debate concerning U.S. policy and procedures in the Caribbean. The author even suggests that control and domination of a canal by the United States would be completely out of character with the democratic tradition of the country. The essay nicely frames the opposition, built on sound legal principles, to U.S. involvement in the Caribbean. As such, Weld's essay fits, in scope, with the essay titled "Latin and Saxon Americans" also published in *The Atlantic Monthly* in December 1889. The author of this essay reflects the tone of the late nineteenth century regarding race and culture: Southern Latin Americans, simply put, were viewed as inferior to their Northern Anglo-Saxon counterparts, and the piece states that Latin Americans were unworthy of being absorbed by the United States. The essay calls for the United States to maintain political and commercial neutrality with respect to Latin Americans, arguing that the differences between the two cultures are so enormous as to make integration or cooperation virtually impossible. The author, Albert G. Browne, concludes by stating, "Let us let South America alone to work out her own salvation, just as we let Europe alone to work out hers." This attitude, of course, was completely at odds with the political climate of the time, which called for more, and not less, commercial integration with the countries of the world, especially those in the western hemisphere. Taken together, Weld and Browne represent a line of thought that would not or could not become American policy in the late nineteenth century. Many Americans distrusted either U.S. objectives in Latin America (Weld) or the Latin Americans themselves (Browne), but thinkers such as Mahan and others who were calling for increased commercial and political relations with the Latin American neighbors would, eventually, win the political battle at home and abroad.

Sidney Webster, in 1893, published "The Diplomacy and Law of the Sea," which is an interesting, thoughtful legal discourse concerning the possible construction of an interoceanic canal, all of the powers involved, and their respective positions and priorities. The author pays special attention to the role of the British, especially concerning construction of the Suez Canal, and concludes, essentially, that given the complex web of international treaties and interests, it would be almost impossible for the United States to "legally" construct and fortify a canal through one of the Central American countries or Colombia.

The four chapters in this part provide a detailed examination of some of the important legal and diplomatic challenges associated with building a canal in Central America: those challenges were openly discussed in the North American press at the end of the nineteenth century, but ultimately, it came down to military force (as Webster implied it might) to determine how the canal would be built. Theodore Roosevelt ran roughshod over international law, international diplomacy, and international treaty obligations, but by the early twentieth century, U.S. commerce and naval might came to depend largely on construction of a canal, given the historic realities and processes of the late 1890s, discussed above. The reality and efficacy of American military power outweighed the niceties of international law and treaty obligation as would be seen in U.S. actions and attitudes in October and November 1903.

13

The Isthmus Canal and American Control

Stuart F. Weld

In 1880, according to the author of this article, the government of the United States made public a principle clearly expressed during the presidency of Grant, that the United States would only support "an American canal under American control." This proclamation is strongly criticized in the article that follows: after examining the legal principles of this idea, considered by the author to be extremely weak, the writer affirms that the expressed attitude is monarchical and absolutist and, as such, completely contrary to the American democratic tradition. Something similar occurred, according to the author, with the Monroe Doctrine of 1823 which prohibited European countries from doing exactly what the United States was proposing via construction of a canal: to use for its exclusive benefit, and, in fact, usurp, the sovereignty of the countries of the Caribbean region.

In the debate upon the Tehuantepec bill in the Senate in February, 1887, after stating what the Monroe doctrine was, and that every soldier and sailor, every life even, in the United States was pledged to its support, Senator Hoar said:

> But this new gloss and perversion which we hear from Senators on the other side of the Chamber, and, I am sorry to say on this side of the Chamber too, that the United States of America has the right to say to a weak South American republic, "You shall not deal with your own territory as you choose; you shall not build a canal, or a railroad, or a public work in the interest of the commerce which goes from sea to sea, unless the United States shall take upon herself the control, shall dictate the terms, shall manage the future conduct of

> that enterprise," is a declaration as repugnant to the law of nations, as repugnant to the purpose of George Canning and John Quincy Adams, and as repugnant to the genius and spirit and honor of the American people as it is to sound morals or sound international law.

In these terms the Massachusetts Senator protested against a doctrine which at the time the French started the undertaking at Panama got possession of public sentiment. It dominated the Republican party and also the Democratic. Based upon principles, or rather assumptions, inconsistent with our institutions, it is equally out of accord with their essence and tendency. The doctrine of American control deserves to be thus stigmatized. Unfortunately, it possessed for five years the favor and support of our government, from 1880 to 1885. In 1885, President Cleveland, in his first annual message, set it aside. Our government simply reverted to the principles which it had previously observed. It is a source of satisfaction that President Harrison said nothing about the doctrine of American control in his inaugural, though it had been propounded on several occasions by his predecessors. The eminently just and fitting statement which he made is that we expect no European state to exercise domination over an American canal. But it has been easier to insist upon this doctrine than to renounce such a right for ourselves. It is easier to say "Hands off!" to Europe than to practice that precept at home. We have not always been ready to maintain that the passage carved through the Cordilleras is to be, as far as use goes, the property of the whole world. And it is therefore gratifying that the inaugural of President Harrison contains no intimation that the doctrine of inequality is to be revived.

In considering the probability or improbability of this revival the following circumstance has weight. Since the period during which American control was the doctrine of the state a great event has changed the letter and prospects of international law. In October, 1888, the European powers signed at Constantinople a treaty which fixes the status of the Suez Canal. It establishes the same principles of equality and liberality which we have ourselves observed, save during the exceptional period referred to. A circumstance which cannot escape an American's attention is that the basic principle adopted by the European monarchies, that of equal rights, constitutes the substance of republican institutions. It was a great step for Europe to take. The contrary doctrine, for a time so inexplicably favored by ourselves, that one state, or two states, may establish over a passage to be used by the whole world a specific domination, and shut out every other from certain privileges, is essentially monarchical. It can be nothing else. Is it possible for us to accept a principle discarded by the absolutism of Europe, and imagine it to be anything else than an anachronism, however adroitly we may adapt it to American ideas? It is not for the New World to inaugurate a monarchical polity just as the Old is abandoning it and adopting the republican principle.

Aside, however, from the confidence inspired by President Harrison's inaugural, aside from such influence as the Suez Convention cannot but exert, another consideration makes in this direction. Unless we conclude to out-french the French and establish a character for instability like that ascribed to them, would it be possible for us to pursue such a shiftless, see-saw policy? A few days prior to the utterance quoted at the beginning of this paper, Senator Hoar said, deprecating a policy so contradictory that nobody could place confidence in it, "It does not comport with the honor of a great and free people to assert one thing yesterday and another today." Shall it be said that in 1850 we asserted principles of liberty and equality in accord with our institutions; that in 1880 we repudiated them, and adopted a monarchical doctrine; that in 1885 we reasserted the principle of justice and right; and that we exemplified the levity of our counsels by making a further change, and making it in the centennial year of the French Revolution? What a time for the assertion of such a doctrine! What a season in which to celebrate a return to the principle of monarchy! It would be hard to determine whether we had a policy or not. A maliciously disposed critic might assert that it was not a policy, but a weather-cock. Such sudden and radical changes might suit the whimsicalities of a despotism, but would be unworthy of an enlightened people. However, if we have a right, as no doubt we have, to change our minds at any stated moment, let us, above all, determine that the change take place from wrong to right, and not from right to wrong; from monarchical ideas to those of republicanism, never in the contrary direction.

These views should be taken for what they are worth. Some will accept them, some may not. But there is a position in which all will concur. As has been said, the matter of American control is not referred to in the inaugural of President Harrison. The members of his administration may not adopt identical views. It is scarcely probable that the Panama or the Nicaragua Canal will be finished in four years. As for the Suez undertaking, its status was not determined till nineteen years after it was opened. Similarly, there is no imperative need of haste in settling the question of the American water-way. But on the other hand, President Harrison may not choose to postpone a settlement. That he can decide this question, and in such a way that no further unsettlement can be thought of, is not improbable. Let us hope that such a settlement of one of the intricate problems of the day is to redound to the honor, rather to the glory, of his administration.

Now, at all events, while uncertainty exists, is the time to inquire into this matter. What is American control? What are its limits? How has it been advocated? What attempts have been made to enforce it? What success have they met with, what failure? Now is the time to get at the root of the question. If upon a third occasion within ten years we propose to right about face, let us understand the purport of this attitude. Let us ask whether it is worthwhile to attempt to inaugurate a change which not a state in the entire world will ratify. Have we ground enough for the act?

The doctrine of American control was propounded in a special message, sent to the Senate, March 8, 1880. Referring to the Isthmus question, President Hayes said, "The policy of this government is a canal under American control." What this control means we shall see as we follow the manner in which the administration of President Hayes and the two succeeding ones tried to carry it out. It is enough to remark here—as implied in part in the quotation already cited—that American control meant, in the purpose of those who advocated it, *virtually* the control of an interoceanic canal by the United States, but in a legal, technical sense its joint control by the United States and the state through which it passed. It was never proposed by our government to admit any other state, whether of Europe or America, into this monopolized co-partnership.

Simultaneously with the promulgation of the doctrine, namely, in the message of March 8th, a position was assumed without basis in justice or common sense. This was subsequently developed in the diplomatic correspondence of the United States, under Secretaries Blame and Frelinghuysen, into a blunder of a positive, unquestionable sort. This blunder, easily demonstrated, consisted in the assertion that under the New Granada treaty of 1848 the United States of Colombia had no right to conclude like treaties with European states. The Executive of the United States, President Polk, in his message to the Senate, which accompanied the draft of the treaty, disclaimed any exclusive views on the part of our government. He explicitly recognized the right of Colombia to conclude such treaties. The only anxiety the President entertained was, that the United States should have the honor of concluding such a treaty before equivalent ones were concluded by other states.* So much for the subsequent ulterior growth of the element referred to in President Hayes's message. In this document, although the New Granada treaty is not by name referred to, a claim of like character is advanced. The President refers to the investment of European capital in an interoceanic canal. This capital must look somewhere, he observes, for protection and security. "No European power," he adds, "can intervene for such protection without adopting measures on this continent which the United States would deem wholly inadmissible." Why inadmissible? Why should it be inadmissible that any power should be invoked by the Colombian government to protect property of vast value, property consecrated to the use of the entire world? Does the right to protect such property devolve upon one and not upon any or all of the states whose individual interest it is that the passage used by the ships of each shall forever remain open and free? As has been demonstrated, the republic of Colombia has as much right to conclude with European states treaties similar to that of 1848 as it had to conclude that treaty with us. Under any such convention, the right of Colombia to invoke the aid of one or more Euro-

*President Polk's message should be consulted. The part referred to is given in "The Isthmus Canal and our Government," in the March *Atlantic*. Here may be found likewise the requisite references to the dispatches of Messrs. Frelinghuysen and Blame.

pean states would be as indisputable as the same under the agreement of 1848. The idea never occurred to any one, at the time that treaty was concluded, that an exclusive sense could attach to it. A contrary interpretation was assigned by the constitutionally appointed powers of the United States, the President and Senate, by whose joint action the proposed convention became one in fact. The endeavor at a later day to tack on to it another meaning has no basis in fact, justice, or common sense. Well may Senator Hoar, in speaking of this whole business of American control, refer to it as "this new gloss and perversion." It is nothing else.

One of the last authorities to be held impartial respecting the Panama Canal, Mr. J. C. Rodrigues—the whole scope of his work entitled *The Panama Canal*, is hostile to that undertaking—says, with reference to the New Granada treaty, page 228:

> As to the treaty of 1848 with Colombia giving the United States any particular advantages of a protectorate over the Isthmus transit, *it is simply an American illusion*. Nothing prevents Colombia from making identical treaties with England, France, and other powers; and when the troops from Washington will one of these days land in Aspinwall, they may find French or English troops already "defending the passage" in virtue of treaty stipulations.

The above was written in 1885, three years prior to the conclusion of the Suez Convention. There is little reason to doubt that when a similar convention is concluded as to Panama the method provided in the former to secure the neutrality of Suez will be adopted here—that is, as to essentials. If the Colombian government should not be able to suppress any insurrectionary movement, it would communicate with the signatory powers, and in conjunction with them take such measures as would be needful. There is no occasion for a conflict of interests—no more at Panama than at Suez.

As regards the assumed right of the United States to object to the conclusion of treaties equivalent to that of 1848, it is perhaps noticeable that the message of President Polk, upon this point wholly conclusive, is not referred to by Rodrigues, nor, for that matter, by Lord Granville in his correspondence with Frelinghuysen and Blame. The fact seems to be that the gloss which American diplomacy tried to fix upon the treaty is so inadmissible, not to say absurd, that neither Granville nor Rodrigues cared to go further than the text. To read Article 35 is sufficient.

An unfortunate element of another kind was introduced into the message of President Hayes. It hardly calls for discussion here. The claim is advanced that the Panama Canal would virtually constitute part of the "coast-line" of the United States. The untenable, in fact contradictory, character of this claim has been shown elsewhere.* The positions assumed in the message of March 8,

*"The Isthmus Canal and our Government," already referred to.

1880, were reiterated by President Hayes in his last annual message, nine months later. But the endeavor to establish American control was not confined to these messages. No empty announcement of the doctrine would suffice. It was to be embodied in and made part of the public law of the continent. A first attempt occurred in February, 1881, a few weeks before the retirement of President Hayes from office. If possible, American control was to be forced upon the government of the United States of Colombia. Not by following this fibrous negotiation, rather by tracing only the principal threads, we may learn what was meant by American control.

Early in 1881 it was plain that the building of an interoceanic canal was to commence. The responsibility which we had incurred in guarantying the neutrality of the Isthmus and sovereignty of Colombia over it would be increased. Our government urged the need of defining, through supplementary stipulations, what this responsibility was and how it should be discharged. This necessity the Colombian government did not recognize. It held that the existing treaty, that of 1848, was sufficient. It was ready, however, to agree to certain additional stipulations, and appointed General Santo Domingo Vila as its plenipotentiary. Mr. Evarts, our Secretary of State, was the negotiator on our part. Each party presented a project of protocol. Even the comparatively moderate one submitted by Santo Domingo, which embodied in part the views of Mr. Evarts, the Colombian government subsequently disavowed. Its envoy, it alleged, had exceeded his instructions. Let us inquire what were the points conceded by Santo Domingo of which his government did not approve. His protocol provided that the two governments should select two places upon the Isthmus where fortifications "permanent or temporary" might be built. Another stipulation provided that these should not be occupied by United States forces except upon occasions when Colombia required our assistance. The first query is whether any necessity existed for considering the erection of fortifications. The Clayton-Bulwer treaty prohibited the building of fortifications upon or in the vicinity of the route to which in particular it referred, the Nicaragua. In the Suez Convention, concluded in October, 1888, precautions are in like manner taken (Article 8) against the erection of fortifications. The tendencies of civilization work undeniably in this direction. Should fortifications be built ostensibly to furnish posts where garrisons might be stationed, so that any insurrectionary disturbance might be promptly suppressed, still the very existence of fortifications would offer a temptation. To this one state or another might yield. Such works might be seized or held to control the passage in the interest of one commonwealth, and against that of another. The Clayton-Bulwer treaty, on the other hand, determined that any such passage should be "forever open and free." The one essential thing in any negotiation was to say nothing about fortifications *except to prohibit them.* The Colombian government was in the right. Why it objected to such a stipulation appears more distinctly when we ascertain what the counter-protocol presented by Mr. Evarts was. The first article provided that the government of Colombia should grant in future no concession for an interoceanic canal, and make no change in any existing one without the consent of the United States. Here was an attempt to encroach upon, to appropriate in part, one of the most valued prerogatives of all governments, the treaty-making power. That such an attempt should have been made is to be explained only by supposing that Mr. Evarts imagined he was dealing with a state so feeble, so devoid of any proper sense of independence, that a little judicious insistence on his part would be enough. He was mistaken. Santo Domingo refused even to discuss such a proposition. Upon this point, at least, he understood his instructions. On the 10th of February, 1881, he addressed Mr. Evarts a note conveying distinctly his views and purpose. In this he observes that when he handed him his protocol "he did not even imagine that the enlightened American government proposed to discuss the right of Colombia as an independent and sovereign nation to conclude conventions of the nature of that which she had concluded with Lucien N. B. Wyse for the construction of an interoceanic canal through her own territory." He continued:

> Although the "whereases" of the draft presented to him are based upon the very obligations contracted by the United States in Article 35 of the treaty of 1846, that is to say upon obligations designed to guaranty the sovereignty of Colombia over the Isthmus, Article 1 of the draft prepared by his excellency the Secretary of State is, in the opinion of the undersigned, in direct derogation of the very sovereignty which it is proposed to guaranty, when it proposes to Colombia to agree that before granting a privilege similar to that which it has granted it needs to secure the con-sent and approval of a foreign state.*

The above is equally straightforward and clear.

Although Santo Domingo had stated that he could not discuss such a proposition, Mr. Evarts was not ready to yield. At first, it is true, he proposed to waive the discussion of Article 1, but he promptly returned to it and urged its acceptance. Santo Domingo, on the day following his first note, addressed him a second. He said:

> The undersigned is sorry not to have succeeded in conveying to his excellency's mind the idea which he had in view, viz., that inasmuch as the draft submitted to his consideration is based upon its first article, and as the undersigned interprets it as not being in harmony with the sovereignty of the country he represents, he has thought that without fresh instructions from his government he cannot continue the discussion touching so important and grave a matter. The government of Colombia could not foresee, when it gave him his instructions, the possibility that when the amplification of the treaty of 1846 should be considered, with a view to specifying the manner and providing the means for the fulfillment of the obligations contracted by the American gov-

*The treaty referred to as that of 1846 was ratified in 1848, and by the latter date we prefer to designate it.

> ernment in connection with the guaranty of the sovereignty of Colombia over the Isthmus, it should be sought, even remotely, to jeopardize or even to call in question its national sovereignty, as, in the opinion of the under-signed, it would be jeopardized if he were to accept as a basis of the discussion of a treaty anything similar to what is contained in Article 1.

The Colombian envoy was a Colombian senator, and referred, at the close of his note, to the necessity of his return to South America. While this consideration may have influenced him, one cannot help surmising that he wished to cut the negotiation short. He was dealing with a government which, whatever its defective knowledge as to the Spanish or even French tongue, did not or would not understand the Anglo-Saxon "no." This information he proposed to impart. In his final note to Mr. Evarts, referring to his departure, he observed that he should be glad to call at the State Department at three o'clock that afternoon, should the Secretary have no prior engagement. He added that he should be "still more glad, on taking leave for the time being, once more to hear the assurances of the fraternal feelings entertained by the great American nation towards its sisters on this continent."

The proposed leave-taking Mr. Evarts accepted. Singular as the conduct of the American Secretary may appear, he persisted, almost as he took the hand of the Colombian envoy, in urging him to stay yet a little longer. He hoped, he said, that they might reach an understanding. As, however, he declined to state *what the basis should be* of a renewed discussion of the subject, the envoy could only refer again to the necessity for his departure. His purpose, he remarked, was to proceed to New York, there to take the South American steamer on the 18th. Mr. Evarts, failing to compass the objects in view, determined by a fresh effort to obtain what part he could. The envoy having departed, he sent a telegram after him. In pursuit of his telegram he dispatched a gentleman in the employ of the Department, Mr. Trescot, of South Carolina. Mr. Trescot was instructed to sign the most favorable protocol it was possible to procure. A final conference occurred in New York. On the 17th, the day before the sailing of the steamer, the signatures were affixed. From this protocol were excluded the objectionable features. In it was inserted the stipulation respecting fortifications to which the Colombian envoy had from the start been ready to agree. Even this moderate instrument, as has been stated, the Colombian government refused to ratify. Reasons have been assigned which seem to justify the decision of the Colombian authorities. One thing was of paramount importance in any such negotiation—not fortifications, but the prohibition of them.

Though the rupture of the negotiations was due specifically to the attempt to encroach upon the treaty-making power, there were other points on which the negotiators could not agree. One had reference to this matter of fortification. Santo Domingo accepted in principle the establishment of such works. These, as we have seen, were to be erected at two points, to be selected by the two governments. Under the terms of Santo Domingo's protocol, however, Colombia might have insisted that these works should be erected neither on the canal nor in its vicinity. Such a course would have accorded with the stipulation of the Clayton-Bulwer treaty. But Mr. Evarts's plan was to plant them upon the canal itself. His design was that these works should be held by the United States and Colombia conjointly, and that the military control of the passage should be vested in these states to the exclusion of every other, either of the eastern or the western hemisphere. All this was in his protocol. In the article which refers to fortifications, Article 3, it is stated that the United States "shall have the right to occupy and fortify such places" at either terminus of the canal and along the line as the United States "may deem necessary." Only further on is the participation of Colombia introduced with reference to the selection of the exact spots. According to this provision, Colombia would have had no power to forbid fortifications upon the canal. It was impossible to see in such a stipulation, in the wording used, anything but that purpose of aggression and encroachment already manifest in the attempt to break the treaty-making power. In the one case it was as plain as in the other. Insistence as to the latter point ruptured the negotiation.

We have not presented every point which the negotiators discussed. What seemed requisite we have produced: points conceded by Santo Domingo, but subsequently disavowed by his government; points urged by Mr. Evarts which Santo Domingo refused even to discuss.

It may be added that in Mr. Evarts's protocol were stipulations which traversed and contradicted others in the convention concluded by the Colombian government with Lucien N. B. Wyse; that is, the Panama Canal Charter. An attempt was made to commit the Colombian government to two contradictory instruments. Such a fact could hardly have encouraged the representative of Colombia to continue the negotiation. Could a state with any sort of self-respect so stultify itself? Santo Domingo observes, in his report to his government, that the United States government "had at last determined to disclose its pretension" to revise the Wyse concession. "This pretension," he adds, he could not allow, without humiliating the "sovereignty" of the state he represented. To convince Mr. Evarts that "it was out of the question to hope that Colombia would consent to such an act of abdication" he wrote the first of the notes already quoted.*

If we consider the nature of the proposals submitted to Colombia, we cannot wonder that she declined to enter into such a compact. According to its terms, the authority conferred was to be joint. But the character of such an agreement between a strong state and a weak one is manifest. Where the genuine authority and control rested was plain. Colombia had no thought of entering into a partnership like that where the beasts went hunting with the lion. It is possible, how-

*The Report of Santo Domingo was published by our government, together with the other documents relating to the negotiation. Resort has been had, in preparing this sketch, to no source outside the official publications of the United States.

ever, that the Colombian government was actuated by diverse motives. Broader views may have been entertained. Such views had been already incorporated by the Colombian government into the charter of the Panama Canal, and it was wise and just to adhere to these.

The course pursued by our envoy at the Colombian capital, Mr. Dichman, was scarcely more satisfactory to the Colombian authorities than the proposals of Mr. Evarts. Mr. Dichman represented at Bogota what Mr. Evarts did in Washington. Mr. Dichman's course became finally so distasteful, not to say offensive, that a request for his recall was forwarded to our State Department. The Colombian government thus took a step analogous, though under circumstances less significant, to that recently taken by this country in the case of an envoy of Great Britain—Lord Sackville.

The diplomat who took Mr. Dichman's place was a man of another cast. He introduced a new and not uninteresting feature into our diplomatic correspondence. Lovers of the picturesque in nature, who appreciate descriptions of it, might read some of the dispatches of Mr. William L. Scruggs with satisfaction, even with zest. In giving an account of his journey to Bogota, perched 8,000 feet above the sea, and of the country in general, he observes as to Colombia, "For boldness and grandeur of natural scenery it is probably without a rival on the globe." So much aesthetic taste, such a growth of refined feeling, as certain dispatches evince—we may refer to his description of certain ranges and the appearance of the moon and stars in a tropical sky, in the dispatch of December 20, 1882—furnish an element as finished and graceful as it is rare in a diplomatic document. Mr. Scruggs was as useful a diplomat as Mr. Dichman. He was perhaps instructed by his government that instead of forcing upon the authorities of Colombia a doctrine as new as it was unpalatable, he should descant rather upon the sights about him. There were the December sunsets, the Southern Cross, the water-falls of the Andes. Such diplomatic methods, if novel, may have had a desired effect. Thus may in some degree have been effaced memories of the "late unpleasantness" between the governments. Mr. Scruggs was the man for the place.*

Such was the negotiation of 1881; such were certain effects. There is not, perhaps, in the diplomacy of the century an attempt to encroach upon the prerogatives of a free state more to be regretted. It was made, not in the interest of broad and liberal views, but of egoistic prejudices. No sort of excuse for it can be alleged.

It is true, however, that when an attempt is made by a powerful state to possess itself of the prerogatives, diplomatic or territorial, of a weak one, there are those who apologize for it. There is hardly a political crime in history—even that most heinous of all, which put the civilized world to shame, the partition of

*One of the early appointments of General Harrison was that of William L. Scruggs as our minister at Caracas.

Poland—but has its apologists and defenders. The doctrine of American control has its adherents. But when Senator Hoar averred that American control was "repugnant to the genius and spirit and honor of the American people" he spoke the truth. Besides this he took a stand which is in the highest sense patriotic. To do right, to advocate the right, is always patriotism.

This consideration—the injustice of an attempt on the part of a powerful state to impose domination upon a lesser—bears so striking a relation to the ideas of the time that it ought to be pointed out. Such aggressions used to be the rule. But a movement of a reverse character has distinguished the present century: not the subjection to greater of lesser nationalities, but their emancipation. Mazzini regarded this movement or tendency as possessed of so radical a character that he predicted it would give its name to the present century. The way in which this prophecy has been fulfilled in the case of his own country, in that of Romania, recently in Bulgaria, even in the case of Belgium, and largely in Hungary speaks for the sagacity and grasp of truth which the great Italian possessed.* Unfortunately, the attempt inaugurated by our government in 1881 ran counter to this principle, respect for the prerogatives, the independence, of minor states. Ought we to think of Europeanizing America, when in so striking a sense Europe has been Americanized? It is a matter for congratulation that the tentative and yet persistent effort described—the attempt to establish in a Spanish-American state a control or domination contrary to the will of the people resulted as it did. It is a fact of weird significance that this endeavor should have taken place in the very year in which, with just circumstance and pomp, we celebrated the downfall of British domination upon this continent. Could the Muse of History have favored us with a smile other than bitter as she recorded the circumstance? Instead of such a policy we ought rather to use a cautious, a persistent vigilance. The United States, the one illustrious commonwealth of America, should set an example consistent, vigorous, and honorable as regards respect for others.**

In connection with this point of view an incident in our policy of 1881 has been omitted. It has reference to the Monroe doctrine. In the instructions given to Santo Domingo it was stated that in the proposed amplification of the treaty of 1848 a reaffirmation of the Monroe doctrine might be inserted. To this doctrine—so the instructions state—"the United States of Colombia *adhere without the slightest reservation*." To this suggestion—if the Colombian envoy made such use of this element of his instructions as they allowed—our government

---

*Another case, that of Greece, preceded Mazzini's prediction. That of Belgium was contemporaneous.

**As for the relation of the nationality principle to the nineteenth century, and the prediction of Mazzini, the *Life, Writings, and Political Principles of Mazzini* may be consulted, page 87. An Introduction by William Lloyd Garrison commends this work to American readers.

gave no heed. The reasons which induced the Colombian government to initiate such a proposal are manifest. That government was aware that the United States was proposing to disregard and set aside those very rights of sovereignty which, according to the Monroe doctrine, it was our province to conserve. The purpose of the Colombian government was to introduce into the proposed convention professions of respect for Colombian sovereignty. These would make the design of the United States more obvious. Nor were the motives of the American Secretary in objecting to such a juxtaposition open to doubt. Could it be for his interest to exhibit in one article of a protocol a purpose to disregard Colombian sovereignty, and at the same time insert a clause so significantly suggestive? According to such insertion, Mr. Evarts would profess a design to protect Colombia from suffering at the hands of others just what he proposed to have her suffer at his own. The case was plain. The American Secretary was in a dilemma. But it was not hard to get out of. He put the Monroe doctrine in his pocket. The Monroe doctrine is one as to which we frequently express ourselves with sincerity and earnestness. At other times it is the most inconvenient luggage to be imagined. At certain junctures we are ready to bestow a tripartite anathema upon the Monroe triumvirate, as we may call it, Canning, Adams, and Monroe, all together. We do what Mr. Evarts did: we put the whole thing in our pockets.

Those who sincerely wish to see the prerogatives of all American states respected can scarcely follow the negotiation of 1881 with satisfaction. The Colombian envoy escaped at last from the wiles of his fellow-diplomat. He reached home, however, only to be denounced by his countrymen, because he had put into the strenuous hand of Mr. Evarts a few crumbs of comfort which he found, after all, he had no right to part with. The protocol was torn up, the whole business brought to a fitting end.

Apropos of the congress of all American states, to meet in Washington in October, a competent writer lately referred as follows to the qualifications of Spanish-American diplomats, and to the disposition, the animus, they may be expected to bring to such a conference.* After speaking of the public men of the United States, he said: "They will have to encounter a sentiment of nationality as proud and strenuous as our own, quick to resent any attempt to disregard or override it. They will meet delegates fully their equals in education, skilled in diplomacy and versed in economic law." Such words might call to mind, were it not in our remembrance, the manner in which the result of the Evarts-Domingo negotiation was received in Colombia. The recall of our minister, Mr. Dichman, was solicited at this time.

Our sketch of American control has been brought down through about a year, from March, 1880, to March, 1881. The protocol signed by Mr. Trescot was dated February 17, 1881. About two weeks remained of President Hayes's administration. General Garfield, the President elect, and Mr. Blame, his Secretary

---

*New York Nation, May 9, 1889.

of State, were aware of the negotiation just concluded. Had President Garfield fully sympathized with the policy of his predecessor—one equally opposed to the views of all American states, except the United States, and to the views of Europe—it would not have been expedient to make an obtrusive statement. The isolated position of the United States counseled reserve. Especially might this be said after the issue of the negotiation just finished. Let us give President Garfield credit, however, for wider views. May not his purpose have been, in the reference to the subject which occurs in his inaugural, while not breaking abruptly with the precedent of his predecessor, to lift our policy towards a more liberal level? It may have been his design to bring the views of the United States more into accord with those of civilization at large. But the change should not be quick or glaring. We may imagine, at any rate, that such was his intent. Assuming this, the declaration made would not be explicit. And it was not. In his inaugural he said, "We will urge no narrow policy, nor seek peculiar or exclusive privileges in any commercial route." This is wholly in accord with the Clayton-Bulwer treaty. These words are followed, however, by others not equally distinct. "But," the President continues, "in the language of my predecessor, I believe it to be 'the right and duty of the United States to assert and maintain such supervision and authority over any interoceanic canal across the isthmus that connects North and South America as will protect our national interests.'" This language might admit of diverse interpretations. Professor T. J. Lawrence, of Cambridge University, England, in discussing the status of the Panama Canal, observes, respecting the entire statement of President Garfield—of which the earlier part disclaims any intent to seek exclusive privileges, and the latter seems not to agree with it—that it is perhaps possible to construe the declaration in accordance with the Clayton-Bulwer treaty.* What in fact is "such supervision and authority" as would "protect our national interests"? Might it not accord with a joint "supervision and authority" exercised by the maritime powers as prescribed in the Suez Convention? Would not this interpretation agree better than any other with the disclaimer made by President Garfield of any purpose to acquire exclusive rights? This was apparently the judgment of Professor Lawrence. At all events, it may be conceded that the position of President Garfield was in advance of that of his predecessor. It indicated a departure from those impassioned views which at first the American people were disposed to harbor. The excitement which had existed and had led to a sort of outburst against the canal was on the wane. Aside from such an explanation, President Garfield seems to have had a better understanding than others of the principles involved,

---

**Essays on some Disputed Questions in Modern International Law*, page 86. It may be said that some of these questions are less disputed now than in 1884, when Professor Lawrence wrote. In 1888 the Suez Convention was concluded.

and a greater readiness to have them carried out. His step was in the right direction.

As much cannot be said of the step taken by Mr. Blame a few months later. In his dispatch dated June 24, 1881, the position was explicitly taken that our government would regard any attempt on the part of European states to negotiate treaties with Colombia equivalent to that of 1848 as unfriendly to the United States. Such a step, Mr. Blame said, "would partake of the nature of an alliance against the United States"! This position, as has been demonstrated, antagonized the understanding and purpose of the United States and New Granada alike at the date of the conclusion of the treaty. The occasion of writing this dispatch was a report that the United States of Colombia were about to conclude such treaties with European states. The purpose was to head her off, to inhibit the exercise of her sovereign rights. This dispatch was the starting-point of a diplomatic discussion between the United States and Great Britain which lasted over two years. This document, of unfortunate historic augury, was written almost at an historic epoch. It was penned only a few days before the second of those fateful shots which within twenty years twice struck down the chief magistrate of the United States. More or less they transformed our policy. As regards the Isthmus question, however, the end of President Garfield's administration and life made no change. For obvious reasons President Arthur did not choose to retain Mr. Blame as Secretary of State. But Mr. Frelinghuysen, his successor, was directed to continue the correspondence. This he did, in the spirit and for the purpose with which it was begun.* The discussion had branched off almost at once from the convention of 1848 to the Clayton-Bulwer treaty. For over two years the not edifying spectacle was presented of an attempt on the part of the United States to get rid of a treaty of which Senator Hoar said—and William H. Seward said the same before him—that it constituted one of the great steps in the world's progress! To such obliquity of judgment, lack of moral grasp and moral sense, had the perversion of the Monroe doctrine brought the government of the United States. Here, at least, as far as this element of American policy went, a radical change was wanted. Fortunately it occurred.

It was not, however, through diplomatic correspondence with England alone that an endeavor was made to get rid of these principles. One of the last acts of President Arthur was the negotiation of a treaty with Nicaragua, by means of which it was proposed to abrogate the convention of 1850. One of the principles which England and the United States had agreed to observe in the case of any interoceanic canal, and especially in the case of one at Nicaragua, was its neutrality. In the proposed Nicaragua treaty of 1884, not a word about neutrality occurs. This element was dropped out. The second of the foundation principles

*President Arthur, in his first annual message (December, 1881), endorsed the strange error of Mr. Blame. Mr. Frelinghuysen's first dispatch was dated May 8, 1882.

of the Clayton-Bulwer treaty was that of equal rights. This likewise it was proposed to disregard. One of the stipulations of the Nicaragua treaty provided that United States vessels, if proceeding from one United States port to another (and this traffic would manifestly absorb the larger part of that in American bottoms), might be favored respecting tolls. These ships might be charged less. No reason seems to exist for establishing a lower rate for this class of vessels; one sure result would be that the commerce of the United States would enjoy a specific and valuable privilege of which most states would be deprived. Let us suppose, however, that a foundation does exist for such a distinction—one between ships engaged in the coasting trade, so called, and those bound for foreign ports. It was a distinction which, according to the principles of the Clayton-Bulwer treaty, should apply to all states alike. Mexico and Colombia, even the Dominion of Canada, might claim its possession. But the proposed treaty did not grant them any such right. This privilege was reserved exclusively for the United States, and that appendage of the United States as far as the treaty went, the state of Nicaragua. After this fashion, as regards the bottom principles of neutrality and equal rights, it was proposed to abrogate the Clayton-Bulwer treaty. The pledges of 1850 were to be flung to the winds. It was with reference to this convention that Senator Hoar said: "Unless this government chooses to abandon her ancient policy, her ancient honor, her ancient faith, we cannot enter upon this great public transaction in Central America in defiance of the obligation of the Clayton-Bulwer treaty."* Fortunately, the United States Senate and the American people were to be spared the disgrace which the conclusion of this convention involved. It failed to receive the requisite two-thirds vote. A few weeks later the term of President Arthur expired.

Concerning the abrogation of the Clayton-Bulwer treaty, the position of paramount importance is that such an abrogation would be an insult to civilization. In this treaty are embodied the higher essence of civilization, its nobler tendencies. The convention of 1850 deserves the encomiums which Senator Hoar and Mr. Seward passed upon it. The question whether in law and techniques it may be held that the treaty has been broken by Great Britain, and that accordingly on that ground we might declare it void, if it have significance, is nevertheless subordinate. As long as Great Britain officially adheres to the treaty—not only adheres to its basic principles, neutrality and equal rights, but has applied these to the Suez Canal by joint convention with the European powers, we ought unhesitatingly to adhere to it ourselves. We should not listen for an instant to any pretext according to which a power, having signed it, might annul her seal. If there be points concerning its observance by Great Britain as to which doubt may be entertained, why should not these be submitted to arbitration? Far the most important matter ever settled by arbitration was determined not long since. Great Britain and the United States were the litigants. Here is a

*Speech in the Senate, February 11, 1887.

case which ought to be settled in the same way, if the parties interested fail to come to an agreement by diplomatic methods. Besides, we should remember, respecting the asserted infraction of the treaty, that among our own statesmen unanimity of opinion is not found.

The administration of President Cleveland held the treaty to be in force. Senator Hoar and authorities of like weight take the same position. At least, no infraction, they say, has occurred since the declaration of President Buchanan in 1860. The Executive then declared that the United States was wholly satisfied with the steps taken by Great Britain in consequence of the complaints of the United States.* In his speech of February 10, 1887, Senator Hoar referred to the two reasons usually alleged in the Senate for considering the treaty void—the occupancy of Belize by Great Britain, and the fact that the treaty related to a special canal then expected to be built, but which was not. He said, "From Clayton himself and his immediate successors through Mr. Seward down to the time of Mr. Blaine, the American government *has stopped itself* from asserting either of those two reasons in any diplomatic discussion." In his judgment, it would not be honorable on our part to try to escape the obligation of the Clayton-Bulwer treaty. We could not do so without violating "the ancient honor and ancient faith" of the United States.

With reference to the allegation that Belize is a part of Central America, and not of Mexico, Mr. Clayton's speech in the Senate, March 8, 1853, should be consulted. It is conclusive. If there be points, however, as to which the statesmen of England and the United States cannot agree, let arbitration decide. Let us employ methods of conciliation and civilization. Let us not think of setting aside one of the noblest landmarks of the century because we may not see all of its appendages with the same eyes.

The attempt, which lasted five years, to subvert our traditional policy suggests reflections of an unfortunate cast. If ever a political party originated in a great principle, and through steadfast adherence to it achieved a triumphant recognition of its validity by the world, that party is the Republican party. The origin of no political organization has been more to its credit. But near the close of the twenty-four years during which this party remained in power it did what it could to overthrow principles of equality and justice which concern, as regards this question, all states and nationalities. These principles the people and government of the United States had, up to the beginning of the undertaking at Panama, recognized and observed. It is true that the Democratic party—this view might be easily enforced—was, especially at the outset, by no means without responsibility. But as the period approached which for the first time in a quarter of a century was to witness a radical change of government, the Republican party became even more rabid in favor of egoism and reaction. The Democratic

*The giving up of the Mosquito protectorate and the surrender of the Bay Islands to Honduras are referred to.

party became less so. The last measure which, prior to its relinquishment of power, the Republican party made an energetic effort to carry was the Nicaragua treaty of 1884. Five weeks before the 4th of March, 1885, the vote occurred. As a body, the Republican Senators voted for the convention, the Democratic Senators against it. There were exceptions on both sides. If we compare the Republican party in its origin with the party when, as the limit of its ascendancy approached, it sought to asperse and annul its former record, the contrast is humiliating. One word tells the story—a falling from moral principle; a falling to the level of temporary expedients and the struggle for advantage. May we not hope that the brief return of the Democratic party to power has produced this good effect, an arrest of further recklessness and degradation?

It is not necessary to analyze the purposes of the Democratic party. We need not decide how far its course was due to motives of expediency or considerations of justice. It may perhaps be said that, having been shut out from power for a quarter of a century, it was ambitious, on resuming ascendancy, to appear as the protagonist of doctrines which concerned the welfare of the whole world and possessed its sanction as well. Whatever the motive, this course the Democratic party took. It should have been taken by the Republican party, but that party refused.

As we have been obliged to criticize with severity the course of President Arthur, it is with satisfaction that we quote from one of his messages, that of December 4, 1882. Referring to the correspondence, not then concluded, between Great Britain and the United States, he said, "It is likely that time will be more powerful than discussion in removing the divergence between the two nations, whose friendship is so closely cemented by the intimacy of their relations and the community of their interests." Precisely this occurred. Time did it. Nor was much time needed. President Cleveland, the successor of President Arthur, possessed one sterling Yankee quality—common sense. He knew what required to be done, and did it. Through his action Great Britain and the United States were brought into accord. At a breath he swept away the whole tissue of assumptions, the absurd pretenses, by which American control had been bolstered up. In place of an egoistic policy he established, or rather reestablished, one by which all states should be entitled to equality of right. Once more it was declared that the Interoceanic Canal of America should be "forever open and free." Never should it become "a point of invitation for hostilities or a prize for warlike ambition."

To the views of President Cleveland may be added those of Mr. Bayard, his Secretary of State. Shortly before Mr. Bayard's retirement they were given to the public as follows:

> Another favorite theme with Mr. Bayard is the neutralization of certain localities which are useful to all the powers, and incapable of defense without disproportionate cost by any one. He instances the neutralization of the Suez Canal by the common consent of the European powers as an example of the im-

> portant benefit to be secured by the application of this principle. Some similar arrangement would have to be entered into to protect the interests of this country, if a ship canal across the Isthmus of Panama is built. It would not be sufficient protection for the United States to have control of such a canal. The only adequate protection is to be secured by neutralization of the canal by consent of all the powers.

This is the exact truth. Fuller security would thus be acquired than if we should pursue a course out of accord with the judgment of other states. American states, as well as European, would repudiate any such policy. Are we voluntarily to place ourselves in antagonism to civilization? Are we to assume the attitude of a state dissatisfied with progress? Shall we turn our backs on the very principles upon which our government is founded?

The mention of President Cleveland and Secretary Bayard ought not to mislead us as to the political significance of these doctrines: their advocacy can be ascribed in no exclusive sense to the Democratic party or Democratic leaders. The honor of believing in them and saying, "These are world-wide doctrines of justice; inevitably they are to prevail," is the property of no party. In all parties those able to take in the significance of progress, the necessities of international comity and right, are believers in and advocates of these principles. We have referred already to the testimonies, as emphatic as any ever uttered, of Senator Hoar and William H. Seward. To their views may be added those of another illustrious American. Admiral Ammen was the intimate friend of General Grant. Widely known through his interest in the interoceanic question and his advocacy of the Nicaragua route, no authority stands higher in the judgment of Americans. In his work upon The American Interoceanic Ship Canal Question he says, "Peoples have arrived at that intelligence that the government of a nation may in its relation to another rather seek to discover and promote common interests than hope to obtain and maintain mean advantages."

In this admirable statement—one of the best expressions of sentiment upon the subject—we are asked not to be upon the watch for "mean advantages;" rather, to make the object of our endeavor benefits which shall be mutual and common—benefits for all. Of a famous poem it has been said that it stood at the high-water mark of the poetry of the present century. It may be said in like manner of the statement of Admiral Ammen that it stands at the high-water mark of the moral declarations of the time. It is not possible that the United States is to depart from a policy so liberal and enlightened.

14

Latin and Saxon America

Albert G. Browne

Commemorating a Pan-American meeting in Washington at the end of 1889, the author of this article calls attention to the dangers that will accumulate for the United States should it choose to accept a political or commercial federation with the Latin American countries. The best policy for the United States concerning Latin America is one of neutrality and nonintervention. The author makes this case by citing arguments used by the founding fathers of the United States.

Additionally, the article examines, in detail, the historical and cultural differences between Saxon and Latin America. The most interesting points of the article are warnings directed toward "innocent" North Americans of the sagacity, intelligence, avarice, and keen understanding of politics characterized by the few upper-class citizens of Latin America. As such, suggests the author, the upper classes feel a mixture of terror and envy toward the United States, represented nicely by the Monroe Doctrine and the events of Panama in the late nineteenth century.

The philosophic study of history teaches that heretofore among mankind no obstacles have been so hard and so slow to be overcome as differences of race accompanied by differences of language and religion. In colonizing this hemisphere there were two currents of immigration thus distinguished, which may be termed Latin and Saxon: the latter flowing chiefly from England, with Holland participating in some but small measure; the former flowing chiefly from Spain and Portugal,* with some participation from France. In modern times, one of these has been reinforced by a great immigration from Germany, and also by an immigration from Ireland, which, though incongruous in race, has been so long assimilated to the Saxon in language and social principles and habits that it is not inharmonious; and the other, in like manner, has been reinforced by a vast number of immigrants from countries bordering on the Mediterranean Sea, particularly from Italy.

For two centuries after the Discovery it was continually doubtful whether the Latin current would not monopolize the New World. Near the close of the next century, the withdrawal of France from the contest, surrendering Canada and ceding Louisiana, fixed the predominance of the Saxon current in the northern continent. During the following half century this predominance was confirmed by the acquisition of Florida and the spoliation of Mexico by our republic; and the last fifty years (completing the fourth hundred from the Discovery) have, in the minds of many of our people, assured the destiny of the Saxon not merely to predominate in North America, but to monopolize it.

It is under these circumstances that the great overshadowing Saxon power of the north has summoned the Latin powers of the south to a conference in the Saxon capital; and they have obeyed the summons with such deluding courtesy that an idea has got into vogue that it is possible to unify them with us in a commercial and political confederation, tributary to our interest and our pride, and antagonistic to the European sources from which all parties to the alliance sprang.

The purpose of this brief article is to incite consideration whether this idea is not a mistake, and whether, unless we are very prudent, the outcome will not more likely be an increase of the dread with which the Latin powers of the hemisphere naturally and reasonably regard us at heart, however specious their profession of respect and friendship. That the conference is not merely commercial in its purposes is manifest from the fact that no European nations possessing American dependencies are bidden to it, although our trade with Canada and with Cuba exceeds that of all the invited participants together.

---

*For convenience, in this article, no distinction will-be made between what issued from Spain and what from Portugal. They will be treated as one in fact, as they were one in substance, and as in fact during a long period of the greatest activity of Spanish colonization Portugal was a Spanish possession. Brazil is an empire trembling on the verge of division into three or four republics. This division and organization would have happened early in the century but for the immigration of the royal family of Braganza. Spasmodic efforts for it have been made repeatedly since, and few publicists doubt that soon after the death of the present respectable Emperor (now far advanced in his sixty-fifth year) they will be renewed and with success.

Some of the foundations of the mistake consist in neglecting the teachings of history already mentioned; ignoring the jealousy with which the modern representatives of the proud race that long was ascendant in the New World regard those by whom their race has been distanced in the competition; misconstruing the quality of their republican government, and interpreting it by ours; overlooking the radical differences between their frame of society and ours, which spring from their union of Church with State, and from the fact that their relation to the Indian population is still by inheritance that of conquerors to subjects, though no longer that of masters to slaves; underrating the keen and selfish intelligence of their ruling classes; failing to comprehend the Oriental fineness and unscrupulousness of their diplomacy; in short, misunderstanding the Latin-American character, and omitting to know that it conceives itself to have a career independent of ours.

The Spaniard preceded the Englishman by a hundred years in occupying America. Long before King Charles First of England granted the Massachusetts charter Spain had girdled the whole of the southern continent and the Gulf of Mexico with colonies, and her possession of the West Indies and the Isthmus secured control of transportation between the oceans, and already she had conceived the project of uniting their waters by a canal. Her precedence in organization was much longer than a century; for during the first fifty years of English colonization there was little attempt of the Mother Country to dictate a political system to her emigrants, and meanwhile the Spanish colonial dominion was systematized by a long line of astute and able viceroys and audiences under direction of the Council of the Indies. In the arts of social life, save so far as they were suppressed or repressed by that direction, Spanish precedence was even more distinguished. While the English colonists remained villagers, whose only public streets were the cow-paths and whose only public parks the cow-pastures; whose climax of luxury in religious edifices was a wooden barn with a steeple of the same material, and to whom, as late as the middle of the eighteenth century, Faneuil Hall was a structure of unrivaled splendor, the Spaniards were founders of cities, laid out with a skill which modern experience has not improved, adorned with vast and solid works of architecture for civil and religious uses which command admiration when tried by the best modern standards, supplied with aqueducts, decorated with alamedas, and often fortified with the greatest military intelligence and the most lavish expenditure. For examples of magnificent cathedrals, those of the cities of Mexico, Puebla, and Lima remain unsurpassed in the New World, and manifold more money was spent by Spain on the fortifications of her galleon port of Carthagena in New Granada than our country has appropriated to those of the port of New York. The advantage of climate and soil also was enormously on the side of the Spaniards. Four fifths of their American domain lay within the tropics, and much of it where the beat of the latitude was tempered by the height of the land, so that its natural products were of every variety; while the English domain was limited to a strip of wilderness on a comparatively sterile northern coast. Of the disparity of the two domains in mineral wealth, and in its development down to the recent era when coal and iron superseded silver and gold in values, there is small need to speak; for greed of the monetary metals was the notorious motive of Spanish dominion, as is familiar to every child. There was nothing in the English colonial possessions to warrant such titles as the Land of Flowers or the Silver River, nothing to impel a search anywhere within their boundaries for the Fountain of Youth or for El Dorado. Another great advantage the Spanish colonists had was in the character of the Indian populations whom they subjugated and enslaved in the West Indies and Mexico and Peru, or adopted and tamed into willing workmen, as in Paraguay. With small exceptions, none of the natives whom they encountered were implacably savage, like those of the northern wilderness. In the viceroyalty of New Spain, and even more in the viceroyalty of Peru, they were so far civilized that they became an immediate help to the conquerors, while the sparse and uncontrollable aborigines who confronted the English settlers were an unmitigated hindrance. The pictures drawn by the historian Prescott (who never visited the countries he described) now are confessed to be touched with fancy, but there is enough of truth in them to demonstrate the intelligence of the labor of the millions who were subjected to the *repartimientos*, *encomiendas*, *mitas*, and other devices by which the Spanish colonists enriched themselves. Nor, in enumerating the constituent parts of their dominion, should the ghastly fact that it was sought, acquired, and administered under the authority and auspices of the Church ever be omitted. Spanish priest and Spanish soldier were inseparable companions, and shared the spoils on terms nearly equal. The tithes for the religious establishments were collected with an exactitude surpassing the collection of the kings fifths. The monuments of clerical wealth so amassed are still the most conspicuous features of all the Spanish settlements from California to Chile; and the division was, on the whole, an equitable one, for the priestly influence over the enslaved population was the strongest security the conquerors had against an insurrection of numbers which bore an even greater proportion to theirs than the natives of Hindostan do to their resident British rulers and army.

It would be easy to enlarge upon the differences between Spanish and English colonization. The subject tempts into dramatic detail. But enough has been said to illustrate them for the present purpose, and to suggest with what feelings the heirs of the one which was so far in advance must contemplate the present ascendancy of the other. For the Spanish-American aristocracies who are represented in this conference at Washington are indeed heirs of the glories of Old Spain as our democracy is of the glories of Old England—heirs of the Roman Empire and the Kingdom of the Visigoths, of the Omayyad Caliphate of Cordova and its Moorish successors, of the splendors of Charles Fifth and gloomy majesty of Philip Second, and of the remembrance that but for the barrenness of an English queen our Mother Land might to-day be a possession of the Spanish Crown. Limited still in South America, save in the Argentine Republic, to almost as scanty settlements back from the coast as a hundred years ago, never acquiring the energy or the numbers necessary to occupy the vast interior, they have beheld the Saxon current in the north sweep from ocean to ocean, and develop into the most powerful nation on the earth, with intelligence generally diffused among the people, with agriculture perfected and industries diversified, with manual labor invested with full political rights and privileges, and with Church absolutely dissociated from State; while five sixths of their own population remain ignorant of letters and incapable of intelligent suffrage, with agriculture positively deteriorated from the times of the Conquest, without manufactures, with little inland transportation save by the natural water-courses, with manual labor despised, and with the Church still so dominant in politics that in a majority of the Latin republics the free public exercise of any but the official religion is prohibited by their constitutions.

If in this contrast sufficient cause for jealousy rather than affection towards us is not already set forth, add the deductions which every Spanish-American mind must draw from the recent declarations of our government that it deems Isthmus communication between the oceans a matter of its own coast-line, although our nearest point of national jurisdiction is still a thousand miles distant. Within the interval thus threatened with impairment of autonomy lie Mexico and the five Central American republics, all Latin in their origin and civilization and language and religion, and heirs of the same traditions as the states of the southern continent. Add also, in the consideration of our probable success in sooner or later executing this doom, the prodigious rate of our increase in population, the still more enormous rate of growth of our material strength, and the dependence of Europe on our plantations and pastures for grain and meat and cotton, and consequent reluctance of Europe to accept any but the gravest occasions to oppose our designs. We are greatly in error if we suppose that the Latin nations of America in our time feel any gratitude to us for the Monroe Doctrine, or regard it with any respect. On the contrary, they would, if they could, proclaim a Monroe Doctrine of their own against ourselves; and it is easily conceivable that at no very distant day European aid may be invoked by them to check our southward progress. Meanwhile, the Doctrine is a convenience to their artful diplomacy, as was illustrated during the recent war between Chile on the one side and Peru and Bolivia on the other, in which the conquering country, first invoking it as a fetish to deter European powers from intervention, next disdainfully rejected our proffers of mediation when that purpose had been accomplished.

We do not begin to comprehend the training, the sagacity, and the pride of the ruling classes of Spanish America—their thorough Machiavellian study of the arts of statesmanship, their monopoly of all the sources of wealth depending on governmental action, the elegance of their social accomplishments, the genuine (though sometimes semi-barbaric) luxury of their social life, the perfection of their knowledge of the world through foreign education and travel, their contempt (not unmixed with terror) of the vulgarity of our northern democracy, their capacity for command, and their hard-hearted willingness to subsist by the sweat of the brows of inferiors. In no Latin country of this hemisphere (unless the Argentine Republic, by reason of its great recent immigration, is an exemption) do they constitute more than a tenth of the population. The other nine tenths are "hewers of wood and drawers of water." The Indian inhabitants of most of these countries still are the majority, and the half-breeds outnumber largely the whites of unmixed blood. There is nothing in our own society, or politics, or literature to enable us to comprehend these ruling classes. The nearest approach to them within our national observation was the slave-holding aristocracy of our Southern States before the civil war. A sentimental disposition prevails among us towards these Latin countries, because all of them, except Brazil, have copied republican forms of government from ours; but if we only will investigate the motive which induced their republican organization, and understand how slow is the progress they have made towards the acquiescence in expressions of the popular will which is the essence of our own republic, we shall find that this sentiment is undue in the large measure in which we bestow it. The occasion of our revolt against England was, to be sure, a selfish one. We rebelled against features of her colonial system which she had copied from the system of Spain. But, underlying the pretext, there was an aspiration for true democratic government which had been fostered among our people for centuries; which reached away back, indeed, to the signing of the compact in the cabin of the Mayflower. No such long-cherished aspiration pervaded the Spanish-Americans. They were incensed by the discriminations which Spain made against them in the bestowal of office and opportunity for gain. The Mother Country filled every colonial office with Spaniards-born, and proscribed the creoles. They also were incensed, as we were, by the commercial code which monopolized their trade to the Mother Country, although this code had been considerably modified the year preceding the battle of Lexington, so as to permit their trade with one another, and was still further relaxed during our Revolutionary War, with the result of developing Buenos Ayres into a flourishing city. But no craving for independence for the sake of self-government was clearly displayed among them until a necessity for it was forced by the confusion of the Spanish kingdom through the ambitions of Napoleon. Then, indeed, this craving sprang to life, and persisted until it satisfied itself, even after the restoration of the legitimate royal rule. But the government instituted in the various republics from Mexico to Chile was not government of the people by the people for the people, but remained government of the many by the few for the few, substituting as the few the creoles in place of the *chapetones*. It could not be otherwise, there being in Spanish America no numerous intelligent middle class, as there is in our Saxon north. But it is not the less a fact which should abate the ignorant sympathy with them that we profess. Indeed, there is not a dependency of the British Crown, where Saxon blood predominates, which is not closer to us in the nature and purpose of its government by the people for the people than is any Latin republic represented in this conference.

Returning now to the purposes of the conference, it will be good for our people to recall to mind the monitions of the farewell address of President Washington:

> The great rule of conduct for us in regard to foreign nations is, in extending our commercial relations, to have with them as little political connection as possible.
>
> It is our true policy to steer clear of permanent alliances with any portion of the foreign world.
>
> Harmony and a liberal intercourse with all nations are recommended by policy, humanity, and interest. But even our commercial policy should hold an equal and impartial hand, neither seeking nor granting exclusive favors or preferences; consulting the natural course of things; diffusing and diversifying by gentle means the stream of commerce, but forcing nothing.

These monitions not only forbid our leaguing with Spanish America against Europe for politics, but also for commerce. The idea of a political league may be fascinating to those who are deceived by the form of government of the Latin republics, and do not penetrate to its substance; but even were the substance democratic (which it is not), such a league would be in direct defiance of the monition to "steer clear of permanent alliances with any portion of the foreign world." The idea of a commercial league with them against Europe may also have fascinations; but even were such a league practicable (which it is not), it would be in direct defiance of the monition to "force nothing," but to "consult the natural course of things." A sufficient reason why it is at present impracticable is the need of foreign capital by Spanish America for its material development, and we have no such capital to spare, in comparison with Europe. Most that we have we require at home for our own development. So long as this need of Spanish America continues with urgency, the "natural course of things" will compel the Latin republics to commercial relations with countries which possess that capital to invest abroad, in preference to those which do not possess it, even if other conditions are equal; and we well know that, besides this, those conditions are not equal, and that we are under further disabilities by reason of our customs-duties on raw materials and our deficiency of shipping, and of the fact that London, not New York, is the financial centre of the world. If the conference teaches us the expediency of abolishing barriers to intercourse which have been erected by our own hands, that will be the utmost reasonable product of it in respect to commerce. As to finance, there is great danger of its assisting to corrupt our currency to a mono-metallic debased silver standard, and it will be fortunate if we escape that peril. As to politics, any relation to them, except absolute independence, in which it may entangle us must prove unsatisfactory, costly, and probably mortifying.

Our rulers do not at all understand Spanish America. Its rulers do more or less understand our country. They are a very superior class of men, much abler and better instructed in the subjects of the conference than are, as a whole, the delegates we have contributed to it, some of whom, in the tour on which the foreigners have been taken (as if they were Apache or Comanche barbarians, to be impressed with unwonted sights), they have come to regard as mercantile "drummers" rather than diplomatic peers. Our straightforward and safe course is to make no gratuitous distinctions, in our political relations, between the Latin-American and other foreign nations; to be friendly with all, but allied with none; and, in Washington's words, "to have with them as little political connection as possible." If we suffer them to draw us into the relation of a permanent arbitrator in their disputes, we shall soon have our hands full of quarrels, and very likely be driven to arms to enforce some of our decisions. For these Latin-American countries are full of occasions for quarreling among themselves: in part from causes which date back to the three conflicting Spanish jurisdictions, civil, military, and ecclesiastical, of which we have a recent instance in the costly war of Brazil, Uruguay, and the Argentine Republic against Paraguay, 1865-70; and in part from rivalry for the hegemony of South America, of which there is a more recent instance in the bloody war of Chile against Peru and Bolivia, 1879-83. Almost their only point of perfectly sympathetic union is their dread of us; and though it might very naturally be argued that this would stop such a project of organized permanent arbitration as is set forth in the official programme of the conference, yet, on the other hand, each of them would be glad of the chance of enlisting us against its adversary. Then, again, if we would draw European nations into disputes with ourselves, we could not pursue a surer way to do so; for the same lack of democratic discipline which induces Latin-American factions to rebel so frequently against decisions of the popular will, in their internal concerns, that many of them are kept in chronic domestic confusion, would be apt to incite the losing party in an arbitrament to invoke European intervention to resist judgments of the international tribunal.

Let us let South America alone to work out her own salvation, just as we let Europe alone to work out hers. That she will work it out successfully, however slowly, there need be no disheartening fear. In spite of present discords, time already has contradicted Bolivar's despairing declaration to Flores sixty years ago, that "America for us" (that is, the people of Spanish descent) "is ungovernable." The number of her statesmen who see that the salvation depends upon inoculating Latin traditions and habits with Saxon principles of truth and liberty and law is multiplying. Already in her temperate zone two countries have proved themselves capable of orderly administration without foreign help—the Argentine Republic and Chile. Time given, with the aid of immigration, the rest are sure to do the same. The eastern slopes of the Andes and upper waters of the vast rivers which pour into the South Atlantic—now the untilled garden of the world—are destined to be the home of a civilization achieved by the Latin race perhaps excelling ours. There is no region of the earth which a mortal eye permitted to anticipate a century, and behold now in a vision as it will be then, can better wish to view.

As to Mexico and the Central American republics, the conference will do great good if it can allay in any measure their sensitiveness, by a disavowal, on the part of our country, of any designs, near or remote, against their autonomy, so emphatically that all Latin America will put faith in the disclaimer. If this would require the executive to modify some of the positions it has taken in administrations preceding that of President Harrison, about Isthmus canalling, pride ought not to stand in the way of a retreat from unjust pretensions. Whenever, if ever, in what President Washington styled "the natural course of things," the surviving Latin countries of the northern continent do fall into our Federal Union, it should not be in the slightest degree by compulsion from our side. We need to realize more clearly than we do that their Latin character makes them an acquisition to be shunned rather than solicited, and that, if destiny condemns us to absorb them as certainly as we shall some day absorb Canada, the longer the day is postponed the better for us. That South America believes this to be their final fate, and will acquiesce if we do not prematurely force the issue, we may be well assured, without any public confessions that would wound Latin pride. As an example of this belief, the president of one of the most enterprising republics of the southern continent, not very long ago, while magnifying the future of his own country and of ours to the writer, in a personal interview, reached to a map and laid his finger upon Panama as the spot (about equally removed now from the boundaries of the one and the other) where he "expected to live to see them meet face to face." But if anybody is very confident of our ability to assimilate annexed Latin populations, let him moderate his confidence by considering how the French-Canadian community, after the exercise of English sway over it for more than a century, still is an undigested lump in the Dominion north of us. Without impugning John Bright's rapturous vision of our continental destiny, let us pray that it be not fulfilled prematurely, nor otherwise than with Peace and Good Will.

15

The Diplomacy and Law of the Isthmian Canals

Sidney Webster

What should be the official position of the U.S. government concerning the possible signing of treaties of neutrality, or the already existent treaties that guarantee free and permanent access of an interoceanic canal through Nicaragua or Panama? The author of this article responds to this question via a study of treaties signed by the United States and through an examination of the British experience with the Suez Canal. Given the difficulties presented by the variety of treaties, the article concludes by suggesting that the transcontinental network of railroads constructed by the United States might actually prove a better model or alternative for moving people and goods across the isthmus.

I

I am asked whether or not the United States now have permanent treaty stipulations with Nicaragua adequate to effectively protect an interoceanic ship-canal through that country constructed by the government or citizens of the United States. The recent internal commotion in Nicaragua, the accompanying revolt against the persons then in power therein, who not long ago gave to a private association of American citizens a canal concession not guaranteed by treaty, and the resulting newspaper comments in Nicaragua on the future of the canal enterprise, have all been of a character to set on foot the inquiry.

I answer it in the negative!

Notwithstanding the lively interest taken by the government of the United States in the construction of an international highway by land or water across the isthmus of the two Americas, nothing practical was accomplished till President Polk, on December 12, 1846, made a treaty with the Republic of New Granada, whose titular designation was in 1861 changed to the United States of Colombia. As its negotiation in 1846 and proclamation in 1848 were contemporaneous with the Mexican war, the acquisition of California and the gold discoveries, it may be inferred that our first treaty preparation to separate the continents by an artificial waterway at Panama, a free navigable route between the two oceans, was inspired by what was then sweeping into our knowledge and our possession on the Pacific coast—now so near by many land routes, but then so inaccessible by land and so remote by sea. Surveys were immediately begun. but the outcome was the Panama Railway, that has been in successful operation during nearly forty years, and is now under French control.

By the thirty-fifth article of the treaty of 1846 the citizens of the United States were put, as to transit across the isthmus, on an equality with New Granadians. As a compensation to New Granada the United States guaranteed "positively and efficaciously" to her the perfect *neutrality* of the before-mentioned isthmus, and the rights of sovereignty and property therein then possessed by New Granada, "with the view" that the free transit promised to the United States may not be interfered with while the treaty exists. The undertaking has already, even with only a railway existing, been burden-some to the United States. It may be very serious if ever a canal shall be in operation, and commercial avidities, ambitions, and strifes of rival peoples and governments shall on that account gather around Colombia. She has interpreted our undertaking as a stipulation that we will defend the railway against local uprisings and civil tumult, and the government at Washington has frequently responded to her calls for aid by a military force landed from one of our men-of-war. In 1862, however, when Colombia asked that three hundred cavalry be sent-thither, Secretary Seward conferred with England and France, setting forth to them that the United States had "no interest in the matter different from that of other maritime powers." Despite the "Monroe doctrine," he invited two great European states to join the United States in guaranteeing time safety of the transit and the authority of the Colombian Confederation. Each replied that as time transit had not been actually interrupted the United States were not yet called on to interfere, but Lord Russell said to Mr. Adams that when the transit shall be really interrupted England will readily cooperate with the government at Washington.

An official opinion has been given by the Attorney-General of the United States to the effect that our guarantee to Colombia covers only "neutrality," in that modern use of the word which relates to an attitude between two or more belligerents, and does not imply a mere protectorate in time of peace.

Perception of the novel and even yet unexplored questions of international law involved, and of the fact that Colombia ever since 1868, as now, might put an end to the treaty of 1846 within a year after giving to us notice of that intention, and, were a canal opened at Panama, might cancel these existing privileges and obligations, has made our Department of State not unwilling to conclude a permanent treaty on more satisfactory terms. In 1856 Secretary Marcy made an endeavor, but New Granada raised insuperable obstacles. The war of secession pushed aside for a time consideration of foreign canals, but in 1868 Secretary Seward caused to be sent to the Senate a new treaty with Colombia, the ratification of which was refused. In 1870 Secretary Hamilton Fish made another effort, but the Congress of Colombia so mutilated the result of the negotiation that it could not be accepted by the United States. A second attempt was made by Mr. Fish, with no better outcome. Various causes contributed to prevent agreement between Washington and Bogota, but probably the chiefest was the very natural conflict of pecuniary interests between, on the one hand, an owner not having the money needed to improve his land, and, on the other hand, a possessor of capital and energy to make the land profitable by incurring serious expenditures, responsibilities, and risks.

Nothing new in regard to the canal was done by Colombia till the concession of March 20, 1878, made by her to Lucien N. B. Wyse, in behalf of the "International Interoceanic Canal Association," of Paris, whose doings have lately lit up again with such lurid light the hazards of even a republic and the statesmen of a republic. That concession was made by Colombia without the consent, and, it has been said, without even the knowledge, of the State Department at Washington. Congress having in 1876, in a spasm of economy, abolished the mission at Bogota, and not having re-established it till the summer of 1878, the Secretary of State had no official channel through which he could be told, and, when told, could protest against, what was going on prejudicial to our interests at Panama.

The efforts in Paris and elsewhere to construct a canal under the Wyse concession moved Secretary Blame in June 1881, to send to our minister at London, and to each of our ministers in Europe, what was in effect a warning to European governments not to enter into a joint guarantee of the neutrality of the interoceanic canal projected across the isthmus of Panama. He therein informed those governments that "a proper guarantee of neutrality" is essential, but the guarantee of the United States will not need "re-enforcement, or accession, or assistance from any other power." A copy of the note was presented to the Foreign Office at London. Lord Granville briefly but most courteously replied by pointing out that the attitude of both governments toward the canal had been and was then fixed by the Clayton-Bulwer convention, and by adding the expression of his confident hope that the United States will observe "*all* the engagements of that treaty." Mr. Blame having made no allusion to the treaty, it may be that its existence, and especially the validity of its eighth section, had for the moment escaped his attention. However that may have been, the note provoked a learned discussion, carried on for two years, which was, however, fruitless in everything excepting a distinctly expressed refusal by the British government to alter or depart from the declaration it had made in the beginning. The refusal distinctly implied that England intended to hold us to the promise made on our behalf in 1850, which was that we will not attempt, either in peace or war, exclusive control over any isthmian canal between the Atlantic and Pacific, but that (quite to the contrary of Mr. Blame's warning) we will unite with Great Britain in establishing "a general principle" applicable to each and every of such canal—namely, the principle of "protection" thereof by each and every government in Europe or America disposed to unite therein, receiving therefor from the proprietors equality of treatment in use of the waterway.

II

There are three canal routes that have had attention—one at Tehuantepec, one at Nicaragua, and another at Panama. The first-named dropped early out of the competition. Owing to the disturbed condition of the state of Nicaragua, created in part by race conflicts and boundary disputes, no efficient work in the way even of surveys or practicable concessions was done on the route till a half-century ago, when, under the auspices of Frenchmen, a beginning was made both at Nicaragua and Suez. Both were resisted by the government at London. The opposition of Lord Palmerston to the endeavors of M. de Lesseps at Suez, under the patronage of France, continued till as late as 1861.

Much that is obscure in British doings at Suez and Nicaragua a half-century ago becomes more plain if one takes account of the personality of Lord Palmerston. He condemned the Webster-Ashburton treaty of 1842 as an "Ashburton surrender to the United States. To Lord Minto he criticized Americans as "an encroaching people." His maxim as Minister of Foreign Affairs was "Never give up a pin's head that you ought to keep and think you can keep; and even if you think that, in the last extremity, you will not be able to keep it, make as many difficulties as you can about resigning it, and manifest a doubt as to whether you should not sooner go to war than resign it."

The preparations of 1849 for a canal in Nicaragua under a concession to the "American Atlantic and Pacific Ship-Canal Company" were stopped by British pretensions on the Mosquito Coast, occupation of San Juan, and by need of pecuniary aid from England. Lord Palmerston denied British intention to hold against the United States exclusive possession of San Juan as the key of the contemplated communication, and offered to unite with them in order to promote by joint influence and mutual co-operation the opening of a channel by Lake Nicaragua, and then declare it a common highway for the use and benefit of all nations. The outcome was the Clayton-Bulwer treaty, negotiated for objects the attainment of which was then indispensable to assure the success of the canal. The needed money was, however, not forthcoming from London. Nicaragua revoked the concession, and there ensued a ten years' controversy over the Clayton-Bulwer treaty and the boundaries of Nicaragua, which were, by the persistent efforts of the United States, finally adjusted in favor of Nicaragua. Our war of secession soon after befell, and public interest in the isthmian routes was temporarily submerged, to reappear in 1867 with the treaty of that year between the United States and the republic of Nicaragua, negotiated by direction of Secretary Seward. At about the same time Nicaragua concluded similar engagements with Great Britain and with France in respect to a canal and its use.

Those treaties are now temporarily in force, and alike manifest the international character of the enterprise. Nicaragua granted thereby "the right of transit" on any and every route, wherever made, by land or sea, through her dominions, and on terms of equality with Nicaragua as to tolls. She distinctly reserved her "sovereignty over the same." She promised a free port at each end. She stipulated that our vessels of war could pass through the canal if the vessels were not to be used against Central American nations friendly to Nicaragua. She covenanted that the United States may, on prescribed conditions, use military force in Nicaragua in order to protect the lives or property of their citizens. What were the United States to do in return? They were, first, to "extend their protection to all such routes of communication as aforesaid;" secondly, "to guarantee the neutrality and innocent use of the same;" and third, "to employ their influence with other nations to induce them to guarantee such neutrality and protection." Thus under three treaties which Nicaragua has made with the United States, Great Britain, and France she has granted to the people of each a transit through any canal on conditions the same as those enjoyed by Nicaraguans.

III

The administration of President Grant desired the construction of a canal either at Panama or Nicaragua, and to that end opened, as has already been seen, negotiations with Colombia, which failed on account of inadmissible conditions exacted by that state. Seven years afterward the Grant administration turned to Nicaragua. The treaty of 1867 existing only for fifteen years, and one year after notice of termination by either party, had proved ineffective. Capital could not be enlisted for a canal. There was needed the more cordial good-will and cooperation of the great powers, made manifest by approving the terms of concessions avid by obligations of guarantee. It was important that the control granted by Nicaragua to those supplying the money should be more explicit and satisfactory. Secretary Hamilton Fish entered on a negotiation with Nicaragua early in 1877. The draught of a new treaty was by him prepared, but Nicaragua refused to concede essential things. It provided for the co-operation of the principal maritime nations in making the canal a neutral pathway consecrated to peace. Its theory of the true interests of the United States in respect to the canal, and of the necessity and method of enforcing its neutrality, was quite unlike that subsequently set forth by Secretary Blame in his circular note of 1881 to our foreign ministers. In 1884 Secretary Frelinghuysen negotiated another canal treaty with

Nicaragua, which was sent to the Senate, but was withdrawn by President Cleveland before the Senate voted finally on its ratification.

IV

Dr. Cardenas, the diplomatic representative who had been sent to Washington in 1876 for negotiation with Mr. Fish of a new treaty, having refused to assent to the draught prepared by the executive branch of the treaty-making power of the United States, and President Grant having rejected in 1877 the conditions imposed by Nicaragua, a plan for concerted legislation by Nicaragua, Costa Rica, and the United States seems to have been devised after what, in 1885, happened to the Frelinghuysen negotiation. Mr. Menocal, then or previously in the service of the United States, and acting in behalf of a private company—the Nicaragua Canal Association, organized on December 3, 1886—entered into a contract with Dr. Cardenas, representing Nicaragua, which was signed April 24, 1887. The government at Washington had no part therein. For the concessions therein made by Nicaragua the association; as subsequently appeared in evidence before the Senate Foreign Affairs Committee, paid to that government one hundred thousand dollars in money, and expended twice as much for surveys. A Nicaragua Canal Construction Company was subsequently organized, on June 10, 1887, under the general laws of Colorado, the capital to be twelve millions; and two months thereafter the association holding the concessions from Nicaragua sold and transferred to that Colorado Construction Company, of which Mr. Warner Miller is president, all the rights and franchises of the association that obtained the concession, including its right to shares and bonds. Congress then incorporated the Maritime Canal Company of Nicaragua.

The Colorado Construction Company thereupon sold for 12 millions of paid-up shares all its property and rights to the new company chartered by Congress, of which Mr. Hiram Hitchcock was and is president. That third owner of the concession and franchise straightway made, on May 24, 1889, a contract with the Colorado Construction Company to build the canal for 200 millions of bonds and 75 millions of shares of the "Maritime Canal Company of Nicaragua," but with a condition that the latter can put an end to the contract by paying all disbursements *plus* ten per cent.

In that condition of the enterprise, which Mr. Menocal had affirmed that 65 millions of dollars would suffice to complete, the Senate Foreign Affairs Committee took it in hand, and after examining witnesses as well as making other diligent inquiries, reported that it was "a clear and specific purpose of the act of Congress that" the political control of the canal shall be retained by the United States; that the corporation is public, not private; that three governments have united to create the corporation and exercise over it "a sovereign control;" and that Nicaragua and Costa Rica have acquiesced in a control of the canal by the United States.

The Foreign Affairs Committee advised the Senate that probably no combination of private individuals can be made adequate to complete the canal. This is its language: "In whatever view the committee could take of the enterprise, there appears grave doubt whether it could be executed without the strong, certain, and powerful support of a great nation, or a combination of nations." Such is the plan of concerted legislation, rather than treaty stipulation, for building a canal in Nicaragua.

The Senate Committee reported a bill which must, one would think, have been a surprise to members of that Democratic party five of whose Presidents—Madison, Jackson, Polk, Pierce, and Buchanan—had vetoed as unconstitutional bills appropriating money for highways and canals *within* the United States. It proposed to limit the number of shares of the "Maritime Canal Company of Nicaragua" at one million of a hundred dollars each; to call in and cancel all shares and bonds issued, as well as satisfy all outstanding liabilities of the company; to authorize a new mortgage on everything, including the franchise, and an issue by the company of 100 millions of new three per cent. bonds, to be deposited in the Treasury of the United States. The Secretary of the Treasury is, after such deposit, and in behalf of the United States, to be required to endorse a guarantee of payment of principal and interest, hand back the bonds to the company, pay the same if the company shall fail so to do, and foreclose the mortgage. The hundred millions in new shares are to be fully paid up—12 millions for the Colorado Construction Company, 7½ millions for Nicaragua and Costa Rica, and the remaining 80½ millions are to become the property of the United States. The President is to appoint ten out of fifteen directors, who are to vote at share-owners' meetings for three others who are to be share-owners. The remaining two directors are to be appointed, one by Nicaragua and one by Costa Rica. That is to be done in face of the stipulation in the concession that in no case shall it be transferred to a "government"!

The Senate Foreign Affairs Committee must be taken to have reported that Congress has constitutional power to raise money by taxation and appropriate the money to dig and operate a ship-canal in a foreign country and outside the territorial jurisdiction of United States over the land or water occupied by the canal and its ocean approaches, even although the seventeenth clause of the eighth section of the first article of the Federal Constitution indicates a clear intent that the Federal government shall hold and exercise exclusive jurisdiction over all places, even in one of our own States, in which "forts, magazines, arsenals, dock yards, and other needful buildings" shall be erected, and although Congress began as early as 1789 to require cession of jurisdiction before erecting even light-houses, and has ever since continued in that way. Mr. Gallatin did, it is true, lead President Jefferson to advocate in 1806-07 a vast national system of internal improvements, including canals, but he deemed a constitutional amendment necessary to bring those objects within the powers of the Federal government. In the Fourteenth Congress Mr. Calhoun raised a special committee of the House to consider "internal improvements," and reported a bill setting aside moneys (derived in some way from the United States Bank) as a fund for constructing roads and canals. The bill was passed by Congress, but its veto was President Madison's last act of official authority. Therein he declares that the power to "*regulate* commerce" did not include a power to dig canals, nor did the power to provide for the common defense and general welfare embrace canal-digging. He put the veto on the ground that a power to dig canals "is not expressly given by the Constitution," and "cannot be deduced from any part of it without an inadmissible latitude of construction"—referring, of course, as he then did, to a time of profound peace, and not to the exigency of actual war and of naval defense; and in 1825 Mr. Jefferson expressed his concurrence with Mr. Madison's views.

I make no comment on the contentions of those who assert or those who deny a power in Congress to levy taxes in order to carry on "a general system of internal improvements." The money expended or land given or credit loaned by the United States to aid in building railways to the Pacific was to promote a public work within our own country—an internal and not an external "improvement."

V

What will be the difference in public law and in the rights of foreign governments between the Panama Railway and the Panama Canal if it shall ever be built? One is a metal road connecting the two oceans, over which transportation is conducted; and the other, if ever made, will be an artificial channel for water, along which vessels can go from one great ocean to the other.

In some current comment and discussion it has been assumed that if there shall be a canal built at Panama under a concession given by Colombia to French-men, or at Nicaragua under a concession given by the republic of that name to Americans, foreign governments may under certain circumstances, and in the absence of treaties, contracts, or special stipulations, have a right, in time of war, to control a use of either of those canals against the will of the owner.

The Suez Canal was dug under a firm an delivered to M. de Lesseps by the Viceroy of Egypt in 1854, and the digging of the Nicaragua Canal is now going on upon much the same plan; and yet, when the Suez Canal had been completed, and before Great Britain had purchased shares therein, that power turned its diplomacy on the canal because of its international qualities. Later on Lord Derby said to Count Schouvaloff that if Russia, then in war with Turkey, exercised the belligerent right to blockade the canal, England could no longer be a neutral, because such interference would be "a menace to India, and a grave injury to the commerce of the world." Lord Derby defended the purchase by England, in 1875, of the canal shares on the plea that the canal came under the "cognizance" of the great powers of Europe; and Great Britain subsequently invited Germany, Austria, Spain, France, Italy, Holland, Russia, and Turkey to unite with her in a convention, stipulating that the Suez Canal shall always be open and free, in time of war as in time of peace, to every vessel of commerce or of war, and not to interfere with such use. A treaty to that effect was signed at Constantinople, October 29, 1888.

If on that international theory, or world-wide commerce theory, foreign governments can, apart from treaties or concessions, insist on such participation in the use of a canal across the American isthmus, no matter by whom it may be owned, then why shall not the United States urge that Nicaragua unite with them in proposing severally to the maritime powers to enter into guarantees and stipulations with reference to the canal and its use as contemplated in the Clayton-Bulwer treaty? Surely such an international understanding would greatly facilitate the loaning of needed funds to the canal company.

Running through all the diplomacy relating to interoceanic canals on either continent there has been distrust of one another among the great maritime powers. It pervades the Clayton-Bulwer treaty. It was manifested between England and France as to Suez. It is seen in the concession by Nicaragua of April 12, 1886, to Mr. Menocal, representing the Nicaragua Canal Association, under which concession, transferred to the Maritime Canal Company, chartered by Congress, excavation for the canal is going on, and Congress is solicited to contribute a hundred millions of three-per-cent United States bonds.

It is stipulated therein that

> the present concession is transferable only to such company of execution as shall be organized by the *Nicaragua Canal Association*, and in no case to governments or to foreign public powers. Nor shall the company cede to any foreign government any part of the lands granted to it by this contract.

And yet the concession permits the building, operating, and business part of the canal to be in the hands of a company "organized in the manner and under the conditions generally adopted for such companies"! Would a transfer of the franchise to the United States by mortgage foreclosure work a forfeiture of the concession?

The distrust and solicitude in respect to a canal at Panama or Nicaragua have related thus far chiefly to war. Hence stipulations touching the guarantee of neutrality. The language of the sixth article of the recent Nicaragua concession to Menocal is a pertinent example and illustration.

That sixth article begins by declaring the proposed canal a neutral place, and that *all* vessels may freely navigate it, but ends by declaring that vessels of war belonging to a government at war with Nicaragua or with any Central American state will be rigorously excluded. Thus, if there be no treaty to the contrary, and a government at war with the United States can get a Central American state as an ally, our ships of war may be excluded from the canal. What the United States can, if they see fit, require—as a condition precedent of pecuniary aid—is a perfect *neutralization* of the canal, as the Suez Canal was neutralized in 1888 by all the great powers, stipulating with one another that the vessels of war of each can always and forever freely use the canal, and that no act of force shall by any of the signatory powers be done in or near the canal.

A protectorate is unlike neutrality, and neutrality is unlike neutralization. England exercised a protectorate over the tribe of Mosquito Indians, but they were not thereby neutralized. "Neutral" and "neutrality" are terms of war. They are the antitheses of intervention and belligerency. When war has begun, new classes of very complex rights and duties, described as neutral rights and duties, supervene for neutrals upon the rights and duties existing before the war so far as the two classes are inconsistent. A definite set of ideas—definite at least among jurists—is now associated with the neutrality of a *state*, but what of a *canal* within that state? Nicaragua does not declare herself (but only the canal and its ports) always neutral "during the term of this concession." She cannot merely by her declaration deprive other governments of their sovereign right to make war on the canal and destroy it. No more can the United States. They were neutrals in the Franco-German war of 1870, but yet were free to become belligerents. Belgium and Switzerland were neutrals, and abstained as did the United States, but Belgium and Switzerland, having been neutralized, had lost the element of freedom to enter the war which the United States possessed. Prussia and France, having consented to neutralize Belgium and Switzerland, had no right to assail them, or either of them.

The only treaty hold Nicaragua has on the United States, or they have on Nicaragua, in regard to the neutrality of the canal, is the treaty of 1867, which can be terminated on a year's notice, and then the United States can as a belligerent violate the neutrality of the canal proclaimed by Nicaragua.

VI

Congress and capitalists are solicited by promoters of the Nicaragua Canal as if it, when dug, will make one navy suffice for our two sea-coasts. A delusion and a snare!

Neutralized—the Nicaragua Canal will of course be to the disadvantage of the United States when at war with any great naval power, by subjecting both our Atlantic and Pacific coasts to peril which menaces either.

Not neutralized, or its neutrality disregarded—the Nicaragua Canal will be at the mercy of the superior naval power, which the United States are not now among all the nations, nor for a long future likely so to become, nor to have a supreme interest in so becoming.

The canal not dug—the United States retain exclusive possession, between the two oceans, of the advantage of railway routes incapable to be cut, or blockaded, or shared by any hostile power.

16

The Strategic Features of the Gulf of Mexico and the Caribbean Sea

A. T. Mahan

This article was written by a naval officer who was widely known for his insistence on strengthening the naval forces of the United States at the end of the nineteenth century. His primary objective was to secure naval routes considered strategic for the commercial domination of the United States in various places around the world. Using a map included with the article, Mahan points out the primary ports and the most important routes in the Gulf of Mexico and Caribbean Sea. Although the author is most concerned, in this article, with the importance of Cuba, the Isthmus of Panama is signaled as a central site in what would hopefully become an "Interior Sea" completely controlled and protected by North Americans.

The importance, absolute and relative, of portions of the earth's surface, and their consequent interest to mankind, vary from time to time. The Mediterranean was for many ages the centre round which gathered all the influences and developments of those earlier civilizations from which our own, mediately or immediately, derives. During the chaotic period of struggle that intervened between their fall and the dawn of our modern conditions, the Inland Sea, through its hold upon the traditions and culture of antiquity, still retained a general ascendancy, although at length its political predominance was challenged, and finally overcome, by the younger, more virile, and more warlike nationalities that had been forming gradually beyond the Alps, and on the shores of the Atlantic and Northern oceans. It was, until the close of the Middle Ages, the one route by which the East and the West maintained commercial relations; for, although the trade eastward from the Levant was by long and painful land journeys, over mountain range and desert plain, water communication, in part, and up to that point, was afforded by the Mediterranean, and by it alone. With the discovery of the passage by the Cape of Good Hope this advantage departed, while at the same instant the discovery of a New World opened out to the Old new elements of luxury and a new sphere of ambition. Then the Mediterranean thrown upon its own productive resources alone, swayed in the East by the hopeless barbarism of the Turk, in the West by the decadent despotism of Spain, and, between the two, divided among a number of petty states, incapable of united, and consequently of potent, action, sank into a factor of relatively small consequence to the onward progress of the world. During the wars of the French Revolution, when the life of Great Britain, and consequently the issue of the strife, depended upon the vigor of British commerce, British merchant shipping was nearly driven from that sea; and but two per cent of a trade that was increasing mightily all the time was thence derived. How the Suez Canal and the growth of the Eastern Question, in its modern form, have changed all that, it is needless to say. Yet, through all the period of relative insignificance, the relations of the Mediterranean to the East and to the West, in the broad sense of those expressions, preserved to it a political importance to the world at large, which rendered it continuously a scene of great political ambitions and military enterprise. Since Great Britain first actively intervened in those waters, two centuries ago, she has at no time willingly surrendered her pretensions to be a leading Mediterranean Power, although her possessions there are of purely military, or rather naval, value.

The Caribbean Sea and the Gulf of Mexico, taken together, form an inland sea and an archipelago. They too have known those mutabilities of fortune which receive illustration alike in the history of countries and in the lives of individuals. The first scene of discovery and of conquest in the New World, these twin sheets of water, with their islands and their main-lands, became for many generations, and nearly to our own time, a veritable El Dorado—a land where the least of labor, on the part of its new possessors, rendered the largest and richest returns. The bounty of nature, and the ease with which climatic conditions, aided by the unwarlike character of most of the natives, adapted themselves to the institution of slavery, insured the cheap and abundant production of articles which, when once enjoyed, men found indispensable, as they already had the silks and spices of the East. In Mexico and in Peru were realized also, in degree, the actual gold-mine sought by the avarice of the earlier Spanish explorers; while a short though difficult tropical journey brought the treasures of the west coast across the Isthmus to the shores of the broad ocean, nature's great highway, which washed at once the shores of Old and of New Spain. From the Caribbean, Great Britain, although her rivals had anticipated her in the possession of the largest and richest districts, derived nearly twenty-five per cent of her commerce, during the strenuous period when the Mediterranean contributed but two per cent.

But over these fair regions too passed the blight, not of despotism merely, for despotism was characteristic of the times, but of a despotism which found no counteractive, no element of future deliverance, in the temperament or in the political capacities of the people over whom it ruled. Elizabeth, as far as she

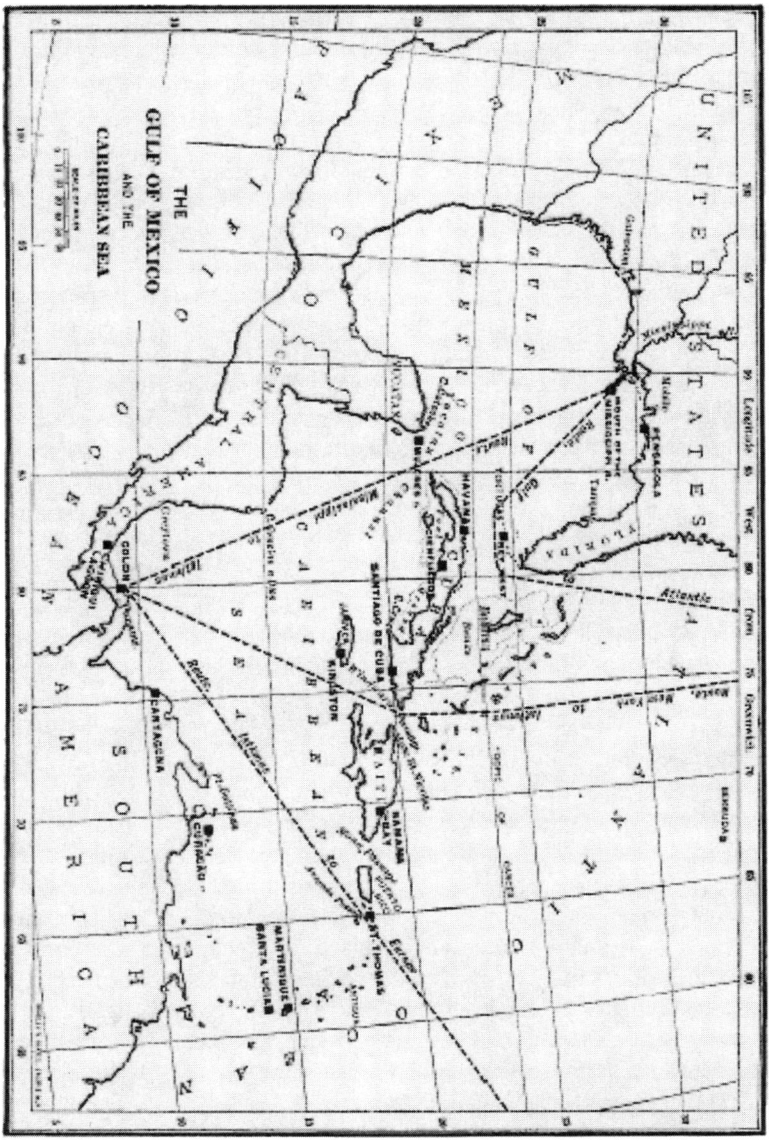

dared, was a despot; Philip II was a despot; but there was already manifest in her subjects, while there was not in his, a will and a power not merely to resist oppression, but to organize freedom. This will and this power, after gaining many partial victories by the way, culminated once for all in the American Revolution. Great Britain has never forgotten the lesson then taught; for it was one she herself had been teaching for centuries, and her people and statesmen were therefore easy learners. A century and a quarter has passed since that warning was given, not to Great Britain only, but to the world; and we today see, in the contrasted colonial systems of the two states, the results, on the one hand of political aptitude, on the other of political obtuseness and backwardness, which cannot struggle from the past into the present until the present in turn has become the past—irreclaimable.

Causes superficially very diverse but essentially the same, in that they arose from and still depend upon a lack of local political capacity, have brought the Mediterranean and the Caribbean, in our own time, to similar conditions, regarded as quantities of interest in the sphere of international relations. Whatever the intrinsic value of the two bodies of water, in themselves or in their surroundings, whatever their present contributions to the prosperity or to the culture of mankind, their conspicuous characteristics now are their political and military importance, in the broadest sense, as concerning not only the countries that border them, but the world at large. Both are land-girt seas; both are links in a chain of communication between an East and a West; in both the chain is broken by an isthmus; both are of contracted extent when compared with great oceans, and, in consequence of these common features, both present in an intensified form the advantages and the limitations, political and military, which condition the influence of sea power. This conclusion is notably true of the Mediterranean, as is shown by its history. It is even more forcibly true of the Caribbean, partly because the contour of its shores does not, as in the Mediterranean peninsulas, thrust the power of the land so far and so sustainedly into the sea; partly because, from historical antecedents already alluded to, in the character of the first colonists, and from the shortness of the time the ground has been in civilized occupation, there does not exist in the Caribbean, or in the Gulf of Mexico—apart from the United States—any land power at all comparable with those great Continental states of Europe whose strength lies in their armies far more than in their navies. So far as national inclinations, as distinct from the cautious actions of statesmen, can be discerned, in the Mediterranean at present the Sea Powers, Great Britain, France, and Italy, are opposed to the Land Powers, Germany, Austria, and Russia; and the latter dominate action. It cannot be so, in any near future, in the Caribbean. As affirmed in a previous paper, the Caribbean is pre-eminently the domain of sea power. It is in this point of view—the military or naval—that it is now to be considered. Its political importance will be assumed, as recognized by our forefathers, and enforced upon our own attention by the sudden apprehensions awakened within the last two years.

It may be well, though possibly needless, to ask readers to keep clearly in mind that the Caribbean Sea and the Gulf of Mexico, while knit together like the Siamese twins, are distinct geographical entities. A leading British periodical once accused the writer of calling the Gulf of Mexico the Caribbean Sea, because of his unwillingness to admit the name of any other state in connection with a body of water over which his own country claimed predominance. The Gulf of Mexico is very clearly defined by the projection, from the north, of the peninsula of Florida, and from the south, of that of Yucatan. Between the two the island of Cuba interposes for a distance of two hundred miles, leaving on one side a passage of nearly a hundred miles wide—the Strait of Florida—into the Atlantic, while on the other, the Yucatan Channel, somewhat broader, leads into the Caribbean Sea. It may be mentioned here, as an important military consideration, that from the mouth of the Mississippi west-ward to Cape Catoche—the tip of the Yucatan Peninsula—there is no harbor that can be considered at all satisfactory for ships of war of the larger classes. The existence of many such harbors in other parts of the regions now under consideration practically eliminates this long stretch of coast, regarded as a factor of military importance in the problem before us.

In each of these sheets of water, the Gulf of Mexico and the Caribbean, there is one position of pre-eminent commercial importance. In the Gulf the mouth of the Mississippi is the point where meet all the exports and imports, by water, of the Mississippi Valley. However diverse the directions from which they come, or the destinations to which they proceed, all come together here as at a great cross-roads, or as the highways of an empire converge on the metropolis. Whatever value the Mississippi and the myriad miles of its subsidiary water-courses represent to the United States, as a facile means of communication from the remote interior to the ocean highways of the world, all centres here at the mouth of the river. The existence of the smaller though important cities of the Gulf coast—Mobile, Galveston, or the Mexican ports—does not diminish, but rather emphasizes by contrast, the importance of the Mississippi entrance. They all share its fortunes, in that all alike communicate with the outside world through the Strait of Florida or the Yucatan Channel.

In the Caribbean, likewise, the existence of numerous important ports, and a busy traffic in tropical produce grown within the region itself, do but make more striking the predominance in interest of that one position known comprehensively, but up to the present somewhat indeterminately, as the Isthmus. Here again the element of decisive value is the crossing of the roads, the meeting of the ways, which, whether imposed by nature itself, as in the cases before us, or induced, as sometimes happens, in a less degree, by simple human dispositions, are prime factors in mercantile or strategic consequence. For these reasons the Isthmus even under the disadvantages of land carriage and transshipment of goods, has ever been an important link in the communications from East to West, from the days of the first discoverers and throughout all subsequent centuries, though fluctuating in degree from age to age; but when it shall be pierced by a canal, it will present a maritime centre analogous to the mouth of the Mississippi. They will differ in this, that in the latter case the converging water routes on one side are interior to a great state whose resources they bear, whereas the roads which on either side converge upon the isthmus lie wholly upon the ocean, the common possession of all nations. Control of the latter, therefore, rests either upon local control of the Isthmus itself, or, indirectly, upon control of its approaches, or upon a distinctly preponderant navy. In naval questions the latter is always the dominant factor, exactly as on land the mobile army —the army in the field—must dominate the question of fortresses, unless war is to be impotent.

We have thus the two centres round which revolve all the military study of the Caribbean Sea and the Gulf of Mexico. The two sheets of water, taken together, control or affect the approaches on one side to these two supreme centres of commercial, and therefore of political and military, interest. The approaches on the other side—the interior communications of the Mississippi, that is, or the maritime routes in the Pacific converging upon the Isthmus—do not here concern us. These approaches, in terms of military art, are known as the "communications." Communications are probably the most vital and determining element in strategy, military or naval. They are literally the most radical; for all military operations depend upon communications, as the fruit of a plant depends upon communication with its root. We draw therefore upon the map the chief lines by which communication exists between these two centres and the outside world. Such lines represent the mutual dependence of the centres and the exterior, by which each ministers to the others, and by severance of which either becomes useless to the others. It is from their potential effect upon these lines of communication that all positions in the Gulf or the Caribbean derive their military value or want of value.

It is impossible to precede or to accompany a discussion of this sort with a technical exposition of naval strategy. Such definitions of the art as may be needed must be given *in loco*, cursorily and dogmatically. Therefore it will be said here briefly that the strategic value of any position, be it body of land large or small, or a seaport, or a strait, depends, 1, upon situation (with reference chiefly to communications), 2, upon its strength (inherent or acquired), and 3, upon its resources (natural or stored). As strength and resources are matters which man can accumulate where suitable situation offers, whereas he cannot change the location of a place in itself otherwise advantageous, it is upon situation that attention must primarily be fixed. Strength and resources may be artificially supplied or increased, but it passes the power of man to move a port which lies outside the limits of strategic effect. Gibraltar in mid-ocean might have fourfold its present power, yet would be valueless in a military sense.

The positions which are indicated on the map by the dark squares have been selected, therefore, upon these considerations, after a careful study of the inherent advantages of the various ports and coast-lines of the Caribbean Sea and the Gulf. It is by no means meant that there are not others which possess merits of various kinds; or that those indicated, and to be named, exhaust the strategic possibilities of the region under examination. But there are qualifying circumstances of degree in particular cases; and a certain regard must be had to political conditions, which may be said to a great extent to neutralize some positions. Some, too, are excluded because overshadowed by others so near and so strong as practically to embrace them, when under the same political tenure. Moreover, it is a commonplace of strategy that passive positions, fortified places, however strong, although indispensable as supports to military operations, should not be held in great number. To do so wastes force. Similarly, in the study of a field of maritime operations, the number of available positions, whose relative and combined influence upon the whole is to be considered, should be narrowed, by a process of gradual elimination, to those clearly essential and representative. To embrace more confuses the attention, wastes mental force, and is a hindrance to correct appreciation. The rejection of details, where permissible, and understandingly done, facilitates comprehension, which is baffled by a multiplication of minutiae, just as the impression of a work of art, or of a story, is lost amid a multiplicity of figures or of actors. The investigation precedent to formulation of ideas must be close and minute, but that done, the unbiased selection of the most important, expressed graphically by a few lines and a few dots, leads most certainly to the comprehension of decisive relations in a military field of action.

In the United States, Pensacola and the Mississippi River have been rivals for the possession of a navy-yard. The recent decision of a specially appointed board in favor of the latter, while it commands the full assent of the writer, by no means eliminates the usefulness of the former. Taken together, they fulfil a fair requirement of strategy, sea and land, that operations based upon a national frontier, which a coastline is, should not depend upon a single place only. They are closer together than ideal perfection would wish; too easily, therefore, to be watched by an enemy without great dispersal of his force, which Norfolk and New York, for instance, are not; but still, conjointly, they are the best we can do on that line, having regard to the draught of water for heavy ships. Key West, an island lying off the end of the Florida Peninsula, has long been recognized as the chief, and almost the only, good and defensible anchorage upon the Strait of Florida, reasonable control of which is indispensable to water communication between our Atlantic and Gulf seaboards in time of war. In case of war in the direction of the Caribbean, Key West is the extreme point now in our possession upon which, granting adequate fortification, our fleets could rely; and, so used, it would effectually divert an enemy's force from Pensacola and the Mississippi. It can never be the ultimate base of operations, as Pensacola or New Orleans can, because it is an island, a small island, and has no resources—not even water; but for the daily needs of a fleet—coal, ammunition, etc.—it can be made most effective. Sixty miles west of it stands an antiquated fortress on the Dry

Tortugas. These are capable of being made a useful adjunct to Key West, but at present they scarcely can be so considered. Key West is 550 miles distant from the mouth of the Mississippi, and 1200 from the Isthmus.

The islands of Santa Lucia and of Martinique have been selected because they represent the chief positions of, respectively, Great Britain and France on the outer limits of the general field under consideration. For the reasons already stated, Grenada, Barbadoes, Dominica, and the other near British islands are not taken into account, or rather are considered to be embraced in Santa Lucia, which adequately represents them. If a secondary position on that line were required, it would be at Antigua, which would play to Santa Lucia the part which Pensacola does to the Mississippi. In like manner the French Guadeloupe merges in Martinique. The intrinsic importance of these positions consists in the fact that, being otherwise suitable and properly defended, they are the nearest to the mother-countries, between whom and themselves there lies no point of danger near which it is necessary to pass. They have the disadvantage of being very small islands, consequently without adequate natural resources, and easy to be blockaded on all sides. They are therefore essentially dependent for their usefulness in war upon control of the sea, which neither Pensacola nor New Orleans is, having the continent at their backs.

It is in this respect that the pre-eminent intrinsic advantages of Cuba, or rather of Spain in Cuba, are to be seen; and also, but in much less degree, those of Great Britain in Jamaica. Cuba, though narrow throughout, is over six hundred miles long, from Cape San Antonio to Cape Maysi. It is, in short, not so much an island as a continent, susceptible, under proper development, of great resources—of self-sufficiency. In area it is half as large again as Ireland, but, owing to its peculiar form, is much more than twice as long. Marine distances, therefore, are drawn out to an extreme degree. Its many natural harbors concentrate themselves, to a military examination, into three principal groups, whose representatives are, in the West, Havana; in the east, Santiago; while near midway of the southern shore lies Cienfuegos. The shortest water distance separating any two of these is 335 miles, from Santiago to Cienfuegos. To get from Cienfuegos to Havana 450 miles of water must be traversed and the western point of the island doubled; yet the two ports are distant by land only a little more than a hundred miles of fairly easy country. Regarded, therefore, as a base of naval operations, as a source of supplies to a fleet, Cuba presents a condition wholly unique among the islands of the Caribbean and of the Gulf of Mexico; to both which it, and it alone of all the archipelago, belongs. It is unique in its size, which should render it largely self-supporting, either by its own products, or by the accumulation of foreign necessaries which naturally obtains in a large and prosperous maritime community; and it is unique in that such supplies can be conveyed from one point to the other, according to the needs of a fleet, by interior lines, not exposed to risks of maritime capture. The extent of the coast-line, the numerous harbors, and the many directions from which approach can be made minimize the dangers of total blockade, to which all islands are subject. Such conditions are in themselves advantageous, but they are especially so to a navy inferior to its adversary, for they convey the power—subject, of course, to conditions of skill—of shifting operations from side to side, and finding refuge and supplies in either direction.

Jamaica, being but one-tenth the size of Cuba, and one-fifth of its length, does not present the intrinsic advantages of the latter island, regarded either as a source of supplies or as a centre from which to direct effort; but when in the hands of a power supreme at sea, as at the present Great Britain is, the questions of supplies, of blockade, and of facility in direction of effort diminish in importance. That which in the one case is a matter of life and death, becomes now only an embarrassing problem, necessitating watchfulness and precaution, but by no means insoluble. No advantages of position can counterbalance, in the long-run, decisive inferiority in organized mobile force—inferiority in troops in the field, and yet much more in ships on the sea. If Spain should become involved in war with Great Britain, as she so often before has been, the advantage she would have in Cuba as against Jamaica would be that her communications with the United States, especially with the Gulf ports, would be well under cover. By this is not meant that vessels bound to Cuba by such routes would be in unassailable security; no communications, maritime or terrestrial, can be so against raiding. What is meant is that they can be protected with much less effort than they can be attacked; that the raiders—the offence—must be much more numerous and active than the defense, because much farther from their base; and that the question of such raiding would depend consequently upon the force Great Britain could spare from other scenes of war, for it is not likely that Spain would fight her single-handed. It is quite possible that under such conditions advantage of position would more than counterbalance a *small* disadvantage in local force. "War," said Napoleon, "is a business of positions;" by which that master of lightning-like rapidity of movement assuredly did not mean that it was a business of getting into a position and sticking there. It is in the utilization of position by mobile force that war is determined, just as the effect of a chessman depends upon both its individual value and its relative position. While, therefore, in the combination of the two factors, force and position, force is intrinsically the more valuable, it is always possible that great advantage of position may outweigh small advantage of force, as 1+5 is greater than 2+3. The positional value of Cuba is extremely great.

Regarded solely as a naval position, without reference to the force thereon based, Jamaica is greatly inferior to Cuba in a question of general war, notwithstanding the fact that in Kingston it possesses an excellent harbor and naval station. It is only with direct reference to the Isthmus, and therefore to the local question of the Caribbean as the main scene of hostilities, that it possesses a certain superiority which will be touched on later. It is advisable first to complete the list, and so far as necessary to account for the selection, of the other points indicated by the squares.

Of these, three are so nearly together at the Isthmus that, according to the rule before adopted, they might be reduced very properly to a single representative position. Being, however, so close to the great centre of interest in the Caribbean, and having different specific reasons constituting their importance, it is essential to a full statement of strategic conditions in that sea to mention briefly each and all. They are, the harbor and town of Colon, sometimes called Aspinwall; the harbor and city of Cartagena, 300 miles to the eastward of Colon; and the Chiriqui Lagoon, 150 miles west of Colon, a vast enclosed bay with many islands, giving excellent and diversified anchorage, the shores of which are nearly uninhabited. Colon is the Caribbean terminus of the Panama Railroad, and is also that of the canal projected, and partly dug, under the De Lesseps scheme. The harbor being good, though open to some winds, it is naturally indicated as a point where isthmian transit may begin or end. As there is no intention of entering into the controversy about the relative merits of the Panama and Nicaragua canal schemes, it will be sufficient here to say that, if the former be carried through, Colon is its inevitable issue on one side. The city of Cartagena is the largest and most flourishing in the neighborhood of the Isthmus, and has a good harbor. With these conditions obtaining, its advantage rests upon the axiomatic principle that, other things being nearly equal, a place where commerce centres is a better strategic position than one which it neglects. The latter is the condition of the Chiriqui Lagoon. This truly noble sheet of water, which was visited by Columbus himself, and bears record of the fact in the name of one of its basins—the Bay of the Admiral—has every natural adaptation for a purely naval base, but has not drawn to itself the operations of commerce. Everything would need there to be created, and to be maintained continuously. It lies midway between Colon and the mouth of the river San Juan, where is Greytown, which has been selected as the issue of the projected Nicaragua Canal; and therefore, in a peculiar way, Chiriqui symbolizes the present indeterminate phase of the Isthmian problem. With all its latent possibilities, however, little can be said now of Chiriqui, except that a rough appreciation of its existence and character is essential to an adequate understanding of Isthmian conditions.

The Dutch island of Curaçao has been marked, chiefly because, with its natural characteristics, it cannot be passed over; but it now is, and it may be hoped will remain indefinitely, among the positions of which it has been said that they are neutralized by political circumstances. Curaçao possesses a fine harbor, which may be made impregnable, and it lies unavoidably near the route of any vessel bound to the Isthmus and passing eastward of Jamaica. Such conditions constitute undeniable military importance; but Holland is a small state, unlikely to join again in a general war. There is, indeed, a float-lug apprehension that the German Empire, in its present desires of colonial extension, may be willing to absorb Holland, for the sake of her still extensive colonial possessions. Improbable as this may seem, it is scarcely more incomprehensible than the recent mysterious movements upon the European chess-board, attributed by common rumor to the dominating influence of the Emperor of Germany, which we puzzled Americans for months past have sought in vain to understand.

The same probable neutrality must be admitted for the remaining positions that have been distinguished: Mujeres Island, Samana Bay, and the island of St. Thomas. The first of these, at the extremity of the Yucatan Peninsula, belongs to Mexico, a country whose interest in the isthmian question is very real; for, like the United States, she has an extensive seaboard both upon the Pacific and—in the Gulf of Mexico—upon the Atlantic Ocean. Mujeres Island, however, has nothing to offer but situation, being upon the Yucatan Passage, the one road from all the Gulf ports to the Caribbean and the Isthmus. The anchorage is barely tolerable, the resources *nil*, and defensive strength could be imparted only by an expense quite disproportionate to the result obtained. The consideration of the island as a possible military situation does but emphasize the fact, salient to the most superficial glance, that, so far as position goes, Cuba has no possible rival in her command of the Yucatan Passage, just as she has no competitor, in point of natural strength and resources for the control of the Florida Strait, which connects the Gulf of Mexico with the Atlantic.

Samana Bay, at the northeast corner of Santo Domingo, is but one of several fine anchorages in that great island, whose territory is now divided between two negro republics—French and Spanish in tongue. Its selection to figure in our study, to the exclusion of the others is determined by its situation, and by the fact that we are seeking to take a comprehensive glance of the Caribbean as a whole, and not merely of particular districts. For instance, it might be urged forcibly, in view of the existence of two great naval ports like Santiago de Cuba and Port Royal in Jamaica, close to the Windward Passage, through which lies the direct route from the Atlantic seaboard to the Isthmus, that St. Nicholas Mole, immediately on the Passage, offers the natural position for checking the others in case of need. The reply is that we are not seeking to check anything or anybody, but simply examining in the large the natural strategic features, and incidentally thereto noting the political conditions, of a maritime region in which the United States is particularly interested; political conditions, as has been remarked, having an unavoidable effect upon military values.

The inquiry being thus broad, Samana Bay and the island of St. Thomas are entitled to the pre-eminence here given to them, because they represent, efficiently and better than any other positions, the control of two principal passages into the Caribbean Sea from the Atlantic. The Mona Passage, on which Samana lies, between Santo Domingo and Puerto Rico, is particularly suited to sailing-vessels from the northward, because free from dangers to navigation. This, of course, in these days of steam, is a small matter militarily; in the latter sense the Mona Passage is valuable because it is an alternative to the Windward Passage, or to those to the eastward, in case of hostile predominance in one quarter or the other. St. Thomas is on the Anegada Passage, actually much used, and which better than any other represents the course from Europe to the Isthmus, just as the Windward Passage does that from the North American Atlantic ports. Neither of these places can boast of great natural strength nor of resources; St. Thomas, because it is a small island with the inherent weaknesses attending all such, which have been mentioned; Samana Bay, because, although the island on which it is large and productive, it has not now, and gives no hope of having, that political stability and commercial prosperity which bring resources and power in their train. Both places would need also considerable development of defensive works to meet the requirements of a naval port. Despite these defects, their situations on the passages named entitle them to paramount consideration in a general study of the Caribbean Sea and the Gulf of Mexico. Potentially, though not actually, they lend control of the Mona and Anegada Passages, exactly as Kingston and Santiago do of the Windward.

For, granting that the Isthmus is in the Caribbean the predominant interest, commercial, and therefore concerning the whole world, but also military, and so far possessing peculiar concern for those nations whose territories lie on both oceans, which it now severs and will one day unite—of which nations the United States is the most prominent—granting this, and it follows that entrance to the Caribbean, and transit across the Caribbean to the Isthmus, are two prime essentials to the enjoyment of the advantages of the latter. Therefore, in case of war, control of these two things becomes a military object not second to the Isthmus itself, access to which depends upon them; and in their bearing upon these two things the various positions that are passed under consideration must be viewed—individually first, and afterwards collectively.

The first process of individual consideration the writer has asked the reader to take on faith; neither time nor space permits its elaboration here; but the reasons for choosing those that have been named have been given as briefly as possible. Let us now look at the map, and regard as a collective whole the picture there graphically presented.

Putting to one side, for the moment at least, the Isthmian points, as indicating the end rather than the precedent means, we see at the present time that the positions at the extremes of the field under examination are held by Powers of the first rank—Martinique and Santa Lucia by France and Great Britain, Pensacola and the Mississippi by the United States.

Farther, there are held by these same states of the first order two advanced positions, widely separated from the first bases of their power, viz., Key West, which is 460 miles from Pensacola, and Jamaica, which is 930 miles from Santa Lucia. From the Isthmus, Key West is distant 1,200 miles; Jamaica, 500 miles.

Between and separating these two groups, of primary bases and advanced posts, extends the chain of positions from Yucatan to St. Thomas. As far as is possible to position, apart from mobile force, these represent control over the northern entrances—the most important entrances—into the Caribbean Sea. No one of this chain belongs to any of the Powers commonly reckoned as being of the first order of strength.

The entrances on the north of the sea, as far as, but not including, the Anegada Passage, are called the most important, because they are so few in number—a circumstance which always increases value; because they are so much nearer to the Isthmus; and, very especially to the United States, because they are the ones by which, and by which alone—except at the cost of a wide circuit—she communicates with the Isthmus, and, generally, with all the region lying within the borders of the Caribbean.

In a very literal sense the Caribbean is a mediterranean sea; but the adjective must be qualified when comparison is made with the Mediterranean of the Old World, or with the Gulf of Mexico. The last-named bodies of water communicate with the outer oceans by passages so contracted as to be easily watched from nearby positions, and for both there exist such positions of exceptional strength—Gibraltar and some others in the former case, Havana and no other in the latter. The Caribbean, on the contrary, is enclosed on its eastern side by a chain of small islands, the passages between which, although practically not wider than the Strait of Gibraltar, are so numerous that entrance to the sea on that side may be said correctly to extend over a stretch of near 400 miles. The islands, it is true, are so many positions, some better, some worse, from which military effort to control entrance can be exerted; but their number prevents that concentration and that certainty of effect which are possible to adequate force resting upon Gibraltar or Havana.

On the northern side of the sea the case is quite different. From the western end of Cuba to the eastern end of Puerto Rico extends a barrier of land for 1,200 miles—as against 400 on the east—broken only by two straits, each fifty miles wide, from side to side of which a steamer of but moderate power can pass in three or four hours. These natural conditions, governing the approach to the Isthmus, reproduce as nearly as possible the strategic effect of Ireland upon Great Britain. There a land barrier of 300 miles, midway between the Pentland Firth and the English Channel—centrally situated, that is, with reference to all the Atlantic approaches to Great Britain—gives to an adequate navy a unique power to flank and harass either the one or the other, or both. Existing political conditions and other circumstances unquestionably modify the importance of these two barriers relatively to the countries affected by them. Open communication with the Atlantic is vital to Great Britain, which the Isthmus, up to the present time, is not to the United States. There are, however, varying degrees of importance below that which is vital. Taking into consideration that, of the 1,200-mile barrier to the Caribbean, 600 miles is solid in Cuba, that after the 50-mile gap of the Windward Passage there succeeds 300 miles more of Haiti before the Mona Passage is reached, it is indisputable that a superior navy, resting on Santiago de Cuba or Jamaica, could very seriously incommode all access of the United States to the Caribbean mainland, and especially to the Isthmus.

In connection with this should also be considered the influence upon our mercantile and naval communication between the Atlantic and the Gulf coasts exercised by the peninsula of Florida, and by the narrowness of the channels separating the latter from the Bahama Banks and from Cuba. The effect of this long and not very broad strip of land upon our maritime interests can be realized best by imagining it wholly removed; or else turned into an island by a practicable channel crossing its neck. In the latter case the two entrances to the channel would have indeed to be assured; but our shipping would not be forced to pass through a long, narrow waterway, bordered throughout on one side by foreign and possibly hostile territories. In case of war with either Great Britain or Spain, this channel would be likely to be infested by hostile cruisers, close to their own base, the very best condition for a commerce-destroying war; and its protection by us under present circumstances will exact a much greater effort than with the supposed channel, or than if the Florida Peninsula did not exist. The effect of the peninsula is to thrust our route from the Atlantic to the Gulf 300 miles to the southward, and to make imperative a base for control of the strait; while the case is made worse by an almost total lack of useful harbors. On the Atlantic, the most exposed side, there is none; and on the Gulf none nearer to Key West than 175 miles,* where we find Tampa Bay. There is, indeed, nothing that can be said about the interests of the United States in an isthmian canal that does not apply now with equal force to the Strait of Florida. The one links the Atlantic to the Gulf, as the other would the Atlantic to the Pacific. It may be added here that the phenomenon of the long, narrow peninsula of Florida, with its strait, is reproduced successively in Cuba, Haiti, and Puerto Rico, with the passages dividing them. The whole together forms one long barrier, the strategic significance of which cannot be overlooked in its effect upon the Caribbean; while the Gulf of Mexico is assigned to absolute seclusion by it, if the passages are in hostile control.

The relations of the island of Jamaica to the great barrier formed by Cuba, Haiti, and Puerto Rico are such as to constitute it the natural stepping-stone by which to pass from the consideration of entrance into the Caribbean, which has been engaging our attention, to that of the transit across, from entrance to the Isthmus, which we must next undertake.

In the matters of entrance to the Caribbean, and of general interior control of that sea, Jamaica has a singularly central position. It is equidistant (500 miles) from Colon, from the Yucatan Channel, and from the Mona Passage; it is even closer (450 miles) to the nearest mainland of South America at Point Gallinas, and of Central America at Cape Gracias-á-Dios; while it lies so immediately in rear of the Windward Passage that its command of the latter can scarcely be considered less than that of Santiago. The analogy of its situation, as a station

*There is Charlotte Harbor, at 120 miles, but it can be used only by medium-sized vessels.

for a great fleet, to that for an army covering a frontier which is passable at but a few points, will scarcely escape a military reader. A comparatively short chain of swift lookout steamers, in each direction, can give timely notice of any approach by either of the three passages named; while, if entrance be gained at any other point, the arms stretched out towards Gallinas and Gracias-á-Dios will give warning of transit before the purposes of such transit can be accomplished undisturbed.

With such advantages of situation, and with a harbor susceptible of satisfactory development as a naval station for a great fleet, Jamaica is certainly the most important single position in the Caribbean Sea. When one recalls that it passed into the hands of Great Britain, in the days of Cromwell, by accidental conquest, the expedition having been intended primarily against Santo Domingo; that in the two centuries and a half which have since intervened it has played no part adequate to its advantages, such as now looms before it; that, by all the probabilities, it should have been reconquered and retained by Spain in the war of the American Revolution; and when, again, it is recalled that a like accident and a like subsequent uncertainty attended the conquest and retention of the decisive Mediterranean positions of Gibraltar and Malta, one marvels whether incidents so widely separated in time and place, all tending towards one end—the maritime predominance of Great Britain—can be accidents, or are simply the exhibition of a Personal Will, acting through all time, with purpose deliberate and consecutive, to ends not yet discerned.

Nevertheless, when compared to Cuba, Jamaica cannot be considered the preponderant position of the Caribbean. The military question of position is quantitative as well as qualitative; and situation, however excellent, can rarely, by itself alone, make full amends for defect in the power and resources which are the natural property of size—of mass. Gibraltar, the synonym of intrinsic strength, is an illustration in point; its smallness, its isolation, and its barrenness of resource constitute limits to its offensive power, and even to its impregnability, which are well understood by military men. Jamaica, by its situation, flanks the route from Cuba to the Isthmus, as indeed it does all routes from the Atlantic and the Gulf to that point; but, as a military entity, it is completely overshadowed by the larger island, which it so conspicuously confronts. If, as has just been said, it by situation intercepts the access of Cuba to the Isthmus, it is itself cut off by its great neighbor from secure communication with the North American Continent, now as always the chief natural source of supplies for the West Indies, which do not produce the great staples of life. With the United States friendly or neutral, in a case of war, there can be no comparison between the advantages of Cuba, conferred by its situation and its size, and those of Jamaica, which, by these qualities of its rival, is effectually cut off from that source of supplies. Nor is the disadvantage of Jamaica less marked with reference to communication with other quarters than the United States—with Halifax, with Bermuda, with Europe. Its distance from these points, and from Santa Lucia, where the resources of Europe may be said to focus for it, makes its situation one of extreme isolation; a condition emphasized by the fact that both Bermuda and Santa Lucia are themselves dependent upon outside sources for anything they may send to Jamaica. At all these points, coal, the great factor of modern naval war, must be stored and the supply maintained. They do not produce it. The mere size of Cuba, the amount of population which it has, or ought to have, the number of its seaports, the extent of the industries possible to it, tend naturally to an accumulation of resources such as great mercantile communities always entail. These, combined with its nearness to the United States, and its other advantages of situation, make Cuba a position that can have no military rival among the islands of the world, except Ireland. With a friendly United States, isolation is impossible to Cuba.

The aim of any discussion such as this should be to narrow down, by a gradual elimination, the various factors to be considered, in order that the decisive ones, remaining, may become conspicuously visible. The trees being thus thinned out, the features of the strategic landscape can appear. The primary processes in the present case have been carried out before seeking the attention of the reader, to whom the first approximations have been presented under three heads. First, the two decisive centres, the mouth of the Mississippi and the isthmus. Second, the four principal routes, connecting these two points with others, have been specified; these routes being, 1, between the Isthmus and the Mississippi themselves; 2, from the Isthmus to the North American coast, by the Windward Passage; 3, from the Gulf of Mexico to the North American coast, by the Strait of Florida; and, 4, from the Isthmus to Europe, by the Anegada Passage. Third, the principal military positions throughout the region in question have been laid down, and their individual and relative importance indicated.

From the subsequent discussion it seems evident that, as "communications" are so leading an element in strategy, the position or positions which decisively affect the greatest number or extent of the communications will be the most important, so far as situation goes. Of the four principal lines named, three pass close to, and are essentially controlled by, the islands of Cuba and Jamaica, viz., from the Mississippi to the Isthmus by the Yucatan Channel, from the Mississippi to the Atlantic coast of America by the Strait of Florida, and from the Isthmus to the Atlantic coast by the Windward Passage. The fourth route, which represents those from the Isthmus to Europe, passes nearer to Jamaica than to Cuba; but those two islands exercise over it more control than does any other one of the archipelago, for the reason that any other can be avoided more easily and by a wider interval than either Jamaica or Cuba.

Regarded as positions, therefore, these two islands are the real rivals for control of the Caribbean and of the Gulf of Mexico; and it may be added that the strategic centre of interest for both Gulf and Caribbean is to be found in the Windward Passage, because it furnishes the ultimate test of the relative power of the two islands to control the Caribbean. For, as has been said before, and cannot be repeated too often, it is not position only, nor chiefly, but mobile force, that is decisive in war. In the combination of these two elements rests the full statement of any case. The question of position has been adjudged in favor of Cuba, for reasons which have been given. In the case of a conflict between the powers holding the two islands, the question of controlling the Windward Passage would be the test of relative mobile strength; because that channel is the shortest and best line of communications for Jamaica with the American coast, with Halifax, and with Bermuda, and as such it must be kept open. If the power of Jamaica is not great enough to hold the passage open by force, she is thrown upon evasion—upon furtive measures—to maintain essential supplies; for, if she cannot assert her strength so far in that direction, she cannot, from her nearness, go beyond Cuba's reach in any direction. Abandonment of the best road in this case means isolation; and to that condition, if prolonged, there is but one issue.

The final result, therefore, may be stated in this way: The advantages of situation, strength, and resources are greatly and decisively in favor of Cuba. To bring Jamaica to a condition of equality, or superiority, is needed a mobile force capable of keeping the Windward Passage continuously open, not only for a moment, nor for any measurable time, but throughout the war. Under the present conditions of political tenure, in case of a war involving only the two states concerned, such a question could admit of no doubt; but in a war at all general, involving several naval powers, the issue would be less certain. In the war of 1778, the tenure, not of the Windward Passage merely, but of Jamaica itself, was looked upon by a large party in Great Britain as nearly hopeless; and it is true that only a happy concurrence of blundering and bad luck on the part of its foes then saved the island. Odds that have happened once may conceivably happen again.

PART V

After Separation

Most Colombians learn, from their grade school teachers, that their province of Panama was "lost" on November 3, 1903, thanks to a hotheaded American President (Theodore "Teddy" Roosevelt) who fumed over the Colombian Senate's rejection of the Hay-Herrán Treaty. A popular Bogotá theatrical production, "I Took Panama" was written in 1974 by Luis Alberto García and staged the same year at the Teatro Popular de Bogotá under the direction of Jorge Alí Triana.[1] The work juxtaposes restless, muscular U.S. Marines in Panama with an elderly political elite at Bogotá, completely out of touch with the popular will or the people of Panama. The play, a political satire, ran for ten years and was revived in the early 1990s. The message of the production is clear: small cliques in Bogotá and Washington have, historically, made political decisions that often have absolutely nothing to do with public will or the good of the Colombian nation at large.

The Hay-Herrán Treaty quickly passed through the U.S. Senate in the spring of 1903 and authorized the United States to finance, construct, and protect a swath of land in Panama seven-miles wide, from ocean to ocean. The Colombian Senate at Bogotá, in no mood to negotiate with the United States given that a civil war known as "The War of the Thousand Days" had just concluded in 1902, rejected the treaty. This resulted in an uprising in Panama City. U.S. naval forces moved in, surrounding the cities of Panama and Colón, effectively neutralizing any Colombian reaction to the Panamanian uprising. Panamanians declared their independence from Bogotá, and the Republic of Panama was born, with the complete support and backing of the United States.

To more fully understand the Panama "uprising" of 1903, it is important to consider Colombian history and the relationship between Bogotá and Panama City. The political class that ruled in Bogotá in 1903 was part of what is known as the "regeneration"; they were a group of conservative politicians who, in 1886, rewrote the constitution of the country, connecting Colombian society strictly to the Roman Catholic Church. Members of this regeneration can be characterized as cautious political conservatives, convinced that civilization and culture radiated out from Catholic Church teachings, Hispanic culture, and the Spanish language. They completely ignored the aspirations of the north coast and the province of Panama, preferring to view those regions of the country as essentially flawed in terms of climate, race, and culture. The north coast and the Province of Panama were much more closely connected to political liberalism and tied intimately to the Caribbean economy and export trade. Travel, for example, between Colón and New Orleans was seven days by boat. To reach Bogotá, the capital of Colombia, from the Panamanian port city of Colón required sailing east to the mouth of the Magdalena River, then a long voyage south, up the river against the northerly flow, and then several days travel from the river town Honda to the capital at 2,600 meters. Total travel time was about one month, depending on climate and other conditions. Panamanians had, since the early 1850s, depended almost completely on trans-isthmian trade and commerce for their livelihood; they received virtually no services from Bogotá, with its political culture that treated the Panamanians with condescension, except, of course, when it came time to collect taxes and other revenues from the province.

For Panamanians, then, construction of a canal—by anyone—became almost an obsession; their livelihood was directly tied to a canal and the benefits it would bring to the region in terms of revenue, taxation, hotel, banking, insurance, and other services that would have to be "sold" at Panama to travelers and commercial enterprises. Panamanians were angered by what they viewed as a completely arbitrary decision at Bogotá in 1903: rejection of the Hay-Herrán Treaty. The anti-Bogotá goals of their "uprising" fit nicely with the policy of Teddy Roosevelt, who referred to the Colombians as "contemptible little creatures" after the Colombian Senate vote. Roosevelt, a man of action, decided that the commercial and military benefits of the canal far outweighed the feelings or political priorities of the Colombian Senate; he also knew that Colombia could not, militarily or otherwise, challenge the U.S. naval forces, so Panama declared independence and was immediately recognized by the United States as a sovereign republic.

Fifteen days after the Panamanian revolution of independence, the true nature of Panamanian sovereignty would be set down in a new treaty signed by U.S. Secretary of State John Hay and the Frenchman Philippe Buneau-Varilla, "an international adventurer who purported to represent Panama's interests."[2] The new treaty allowed for the United States to control and defend a ten-mile strip across the isthmus, and construction of the canal began almost immediately afterwards, culminating in the opening of the canal in 1914, shortly before the beginning of the World War I.

The heavy-handedness of the Roosevelt administration's treatment of Colombia offended not just Colombians, but all of Latin America. Colombian-U.S. diplomatic relations were frozen until the early 1920s when discovery of oil in Colombia, and payment of a 25 million dollar indemnity by the United States beginning in 1922, appears to have lubricated the oxidized wheels of diplomacy.

The two chapters in this final part contain articles from November 1904 (*Harper's*) and April 1905 (*The Atlantic Monthly*); both articles were published shortly after the events of November 1903 and, as such, should be seen as early attempts to wrestle with the new aggressive policy of the United States toward Latin America and place that policy within the stricture of international law and/or U.S. diplomacy. The chapter by John Bassett Moore is especially fascinating in that the author claims that the policy of nonintervention is (despite intervention in Cuba and Panama) still very much the law and priority of the United States of America. However, that same year, in 1904, President Theodore Roosevelt expressed a doctrine of intervention in what would become known as "the Roosevelt Corollary to the Monroe Doctrine." That doctrine stated that "chronic wrongdoing, or an impotence which results in a general loosening of the ties of civilized society, may in America, as elsewhere, ultimately require intervention by some civilized nation."[3] Clearly, the Roosevelt Corollary was a doctrine of intervention, and the policy of the Roosevelt Administration undermines the academic treaties offered by Moore in *Harper's* magazine. The Dole article, published five months after Moore's, is compelling in that the author criticizes the Monroe Doctrine as essentially outdated by the early twentieth century and questions whether the United States has the legal right to "bar our neighbors from lands in which we have no shadow of a title." Dole, no friend to Latin America, cynically suggests that the German presence in Latin America would be civilizing and uplifting, and, demonstrating the naïveté of American scholars at the time, writes that "Germans are doubtless coming in considerable numbers into the temperate countries of South America. They are a most desirable kind of immigrant. Wherever they go a higher civilization goes with them. Life and property are safer."

Notes

1. Manuel Zapata Olivella et al., *Teatro Colombiano Contemporáneo*, Madrid: Fondo de Cultura Económica, pp. 417-506.

2. E. Bradford Burns and Julia A. Charlip, *Latin America: A Concise Interpretive History*, 7th ed., Englewood Cliffs, N.J.: Prentice Hall, 2002, p. 174.

3. Ibid. p. 175.

17

Non-Intervention and the Monroe Doctrine

John Bassett Moore*

Moore, a close associate of President Theodore Roosevelt and a renowned professor of international law and diplomacy at Columbia University, published a series of articles after the "Separation of Panama" in 1903 that were widely circulated in an attempt to explain the central principles of the foreign policy of the United States. Two of the most important themes for Moore involved the Monroe Doctrine and the doctrine of nonintervention. The author explains the intervention of the United States in Cuba as a lamentable but inevitable exception to the principle of nonintervention and, concerning Panama, the events of 1903 occurred in accordance with the best traditions of U.S. foreign policy. Such traditions include defending sovereignty, quickly accepting the will of all peoples who express, with acts, their desire for independence while organizing and helping to sustain a new state. Thus, concludes the author, neither the Cuban nor the Panamanian case should cause alarm in the international community given that the official policy of the United States remains a principle of nonintervention and support for the Monroe Doctrine.

Among the rules of conduct prescribed for the United States by the statesmen who formulated its foreign policy, none was conceived to be more fundamental or more distinctively American than that which forbade intervention in the political affairs of other nations. The right of the government to intervene for the protection of its citizens in foreign lands on the high seas never was doubted; nor was such action withheld in proper cases. But, warned by the spectacle of

*Professor of International Law and Diplomacy, Columbia University.

the great European struggles that had marked the attempts of nations to control one another's political destiny, the statesmen of America, believing that they had a different mission to perform, planted themselves upon the principle of the equality of nations as expounded by Grotius and other masters of international law. This principle was expressed with peculiar felicity and force by Vattel, who declared that nations inherited from nature "the same obligations and rights," that power or weakness could not in this respect produce any difference, and that a "small republic" was "no less a sovereign state than the most powerful kingdom." The same thought was tersely phrased by Chief-Justice Marshall, in his celebrated affirmation: "No principle is more universally acknowledged than the perfect equality of nations. Russia and Geneva have equal rights." And as the Declaration of Independence proclaimed life, liberty and the pursuit of happiness to be "unalienable rights" of individual men, so the founders of the American republic ascribed the same rights to men in their aggregate political capacity as independent nations.

While the principle of non-intervention formed an integral part of the political philosophy of American statesmen, its practical importance was profoundly impressed upon them by the narrowness of their escape from being drawn, by the alliance with France, into the vortex of the European conflicts that grew out of the French Revolution. Even before American independence was acknowledged by Great Britain, American statesmen scented the dangers that lurked in a possible implication in European broils. "You are afraid," said Richard Oswald to John Adams, "of being made the tool of the powers of Europe." "Indeed I am," said Adams. "What powers?" inquired Oswald. "All of them," replied Adams; "it is obvious that all the power of Europe will be continually maneuvering with us to work us into their real or imaginary balances of power. . . . But I think that it ought to be our rule not to meddle." In 1793 the revolutionary government of France, apparently doubting the applicability of the existing alliance with the United States to the situation in Europe, submitted a proposal for "a national agreement, in which two great peoples shall suspend their commercial and political interest and establish a mutual understanding to defend the empire of liberty, wherever it can be embraced." This proposal the American government declined; and its response found practical embodiment in its acts. The reasons for the policy of non-intervention and neutrality, to which the administration of the time so sedulously adhered, were eloquently summed up by Washington in that immortal political legacy, his Farewell Address. "The great rule of conduct for us, in regard to foreign nations," said Washington, "is, in extending our commercial relations, to have with them as little political connection as possible. So far we have already formed engagements, let them be fulfilled with perfect good faith. Here let us stop." The same thought was conveyed by Jefferson, in his first inaugural address, in the apothegm, "Peace, commerce, and honest friendship with all nations, entangling alliances with none."

The policy of non-intervention embraced matters of religion as well as of politics. By the first amendment to the Constitution of the United States, Congress was expressly forbidden to make any law "respecting an establishment of religion, or prohibiting the free exercise thereof." This inhibition against governmental interference with religious opinions and practices was in its spirit extended to the intercourse of the United States with foreign nations. In Article IX of the treaty between the United States and Tripoli, which was concluded on November 4, 1796, during the administration of Washington, we find this significant declaration: "As the Government of the United States of America is not in any sense founded on the Christian religion; as it has in itself no character of enmity against the laws, religion, or tranquillity of Mussulmen; . . . it is declared by the parties, that no pretext arising from religious opinions shall ever produce an interruption of the harmony existing between the two countries." With the omission of the introductory phrase, a similar declaration was inserted in the treaty with Tripoli of 1805, and in the treaties with Algiers of 1815 and 1816. A stipulation less broad in its tolerance appears in Article XXIX of the treaty between the United States and China, signed at Tientsin, June 18, 1858. This article, after reciting that the principles of the Christian religion are "recognized as teaching men to do good, and to do to others as they would have others do to them," provides that "any person, whether citizen of the United States or Chinese convert, who, according to these tenets, peaceably teach and practice the principles of Christianity, shall in no case be interfered with or molested." By Article IV, however, of the Burlingame treaty of 1868, this stipulation is mentioned as an introduction to the declaration that it is "further agreed that citizens of the United States in China of every religious persuasion, and Chinese subjects in the United States, shall enjoy entire liberty of conscience, and shall be exempt from all disability or persecution on account of their religious faith or worship in either country." In harmony with this principle was the simple declaration in the treaty with Siam of 1856, and in the treaty with Japan of 1858, that Americans in those countries should "be allowed the free exercise of their religion." They were to be protected, not as the adherents or the propagandists of any particular faith, but as American citizens. As was once said by Mr. Cass, it was the policy of the United States "not merely to protect a Catholic in a Protestant country, a Protestant in a Catholic country, a Jew in a Christian country, but an American in all countries."

The policy of non-intervention, which guided the United States during the wars growing out of the French Revolution, was severely tested in the struggle of the Spanish colonies in America for independence; but, under the guardian care of Monroe and John Quincy Adams, it was scrupulously adhered to. In view of the circumstance, it is strange that one of the greatest perils by which, after the days of the alliance with France, the maintenance of the policy was ever apparently threatened should have grown out of a political contest in Europe. The struggle of the Greeks for independence evoked much sympathy in

America as well as in England; but the struggle of the Hungarians, under the leadership of Kossuth, for emancipation from Austria rule, gave rise in the United States to manifestations of feelings that were unprecedented. The Hungarian revolution came at a time when the spirit of democracy, which distinguishes the political and social development of the nineteenth century, was especially active; but the widespread interest felt in the United States in the Hungarian movement was greatly intensified by reason of the popular assumption that the declaration of Hungary's independence, although it in reality left the question of a permanent form of government wholly in abeyance, was the forerunner of a republic. It was, however, only after the arrival of Kossuth in the United States that the excitement reached its greatest height. In June, 1849, Mr. A. Dudley Mann was appointed by the President as a "special and confidential agent of the United States to Hungary"; but before he reached his destination Russia had intervened in aid of Austria, and the revolution had practically come to an end. When the revolution was crushed, Kossuth and many of his associates sought refuge in Turkey. By a joint resolution of Congress of March 3, 1851, the President was requested, if it should be the wish of these exiles to "emigrate" to the United States, to authorize the employment of a public vessel to convey them to America. In conformity with this request the U.S.S. *Mississippi* was sent to the Dardanelles; but the exiles had scarcely embarked when it was found that Kossuth had other views than that of coming to America as an emigrant. At Gibraltar he left the *Mississippi* and proceeded to London for the purpose of conferring with revolutionary exiles in that city; and he afterwards sailed for America in the steamer *Humboldt* from Southampton. He arrived at New York on the 14th of December, 1851.

He soon dissipated all doubts as to the object of his mission. In his public addresses he cast all reserve, and in his "official capacity" as the representative of Hungary made an appeal for aid. He affirmed that the consideration of distance should not deter the United States in the case of Hungary, any more than in that of Cuba, from interfering against European invasion. Cuba was six days distant from New York; Hungary was eighteen. Was this, he asked, a circumstance to regulate the conduct and policy of a great people? The people, wherever he went, seemed enthusiastically to give a negative answer. His journey to Washington was in the nature of a triumphal progress. When presented to the President, he made a direct appeal for intervention. President Fillmore, with courtesy and dignity, but with equal candor, repelled the solicitation. But, for his disappointment at the White House, Kossuth found consolation in his reception by Congress, though it in the end proved to be wholly illusory. He was received both by the Senate and by the House, and was banqueted by Congress. The first effective check to the popular excitement was given by Henry Clay, who refused to countenance the prevailing agitation. Kossuth more than once expressed a desire to meet him, and Clay, though in feeble health, at length granted him an interview. "For the sake of my country," said Clay, addressing Kossuth, "you must allow me to protest against the policy you propose to her." "Waiving the grave and momentous question of the right of one nation to assume the executive power among nations, for the enforcement of international law," Clay pointed out the practical difficulties that stood in the way of affording to Hungary effective aid against Austria and Russia. He also enlarged upon the evil example that would be afforded by the United States to other powers in departing from its "ancient policy of amity and non-intervention"; and after declaring that the United States had, by adhering to that policy, "done more for the cause of liberty in the world than arms could effect," he concluded: "far better is it for ourselves, for Hungary, and for the cause of liberty, that, adhering to our wise and pacific system and avoiding the distant wars of Europe, we should keep our lamp burning brightly on this western shore, as a light to all nations, than to hazard its utter extinction amid the ruins of fallen or falling republics in Europe." The Kossuth danger passed away even more suddenly than it had arisen. After he left Washington, he addressed a letter to the presiding officers of the two Houses of Congress, in which he expressed the hope that the United States would pronounce in favor of the law of nations and of international rights and duties. A motion to print this letter was carried in the Senate by only one vote, and the arguments in support of the motion were almost exclusively confined to considerations of courtesy. Indeed, the sudden collapse of Kossuth enthusiasm in high places after his departure from the capital would have been inexplicable if the open opponents of his policy of intervention had found any one to meet them on the ground.

It may be said that the most pronounced exception ever made by the United States, apart from cases arising under the Monroe Doctrine, to its policy of non-intervention is that which was made in the case of Cuba. At various times since the United States became an independent nation conditions in Cuba had been such as to invite interference either for the purpose of correcting disorders which existed there, or for the purpose of preventing Cuba from falling a prey to some of Spain's European enemies. During the Ten Years' War in Cuba, from 1868 till 1878, intervention by the United States was prevented on several occasions only by the powerful influence of President Grant, counseled and supported by his Secretary of State, Hamilton Fish. In its abstention the administration was aided by the situation at home, which afforded daily admonition of the difficulties that might attend the reestablishment of order in a large and populous island where the process of emancipation was still going on. In 1895 the situation was changed in the United States as well as in Cuba. American interests on the island had also increased. The second insurrection was, besides, more active than the first, and spread over a wider area. If the conflict were left to take its course, the ruin of the island was apparently assured. The United States tendered its good offices; but the offer was not productive of any tangible result. In his annual message of December 7, 1896, President Cleveland declared that, when Spain's inability to suppress the insurrection had become manifest, and the struggle had degenerated into a hopeless strife involving useless sacrifice of life and the destruction of the very subject-matter of the conflict, a situation would be presented in which the obligation to recognize the sovereignty of Spain would be "superseded by higher obligations."

Conditions continued to grow worse. The distress produced by the measures of concentration, under the rule of General Weyler, excited strong feeling in the United States, and prompted President McKinley to request Spain to put an end to existing conditions and restore order. General Weyler was afterwards succeeded by General Blanco, and it was announced than an autonomous régime would be instituted. But neither the offer of autonomy nor the actual institution of an autonomous government produced peace. The insurgents, embittered by the three years' conflict, rejected the programme of autonomy with substantial unanimity, while the distinctively Spanish element of the population viewed it with disapprobation and withdrew from polities.

In this delicate situation the intervention of the United States was precipitated by certain startling events. The incident created by the surreptitious publication of the letter of Señor Dupuy de Lome, Spanish minister at Washington, to Señor Canalejas, in which President McKinley was aspersed and the reciprocity negotiations between the two countries were exhibited as a sham, had just been officially declared to be closed, when the U.S.S. *Maine* was blown up at Havana, and 266 of her crew perished. Shallow and short-sighted reasoners have wished to treat the destruction of the *Maine* as the justification and the cause of the intervention of the United States. The government of the United States, however, did not itself take that ground. It is true that the case of the *Maine* is mentioned in the preamble to the joint resolution of Congress by which the intervention of the United States was authorized; but it is recited merely as the culmination of "abhorrent conditions," which had existed for more than three years. The destruction of the *Maine* doubtless kindled the intense popular feeling without which wars are seldom entered upon; but the government of the United States never charged—on the contrary, it refrained from charging—that the catastrophe was to be attributed to "the direct act of a Spain official." Its intervention rested upon the ground that there existed in Cuba conditions so injurious to the United States, as a neighboring nation, that they could no longer be endured. Its action was analogous to what is known in private law as the abatement of a nuisance. On this ground the intervention was justified by the late Alphonse Rivier, one of the most eminent publicists in Europe, and on this ground its justification must continue to rest.

Any exposition of the American doctrine of non-intervention would be incomplete that failed to notice the rule of the United States with regard to the recognition of new governments—a rule which is indeed a corollary of that doctrine. In Europe, governments had been treated as legitimate or illegitimate, according to what was conceived to be the regularity or the irregularity of the succession of their rulers. The attitude of the United States on this question was early defined when the National Convention in France proclaimed a republic. On the occasion Jefferson, as Secretary of State, in a letter to Gouverneur Morris, of March 12, 1793, which has become a classic, said: "We surely cannot deny to any nation that right whereon our own government is founded, that every one may govern itself according to whatever form it pleases, and change these forms at its own will; and it may transact its business with foreign nations through whatever organ it thinks proper, whether king, convention, assembly, committee, president, or anything else it may choose. The will of the nations is the only thing essential to be regarded." In a word, the United States maintained that the true test of a government's title to recognition is not the theoretical legitimacy of its origins, but the fact of its existence as the apparent exponent of the popular will. And from this principle, which is now universally accepted, it necessarily follows that recognition can properly be accorded only when the new government has demonstrated its ability to exist. Recognition extended at an earlier stage of the revolution savors of an action of intervention, and as such must be defended on its merits, as is clearly set forth in President Roosevelt's message on January 4, 1904, in relation to the recognition of the Republic of Panama.

In connection with the principle of non-intervention, a prominent place must be given to the Monroe Doctrine, the object of which was to render intervention unnecessary by precluding the occasions for it. On September 26, 1815, the Emperors of Austria and Russia and the King of Prussia signed at Paris a personal league commonly called the Holy Alliance, the design of which was declared to be the administration of government, in matters both internal and external, according to the precepts of justice, charity, and peace. To this end the allied monarchs, "looking upon themselves as delegated by Providence" to rule over their respective countries, engaged to "lend one another, on every occasion and in every place, assistance, aid, and support." In the course of time, as revolt against the arrangements of the Congress of Vienna spread and grew more pronounced, the alliance came more and more to assume the form of a league for the protection of the principle of legitimacy—the principle of divine right of kings as opposed to the rights of the people—against the encroachments of liberal ideas. Congresses were held at Ais-la-Chapelle, Troppau, and Laybach, for the purpose of maturing a programme to that end. The league was joined by the King of France; but England, whose Prince regent had originally given it his informal adhesion, began to grow hostile.

Her own government, with its free and parliamentary institutions, was founded on a revolution; and the allies, in the circular issued at Troppau, had associated "revolt and crime," and had declared that European powers "had an undoubted right to take a hostile attitude in regard to those states in which the overthrow of the government might operate as an example." In a circular issued at Laybach they denounced "as equally null, and disallowed by the public law of Europe, any pretended reform effected by revolt and open force." In October,

1822, they held a congress at Verona for the purpose of concerting measures against the revolutionary government in Spain; and in yet another circular announced their determination "to repel the maxim of rebellion, in whatever place and under whatever form it might show itself." Their ultimate object was more explicitly stated in a secret treaty in which they engaged mutually "to put an end to the system of representative governments" in Europe, and to adopt measures to destroy "the liberty of the press." Popular movements were forcibly suppressed in Piedmont and Naples; and in April, 1823, France, acting for the allies, invaded Spain for the purpose of restoring the absolute monarch Ferdinand VII. Before the close of the summer such progress had been made in this direction that notice was given to the British government of the intention of the allies to call a congress with a view to the termination of the revolutionary governments in Spanish America.

At this time Lord Castlereagh, who had always been favorably disposed towards the alliance, had been succeeded in the conduct of the foreign affairs of England by George Canning, who reflected the popular sentiment as to the policy of the allied powers. The independence of the Spanish-American governments, which had now been acknowledged by the United States, had not as yet been recognized by Great Britain. But English merchants, like those of the United States, had developed a large trade with the Spanish-American countries—a trade which the restoration of those regions to a colonial condition would, under the commercial system then in vogue, have cut off and destroyed.

In view of this common interest, Canning, towards the close of 1823, began to sound Richard Rush, the American minister at London, as to the possibility of a joint declaration by the two governments against the intervention of the allies in Spanish America. Canning once boasted that he had called into being the New World to redress the balance of the Old. The meaning of this boast can be understood only in the light of his proposals. In a "private and confidential" note to Rush, of August 23, 1823, he declared: "1. We conceive the recovery of the colonies of Spain to be hopeless. 2. We conceive the question of the recognition of them, as independent states, to be one of time and circumstances. 3. We are, however, by no means disposed to throw any impediment in the way of an arrangement between them and the mother country by amicable negotiation. 4. We aim not at the possession of any portion of them ourselves. 5. We could not see any portion of them transferred to any other power with indifference."

If these opinions and feelings were shared by the United States, Canning thought the two governments should declare them in the face of the world, as the best means to defeating the project, if any European power should cherish it, of subjugating the colonies in the name of Spain, or of acquiring any part of them itself by cession or by conquest. He therefore desired Rush to act upon his proposals at once, if he possessed the power to do so. It was said of Richard Rush by an eminent Senator that, in the course of an unusually long and important career, he "never said a word that was improper, nor betrayed a thought that might peril his country's fortunes." On the present occasion he acted with his usual good judgment. His powers did not embrace the making of such a declaration as Canning desired; but, while he expressed the opinion that Canning's sentiments, except as to independence, which the United States had already acknowledged, were shared by his government, he lost no time in reporting the matter to the President. Monroe, on receiving the correspondence, hastened to take counsel upon it. Jefferson, whose opinion was solicited, replied: "Our first and fundamental maxim should be never to entangle ourselves in the broils of Europe; our second, never to suffer Europe to intermeddle with cisatlantic affairs." He was disposed to look with favor upon cooperation with England in the direction suggested, and Madison shared his opinion. In the cabinet of Monroe, Calhoun inclined to invest Rush with power to join England in a declaration, even if it should pledge the United States not to take either Cuba or Texas. The President at first was inclined to Calhoun's idea of giving Rush discretionary powers, but this was opposed by John Quincy Adams, who maintained that we could act with England only on the basis of the acknowledged independence of the Spanish-American states. The views of Adams prevailed. His basal thought was the right of self-government, which he believed it to be the duty and the interest of the United States to cherish and support. He thought that the United States should let England make her own declaration. This England did, without waiting for the decision of the United States. On October 9, 1823, Canning, in an interview with Prince de Polignac, French ambassador, declared that while Great Britain would remain "neutral" in any war between Spain and her colonies, the "junction" of any foreign power with Spain against the colonies would be viewed as constituting "entirely a new question," upon which Great Britain "must take such decision" as her interests "might require."

In his annual message to Congress of December 2, 1823, President Monroe devoted to the subject a long passage. The substance of it is, however, conveyed in a few sentences. After adverting to the abstention of the United States from European wars and the dangers to be apprehended from the system of the allied powers, he declared: "We owe it, therefore, to candor and to the amicable relations existing between the United States and those powers, to declare that we should consider any attempt on their part to extend their system to any portion of this hemisphere as dangerous to our peace and safety. With the existing colonies or dependencies of any European power we have not interfered and shall not interfere. But with the governments who have declared their independence and maintained it, and whose independence we have, on great consideration and on just principles, acknowledged, we could not view any interposition for the purpose of oppressing them, or controlling in any other manner their destiny, by any European power, in any other light than a manifestation of an unfriendly disposition towards the United States."

The sentences just quoted specially relate to the aims of the Holy Alliance; but there is another passage in the message which is also often cited as embodying the Monroe Doctrine. In 1821, the Emperor of Russia issued a ukase, by which he assumed, as owner of the shore, to exclude foreigners from carrying on commerce and from navigating and fishing within a hundred Italian miles of the northwest coast of America, from the Bering Strait down to the 51st parallel of north latitude. As this assertion of title embraced territory which was claimed by the United States as well as by Great Britain, both those governments protested against it. In consequence the Russian government proposed to adjust the matter by amicable negotiation; and instructions to that end were prepared by John Quincy Adams for the American ministers at London and St. Petersburg. At a meeting of the cabinet on June 28, 1823, while the subject was under discussion, Adams expressed the opinion that the claim of the Russians could not be admitted, because they appeared to have no "settlement" upon the territory in dispute; and on July 17 he informed Baron Tuyl, then Russian minister at Washington, "that we [the United States] should contest the right of Russia to any territorial establishment on this continent, and that we should assume distinctly the principle that the American continents are no longer subjects of *any* new European colonial establishments." With reference to this subject, President Monroe, in the message above quoted, said: "In the discussion to which this interest has given rise, and in the arrangements by which they may terminate, the occasion has been judged proper for asserting as a principle in which the rights and interests of the United States are involved, that the American continents, by the free and independent condition which they have assumed and maintain, are henceforth not to be considered as subjects for future colonization by any European powers."

By the term "future colonization" President Monroe evidently intended to convey the same meaning as was expressed by the terms "settlement" and "colonial establishments" previously employed by Adams. They were used to denote, what they were then commonly understood to mean, the acquisition of title to territory by original occupation and settlement. But in the course of time the phrase "future colonization" came to receive a broader interpretation. President Polk, in his annual message of December 2, 1845, declared that, while existing rights of every European nation should be respected, it should be "distinctly announced to the world as our settled policy that no future European colony or dominion shall, with our consent, be planted or established on any part of the North-American Continent." By pronouncing against the establishment by a European power of any "dominion"—a term which included even the voluntary transfer of territory already occupied—President Polk expressed a conception which has come generally to prevail, and which is embodied in the popular phrase, "No more European colonies on these continents." The same meaning is conveyed in the phrase, "America for the Americans," which signifies that no European power shall be permitted to acquire new territory or to extend its dominions in the Western Hemisphere.

In this sense, but apparently with the qualification in the particular case that only a forcible acquisition of territory was forbidden, the Monroe Doctrine was invoked by President Cleveland in respect of the Venezuelan boundary question. This incident, as is well known, grew out of a long-standing dispute between Great Britain and Venezuela, which was the continuation of a dispute two centuries old between the Netherlands and Spain as to the limits of the Dutch and Spanish settlements in Guiana. In 1844 Lord Aberdeen proposed to Venezuela a conventional line, beginning at the river Moroco. This proposal was declined; and, chiefly in consequence of civil commotions in Venezuela, negotiations remained practically in abeyance till 1876. Venezuela then offered to accept the Aberdeen line; but Lord Grenville suggested a boundary farther west; and in subsequent negotiations the British demand was extended still farther in that direction. Venezuela, representing that this apparent enlargement of British dominion constituted a pure aggression on her territorial rights, invoked the aid of the United States on the ground of the Monroe Doctrine. Venezuela asked for arbitration, and in so doing included in her claim a large portion of British Guiana. Great Britain at length declined to arbitrate unless Venezuela would first yield all territory within a line westward of that offered by Lord Aberdeen. In these circumstances, Mr. Olney, as Secretary of State, in instructions to Mr. Bayard, American Ambassador at London, on July 20, 1895, categorically inquired whether the British government would submit the whole controversy to arbitration. In these instructions Mr. Olney declared that the Monroe Doctrine did not establish a "protectorate" over other American States; that it did not relieve any of them "from its obligations as fixed by international law nor prevent any European power directly interested from enforcing such obligations or from inflicting merited punishment for the breach of them"; but that its "single purpose and object" was that "no European power or combination of European powers" should "forcibly deprive an American state of the right and power of self-government, and of shaping for itself its own political fortunes and destinies." This principle he conceived to be at stake in the dispute between Great Britain and Venezuela, because, as the dispute related to territory, it necessarily imported "political control to be lost by one party and gained by the other."

"Today," declared Mr. Olney, "the United States is practically sovereign on this continent, and its fiat is law upon the subjects to which it confines its interposition." All the advantages of this superiority were, he affirmed, at once imperiled if the principle should be admitted that European powers might convert American states into colonies or provinces of their own. Lord Salisbury declined unrestricted arbitration; and when his answer was received, President Cleveland, on December 17, 1895, laid the correspondence before Congress. "If a European power, by an extension of its boundaries, takes possession of the territory of one of our neighboring republics against its will and in derogation of its rights," it was, said President Cleveland, the precise thing which President Monroe had declared to be "dangerous to our peace and safety"; but, he added, "any adjustment of the boundary which that country [Venezuela] may deem for her advantage and may enter into or her own free will cannot, of course, be objected by the United States."

He then recommended the appointment by the United States of a commission to investigate the merits of the controversy, and declared that, if the title to the disputed territory should be found to belong to Venezuela, it would be the duty of the United States "to resist by every means in its power, as a willful aggression upon its rights and interests, the appropriation by Great Britain of any land or the exercise of governmental jurisdiction over any territory which, after investigation, we have determined of right belongs to Venezuela."

This declaration produced great excitement, in the United States as well as in England. So far as it seemed to imply, as the language has often been constructed to do, that the United States possessed the right, by means of an *ex parte* commission, appointed by itself and composed of its own citizens, authoritatively to fix the boundary between two other independent nations, it went beyond the immediate necessities of the case. If the commission had ever reported, its conclusions probably would have been treated as advisory rather than definitive, and would have been made the basis of further correspondence with both governments.

The actual position insisted upon in Mr. Olney's instructions to Mr. Bayard, as well as in the rest of President Cleveland's message, was that the United States would resist the palpable and substantial seizure and appropriation by Great Britain of Venezuelan territory. This position was quite in harmony with the spirit of the Monroe Doctrine. Congress unanimously provided for the appointment of a commission of investigation; but the commission, immediately after its organization, addressed to Mr. Olney, through its president, Mr. Justice Brewer, a letter setting forth its peaceful and non-partisan character and the desirability of securing the cooperation of Great Britain and Venezuela in obtaining evidence. At the close of his letter, Mr. Justice Brewer observed: "The purposes of the pending investigation are certainly hostile to none, nor can it be of advantage to any that the machinery devised by the government of the United States to secure the desired information should fail of its purpose."

This statement was communicated to Great Britain as well as to Venezuela, and both governments promptly responded to the appeal. The labors of the commission were, however, brought to a close by the conclusion of a treaty of arbitration, signed by Great Britain and Venezuela, but negotiated between Great Britain and the United States, the predominant feature of which was the application of the principle of prescription, under the definite rule that fifty years' adverse holding of a district, either by exclusive political control or by actual settlement, should suffice to constitute national title. The adoption of the principle of prescription, on which the arbitrators would necessarily have acted, even if it had not been incorporated into the treaty, at once rendered nugatory the greater part of the Venezuelan claim. Although the extreme British claim was not allowed, the territorial results of the arbitration were decidedly favorable to that government. It must, however, be conceded that the most important political result of the Venezuelan incident was not the decision upon the territorial question, but the official adoption of the Monroe Doctrine by the Congress of the United States, and its explicit acceptance by the principal maritime powers of Europe.

The latest official exposition of the Monroe Doctrine was given by President Roosevelt in his annual message of December 3, 1901, in which he said: "The Monroe Doctrine is a declaration that there must be no territorial aggrandizement by any non-American power at the expense of any American power on American soil. It is in no wise intended as hostile to any nation in the Old World. . . .This doctrine has nothing to do with the commercial relations of any American power, save that it in truth allows each of them to form such as it desires. . . .We do not guarantee any state against punishment if it misconducts itself, provided that punishment does not take the form of the acquisition of territory by any non-American power." An occasion for the practical application of this definition soon arose. On December 11, 1901, the German ambassador at Washington left at the Department of State a memorandum in which it was stated that the German government proposed to take certain coercive measures against Venezuela, for the satisfaction of claims, based partly on breaches of contract and partly on violent wrongs, which it had been found to be impracticable otherwise to bring to a settlement. At the same time the memorandum declared that "under no circumstances" would the German government consider in its proceedings "the acquisition or the permanent occupation of Venezuelan territory." In acknowledging the receipt of this memorandum, on the 16th of December, Mr. Hay adverted to the fact that the German ambassador, on his recent return from Berlin, had conveyed personally to the President, and had afterward repeated to himself, the assurance of the German Emperor that the imperial government had no purpose or intention to make even the smallest acquisition of territory on the South-American continent or the adjacent islands; and in view of this circumstance, and of the further assurance given in the memorandum, Mr. Hay declared that the President, while "appreciating the courtesy of the German government in making him acquainted with the state of affairs referred to," did not regard himself "as called upon to enter into the consideration of the claims in question." The coercive measures contemplated by the German government were postponed for a year, and were then taken in conjunction with the British government, which also made to the United States, on November 13, 1902, a frank communication of its purposes. To this communication Mr. Hay replied that "the government of the United States, although it regretted that European powers should use force against Central and South American governments, could not object to their taking steps to obtain redress for injuries suffered by their subjects, provided that no acquisition of territory was contemplated." In the hostilities with Venezuela that ensued the assurances of the powers were honorably kept, but peaceful relations were honorably kept, but peaceful relations were eventually restored through the frank exercise of the friendly offices of the United States.

In popular discussions the position has sometimes been urged that it is a violation of the Monroe Doctrine for a European power to employ force against an American republic for the purpose of collecting a debt or satisfying a pecuniary demand, no matter what may have been its origin. For this supposition, which is discredited by the declarations and the acts of President Roosevelt and Mr. Hay, there appears to be no official sanction. It is true that in Wharton's *International Law Digest* under the head of the "Monroe Doctrine," two alleged manuscript instructions by Mr. Blaine to the American minister at Paris, of July 23 and December 16, 1881, are cited as authority for the statement that "the government of the United States would regard with grave anxiety an attempt on the part of France to force by hostile pressure the payment by Venezuela of her debt to French citizens." The citation, however, is wholly inadvertent. Both instructions are published in the volume of foreign relations for 1881; and they refer, not to "hostile pressure," but to a rumored design on the part of France of "taking forcible possession of some of the harbors and a portion of the territory of Venezuela in compensation for debts due to citizens of the French Republic." Even in regard to this they nowhere express "grave anxiety," but merely argue that such a proceeding would be unjust to other creditors, including the United States, since it would deprive them of a part of their security; while they avow the "solicitude" of the government of the United States "for the higher object of adverting hostilities between two republics for each of which it feels the most sincere and enduring friendship."

In 1861 the United States formally admitted the right of France, Spain, and Great Britain to proceed jointly against Mexico for the satisfaction of claims. "France," said Mr. Seward on that occasion, in an instruction to the American minister at Paris, of June 26, 1862, "has a right to make war against Mexico, and to determine for herself the cause. We have the right and the interest to insist that France shall not improve the war she makes to raise up an anti-republican or anti-American government, or to maintain such a government there." In a similar vein, Mr. Seward, writing to the American minister in Chile, on June 2, 1866, with reference to the hostilities then in progress between Spain and the republics of the west coast of South America, and particularly to the bombardment of Valparaiso by the Spanish fleet, declared that the United States did not intervene in wars between European and American states "if they are not pushed, like the French war in Mexico, to the political point"; that the United States had no "armies for the purpose of aggressive war; no ambition for the character of a regulator."

A tendency is often exhibited to attach decisive importance to particular phrases in President Monroe's message of 1823, or to the special circumstances in which they originated, as if they furnished a definitive test of what should be done and what should be omitted under all contingencies. The verbal literalist would, on the one hand, make the United States an involuntary party to all controversies between European and American governments, in order that the latter may not be "oppressed"; while the historical literalist would, on the other hand, treat Monroe's declarations as obsolete, since the conditions to which they specially referred no longer exist. But when we consider the mutations in the world's affairs, these modes of reasoning must be confessed to be highly unsatisfactory. The "Monroe Doctrine" has in reality become a convenient title by which is denoted a principle that doubtless would have been wrought out if the message of 1823 had never been written—the principle of the limitation of European power and influence in the Western Hemisphere. We have seen, in the first part of this series, that as early as 1778 the Continental Congress, in the treaty of alliance with France, obtained from its ally the renunciation of any claim to the British possessions in North America. When Washington, in his Farewell Address, observed that Europe had "a set of primary interest, which to us have none, or a very remote relation," he lent emphasis to the thought that it was desirable so far as possible to dissociate America from the vicissitudes of European polities. Giving to this thought a further reach, Jefferson, while President, in 1808, declared: "We shall be satisfied to see Cuba and Mexico remain in their present dependence, but very unwilling to see them in that of either France or England, politically or commercially. We consider their interest and ours as the same, and the object of both must be to exclude European influence from this hemisphere." On January 15, 1811, twelve years before Monroe's message was published, Congress, in secret session, "taking into view the peculiar situation of Spain and her American provinces," and "the influence which the destiny of the territory adjoining the southern border of the United States might have upon their security, tranquility, and commerce," resolved that the United States could not "without serious inquietude see any part of said territory pass into the hands of any foreign power"; and the President was authorized to occupy all or any part of the Floridas, "in the event of an attempt to occupy the same, or any part thereof, by any foreign government."

In the long struggle, which was eventually crowned with success, to exclude European domination from the interoceanic canal routes, and to secure the construction of a neutralized canal under American auspices, American statesmen no doubt were aided by the authority of Monroe's declarations, but were by no means dependent upon them. It is a remarkable fact that Seward, neither in the formal demand upon France in 1865 to desist from armed intervention in Mexico for the purpose of overthrowing the domestic republican government under Juarez and establishing on its ruins the foreign imperial government under Maximilian, nor in any of the official correspondence relating to the subject, mentioned the "Monroe Doctrine," although his action came within the letter as well as the spirit of the message of 1823. President Polk, on the other hand, in pronouncing against the acquisition of few "dominion" in North America by a European power, although he was well within the limits of the "Monroe Doctrine" as it is now understood, invoked a passage that fell far short of sustaining his position. It would be easy to cite many similar examples.

The Monroe Doctrine, as a limitation upon the extension of European power and influence on the American continents, is now generally recognized as a principle of American policy. To its explicit acceptance by Great Britain and Germany there may be added the declaration which was spread by unanimous consent upon the minutes of the Hague Conference, and which was permitted to be annexed to the signature of the American delegates to the convention for the peaceful adjustment of international disputes, that nothing therein contained should be so constructed as to require the United States "to depart from its traditional policy of not entering upon, interfering with, or entangling itself in the political questions or internal administrations of any foreign state," or to relinquish "its traditional attitude toward purely American questions."

18

The Right and Wrong of the Monroe Doctrine

Charles F. Dole

The author of this article asks whether the conditions that brought about the Monroe Doctrine in 1823 were still valid in 1905. Additionally, the author affirms that as a mere "pronouncement" the doctrine is not official since it was never approved by the U.S. Congress. The Monroe Doctrine grew out of a paragraph in a presidential speech. Dole questions European power and interests and suggests that, at the beginning of the twentieth century, certain European states might have the military power and desire to invade some of the American nations. Still, in a cynical sense, the author suggests that, given the "circumstances" of some of the Latin American nations, the presence of Germany in Latin American might actually bring benefits, similar to the benefits of the U.S. presence in the Philippines. The author's central concern, though, is to question whether the Monroe Doctrine is really nothing more than a wish, by the United States, to establish a protectorate in Latin America. Through criticism of the Monroe Doctrine, Dole hopes to avoid what he sees as "a dangerous concession to permit a single state, however civilized it deems itself, to assume the right to become a knight-errant, to adjust wrongs in the world, and incidentally to be sheriff, judge and jury on its own motion."

Among the magical words that hypnotize men's minds and keep from asking intelligent questions, the Monroe Doctrine has a sovereign charm in American politics. Secretary Hay has coupled the mention of this Doctrine with the Golden Rule. Let us venture to ask a few straight questions, and not be afraid to go wherever the honest answer to our questions may carry us.

First, what was the substance of the original Monroe Doctrine in 1823, when it was promulgated? The Spanish American colonies had then revolted, and we had recognized their independence. There was a boundary question between the United States and Russia. We were a young republic, trying a great experiment in the eyes of a critical and unfriendly world. A "Holy Alliance" organized at the instance of Russia, with a really beautiful programme for the good order of Europe, threatened to be turned into an instrument of mischief and oppression, and even to help Spain to recover her possessions in America. It is likely that, as in many other instances of human alarm, nothing dangerous would have happened. But our government naturally felt nervous, and raised its cry of warning in the form of the Monroe Doctrine. This was merely a declaration, made by the President in his message to Congress, to the effect that the United States would hold it unfriendly in the European powers to take any aggressive action in this continent. Important as the subject now seems, it involved no vote in Congress, nor the careful discussion that an actual vote generally involves. It is doubtful whether many Americans who read Monroe's Message gave serious thought to the passages which were destined to give his name prominence. But Americans would have generally agreed in their disinclination to see monarchies set up in the New World, or to suffer any kind of undemocratic system to be brought over here from Europe.

It is noteworthy that the bare statement of the attitude of the United States, without any show of force or preparation for war, was sufficient to secure respectful treatment from the European powers. President Monroe did not feel called upon to ask appropriations for an increase in the navy in order to "back up" his doctrine. The United States did not possess a formidable navy till it had to build one in the period of the Civil War.

It should also be remarked that England, doubtless for commercial reasons, forwarded our government in its attitude in behalf of the independence of the South American republics. Few would have dreamed at that time that the Monroe Doctrine would ever be used as a menace against England.

See now what enormous political changes have come about within eighty years. Except Russia, there is not an autocratic government left of all the nations who composed the short-lived Holy Alliance. All the others, even Austria and Spain, have adopted constitutional methods. Their people have everywhere been given more or less democratic representation. Spain does not contemplate winning back her colonies. We possess by amicable purchase the very territory over which there was once risk of a boundary dispute with Russia. So far from fearing the extension of autocratic and oppressive governments from Europe to America, the European governments are daily brought to face new demands on the part of their people in the direction of democratic experiments. Autocratic militarism all over the world stands on the defensive. It is becoming recognized as economically and politically intolerable. A great international court has been established on purpose to put an end to war between the nations. It has begun to be used and respected.

Meanwhile the world has become one in geography and international relations. We are practically nearer the shores of Europe than we are to South America. We have larger and closer interests with China and Japan than we have with Chile and Guatemala.

Let us try now to find what European power, if any, threatens to bring the methods of oppression and tyranny to our continent, or in any way to menace the welfare of the United States. Russia, as we have observed, is out of the question, having voluntarily withdrawn from this continent. She allowed her proud flag to be hauled down in Alaska without the slightest loss of honor.

England is our best friend in all the world. Let us never admit jealousy or suspicion between us. For three thousand miles our territory and the Dominion of Canada march together. By mutual consent neither of us has a ship of war upon the Great Lakes. Let us see to it that we never put warships there. We are obviously safer without them. Like two strong men, dwelling on adjacent farms, we are mutually safeguarded, not by building suspicious fences against each other and purchasing weapons in view of the possibility of our wishing to fight, but rather by assuming that we shall never be so foolish as to injure each other. If we ever disagree, we do not purpose to degrade ourselves by fighting. So far as England is concerned, we may venture boldly to declare that the United States does not need a fort nor a battleship. We contemplate her time-honored naval station at Halifax as complacently as travelers view the collection of ancient armor in the Tower of London. Moreover, as regards the Monroe Doctrine, the last thing which England could possibly attempt, with her own popular constitutions, would be to abridge the liberties of Americans, either North or South.

Summon now the Republic of France, and interrogate her as to her designs and ambitions touching the affairs of America. Probably few Americans could name her cisatlantic possessions, so inconspicuous are they. They are costing the French treasury a steady outgo. No intelligent nation would take the gift of them, especially of Martinique, with its tempestuous volcanoes. France has had little experience with American colonies cheerful enough to stir her to desire the risk of a disagreement with the United States for the sake of gaining more territory. Never-the-less, we must admit that we had rather live under the rule of France than in most of the States of South or Central America. From no point of view does France threaten to establish a tyranny over any of the population in the New World.

We hear of Italians in South America. They have emigrated to the Argentine Republic. Does this fact make the slightest demand upon the United States to build iron ships to guard against the friendly government of Victor Emmanuel? On the contrary, the more Italians in the Argentine Republic the better we like it. They are more enterprising and industrious than either the Spaniards or the natives, and there is plenty of room for all who wish to go there. It is conceivable that Italy, saddled with ruinous debt and with a fearful burden of European militarism, should undertake a war of conquest in South America? If this were conceivable, does any one suppose that Italian rule down there, supposing it to prevail, would be less enlightened, or less righteous, than Spanish-American rule has been under the delusive name of "republic"? The people of the United States cannot know Italy, or her political conditions, and feel the slightest apprehension that she is capable of extending to our continent methods of government inimical to our peace.

No other nation in Europe remains, about whose designs in our continent the American people have the need to lose a wink of sleep, except Germany. If the plain truth were told by the alarmists, Germany is very nearly the one power in Christendom on whose account we are called upon to pay a naval "insurance fund" of a hundred millions of dollars a year. The talk about a "German peril" would be laughable, if millions of poor people did not need the money which such incendiary talk cost us; or worse yet, if this ceaseless talk about possible war with a great nation were not irritating to every one concerned, and naturally provocative of ill feeling.

Why indeed should we imagine mischief from Germany? To hear certain speakers and writers, one would suppose that Germany—instead of being a land of arts and laws, of universities and free institutions, with a vast network of worldwide trade—was overrun, as of old, by barbarous hordes breathing violence and robbery. Germany, in fact, has no quarrel or enmity against the kindred people of the United States. Germany is richer every day by reason of the prosperity of our country. The export and import trade between the United States and Germany amounted in 1903 to over three hundred and ten millions of dollars, more than double our whole trade with South America in the same year—a half more than our trade with all Asia. The boasted "open door" into the Chinese Empire only allowed the passage both ways of about forty-five millions of dollars' worth of products—less than one sixth of our trade with Germany.* Does any one think that Germany would lightly quarrel with the source of so much bread and butter? For what possible use? She could not conquer and slave us, nor does she wish to. We have no boundary lines on the planet to make friction between us. We may say again stoutly, as in the case of England, we are safer from any possible attack from Germany without a ship or a fort than we are with the largest navy that Captain Mahan could desire. For in the one case we should be sure to avoid needless disputes, and should be more than willing on both sides to put any question that might ever arise between us to arbitration; whereas in the other case, standing with loaded guns as it were, some trifling explosion of an angry man's temper might involve the two nations in strife.

*The value of the total trade to and from the Philippine Islands in the same year would have been more than used up in building three battleships.

It may be asked whether there is not grave risk that Germany may endeavor to plant colonies in South America, or to interfere in some way with the affairs of the South American people. We hardly need more than to repeat the paragraph touching this kind of contingency on the part of Italy. Germans are doubtless coming in considerable numbers into the temperate countries of South America. They are the most desirable kind of immigrant. Wherever they go a higher civilization goes with them. Life and property are safer. A more efficient type of government is demanded. All this is surely for the interest of the United States. We can only be glad for any influences which will tone up the character of the South and Central American states. If they were all Germanized, the whole world, including the United States, would be permanently richer. In fact, the ties of trade and friendship between us and a possible Germanized state in South America would normally tend to be closer than they seem likely to be with the Spanish-American peoples.

Neither is there the slightest evidence that Germany would ever threaten to introduce tyrannical forms of government into South America, or to oppress the native peoples. Indeed, so far as it is good for the United States to govern the Philippine Islands for the betterment of their people, the same argument holds in favor of any reasonable method, for example, through purchase or by the final consent of the people, for the extension of German law and political institutions into ill-governed South American states. I do not care to press this argument, which is only valid for those Americans who believe in our colonial experiment. But the argument is far stronger for possible German colonies than it is for the United States, inasmuch as South America is a natural and legitimate field for German immigration, being largely a wilderness, while no large number of Americans will ever care to settle in the Philippine Islands. The time may naturally come when Germany would have the same kind of interest in the welfare of her people beyond the seas that England has in that of the Englishmen in South Africa. There can be no good reason why the United States should look upon such an interest with jealousy or suspicion. For we are unlikely to have any legitimate colonial interest in the southern half of our continent.

Meanwhile, the whole history of colonial settlements goes to show the futility of holding colonies with which the home government is not bound by the ties of good will. Thus Canada and Australia uphold the British Empire, because they possess practical freedom; while England has to spend hundreds of millions of dollars a year, badly needed by her own poor people, merely in order to keep her hold over India. All precedents go to show that the Empire of Germany would only weaken herself, in case she should endeavor to meddle in South America against the interest and the good will of the people there.

Let us ask another question, hitherto too little is considered. On what ground of rights is the United States justified in continuing to assert the Monroe Doctrine? We may warn trespassers off our land. Have we the right to bar our neighbors from lands to which we have no shadow of a title? Suppose that we may do this as the stronger people, for the sake of humanity, to protect weaker people from oppression. It is surely a dangerous concession to permit a single state, however civilized it deems itself, to assume the right to become a knight errant, to adjust wrongs in the world, and incidentally to be sheriff, judge, and jury on its own motion. But grant this concession for a moment in favor of the United States. While it may have been true eighty years ago that the American people were filled with sympathy for the republics which revolted from Spain, it would be hypocrisy to claim to-day that our people are seriously concerned over the troubles of their South American neighbors. We are rather apt to say that they are unfit to govern themselves. The United States to-day holds eight millions of people on the other side of the globe, very like the South Americans, on the distinct ground that they are not yet fit for independence. Our own course, therefore, bars us from sensitiveness over the perils which South America suffers from the bare possibility of the interference of European states.

Moreover, we have shown that there is no state in Europe which has in mind to do any wrong to South America. So far as the promise of higher civilization goes, the planting of bona fide colonies in the vast areas of the southern continent signifies good to humanity.

We must fall back upon a totally different line of reasoning in order to find the only legitimate defense of our Monroe Doctrine. The argument is this: that a nation has the right to safeguard herself against the menace of aggression. Concede that this might have been a sound argument when the Monroe Doctrine was first proclaimed. Our government saw a peril in the setting up of a European system of despotism on this continent. We have made it clear, however, that this peril which disturbed our fathers appears to have vanished forever. No one can show what actual danger to our liberties is threatened by any governmental system that European powers can set up in South America. Let us not even imagine that we are in fear of such a chimerical peril. We have no fear that Germany wishes to harm us while she stays at home in Europe. We have no more ground to fear if Germany were by some magic to fill South America as full of sturdy German people as Canada is now full of friendly English, Scotch, and Frenchmen. The better civilized our neighbors are, the less peril do they threaten to our liberties.

Let us then disabuse our minds of any fear of European aggression, to injure American liberties.

But it may be argued that the European governments, as was shown in the late Venezuelan episode, may prove disagreeable in their efforts to collect debts due to their subjects, or, on occasion, in safeguarding the rights of their colonists in the disorderly South American states. The condition of these states, it is urged, offers points of serious friction between us and our European neighbors. The class of issues here raised stands quite aside from the original intent of the Monroe Doctrine. Here is the need of new international law, of the services of the Hague Tribunal, very likely of the establishment of a permanent Congress of

Nations. How far ought any nation to undertake by warships and armies to collect debts for venturesome subjects who have speculated in the tumultuous politics of semi-civilized peoples? How far is the real welfare of the world served by punitive expeditions dispatched in the name of missionaries, travelers, and traders, who have chosen to take their own lives in their hands in the wild regions of the world? There is no call for a Monroe Doctrine on these points. The issue is international, not American. The question is not so much whether France and England may send a fleet to take the customs duties of a dilapidated South American port, as it is, what course ought any government to take when wily promoters ask its assistance in carrying out their schemes in Bogota or Caracas, or Pekin; or again (an equally pertinent question), what remedy, if any, international law ought to give when one of our own cities or states defaults its bounds held in Paris or Berlin.

Grant that it is uncomfortable to our traders in South America to see European sheriffs holding ports where we wish to do business. We evidently have no right to protest against other nations doing whatever we might do in like circumstances. If we can send armored ships to South America, all the others can do so. If we like to keep the perilous right to collect debts, we must concede it to the others. We may not like to see strangers, or even our own neighbors, taking liberties and quarreling in the next field to our own. But who gives us the right forcibly to drive them out of a field which we do not own? The rule here seems to be the same for the nation as for the individual.

In other words, whatever the Monroe Doctrine historically means, it no longer requires us to stand with a show of force to maintain it. In its most critical form, when it meant a warning against despotism, it only needed to be proclaimed, and never to be defended by fighting ships. In the face of governments practically like our own, the time has come to inquire whether there remains any reasonable issue under the name of the Monroe Doctrine, over which the American people could have the least justification for a conflict of arms with a European government. The interests of the United States in South America are not different from those of other powers, like England and Germany. They are substantially identical interests; they are all obviously involved together with the improvement of material, political, and moral conditions in the South American states.

We have sought so far such an interpretation of the Monroe Doctrine as may honorably go in company of the Golden Rule, or, in other words, of international justice. There remains, however, a possible new definition of the Doctrine, which should be fairly faced. There is an idea in the air that the United States holds a certain protectorate or suzerainty over the whole continent of America. A manifest destiny is thought to be working in favor of the dominion or suzerainty of a single power from the Arctic Ocean to Patagonia. Porto Rico is ours. Cuba is almost ours. Many believe that Canada will some time desire to be with us. No people to the south of us show stable promise of what we call good government. The new Canal at Panama affords additional reasons for our control of the continent. Boundless resources are yet to be developed in the virgin continent. We are the people who can provide the brains, the capital, and the political security requisite for the exploitation of practically a seventh of the surface of the earth.

The new Monroe Doctrine comes thus to mean, frankly, that we want, or at least may some time want, all America for ourselves. We give due notice in advance of our claim of preemption. What else does the Monroe Doctrine mean, that there should be the pretense of a necessity to fight for it? What else does our President mean by his note of repeated warning to the republics of South and Central America that they must "behave themselves"?

Few persons seriously expect that South Americans are ready to "behave themselves" to order, to pay their foreign debts, and keep their promises punctually, and to make no disturbances to the inconvenience of their neighbors. If Europe must not be suffered to discipline them, must we not give them their lessons? The recent movement to assume a receivership at Santo Domingo, to collect and pay Dominican taxes for the benefit of bond-holders both at home and abroad, brings the new doctrine into practical effect. Here and nowhere else looms up the need of new battleships and a hundred millions of dollars a year for the navy. It is in regard to South America, and for the extension of the Monroe Doctrine to a control over the continent, that we discover in the political horizon all manner of colossal foreign responsibilities and the possibilities of friction and war.

The new Monroe Doctrine may kindle one's imagination; it may stir the ambition of our people; it may tempt some of them with a glamour of power and wealth. We may fancy that we would like to be the suzerain power of the continent, with United States officials in authority in every Spanish and Portuguese American capital. The stern ancient question presses: What right has the United States to assume a protectorate, and much less any form of sovereignty, over South America? The South American governments are as independent as our own. There are no traditions common between us to constitute us an acknowledged Lord Protector over them. On the contrary, our conduct toward Colombia and the Philippines, and the extraordinary utterances of some of our public men, seem to have already produced a certain nervousness among our Spanish-American neighbors.

Neither does international law, which has never in the past given the Monroe Doctrine any clearly acknowledged footing, admit the right of the United States to mark off the American continent as its own preserve, and to stand, like a dog in the manger, to warn other friendly peoples from entering it.

Moreover, the millions of the plain American people, who toil and pay the taxes to the tune of about forty dollars a year for every average family, have no valid interest whatever in spending the money or the administrative ability of the country in dubious enterprises beyond the seas, at the behest of ambitious capitalists or politicians, who aim to open markets and run satrapies by the use of national battleships. The people, who need indefinite services for the expansion of their welfare and happiness at home, have never even been asked to consider, much less to approve, a policy which threatens to dissipate the activities of their government over the length of the continent. The new Monroe Doctrine is a menace to the interests of every American workingman. It is the old story. The few usurp the power of the many to work their own ends.

In short, so far as we are good friends of the South American peoples, so far as we are friends of our kinsmen over the seas on the continent of Europe, so far as our intentions in South America are honestly humane and philanthropic, we have no need whatever of the Monroe Doctrine any longer. On the side of our common humanity all our interests are substantially identical. On the other hand, so far as we purpose to exploit the continent for our selfish interests, so far as we aim at the extension of our power, so far as we purpose to force our forms of civilization and our government upon peoples whom we deem our "inferiors", our new Monroe Doctrine rests upon no grounds of justice or right, it has no place with the Golden Rule, it is not synonymous with human freedom, it depends upon might, and it doubtless tends to provoke jealousy, if not hostility and war.

Selected Bibliography of Titles in English and Spanish

Araúz, Celestino Andrés, and Patricia Pizzurno. *Relaciones entre Panamá y los Estados Unidos: historia del Canal Interoceánico desde el siglo XVI hasta 1903.* Panamá: Autoridad del Canal de Panamá, 1999.

Arbeláez, Octavio, et al. *Documentación histórica del Canal de Panamá.* Bogotá: Universidad Javeriana, 1989.

Barry, Tom, John Lindsay-Poland, Marco A. Gandansegui, and Peter Simonson. *Inside Panama.* Albuquerque, N.M.: Resource Center Press, 1995.

Black, George. *The Good Neighbor: How the United States Wrote the History of Central America and the Caribbean.* New York: Pantheon Books, 1988.

Brand Herrera, Nubia Rosa. *La reconciliación de Colombia y Panamá.* Santa Fe de Bogotá: Antares, 1996.

Domínguez Ossa, Camilo A, Guido Barona Becerra, Apolinar Figueroa Casas, and Agusto J. Gómez López, edición, análisis y comentarios. *Geografía Física y Política de la Confederación Granadina. Vol.VI: Estado del Istmo de Panamá, Provincias de Chiriquí, Veraguas, Azuero y Panamá.* Obra dirigida por el General Agustín Codazzi (1854). Bogotá: Universidad Nacional de Colombia, 2002.

Coleman, Kenneth M., and George C. Herring. *The Central American Crisis: Sources of Conflict and the Failure of U.S. Policy.* Wilmington, Del.: Scholarly Resources, 1985.

Collin, Richard H. *Theodore Roosevelt's Caribbean: The Panama Canal, the Monroe Doctrine, and the Latin American Context.* Baton Rouge: Louisiana State University Press, 1990.

Conniff, Michael L. *Panama and the United States: The Forced Alliance.* Athens: University of Georgia Press, 1992.

Conte Porras, Jorge. *Antología de pensamiento constitucional del Istmo de Panamá en el siglo XIX.* Bogotá: Banco de la República, 1986.

Davis, Harold Eugene, et al. *Latin American Diplomatic History: An Introduction.* Baton Rouge: Louisiana State University Press, 1977.

Dent, David W. *The Legacy of the Monroe Doctrine: A Reference Guide to U.S. Involvement in Latin America and the Carribean.* Westport, Conn.: Greenwood Press, 1999.

Diago Heilbron, Santiago Andrés. *Historia de los tratados entre los Estados Unidos, Gran Bretana, Nicaragua y Colombia sobre el Canal de Panamá.* Bogotá: Universidad Javeriana, 1987.

Díaz Espino, Ovidio. *How Wall Street Created a Nation: J.P. Morgan, Teddy Roosevelt, and the Panama Canal.* New York: Four Walls Eight Windows, 2001.

Díaz Callejas, Apolinar. *Colombia-Estados Unidos: entre la autonomía y la subordinación: De la independencia de Panamá.* Santafé de Bogotá: Planeta, 1997.

Dodd, Thomas J., ed. *La crisis de Panamá: cartas de Tomás Herrán 1900-1904.* Bogotá: Banco de la República, 1985.

Dolan, Edward F. *Panama and the United States: Their Canal, Their Stormy Years.* New York: F. Watts, 1990.

Farnsworth, David N., and James W. McKenney. *U.S.-Panama Relations, 1903-1978: A Study in Linkage Politics.* Boulder, Colo.: Westview Press, 1983.

Falcoff, Mark, and Richard Millett. *Searching for Panama: The U.S. Panama Relationship and Democratization.* Washington, D.C.: Center for Strategic and International Studies, 1993.

Falcoff, Mark. *Panama's Canal: What Happens When the United States Gives a Small Country What It Wants.* Washington, D.C.: AEI Press, 1998.

Gori, José Joaquín. *Derechos de Colombia en el Canal de Panamá.* Bogotá: Temis, 1982.

Hill, Howard Copeland. *Roosevelt and the Caribbean.* New York: Russell and Russell, 1965.

Isaza Calderón, Baltasar. *Historia de Panamá, 1821-1916: Carlos A. Mendoza y su generación.* Panamá: Academia Panameña de la Historia, 1982.

Joseph, G.M., Catherine LeGrand, and Ricardo Donato Salvatore. *Close Encounters of Empire: Writing the Cultural History of U.S.-Latin American Relations.* Durham: Duke University Press, 1998.

Knight, Franklin W. *The Caribbean: The Genesis of a Fragmented Nationalism.* New York: Oxford University Press, 1978.

Lael, Richard L. *Dilemma over Panama: United State-Colombian Relations, 1903-1922.* Chapel Hill: University of North Carolina Press, 1976.

LaFeber, Walter. *Inevitable Revolutions: The United States and Central America.* New York: Norton, 1983.

———. *The Panama Canal: The Crisis in Historical Perspective.* New York: Oxford University Press, 1989.

Langley, Lester D. *Struggle for the American Mediterranean: United States-European Rivalry in the Gulf-Caribbean, 1776-1904.* Athens: University of Georgia Press, 1976.

Lemaitre Román, Eduardo. *Panamá y su separación de Colombia,* 4ª. Ed. Santafé de Bogotá: Amazonas, 1993.

Leonard, Thomas M. *United States-Latin American Relations: 1850-1903: Establishing a Relationship.* Tuscaloosa: University of Alabama Press, 1999.

Lindop, Edmund. *Panama and the United States: Divided by the Canal.* New York: Twenty-First Century Books, 1997.

Liss, Sheldon B. *The Canal: Aspects of United States-Panamanian Relations.* South Bend: University of Notre Dame Press, 1967.

Major, John. *Prize Possession: The United States and the Panama Canal, 1902-1979.* New York: Cambridge University Press, 1993.

Mendoza, Carlos Alberto, and Vicente Stamato. *1903 en la prensa panameña y los infaustos años precedentes*. Bogotá, Alcaldía de Panamá: Biblioteca del Centenario, 2001.

Morales Benítez, Otto. *Sanclemente, Marroquín, el liberalismo y Panamá*. Santa Fe de Bogotá: Stamato, 1998.

Musicant, Ivan. *The Banana Wars: A History of the United States Military Intervention in Latin America from the Spanish-American War to the Invasion of Panama*. New York: Macmillan, 1990.

Ortega Durán, Oyden. *La lucha por el canal*. Panamá: s.n., 1986.

Pearce, Jenny. *Under the Eagle: U.S. Intervention in Central America and the Caribbean*. London: Latin American Bureau, 1982.

Pizzurno Gelos, Patricia. *Antecedentes, hechos y consecuencias de la guerra de los mil días en el Istmo de panamá*. Panamá: s.n., 1990.

Plazas Olarte, Guillermo. *La separación de Panamá desde el punto de vista militar*. Bogotá: ABC, 1987.

Randall, Stephen J. *Colombia and the United States: Hegemony and Interdependence*. Athens: University of Georgia Press, 1992.

Ryan, Paul B. *The Panama Canal Controversy: U.S. Diplomacy and Defense Interests*. Stanford, Calif.: Hoover Institution Press, 1977.

Uribe Vargas, Diego. *Los últimos derechos de Colombia en el Canal de Panamá: el tratado Uribe Vargas-Ozores*. Bogotá: Universidad Nacional de Colombia, 1993.

Vazquez Carrizosa, Alfredo. *Relatos de historia diplomáticas de Colombia*. Santa Fe de Bogotá: CEJA, 1996.

Woodward Jr., Ralph Lee. *Central America: A Nation Divided*, 2nd ed. New York: Oxford University Press, 1985.

Zimbalist, Andrew S., and John Weeks. *Panama at the Crossroads: Economic Development and Political Change in the Twentieth Century*. Berkeley: University of California Press, 1991.

Credits

Chapter 1 is reprinted from *Harper's Monthly Magazine*, 11, no. 65 (October 1855): 616-622.
Chapter 2 is reprinted from *Harper's Monthly Magazine*, 18, no. 104 (January 1859): 145-169. This article is the fourth part of a series of five related with the same trip to Panama and published by *Harper's* as follows: first part, 16, no. 94 (March 1858): 457-471; second part, 16, no. 95 (April 1858): 577-593; third part, 17, no. 97 (June 1858): 19-39; fifth part, 19, no. 112 (September 1859): 433-454.
Chapter 3 is reprinted from *Harper's Monthly Magazine*, 10, no. 58 (March 1855): 433-458. This article is the first part of two published by *Harper's* as follows: second part, 10, no. 60 (May 1855): 745-764.
Chapter 4 is reprinted from *Harper's Monthly Magazine*, 11, no. 65 (October 1855): 577-590. This article is the first part of two published by *Harper's* as follows: second part, 11, no. 66 (November 1855): 744-763.
Chapter 5 is reprinted from *Harper's Monthly Magazine*, 22, no. 128 (January 1861): 198-209.
Chapter 6 is reprinted from *Harper's Monthly Magazine*, 47, no. 282 (November 1873): 801-820.
Chapter 7 is reprinted from *Harper's Monthly Magazine*, 63, no. 378 (November 1881): 905-911.
Chapter 8 is reprinted from *Harper's Monthly Magazine*, 1, no. 1 (June 1850): 79-81.
Chapter 9 is reprinted from *Harper's Monthly Magazine*, 96, no. 573 (February 1898): 351-358.
Chapter 10 is reprinted from *Harper's Monthly Magazine*, 96, no. 576 (May 1898): 837-846.
Chapter 11 is reprinted from *The Atlantic Monthly*, 86, no. 518 (December 1900): 844-848.
Chapter 12 is reprinted from *Harper's Monthly Magazine*, 103, no. 614 (July 1902): 283-284.
Chapter 13 is reprinted from *The Atlantic Monthly*, 64, no. 383 (September 1889): 289-303.
Chapter 14 is reprinted from *The Atlantic Monthly*, 64, no. 386 (December 1889): 834-840.

Chapter 15 is reprinted from *Harper's Monthly Magazine*, 87, no. 520 (September 1893): 602-609.
Chapter 16 is reprinted from *Harper's Monthly Magazine*, 95, no. 569 (October 1897): 680-691.
Chapter 17 is reprinted from *Harper's Monthly Magazine*, 109, no. 654 (November 1904): 857-869.
Chapter 18 is reprinted from *The Atlantic Monthly*, 95, no. 4 (April 1905): 567-573.

Index

About the Editors

Michael LaRosa is associate professor of history at Rhodes College in Memphis. He is the author of *De la derecha a la izquierda: La Iglesia Católica en la Colombia Contemporánea* (2000). He edited, with Frank O. Mora, *Neighborly Adversaries: Readings in U.S.-Latin American Relations* (1999).

Germán R. Mejía is professor of history at the Pontificia Universidad Javeriana, Bogotá, Colombia. He is the author of *Los años del cambio: Historia urbana de Bogotá, 1820-1910*, which won a Colombian national book award in 1999 under the category "best book in Social Sciences, Sociology, and Politics." He edited, with Fabio Zambrano, *La ciudad y las ciencias sociales* (2000).

LaRosa and Mejía edited *Colombia en el siglo XIX* (with Mauricio Nieto) in 1999.